The Gilded Age and Progressive Era

Uncovering the Past: Documentary Readers in American History
Series Editors: Steven Lawson and Nancy Hewitt

The books in this series introduce students in American history courses to two important dimensions of historical analysis. They enable students to engage actively in historical interpretation, and they further students' understanding of the interplay between social and political forces in historical developments.

Consisting of primary sources and an introductory essay, these readers are aimed at the major courses in the American history curriculum, as outlined further below. Each book in the series will be approximately 225–250 pages, including a 25–30-page introduction addressing key issues and questions about the subject under consideration, a discussion of sources and methodology, and a bibliography of suggested secondary readings.

Published

Paul G.E. Clemens
The Colonial Era: A Documentary Reader

Sean Patrick Adams
The Early American Republic: A Documentary Reader

Stanley Harrold
The Civil War and Reconstruction: A Documentary Reader

Steven Mintz
African American Voices: A Documentary Reader, 1619–1877

Robert P. Ingalls and David K. Johnson
The United States Since 1945: A Documentary Reader

Camilla Townsend
American Indian History: A Documentary Reader

Steven Mintz
Mexican American Voices: A Documentary Reader

Brian Ward
The 1960s: A Documentary Reader

Nancy Rosenbloom
Women in American History Since 1880: A Documentary Reader

Jeremi Suri
American Foreign Relations Since 1898: A Documentary Reader

Carol Faulkner
Women in American History to 1880: A Documentary Reader

David Welky
America Between the Wars, 1919–1941: A Documentary Reader

William A. Link and Susannah J. Link
The Gilded Age and Progressive Era: A Documentary Reader

The Gilded Age and Progressive Era

A Documentary Reader

Edited by
William A. Link
and Susannah J. Link

A John Wiley & Sons, Ltd., Publication

This edition first published 2012
© 2012 Blackwell Publishing Limited

Blackwell Publishing was acquired by John Wiley & Sons in February 2007. Blackwell's publishing program has been merged with Wiley's global Scientific, Technical, and Medical business to form Wiley-Blackwell.

Registered Office
John Wiley & Sons Ltd, The Atrium, Southern Gate, Chichester, West Sussex, PO19 8SQ, UK

Editorial Offices
350 Main Street, Malden, MA 02148–5020, USA
9600 Garsington Road, Oxford, OX4 2DQ, UK
The Atrium, Southern Gate, Chichester, West Sussex, PO19 8SQ, UK

For details of our global editorial offices, for customer services, and for information about how to apply for permission to reuse the copyright material in this book please see our website at www.wiley.com/wiley-blackwell.

The right of William A. Link and Susannah J. Link to be identified as the authors of the editorial material in this work has been asserted in accordance with the UK Copyright, Designs and Patents Act 1988.

Wiley also publishes its books in a variety of electronic formats. Some content that appears in print may not be available in electronic books.

Designations used by companies to distinguish their products are often claimed as trademarks. All brand names and product names used in this book are trade names, service marks, trademarks or registered trademarks of their respective owners. The publisher is not associated with any product or vendor mentioned in this book. This publication is designed to provide accurate and authoritative information in regard to the subject matter covered. It is sold on the understanding that the publisher is not engaged in rendering professional services. If professional advice or other expert assistance is required, the services of a competent professional should be sought.

Library of Congress Cataloging-in-Publication Data

The Gilded Age and Progressive Era : a documentary reader / edited by William A. Link and Susannah J. Link.
    p.   cm. – (Uncovering the past : documentary readers in American history ; 12)
    Includes bibliographical references and index.
    ISBN 978-1-4443-3138-7 (hardback) – ISBN 978-1-4443-3139-4 (paperback)
1. United States–History–1865-1921–Sources.   2. United States–Politics and government–1865-1933–Sources.   3. United States–Social conditions–1865-1918–Sources.
4. Progressivism (United States politics)–Sources.   I. Link, William A.   II. Link, Susannah J.
    E661.G455 2012
    973.8–dc23

                                                                2011034658

A catalogue record for this book is available from the British Library.

Set in 10/12.5pt Sabon by SPi Publisher Services, Pondicherry, India
Printed in Singapore by Ho Printing Singapore Pte Ltd

Contents

Series Editors' Preface

Primary sources have become an essential component in the teaching of history to undergraduates. They engage students in the process of historical interpretation and analysis and help them understand that facts do not speak for themselves. Rather, students see how historians construct narratives that re-create the past. Most students assume that the pursuit of knowledge is a solitary endeavor; yet historians constantly interact with their peers, building upon previous research and arguing among themselves over the interpretation of documents and their larger meaning. The documentary readers in this series highlight the value of this collaborative creative process and encourage students to participate in it.

Each book in the series introduces students in American history courses to two important dimensions of historical analysis. They enable students to engage actively in historical interpretation, and they further students' understanding of the interplay among social, cultural, economic, and political forces in historical developments In pursuit of these goals, the documents in each text embrace a broad range of sources, including such items as illustrations of material artifacts, letters and diaries, sermons, maps, photographs, song lyrics, selections from fiction and memoirs, legal statutes, court decisions, presidential orders, speeches, and political cartoons.

Each volume in the series is edited by specialists in the field who are concerned with undergraduate teaching. The goal is not to offer a comprehensive selection of material but to provide items that reflect major themes and debates; that illustrate significant social, cultural, political, and economic dimensions of an era or subject; and that inform, intrigue, and inspire undergraduate students. The editors of each volume have written an introduction that discusses the central questions that have occupied historians in this field and the ways historians have used primary sources to answer them. In addition, each introductory essay contains an explanation of the kinds of materials available to investigate a particular subject, the methods by which scholars analyze them, and the considerations that go into interpreting them. Each source selection is introduced by a short headnote that gives students the necessary information and a context for understanding the document. Also, each section of the volume includes questions to guide student reading and stimulate classroom discussion.

William Link's and Susannah Link's *The Gilded Age and Progressive Era* offers a superb array of documents dealing with political, social, economic, cultural, and diplomatic developments following the end of Reconstruction to World War I, the so-called Gilded Age and Progressive periods. The Gilded Age featured the growth of modern America through the creation and expansion of large-scale industrial and corporate enterprises that dominated the political and economic landscapes. During the period after the Civil War, the United States succeeded in subduing Native American tribes that blocked the material ambitions of homesteaders, miners, railroads, an assortment of entrepreneurs, and corporate interests seeking to exploit the opportunities and resources of the West. The rapid industrialization in the 1880s and 1890s created enormous wealth and concentrated it in the hands of a very few. At the same time, the rapid growth of big business resulted in widespread poverty among the many workers whose wages, employment, and living conditions kept them from sharing in prosperity. The shift toward rapid industrialization also created burgeoning cities, which attracted impoverished farmers seeking to find success. Joining them in teeming cities were millions of immigrants, mainly from southern and eastern Europe, hoping to escape from poverty or religious and political persecution. Instead of providing glittering riches, the Gilded Age brought them unhealthy and crowded housing, poorly paid jobs, and a good deal of discrimination.

Given the sweeping changes that industrialization produced, workers and farmers organized themselves into labor unions and agricultural alliances to gain power, improve their economic conditions, and create a fairer and more representative society. Although they met with limited success, reform did emerge in the nation in the first two decades of the twentieth century. Loosely organized around the idea of progress, various representatives of business, professional, and working-class groups, known as progressives, sought to use local, state, and national governments to regulate wasteful and ruthless business and financial practices; adopt methods to make the government operate more efficiently; improve working, living, and health conditions; and impose middle-class moral standards on impoverished immigrants dwelling in large cities. Although most women could not vote, they did play a large role in promoting progressive reform through community organizing and lobbying. Further, during the Gilded Age and Progressive Era, black southerners experienced racial segregation, disfranchisement, and lynching, but African Americans, such as W.E.B. Du Bois, joined reformers to challenge these brutal conditions.

The other major characteristic of modern American during the Gilded Age and Progressive Era came in the United States building an overseas imperial empire, one that led the nation into two wars. Imperialists like Theodore Roosevelt envisioned an expanded role for the United States in world affairs, departing from its anticolonial tradition, to ensure commercial markets and gain power to create a stable world order for American economic enterprises and national security. Triumphing over opponents of overseas expansion, imperialists succeeded in 1898 in persuading the United States to enter a war against Spain in Cuba and the Philippines, which resulted in control over new territory. Having gained a significant foothold in international relations, the United States chose in 1917 to fight in World War I, a war that not only improved its world economic position but would also create the basis for tragic future conflicts.

Delving into this exciting and transformative historical period, William Link and Susannah Link furnish an array of rich documents with headnotes and questions in each chapter that will encourage students to create history and show that facts do not speak for themselves. Students can analyze the views of politicians, businessmen, journalists, photographers, intellectuals, novelists, ministers, judges, reformers, and ordinary people – farmers and workers, women and men, and black, white, Mexican, and Native Americans – as they grappled with the opportunities and challenges of industrialization, urbanization, imperialism, and war.

Steven F. Lawson and Nancy A. Hewitt,
Series Editors

Acknowledgments to Sources

The editors and publisher gratefully acknowledge the permission granted to reproduce the copyright material in this book:

1.4.1: Library of Congress, Prints and Photographs Division, LC-DIG-nclc-01583.

1.4.2: Library of Congress, Prints and Photographs Division, LC-DIG-nclc-01464.

3.4.1: Image © Library of Congress, Prints and Photographs Division. Photograph by Richard K. Fox.

3.4.2: Library of Congress, Prints & Photographs Division, NYWT&S Collection.

3.4.3, 7.4.1, 7.4.2: Library of Congress, Prints and Photographs Division.

5.4.2: Bettmann/Corbis, photo T.H. Lindsey.

6.3: Getty Images/Hulton Archive.

7.6: First paragraph from http://ccarnet.org/Articles/index.cfm?id=39& pge_id=1606, accessed July 7, 2011. © Central Conference of American Rabbis.

9.5.1 and 9.5.2: North Carolina Collection, University of North Carolina at Chapel Hill Library.

5.4.1, 10.4.1, 10.4.2, 10.4.3: photos Bettmann/Corbis.

11.4: from Margaret Sanger, "Morality and Birth Control," February, 1918, Margaret Sanger Papers Project (http://www.nyu.edu/projects/sanger/secure/

documents/speech_morality_and_bc.html). Courtesy of the Margaret Sanger Papers, New York University.

12.3: from interview with Helen Valeska Bary, December 29, 1972–January 14, 1973, Suffragists Oral History Project, Regional Oral History Office, Bancroft Library, UC-Berkeley.

13.4: US Naval History and Heritage Commands photograph, Collection of Roy D. France, photo by C.E. Waterman.

14.2: from Eugene V. Debs, *Eugene V. Debs Speaks*, ed. Jean Y. Tussey (New York: Pathfinder Press, 1970), pp. 243–79. Copyright © 1970 by Pathfinder Press. Reprinted by permission.

14.4: from Arthur S. Link *et al.* (eds), *The Papers of Woodrow Wilson*, 69 vols (Princeton, NJ: Princeton University Press, 1966–93), Vol. 45, pp. 534–9. Reprinted by permission of Princeton University Press.

Introduction

On May 10, 1876, Americans began to celebrate a birthday – their own. On the hundredth anniversary of the creation of the American republic – May 10, 1776, was the date that Congress authorized the drafting of a Declaration of Independence – Philadelphia hosted the "International Exhibition of Arts, Manufactures and Products of the Soil and Mine." Describing the opening ceremonies, a correspondent from the *Chicago Tribune* wrote that, for "miles and miles, from housetops, from windows, from doorways and [railroad] car roofs, and even from the heads of numberless horses, our national standard has been displayed." Bells rang across Philadelphia to announce opening day, and the festivities attracted a crowd estimated as large as 200,000 people. President Ulysses S. Grant, along with congressmen, members of the Supreme Court, and the emperor and empress of Brazil, attended the Centennial's opening. Grant delivered an address that "could not be heard very far," and the crowd became "somewhat disorderly." But at noon, when the Exposition was declared open, the crowd eagerly investigated the 236-acre tract of Fairmount Park that overlooked seven miles of the Schuylkill River about a mile and a half from the Philadelphia city center.[1]

---

[1] "Centennial," *Chicago Tribune*, May 11, 1876; J.S. Ingram, *Centennial Exposition Described and Illustrated: Being a Concise and Graphic Description of This Grand Enterprise Commemorative of the First Centenary of American Independence* (Philadelphia: Hubbard Bros, 1876), pp. 105–6.

The Gilded Age and Progressive Era: A Documentary Reader, First Edition.
Edited by William A. Link and Susannah J. Link.
© 2012 Blackwell Publishing Ltd. Published 2012 by Blackwell Publishing Ltd.

The Philadelphia Centennial Exposition became the United States' first major world's fair, featuring exhibitions from 37 nations and including 250 pavilions. Fantastically popular, the exhibition eventually attracted more than nine million visitors – the largest attendance of any world's fair ever previously held. The event celebrated the survival of the Republic after the grave crisis of the Civil War. But the Centennial also looked forward in time. Many of the exhibits trumpeted technology, industrial change, and the transportation revolution. The centerpiece of the Exposition, the Main Building, was a massive structure 1,880 feet long and 464 feet wide. Constructed of iron, wood, and glass at the cost of $1.6 million, it possessed floor space of more than 21 acres, with 75-foot high towers on its four corners. Four other main exhibition halls dominated the grounds. Agricultural Hall, located on ten acres of the northern side of the fairgrounds, exhibited steam-powered agricultural machinery and advertised the new science of agriculture. Stockyards were maintained in a separate building with horses, cattle, swine, sheep, and poultry. Horticultural Hall, built of glass and iron, featured extensive marble and brick work and parterres of flowers and plants, fountains, and promenades in all directions. The hall featured exotic trees, shrubs, and flowers, along with gardening tools and accessories and greenhouses. Memorial Hall, constructed of granite with a dome of iron and glass 150 feet high, housed sculpture, paintings, lithographs, and photographs.

Machinery Hall, the second-largest building, stressed innovation. One of its most popular exhibitions was the Lockwood Envelope Machine, that "very perfect and interesting machinery for making envelopes by the million," which manufactured envelopes at the rate of 120 per minute and 60,000 a day.[2] With 14 acres of floor space, the hall displayed modern machinery and the wonders of technological progress. The largest steam engine in the world, the Corliss Engine, a popular attraction in Machinery Hall, was described by a contemporary as "an athlete of steel and iron." Containing 70 miles of belts and shafts that powered looms, drills, and pumps, it provided a fascinating example of the new importance of machinery in American life. "How the American's heart thrills with pride and love of his land as he contemplates the vast exhibition of art and prowess here," commented California poet Joaquin Miller, and the exhibition represented to him an "acorn from which shall grow the wide-spreading oak of a century's growth."[3] There were also other structures that were part of the

---

[2]   Ingram, p. 162.
[3]   Robert W. Rydell, *All the World's a Fair: Visions of Empire at American International Expositions* (Chicago: University of Chicago Press, 1984), p. 16.

Centennial: 17 buildings representing states; six cigar pavilions; and nine buildings with exhibitions from foreign nations. Individual companies such as Singer Sewing Machine advertised their wares. And the exhibition contained a Woman's Pavilion, dedicated to the "exclusive exhibition of woman's art, skill and industry."[4]

The Centennial grounds showed off new standards of modern urban planning, with intersecting grand avenues. Encircled by a fence extending 16,000 feet, the grounds contained seven miles of walks and drives and a 5½-mile narrow-gauge railroad. Elsewhere, the fair transported visitors on steamboats, carriages, and streetcars, and even an elevated monorail. The Belmont Hill Tower elevator carried visitors 185 feet up to a platform for a view of the exposition, while elevators – a new technology – were used throughout the Centennial to move people and goods. An array of new products – including Christopher B. Sholes's Remington typewriter and Alexander Graham Bell's telephone – were first unveiled at the Centennial. The fair displayed, according to one account, "the great progress in the arts, sciences, and mechanical skill made in a single century, and demonstrated that we are but little behind older nations in any one branch, while in some we scarcely have a rival."[5]

With the conclusion of the Civil War and Reconstruction, a new, more integrated nation-state came into focus across the American continent. To some extent, the nationalization of American life during the Gilded Age and Progressive Era became a prevailing theme characterizing the period from the 1870s to World War I. The Civil War had settled the constitutional question of whether Americans belonged to a collection of semi-autonomous states or to a single nation. After 1865, through conscious efforts, a clear assertion of American nationality led to its coherent definition in public life, economic growth, and culture.

The completion of a national transportation network made possible the connection of separate regions. Seven years to the day before the Philadelphia Centennial opened, on May 10, 1869, the first transcontinental railroad was completed, when railroad officials from the Union Pacific and Central Pacific drove in a ceremonial last spike and declared the line to be finished. The completion of a transcontinental railroad coincided with rapid growth in the nation's transportation infrastructure. Before the Civil War, railroad lines were scattered and generally confined to coastal areas, but thereafter they rapidly penetrated the American interior. By 1900, more

4   Ingram, p. 116.
5   "Our Centennial," *Chicago Tribune*, December 6, 1876.

than 200,000 miles of railroad track existed, and few communities did not live in some proximity to a railroad.

Nothing personified the integration that accompanied railroads more than the standardization of time. Until the late nineteenth century, the time appearing on Americans' clocks and watches varied by as much as 20 or 30 minutes, and localities usually decided on their own which time they would observe. But with the spread of railroads, the need to establish consistent timetables for scheduling became an imperative. A group of railroad super- intendents organized the Time Table Convention in 1872, and in 1875 it renamed itself the General Time Convention. In 1881, William F. Allen, as secretary of this organization, pushed hard for standardization of time. In 1883, the major railroad companies agreed to establish four time zones with standard times consistently with England's Greenwich mean time, which the British railroads had established as that nation's standard time. In the United States, the transition was announced and accomplished at noon on November 18, 1883. In the Pennsylvania Railroad Station in Jersey City, New Jersey, curious onlookers watched as signs indicating "New York Time" and "Philadelphia Time" – Philadelphia was a minute slower – were replaced with a single "Standard Time." In Atlanta, meanwhile, clocks were turned back 20 minutes behind what locals called "true Atlanta time." "By turning back our watches in this city 22 minutes," said the *Atlanta Constitution*, "we have the time of a vast sweep of country – of the great heart of this land."[6]

It is possible to overstate the extent of nationalization in the Gilded Age and Progressive Era. The United States remained a nation of great geograph- ical diversity, with persisting differences among states and regions. Two par- ticular examples of differences were the semi-colonial dependencies of the South and the West. The peculiarities of the social system of the South and its defeat in the Civil War set the region apart. Though it experienced urban- ization, the South remained more rural and more agricultural than the rest of the country. Its rural population was poor, significantly poorer than Americans elsewhere. At the end of the Civil War in 1865, four million for- merly enslaved African Americans attempted to assert their freedom, despite white oppression, widespread poverty, and an economy dominated by mon- oculture in farming and a persisting plantation system. The struggle to establish a new racial hierarchy which whites dominated was a central part of the South's post-emancipation history. The American West also differed from the rest of the country. The Trans-Mississippi West attracted migrants

---

[6] "The New Time," *Atlanta Constitution*, November 13, 1883.

from the United States and Europe, as well as Asia and Mexico. Race and ethnicity were important, as Anglos attempted to assert their control. Uniquely, it was also home both to an Indian population that was subdued and had experienced the ravages of federal policies designed to reduce its cultural independence and integrity, and people of Mexican descent who were subdued by the arrival of Anglo-American cultural and economic supremacy.

Despite the geographical diversity of the United States, economic growth created new opportunities. A new super-rich class of entrepreneurs achieved fantastic wealth. Born in 1797, Cornelius Vanderbilt amassed a large fortune in the steamboat business, which he then plowed into railroads. By the Civil War, he controlled the New York Central line – and much of the transportation business in the Northeast. On his death, he left his son, William, a large fortune of $95 million – and established the Vanderbilts as among the richest families in America. Immigrating to the United States from Scotland at age 13, Andrew Carnegie worked his way up to the position of manager on the Pennsylvania Railroad. After the Civil War, he invested in the iron industry in Pittsburgh and was among the first industrialists to exploit a new technology, the Bessemer process, that permitted steel manufacturing. Perhaps the most famous industrialist of his age was John D. Rockefeller. Born in western New York in 1839, Rockefeller made his fortune in Cleveland, Ohio, where he established a business before the Civil War as a commission merchant. An oil boom ensued in western Pennsylvania after the discovery of petroleum in Titusville, Pennsylvania, in August 1859. In the late 1860s, Rockefeller established a business to refine crude oil into kerosene, then one of the leading sources of indoor illumination. Creating the Standard Oil Company in 1870 and the Standard Oil Trust in 1882, Rockefeller extended control over the entire oil industry – from production to refining to distribution. By 1912, the Rockefeller fortune was estimated to be close to $1 billion – a fantastic sum for that age.

These individual stories form part of a larger pattern: the rise of large business enterprise and the expanding impact of the market economy upon American life. The railroads became the first forms of business to expand beyond state and local borders, but the growth of railroads and what is known as the Transportation Revolution spurred the national reach of other business activity. With a protective legal and political structure – a national government providing little regulation and a Supreme Court which defined business enterprise as a semi-independent activity – there were few political obstacles to the growth of larger business enterprises. During the 1880s, the organization of "big business" began to dominate the scene, with an ability to mass-produce commodities and to distribute them widely. Big business employed a new corporate structure, which enabled enterprises to raise large amounts of capital through stock and bond offerings and provided a more stable legal structure for operating in national and international markets.

The rise of big business provides only one dimension of the radically altered social landscape of late nineteenth-century America. The era's economic growth spurred migration of Americans from farms and rural communities to towns and cities, and a profound demographic shift occurred as the United States became a more urban nation. Migrants moved to the new jobs that were created in urban America; the migrant population contributed to the rapid growth and dense population evident in towns and cities, which expanded spatially in order to accommodate their new inhabitants. The extent of urbanization was most significant in the North and Midwest, the centers of industrial manufacturing. There, especially, much of the work force in the factories, mills, and mines of industry was composed of the 25 million immigrants who arrived in the United States between 1871 and 1914. Some eleven million immigrants passed through Ellis Island, in New York harbor, between its opening as an immigration station in 1892, and 1940.

The flood of immigrants was aided by improved transportation after the Civil War: whereas more than 95 percent in 1856 came on sailing ships, in 1873 more than 95 percent traveled by steam. A majority of these came from southern and eastern Europe, especially the poor sections of southern Italy and Sicily, along with people escaping political oppression and poverty in the Russian, Austro-Hungarian, and Ottoman empires. Thousands of these "new" immigrants – so-called because they differed from previous immigrants from northern Europe – came to major metropolitan areas such as New York and Chicago. By 1910, more than 75 percent of New York's inhabitants were either immigrants or the children of immigrants. The majority of Asian and Mexican immigrants traveled to the American West, but both groups suffered restrictions unlike anything experienced by European immigrants. In 1882, the Chinese Exclusion Act banned immigration by Chinese laborers and prohibited Chinese from obtaining citizenship, while Japanese were excluded from citizenship by order of the US Attorney General in 1906. Japanese immigrants were prohibited from owning land in California by an act of the state legislature in 1913.

Cities became the centers of working-class life, with a distinctive culture emerging there. The industrialization of the workplace completely altered the way that workers conducted themselves in their jobs, how they oriented their days, and how much control they possessed over their surroundings. Innovations in manufacturing, mining, and other extractive industries resulted in much greater productivity but much less autonomy by workers, who struggled for control against the near-absolute authority of Gilded Age industrial capitalists, and labor strife was characteristic of this era. A continuing struggle between workers and owners dominated the history of industrialization.

While metropolitan areas such as New York and Chicago created institutions of "high" culture – operas, museums, and libraries – they also saw the rapid expansion of popular culture and new spaces where workers could congregate. The rise of professionalized sports, such as baseball, provided one such space, and ballparks became a focus of urban life. New amusement parks – the best and biggest example at Coney Island, in New York City – attracted a working-class audience in urban America. Dance halls and theaters, which featured new music and drama, were another center, and these new forms of culture challenged traditional notions of sexuality and public performance. To some extent, it provided new opportunities for women in the urban spaces of Gilded Age America.

The urban–industrial centers thus became cultural havens for the American working class. With the advent of cheap printing presses during the Gilded Age, a readership developed for popular literature – dime novels and magazines geared to working-class audiences. Organized labor maintained an extensive network of newspapers presenting a working-class point of view and the perspective of immigrants. Other publications appealed to working-class audiences as well. Story papers, which published five to eight stories a week for about five cents, carried serial accounts of fiction featuring westerns, romances, and adventures. Even more important during the Gilded Age and Progressive Era were dime novels, short pieces of fiction that emphasized violent, suggestive sexual themes and sensationalism – combined with middle-class morality. Publishers of dime novels also began to offer briefer pamphlet versions (a third of the size of the novels), which sold for a nickel and reached an even wider audience. The heroes of the stories were working-class men and women and reflected the conditions of urban life, while the enemies were frequently the wealthy. Often the central characters were women, and popular literature projected different views of gender.

Much of the national self-definition occurring during the Gilded Age and Progressive Era concerned the status of Americans in the world. Historically, the United States was isolated by thousands of miles of ocean, and slow transportation and communication, from Europe, Asia, and Africa. During this period, however, the world became a smaller place. Steamships, by 1900, traveled across the North Atlantic in less than a week; liners easily and cheaply carried goods south to Latin America and west to Asia.

A global communications revolution occurred after the Civil War. In 1866, the British laid the first transatlantic cable, and by the 1870s it had communications links to its imperial possessions in Africa and Asia. The Spanish-American War of 1898 was fought with the benefit of telegraphic communication, by means of cables that linked Washington and the Pacific Fleet across the Atlantic and Indian oceans. Not until 1903 was the first transpacific cable laid.

The emergence of the United States as an economic superpower meant that its global interests grew substantially by the early twentieth century. In the aftermath of the Spanish-American War, the United States created a formal empire consisting of colonies in Puerto Rico and the Philippines and new possessions in the Pacific Islands, along with an official protectorate in Cuba and unofficial protectorates around the Caribbean basin. An informal empire consisting of expanding financial interests in Latin America and Asia became increasingly important.

A major theme of this volume involves the transformative effects of reform and war. The Progressive Era brought a wholesale restructuring of social and political institutions, largely in response to the economic and social transformations of the post-Reconstruction era, and reform became a driving force during the early twentieth century. Progressive Era reformers were united by a common anxiety about industrialism and what the new economic system meant for the social and political fabric. Reformers were generally opposed to monopolies, and they sought ways to regulate uncontrolled capitalism in the marketplace. The industrial revolution had expanded wealth but had also exposed social divisions to an unprecedented extent. Reformers, aware of the harsh realities of industrial life, feared a widening gap between rich and poor. They thus focused their efforts on alleviating the social consequences of industrial society, for immigrants, workers, the poor, and especially for children. They feared political corruption, in some measure a result of the inability of the political system to keep up with new economic forces. Reformers were animated by the Social Gospel – the new Protestant faith in the ability of human society to solve social problems. Progressives were also united around cosmopolitan values – a faith in science, a belief in progress, and a desire to find new sources of social cohesion.

Women, especially middle-class women, occupied a prominent position in the ranks of reformers, and progressivism provided a forum for a newly assertive public presence in campaigns for education, playgrounds, and restricting child labor. Many of these same women reformers led the way in obtaining woman suffrage. Reform in the early twentieth century focused especially on refashioning social relationships, reconstructing the political system, and injecting a new sense of nationality. Perhaps the most important force for change in the early twentieth century, however, was war – and the United States' new presence abroad. America became an imperial power after the conclusion of the Spanish-American War of 1898, but it was increasingly drawn into world events, eventually intervening in 1917 in the European war. Especially important were the domestic implications of imperialism and war – and how forces of nationalism, ethnic identity, and racism shaped Americans' perceptions of the world, and how the decision to intervene was hotly contested and opposed in an extensive national debate.

The Gilded Age and Progressive Era thus compelled Americans to consider their place in the world. The new technological forces evident in communication and transportation had made the world much smaller – and more accessible to American economic dominance and financial control. The Spanish-American War made the United States, for the first time in its history, the possessors of overseas colonies. Yet the more important manifestation of American imperialism was the spread of financial control and domination of overseas markets. This new position as a formal and informal imperial power certainly meant new responsibilities. Not all Americans were comfortable with having an overseas empire, however limited, and not all Americans wanted to become more involved in European disputes. With the outbreak of general war in Europe in 1914, Americans were forced to confront the meaning of their nationality and their relationship to the rest of the world.

This volume gathers documents related to the Gilded Age and Progressive Era, the large period in American history between Reconstruction and World War I. These documents are suited to classroom use, with 14 chapters, each containing roughly four or five documents. For purposes of clarity, the volume is broken into five parts organized around some important themes of this historical period. Within each part, chapters provide thematic and chronological topics suited for instructors and students.

The documents illustrate the variety of experiences and themes involved in the transformation of American political, economic, and social systems during this period. We have tried to present perspectives of race, class, gender, and culture – central to understanding the experiences of the Gilded Age and Progressive Era. The volume begins with a look at the American frontier after Reconstruction in the South and West, and cultural interactions between whites and Native Americans, African Americans, Hispanics, and Asians. We next present different perspectives on the transformations that arrived with industrialization, including the rise of large corporations, the sudden emergence of a large moneyed class as contrasted with the persistence of poverty in urban–industrial areas, and the arrival of different groups of new, heretofore "alien" immigrants to the United States. In the third part of the book, we present documents that reveal the social and political crisis that gripped the United States at the end of the nineteenth century in terms of populism, race, and labor. The final sections of the book provide documents for students on reform and war, and in these sections we provide perspectives from different groups about how these forces transformed America.

Prelude: Mark Twain and the Gilded Age[1]

Mark Twain and Charles Dudley Warner, from *The Gilded Age*, 1873

Samuel L. Clemens (1835–1910), who wrote under the name Mark Twain, was a leading novelist, humorist, and personality of the last half of the nineteenth century. Among his many writings, The Adventures of Tom Sawyer *(1876) and* The Adventures of Huckleberry Finn *(1884) were among his most popular. Born in Florida, Missouri, Clemens learned the trade of printing, and worked in New York, Philadelphia, and Cincinnati. Traveling to the West Coast by stagecoach in 1861, Twain spent the Civil War years in San Francisco, where he worked as a journalist. He continued to travel widely and published accounts of his travels to Europe in* Innocents Abroad *(1869) and to the American West in* Roughing It *(1872).*

The Gilded Age was co-authored with Charles Dudley Warner, and it represents Twain's first attempt at fiction. This tongue-in-cheek account of the city of Washington, DC, has all the marks of Twain's brand of humor. This excerpt from the longer novel written jointly by Twain and Warner conveys a sense of the capital as a backwater city aiming to be sophisticated and cultured. This section of the book satirizes the political corruption

---

[1] Mark Twain and Charles Dudley Warner, *The Gilded Age: A Tale of Today* (New York and London: Harper & Brothers, 1915 [1873]), excerpted from Chapter XXIV.

The Gilded Age and Progressive Era: A Documentary Reader. First Edition.
Edited by William A. Link and Susannah J. Link.
© 2012 Blackwell Publishing Ltd. Published 2012 by Blackwell Publishing Ltd.

during the Grant administration, but the phrase that the authors coined to illustrate the excesses of the late nineteenth century, "the Gilded Age," also refers to economic excesses of the period.

Washington is an interesting city to any of us. It seems to become more and more interesting the oftener we visit it. Perhaps the reader has never been there? Very well. You arrive either at night, rather too late to do anything or see anything until morning, or you arrive so early in the morning that you consider it best to go to your hotel and sleep an hour or two while the sun bothers along over the Atlantic. You cannot well arrive at a pleasant intermediate hour, because the railway corporation that keeps the keys of the only door that leads into the town or out of it take care of that. You arrive in tolerably good spirits, because it is only thirty-eight miles from Baltimore to the capital, and so you have only been insulted three times (provided you are not in a sleeping car—the average is higher there): once when you renewed your ticket after stopping over in Baltimore, once when you were about to enter the "ladies' car" without knowing it was a lady's car, and once when you asked the conductor at what hour you would reach Washington.

You are assailed by a long rank of hackmen who shake their whips in your face as you step out upon the sidewalk; you enter what they regard as a "carriage," in the capital, and you wonder why they do not take it out of service and put it in the museum: we have few enough antiquities, and it is little to our credit that we make scarcely any effort to preserve the few we have. . . .

You naturally wish to view the city; so you take an umbrella, an overcoat, and a fan, and go forth. The prominent features you soon locate and get familiar with; first you glimpse the ornamental upper works of a long, snowy palace projecting above a grove of trees, and a tall, graceful white dome with a statue on it surmounting the palace and pleasantly contrasting with the background of blue sky. That building is the capitol. . . .

You stand at the back of the capitol to treat yourself to a view, and it is a very noble one. You understand, the capitol stands upon the verge of a high piece of table land, a fine commanding position, and its front looks out over this noble situation for a city—but it don't see it, for the reason that when the capitol extension was decided upon, the property owners at once advanced their prices to such inhuman figures that the people went down and built the city in the muddy low marsh behind the temple of liberty; so now the lordly front of the building, with its imposing colonnades, its projecting, graceful wings, its picturesque groups of statuary, and its long terraced ranges of steps, flowing down in white marble waves to the ground, merely looks out upon a sorrowful little desert of cheap boarding houses. . . .

The capitol is a very noble and a very beautiful building, both within and without, but you need not examine it now. Still, if you greatly prefer going into the dome, go. Now your general glance gives you picturesque stretches of gleaming water, on your left, with a sail here and there and a lunatic asylum on shore; over beyond the water, on a distant elevation, you see a squat yellow temple which your eye dwells upon lovingly through a blur of unmanly moisture, for it recalls your lost boyhood and the Parthenons done in molasses candy which made it blest and beautiful. Still in the distance, but on this side of the water and close to its edge, the Monument to the Father of his Country towers out of the mud—sacred soil is the customary term. It has the aspect of a factory chimney with the top broken off. The skeleton of a decaying scaffolding lingers about its summit, and tradition says that the spirit of Washington often comes down and sits on those rafters to enjoy this tribute of respect which the nation has reared as the symbol of its unappeasable gratitude. The Monument is to be finished, some day, and at that time our Washington will have risen still higher in the nation's veneration, and will be known as the Great-Great-Grandfather of his Country. The memorial Chimney stands in a quiet pastoral locality that is full of reposeful expression. With a glass you can see the cow-sheds about its base, and the contented sheep nibbling pebbles in the desert solitudes that surround it, and the tired pigs dozing in the holy calm of its protecting shadow.

Now you wrench your gaze loose, and you look down in front of you and see the broad Pennsylvania Avenue stretching straight ahead for a mile or more till it brings up against the iron fence in front of a pillared granite pile, the Treasury building—an edifice that would command respect in any capital. The stores and hotels that wall in this broad avenue are mean, and cheap, and dingy, and are better left without comment. Beyond the Treasury is a fine large white barn, with wide unhandsome grounds about it. The President lives there. It is ugly enough outside, but that is nothing to what it is inside. Dreariness, flimsiness, bad taste reduced to mathematical completeness is what the inside offers to the eye, if it remains yet what it always has been.

The front and right hand views give you the city at large. It is a wide stretch of cheap little brick houses, with here and there a noble architectural pile lifting itself out of the midst—government buildings, these. If the thaw is still going on when you come down and go about town, you will wonder at the short-sightedness of the city fathers, when you come to inspect the streets, in that they do not dilute the mud a little more and use them for canals.

If you inquire around a little, you will find that there are more boardinghouses to the square acre in Washington than there are in any other city in the land, perhaps. If you apply for a home in one of them, it will seem odd to you to have the landlady inspect you with a severe eye and then ask you if you are a member of Congress. Perhaps, just as a pleasantry, you will say yes. And then she will tell you that she is "full." Then you show her her advertisement in the morning paper, and there she stands, convicted and ashamed. She will try to blush, and it will be only polite in you to take the effort for the deed. She shows you her rooms, now, and lets you take one—but she makes you pay in advance for it. That is what you will get for pretending to be a member of Congress. If you had been content to be merely a private citizen, your trunk would have been sufficient security for your board. If you are curious and inquire into this thing, the chances are that your landlady will be ill-natured enough to say that the person and property of a Congressman are exempt from arrest or detention, and that with the tears in her eyes she has seen several of the people's representatives walk off to their several States and Territories carrying her unreceipted board bills in their pockets for keepsakes. And before you have been in Washington many weeks you will be mean enough to believe her, too.

Of course you contrive to see everything and find out everything. And one of the first and most startling things you find out is, that every individual you encounter in the City of Washington almost—and certainly every separate and distinct individual in the public employment, from the highest bureau chief, clear down to the maid who scrubs Department halls, the night watchmen of the public buildings and the darkey boy who purifies the Department spittoons—represents Political Influence. Unless you can get the ear of a Senator, or a Congressman, or a Chief of a Bureau or Department, and persuade him to use his "influence" in your behalf, you cannot get an employment of the most trivial nature in Washington. Mere merit, fitness and capability, are useless baggage to you without "influence." The population of Washington consists pretty much entirely of government employees and the people who board them. There are thousands of these employees, and they have gathered there from every corner of the Union and got their berths through the intercession (command is nearer the word) of the Senators and Representatives of their respective States. It would be an odd circumstance to see a girl get employment at three or four dollars a week in one of the great public cribs without any political grandee to back her, but merely because she was worthy, and competent, and a good citizen of a free country that "treats all persons alike." Washington would be mildly thunderstruck at such a thing as that. If you are a member of Congress, (no offence,) and one of your constituents who doesn't know anything, and does not want to go into the bother of learning something, and has no money, and no employment, and can't earn a living, comes besieging you for help, do you say, "Come, my friend, if your services were valuable you could get employment elsewhere—don't want you here?" Oh, no: You take him to a Department and say, "Here, give this person something to pass away the time at—and a salary"—and the thing is done. You throw him on his country. He is his country's child, let his country support him. There is something good and motherly about Washington, the grand old benevolent National Asylum for the Helpless.

The wages received by this great hive of employees are placed at the liberal figure meet and just for skilled and competent labor. Such of them as are immediately employed about the two Houses of Congress, are not only liberally paid also, but are remembered in the customary Extra Compensation bill which slides neatly through, annually, with the general grab that signalizes the last night of a session, and thus twenty per cent is added to their wages, for—for fun, no doubt.

Part I   New Frontiers

Chapter 1   The New South

1 Henry W. Grady, "The New South," 1886[1]

As editor of the Atlanta Constitution, *Henry W. Grady (1850–1889)
was an important voice for reconciliation with the North and a strong
proponent of the New South creed. Along with many other boosters
active in the US South after Reconstruction, Grady enthusiastically
embraced railroads, industrialization, and the commercialization of
agriculture as part of a broad program of modernization. Like other
boosters, Grady tended to minimize the adverse consequences of
modernization, the harsh results of industrialization, the dislocation
of rural southerners, and the widening income gap between rich and
poor – and he said little about racial oppression that was so was prevalent
in the post-Civil War era.*

*In his 39 years of life, Grady helped to promote the city of Atlanta as the
premier industrial and business hub in the South. The newspaper became his
vehicle for conveying his enthusiasm for a variety of causes, among them his
support for Democratic politics, for the railroad, and for agricultural
diversification away from cotton. He portrayed race relations as harmonious,
which pleased white southerners but failed to convince northern businessmen
to overlook the evidence of black disfranchisement and white violence*

[1] Edwin DuBois Shurter, ed., *The Complete Orations and Speeches of Henry W. Grady*
(New York: Hinds, Noble, & Eldredge, 1910), pp. 7–22.

The Gilded Age and Progressive Era: A Documentary Reader, First Edition.
Edited by William A. Link and Susannah J. Link.
© 2012 Blackwell Publishing Ltd. Published 2012 by Blackwell Publishing Ltd.

toward blacks. In this speech, which Grady delivered to a northern audience in 1886, he explains how the South was changing and how it was moving toward a different future.

To the New England Club in New York, 1886

We have established thrift in city and country. We have fallen in love with work. We have restored comfort to homes from which culture and elegance never departed. We have let economy take root and spread among us as rank as the crabgrass which sprung from Sherman's cavalry camps, until we are ready to lay odds on the Georgia Yankee as he manufactures relics of the battlefield in a one-story shanty and squeezes pure olive oil out of his cotton seed, against any down-easter that ever swapped wooden nutmegs for flannel sausage in the valleys of Vermont.[2] Above all, we know that we have achieved in these "piping times of peace" a fuller independence for the South than that which our fathers sought to win in the forum by their eloquence or compel in the field by their swords.

It is a rare privilege, sir, to have had part, however humble, in this work. Never was nobler duty confided to human hands than the uplifting and upbuilding of the prostrate and bleeding South—misguided, perhaps, but beautiful in her suffering, and honest, brave and generous always. In the record of her social, industrial and political illustration we await with confidence the verdict of the world.

But what of the negro? Have we solved the problem he presents or progressed in honor and equity toward solution? Let the record speak to the point. No section shows a more prosperous laboring population than the negroes of the South, none in fuller sympathy with the employing and land-owning class. He shares our school fund, has the fullest protection of our laws and the friendship of our people. Self-interest, as well as honor, demand that he should have this. Our future, our very existence depend upon our working out this problem in full and exact justice. We understand that when Lincoln signed the emancipation proclamation, your victory was assured, for he then committed you to the cause of human liberty, against which the arms of man cannot prevail—while those of our statesmen who trusted to make slavery the corner-stone of the Confederacy doomed us to defeat as far as they could, committing us to a cause that reason could not defend or the sword maintain in sight of advancing civilization.

---

[2]   Grady here referred to northerners and southerners equally willing to hustle to make a profit – by whatever means.

Had Mr. Toombs³ said, which he did not say, "that he would call the roll of his slaves at the foot of Bunker Hill," he would have been foolish, for he might have known that whenever slavery became entangled in war it must perish, and that the chattel in human flesh ended forever in New England when your fathers—not to be blamed for parting with what didn't pay—sold their slaves to our fathers—not to be praised for knowing a paying thing when they saw it. The relations of the southern people with the negro are close and cordial. We remember with what fidelity for four years he guarded our defenseless women and children, whose husbands and fathers were fighting against his freedom. To his eternal credit be it said that whenever he struck a blow for his own liberty he fought in open battle, and when at last he raised his black and humble hands that the shackles might be struck off, those hands were innocent of wrong against his helpless charges, and worthy to be taken in loving grasp by every man who honors loyalty and devotion. Ruffians have maltreated him, rascals have misled him, philanthropists established a bank for him, but the South, with the North, protests against injustice to this simple and sincere people. To liberty and enfranchisement is as far as law can carry the negro. The rest must be left to conscience and common sense. It must be left to those among whom his lot is cast, with whom he is indissolubly connected, and whose prosperity depends upon their possessing his intelligent sympathy and confidence. Faith has been kept with him, in spite of calumnious assertions to the contrary by those who assume to speak for us or by frank opponents. Faith will be kept with him in the future, if the South holds her reason and integrity.

But have we kept faith with you? In the fullest sense, yes. When Lee surrendered—I don't say when Johns[t]on⁴ surrendered, because I understand he still alludes to the time when he met General Sherman last as the time when he determined to abandon any further prosecution of the struggle—when Lee surrendered, I say, and Johns[t]on quit, the South became, and has since been, loyal to this Union. We fought hard enough to know that we were whipped, and in perfect frankness accept as final the arbitrament of the sword to which we had appealed. The South found her jewel in the toad's head of defeat. The shackles that had held her in narrow limitations fell forever when the shackles of the negro slave were broken. Under the old regime the negroes were slaves to the South; the South was a slave to the system. The old plantation, with its simple police regulations and feudal

³ Robert Toombs (1810–1885), Georgia Senator and Confederate Secretary of State.
⁴ General Joseph E. Johnston, commander of Confederate forces defending Atlanta, May–August 1864.

habit, was the only type possible under slavery. Thus was gathered in the hands of a splendid and chivalric oligarchy the substance that should have been diffused among the people, as the rich blood, under certain artificial conditions, is gathered at the heart, filling that with affluent rapture but leaving the body chill and colorless.

The old South rested everything on slavery and agriculture, unconscious that these could neither give nor maintain healthy growth. The new South presents a perfect democracy, the oligarchs leading in the popular move-ment—a social system compact and closely knitted, less splendid on the surface, but stronger at the core—a hundred farms for every plantation, fifty homes for every palace—and a diversified industry that meets the complex need of this complex age.

The new South is enamored of her new work. Her soul is stirred with the breath of a new life. The light of a grander day is falling fair on her face. She is thrilling with the consciousness of growing power and prosperity. As she stands upright, full-statured and equal among the people of the earth, breathing the keen air and looking out upon the expanded horizon, she understands that her emancipation came because through the inscrutable wisdom of God her honest purpose was crossed, and her brave armies were beaten.

2 Henry McNeal Turner on African American Civil Rights, 1889[5]

Henry McNeal Turner (1834–1915) was born a free black in Newberry Courthouse, South Carolina, and was largely self-educated. Eventually becoming a preacher in the black African Methodist Episcopal (AME) church, he served as an evangelist during the 1850s and eventually moved north to St Louis, Washington, DC, and Baltimore. In 1863, he helped to organize a regiment of black troops, serving as its chaplain. After the end of the Civil War, Turner moved to Georgia, and became an organizer for AME churches around the state. Meanwhile, he became an important leader in the Republican party, participating in Georgia's Reconstruction constitutional convention in 1868. In 1880, he became an AME bishop, and he remained a fearless advocate of African American civil and political rights.

In these two letters, published in the New York Voice *and the* Christian Record, *Turner protested the decision of the Supreme Court in the Civil Rights Cases (1883), which rendered the Civil Rights Act of 1875*

---

[5]   Henry McNeal Turner, *Civil Rights: The Outrage of the Supreme Court of the United States upon the Black Man* (Philadelphia: Publication Department AME Church, 1889).

unconstitutional. He wrote in a political environment in which the position
of African Americans was besieged by white supremacists. Increasingly, their
northern allies were abandoning them to white political control that
occurred with the end of Reconstruction.

Amidst multitudinous duties I find, calling my attention, your note of recent date, asking me to briefly refer to the "Civil Rights Decisions," which, since their delivery has drawn from me expressions which many are pleased to call severe adverse strictures upon the highest court in this country, and upon all of its judges save one, Mr. Justice Harlan.[6] It is to me a matter of that kind of surprise called wonder suddenly excited, to find a single, solitary individual who belongs in the United States, or who has been here for any considerable time, unacquainted with those famous FIVE DEATH DEALING DECISIONS. Indeed, sir, those decisions have had since the 15th day of October, A. D., 1883, the day of their pronouncement, more of my study than any other civil subject. I incline to the opinion that I have an argument which, taken as a concomitant of the learned dissenting sentiments of that eminent jurist, Mr. Justice Harlan, would to a rational mind, make the judgment of Justice Bradley[7] and his associates a deliquescence—a bubble on the wave of equity—a legal nothing. You bid me in my reply to observe brevity. Shortness and conciseness seems to be the ever present rule, when the Negro and his case is under treatment. However, I am satisfied that in saying this, I do not convey your reason for commanding me to condense, "boil down." The more I ponder the non-agreeing words of that member of our chief assize, who had the moral courage to bid defiance to race prejudice, the more certain am I that no words of mine, condemnatory of that decision, has been sufficiently harsh.

March 1st, 1875, Congress passed an act, entitled, "An act for the prevention of discrimination on the ground of race, color or previous condition of servitude," said act being generally known as the Civil Rights Bill,....

No sane man can read the record, law and authorities relating to these cases, without forming a conclusion that cannot be brushed away, that the bench of judges were narrow even to wicked ingeniousness, superinduced by color-phobiism [*sic*]. Sane men know that the gentlemen in Congress who voted for this act of 1875, understood full well the

---

[6]   John Marshall Harlan (1833–1911), a Supreme Court justice who dissented from the majority decision in the case.

[7]   Joseph P. Bradley (1813–1892), appointed to the court in 1870, who delivered the majority decision in the case.

condition of our country, as did the powers amending the Constitution abolishing slavery. The intention was to entirely free, not to partly liberate.

The desire was to remove the once slave so far from his place of bondage, that he would not even remember it, if such a thing were possible. Congress stepped in and said, he shall vote, he shall serve on juries, he shall testify in court, he shall enter the professions, he shall hold offices, he shall be treated like other men, in all places the conduct of which is regulated by law, he shall in no way be reminded by partial treatment, by discrimination, that he was once a "chattel," a "thing." Certainly Congress had a right [to] do this. The power that made the slave a man instead of a "thing" had the right to fix his status. The height of absurdity, the chief point in idiocy, the brand of total imbecility, is to say, that the Negro shall vote a privilege into existence which one citizen may enjoy for pay, to the exclusion of another, coming in the same way, but clothed in the vesture covering the earth when God first looked upon it. Are colored men to vote grants to railroads upon which they cannot receive equal accommodation? When we ask redress, we are told that the State must first pass a law prohibiting us from enjoying certain privileges and rights, and that after such laws have been passed by the State, we can apply to the United States courts to have such laws declared null and void by quo warranto proceedings.[8] The Supreme Court, when applied to, will say to the State, you must not place such laws on your statute book. You can continue your discrimination on account of color. You can continue to place the badge of slavery on persons having more than one-eighth part of Negro blood in their veins, and so long as your State Legislatures do not license you so to do, you are safe. For if they, (the Negroes) come to us for redress, we will talk about the autonomy of the State must be held inviolate, referring them back to you for satisfaction.

Do you know of anything more degrading to our country, more damnable? The year after this decision the Republican party met with defeat, because it acquiesced by its silence in that abominable decision, nor did it lift a hand to strike down that diabolical sham of judicial monstrosity, neither in Congress nor the great National Convention which nominated Blaine and Logan. God, however, has placed them in power again, using the voters and our manner of electing electors as instruments in his hands. God would have men do right, harm no one, and to render to every man his just due. Mr. Justice Harlan rightly says that the Thirteenth Amendment intended that the white

---

[8]   "Quo warranto" referred to claims asserting that individual or governmental officials were wrongfully exercising their powers.

race should have no privilege whatsoever pertaining to citizenship and freedom, that was not alike extended and to be enjoyed by those persons who, though the greater part of them were slaves, were invited by an act of Congress to aid in saving from overthrow a government which, theretofore by all of its departments, had treated them as an inferior race, with no legal rights or privileges except such as the white race might choose to grant. It is an indisputable fact that the amendment last mentioned may be exerted by legislation of a direct and primary character for the eradication, not simply of the institution of slavery, but of its badges and incidents indicating that the individual was once a slave. The Supreme Court must decide the inter-State commerce law to be unconstitutional on account of interference with the State's autonomy, for it must be remembered that Mrs. Robinson,[9] a citizen of Mississippi, bought a ticket from Grand Junction, Tennessee, to Lynchburg, Virginia, and when praying for satisfaction for rough and contumacious treatment, received at the hands of the company's agent, she was informed by the Court, that the Court was without power to act. Congress had constitutional power to pursue a runaway slave into all the States by legislation, to punish the man that would dare to conceal the slave. Congress could find the poor fellow seeking God's best blessing to man, liberty, and return him to his master, but Congress cannot, so say our honorable Court, give aid sufficient to the poor black man, to prove beyond all doubt to him that he is as free as any other citizen. Mr. Justice Harlan says: "The difficulty has been to compel a recognition of the legal right of the black race to take the rank of citizens, and to secure the enjoyment of privileges belonging under the law to them as a component part of the people for whose welfare government is ordained. At every step in this direction, the Nation has been confronted with class tyranny, which is of all tyrannies the most intolerable, for it is ubiquitous in its operation, and weighs perhaps most heavily on those whose obscurity or distance would draw them from the notice of a single despot. To-day it is the colored race which is denied by corporations and individuals wielding public authority, rights fundamental in their freedom and citizenship. AT SOME FUTURE TIME IT MAY BE THAT SOME OTHER RACE WILL FALL UNDER THE BAN OF RACE DISCRIMINATION." This last preceding sentence sounds like prophecy from on high. Will the day come when Justice Bradley will want to hide from his decree of the 15th day of October, 1883, and say *non est factum*? I conclude with great reluctance these brief lines, assuring you that the subject is just opened and if desired by you, I will be glad to give it elaborate attention.

---

[9] One of the plaintiffs in the case.

I ask no rights and privileges for my race in this country, which I would not contend for on behalf of the white people were the conditions changed, or were I to find proscribed white men in Africa where black rules.

A word more and I am done, as you wish brevity. God may forgive this corps of unjust judges, but I never can, their very memories will also be detested by my children's children, nor am I alone in this detestation. The eight millions of my race and their posterity will stand horror-frozen at the very mention of their names. The scenes that have passed under my eyes upon the public highways, the brutal treatment of helpless women which I have witnessed, since that decision was proclaimed, is enough to move heaven to tears and raise a loud acclaim in hell over the conquest of wrong. But we will wait and pray, and look for a better day, for God still lives and the LORD OF HOSTS REIGNS.

I am, sir, yours, for the Fatherhood of God, and the Brotherhood of man.

H. M. TURNER.

Atlanta, Georgia,
January 4th, 1889.

3 William D. Kelley, from *The Old South and New*, 1888[10]

William Darrah Kelley (1814–1890) was a longtime congressman and lawyer from Philadelphia, Pennsylvania. A speech he delivered in 1854, denouncing the slave trade, brought him widespread attention at a time when the extension of slavery to the new US territories was a subject of intense national debate. When the Missouri Compromise was overturned, Kelley left the Democratic party and helped to found the new Republican party, which was dedicated to stopping the extension of slavery. His steady support for the Pennsylvania iron and steel industry earned him the nickname of "Pig Iron" Kelley. He served in the US House of Representatives from 1861 until his death in 1890. After the Civil War, Kelley was a staunch radical Republican, and he supported black suffrage and civil rights in the South. This account of the South comes from his visits and observations that were published as The Old South and the New *in 1888.*

In this document, Kelley examines the prospects for change in the post-Civil War South. Like many other northerners, Kelley was taken with the possibilities of economic development in the South in railroads, mining, and industrialization. Indeed, his analysis sounds very familiar to the treatment provided by Atlanta's Henry W. Grady.

---

[10]   William D. Kelley, *The Old South and the New* (New York and London: G.P. Putnam's Sons, 1888), pp. 1–14.

Letter I

The South in 1867—Nashville, Cowan, South Pittsburg, Chattanooga, Birmingham, Anniston, and Atlanta in 1887

Washington, D. C., December 15, 1886

I gladly comply with your request for a communication on the resources, progress, and prospects of the South as seen during my recent visit to Tennessee and Alabama, and while making a trip through Northeastern Georgia and across South Carolina on the Piedmont Air Line road, en route from Atlanta to Washington.

I have points of comparison in vivid recollections of visits to these States in 1867, and to Florida and Georgia in 1875. The progress in wealth, in the means of individual comfort, and in productive power made by those portions of the country with which I can thus institute comparisons has been marvellous. In 1867 the South was a land of desolation, her fields were fenceless and uncultivated, and her people were without reproductive stock, or that with which to impel modern agricultural implements, if these had been bestowed upon them gratuitously. They were, numerically speaking, without seed for food crops, except such as had been bestowed upon them by personal friends, or the government through the Freed- men's Bureau and the agencies of the Agricultural Department.

The war had undoubtedly been the proximate cause of these deplorable conditions; but it was not their primary cause, as investigation discloses the fact that this was to be found in the economic opinions and industrial system that had dominated the South before the war, and under which she neither had nor could have populous towns or a great city, which her leaders regarded as great sores. Without such aggregations of people, no development of her boundless and infinitely varied mineral resources could be had. These were, in fact, treated as of little value, and as involving in their possible development dangers to the prevailing system of field labor. In the absence of cities and of mining and manufacturing populations, the productions of the South were restricted to a few great staples, such as cotton, rice, sugar, and tobacco; and in the inevitable absence of fertilizers, which in those days were chiefly derived from the barnyard, and the refuse of towns and cities, these crops were so exhausting as to require the land to be recuperated by being permitted to lie fallow for twenty or more years, so that each planter was required to own vast bodies of land in order to have at all times a plantation susceptible of profitable cultivation. As the labor on these large estates was performed by slaves, there was no employment for the white families, who occupied small patches of poor land, and most of whom derived a precarious living from the game and fish they might take, and from such cotton or tobacco as in the absence of implements and barnyards they could extort from their exhausted acres.

Referring to the poverty of the people and contrasting it with the incalculable value of the mineral wealth with which their State abounded, I appealed to an audience of thousands of people at Montgomery, Alabama, in May, 1867, to relieve themselves from the drudgery of ill-paid manual toil, and the penury it entailed upon them, by exchanging part of their land for capital with which to develop the coal, iron ore, and limestone to be found in or near to that which they might retain. By recurring to my remarks, as reported by a citizen of Alabama in the *Montgomery Sentinel*, I find that I said:

"It is in the interest of our country that I speak when I ask you how you use the advantages with which nature has so bounteously provided you, and tell you that you have impoverished yourselves by treating them with contempt. We turn our coal and iron to most profitable account. You permit yours to slumber in their native earth. Availing ourselves of their power, one man with us does the work of a hundred with you. One little girl, tending a machine in a factory, will spin or weave more cotton in a day than one of your women will in a year by the ancient method of the wheel and the hand-loom. You have not deemed your mineral wealth worthy of consideration. In your devotion to your peculiar system of labor, you have forgotten that iron and coal are the most potent agents of modern civilization. Mere muscular power has become a thing of secondary consideration. Iron is the muscle of modern civilization, and coal—ignited coal—is the nervous force that animates it."

In view of the immense development of the coal and iron ore of these States, and the increase in number and extent of industrial centres I saw in Tennessee and Alabama, the States in which I had most frequently spoken in 1867, the recollection of the remarks just quoted made me fear that well-instructed men among my auditors must have felt that I was treating them as children, and giving them what might be regarded as a kindergarten lesson in the elements of the civilization of the latter half of the nineteenth century. Certain it is that they have outgrown the need of such elementary suggestions. The changes wrought in the meantime have been marvellous, and may justly be regarded as the work of Titans.

The systems of railroad that now traverse the South are as perfect in the construction of road-bed, track, and bridges, and in passenger cars and the means provided for the transportation of freight, as those of the North. Lateral roads branch from them into such valleys as are known to be specially rich, not in iron alone, but in other minerals, some of which are found in such profusion and juxtaposition as to seem to defy geologic laws as elsewhere illustrated. . . .

My attention was first drawn to the striking contrast between the neat, commodious, and well-painted homes of the negro laborers engaged in mining, smelting, and mechanical pursuits, and the cabins in which the poor white growers of cotton live now, as they did before the war. ...But the establishment which interested me as much as any in Chattanooga was a Bessemer steel-nail works, of which Mr. James Duncan, formerly of the Cambria Works, of Johnstown, Pennsylvania, is superintendent, and, I think, proprietor. . . . Here I found unexpected evidence of the industry and mechanical skill of some of these colored boys, in attestation of which I purchased from one of them a steel paper-cutter made from a railway spike with such imperfect tools as he had himself constructed. The maker disliked to part with this evidence of his skill, because it had not received the finishing touches, and the blade was less smooth and polished than he had intended to make it. I also secured a lady's button-hook, made from a spike with the same artless tools by the same lad. Mr. Duncan assured us that for the privilege of testing their skill and improving it some of the boys would devote more than half of the hour allowed for dinner to this work, and that the only limitation upon the number of articles they might produce was that they should work at them during dinner-time only, and should report the fact whenever they required another spike. The establishment of an industrial-art school in the midst of a population like these Chattanooga nail-makers would soon produce gratifying evidence of the adaptation of negro labor to mechanical pursuits requiring a high degree of skill. Chattanooga, in addition to its productive industries, is also a large distributer of groceries and dry goods, and evidently has a commercial future.

Birmingham lacks the advantages Chattanooga derives from its situation on a river. It is an interior town. When the war closed, its site was a tenantless wilderness, but it is now an industrial centre, the energy of whose more than 25,000 inhabitants and the resources, found chiefly within a few miles of the city limits, which they have made tributary to their prosperity, would be a marvel in any country. . . .

It is a noteworthy fact that Anniston has a direct trade with China, at least to the extent of part of the productions of its cotton-mill. It was indeed a surprise to find bales of goods marked and branded for direct shipment from this interior town in Alabama, the history of which runs through less than seventeen years, to a commercial correspondent in

China. The ores used in the furnaces at Anniston, Ironaton, and Jenifer are procured from mines belonging to the companies, and the wood from which charcoal, the only fuel used in the furnaces and shops, is derived from the mountain spurs which are distant far enough from the Inn, as viewed from its broad verandas, to give the scene the character of an enchanted valley. ...

Space will not permit me to say anything definite about the marble deposits which extend through Tennessee, Alabama, and Georgia, and embrace almost every variety of marble. I may, however, mention an illustrative fact. In passing by the Woodstock furnaces, the attention of our party was attracted by a pile of broken marble of singular whiteness, pieces of which bore such an appearance of polish, as to create the impression that they were fragments of a manufactured article. This, however, was not the case. They had been brought there to be used as flux. The quarry from which they had been taken was the one selected to furnish the block of marble Alabama was to contribute to the Washington monument. When it had been finished and properly inscribed, the block was forwarded and received by the builders of the monument, and having been scrutinized and submitted to the judgment of experts, it was returned with a communication stating that the law required the stone from each State to be a specimen of its own resources, and that this was Italian marble. So firm was this conviction that it required the certificates upon honor of the governor of the State, of senators and members of Congress, and the affidavits of parties connected with the quarry to convince the experts who had the erection of the monument in charge that it was not Italian, but Alabama marble. . . .

In 1867 I saw the ruins of what had been the little city of Atlanta, which had prided itself upon the amount of cotton its merchants handled annually. It was literally in ruins—I may say in ashes; but as I looked upon it now I saw that I had then looked upon the ashes from which a phoenix was to rise. The census of 1880 found more than 50,000 people in Atlanta, and the number has certainly increased since then. That they are prosperous people is attested by every thing you behold in Atlanta. Into and out of its union depot pass the cars of eight through-line railroads, to which three important ones are now being added. The Kimball House, which is one of the best- appointed hotels in the country, cost considerably more than a million of dollars for its reconstruction after its destruction by fire in 1883. The office from which the *Constitution* issues its many thousand papers daily is impressive alike by its extent and architectural beauty. The Markham House and other fine hotels cluster about the depot and the

Kimball House. The evening was cold and the streets were sleety, but it was the only chance I would have to see any thing of Atlanta. I therefore walked far enough to see some of the great business houses of the city, and, by the aid of street railroads, saw something of the portion in which the elegant residences of Atlanta's millionaires are found. As we left in the morning, we discovered pregnant proof that the growth of Atlanta had exceeded the expectations of its earlier settlers, for factories, warehouses, freight depots, and other massive buildings are rapidly enclosing the beautiful cemetery, which, when laid out, was evidently believed to be too remote from the town for the possible encroachment of its stirring life upon this quiet city of the dead.

In having complied with your request, and thus told the readers of the *Manufacturers Record* what I saw in my brief visit to Tennessee, Alabama, and Georgia, I have given them but faint intimations of the resources of the South, of the impulses that now animate her, and of the rapid strides with which the spirit of the nineteenth century is changing not only the aspect of the country but the purposes and aspirations of her people.

4 Lewis Hine, Photographs of Southern Textile Workers, 1908–09

Lewis W. Hine (1874–1940) was a sociologist and a photographer who documented several important subjects in American life, among them labor, immigrants, and child labor. Born in Oshkosh, Wisconsin, he enrolled at the University of Chicago in 1900. A year later, he relocated to New York City, and, while working at the Ethical Culture School, began work in photography while earning a degree at New York University. As a sociological photographer, he began examining various aspects of American life. His photographs of immigrants on Ellis Island, which he took in 1904, documented the entry point in New York Harbor for European immigrants. The Ellis Island photographs reflect his efforts to portray the working classes and immigrants sympathetically.

In 1908, Hine was assigned by the National Child Labor Committee to take photographs of children at work in factories, mines, and on farms. These photographs are a small selection from his work documenting the use of children in southern cotton factories during the early twentieth century. His photographs created public awareness of the deprivation caused by child labor and were instrumental in the demand for child labor laws.

Figure 1.1 "Little Spinner in Globe Cotton Mill. Augusta, Ga. The overseer admitted she was regularly employed."
Source: Photograph by Lewis W. Hine. Library of Congress, Prints and Photographs Division, LC-DIG-nclc-*01583*.

Figure 1.2   "Girls as Mill Workers, 1908. Spinners & doffers in Mollahan Mills, Newberry, S.C. Many others as small," December 1908.
Source: Photograph by Lewis W. Hine. Library of Congress, Prints and Photographs Division, LC-DIG-nclc-01464.

Discussion Questions: Chapter 1

1   How did Henry Grady regard Confederate defeat, 20 years after the end of the Civil War?
2   In Kelley's view, what accounted for the dramatic economic changes that had occurred between his previous and his most recent visits to the South?
3   Compare Grady's, Turner's, and Kelley's views of African Americans in the New South.
4   What are Grady's attitudes toward the Old South? What were its values, and how does he reject them?
5   What objections did Turner have to the *Civil Rights Cases* decision?

Chapter 2   The New West

1 T.S. Kenderdine, from *California Revisited, 1858–1897*, 1898[1]

*Thaddeus S. Kenderdine (1836–1922) traveled to California twice, in 1858
and in 1897, and, in the following account, he chronicles the changes he
observed during his second trip west. He traveled from San Francisco south
to the area around Los Angeles and back up through the Sacramento Valley
and gold country before heading east again. Beginning with the Gold Rush
of the 1850s, California, in particular, had grown and changed in his 40-year
absence. The railroads dominated western business and politics, and farmers
had begun to fight back. In order to obtain a cheap source of labor, the
railroad owners had imported large numbers of Chinese workers to build the
lines, which helped to create racial tensions and led to the passage of laws
excluding Chinese from immigrating to the state. California Indian tribes
had been pushed onto reservations made up of marginal lands, where their
numbers continued to decline.*

[1] (Newtown, PA, 1898), pp. 160–99.

The Gilded Age and Progressive Era: A Documentary Reader, First Edition.
Edited by William A. Link and Susannah J. Link.
© 2012 Blackwell Publishing Ltd. Published 2012 by Blackwell Publishing Ltd.

We soon came to another divide, this time where we crossed the Sierra Madre—the Mother Mountain. Heavy grades, sharp, over-lapping curves, whence we look down to deep valleys with mining camps and irrigated strips of cultivated ground in their bottoms; and then through a 7000 foot tunnel, and we swiftly descend to the Los Angeles valley. The scene is changing, and in place of brown mountain ranges and desolate valleys we are amid such scenes as cheered the hearts of Napoleon's soldiers as they tramped down the Alps to Italy—except our mountain, instead of being snow-clad, was browned with drouth. Orange orchards and groves of olives showed themselves around us, and far ahead the vales and plains were green with irrigated fruit lands. Descending more and more, we came to the Los Angeles river and, skirting it a while, we at length came to straggling suburbs, and crossing the river were in a few minutes under the roof of the Arcade depot, and in the City of Angels—once so called, but now a city of hustling mortals.

How can I compare this place of 100,000 people; a railroad centre, whence steam and electric ways converge from all direction; 175 miles of graveled and asphalt avenues which street cars traverse to a large extent; magnificent stores and private residences in the city's heart, and in the suburbs neat cottages surrounded by tropical plants and flowers; watered by artesian wells and mountain streams and lighted by electricity? No better way than by my description in '58, after speaking of the business portion.

"The streets of old Los Angeles have a singular look. The houses are built of blocks of sun-dried clay, called adobes; roofed with tiles and sometimes reeds, or tules, from the marshes. Over the last is spread a coating of pitch from bitumen beds near the town. In the summer this melts, and running down the white fronts gives them a variegated look. These ranges of houses are occasionally pierced by gateways which open to gardens where orange trees and grape vines show their fruit in their seasons. While the Americans were in the lead there was a large percentage of a different element— Mexicans, Indians and Chinese. Occasionally a troop of faggot-laden donkeys[2] would come stringing into the town from the adjacent mountains, while now and then a slow moving team of oxen, on the road to the coast with pipes of wine, was seen. At an opposite gate came Mexican horsemen with large hats; 'serapes' on shoulder and lasso on saddle, with big spurs a- jingle, raising clouds of dust. Mid-stream, in the Los Angeles river, I saw women washing clothes by beating and wringing them; a picturesque scene."

....A visit to "Spanish-town," as the section around and south of the Plaza is called, is of much interest. The greater part of the old adobes are standing;

---

[2]   Faggots are bundles of sticks used for fuel.

but their one-time Mexican tenants are mainly died away, and Chinamen, or people of like low caste, have replaced them. Some of the old buildings are in fair condition; but many are going to ruin. The Pico House, in General Pico's time a pretentious mansion, from being of two- stories, is the most imposing of the lot, and even this is a victim of Chinese invasion. The greater part of these slant-eyed fellows is truckers,[3] renting patches of land in the suburbs. Through their economical, patient, careful ways they have driven the Americans from vegetable rising in California. They are adapted to the irrigating necessities of the southern end of the state and by the use of hand pumps, artesian wells, or corporation water are making arid plains and hillsides teem with edible growth. They do not, however, put their marketing in attractive shape, but as it is sold at low prices that does not seem an objection. At first they abused their horses, but a few fines from the S. P. C. A.[4] taught these frugal-minded heathens a lesson. As the Celestials[5] drive in to town in the evenings with their loads of truck on rickety wagons, drawn by rough horses in patched up harness, they form a curious picture. As soon as night comes on they begin their low pleasures, and shuffle and skurry along to gambling house, opium joint and theatre. The last we did not enter, but stood at the door awhile listening to the screaming voices of the actors, the clangor of drums and gongs, and occasional strains of barbaric music from brass and reed instruments. They sounded like wails from lost souls. We were curious to go inside but did not think the dirty coolies[6] crowding up the stairs suitable company and passed on. There is a Joss house[7] here, but not much favored; showing that John is getting "allee samee Meli- can man."

. . . . Long Beach is the finest bathing place on the coast, but on account of the cool air not to compare with similar resorts East. This seems strange considering the tropical vegetation and hot mid-days of Southern California; but on the shore it is cool day and night at this point. The rising of the heated air from the vast desert areas east of the Sierra Nevadas causes a vacuum which is supplied by the sea-air, and while this is warmed on its way its freshness is felt along shore to a delightful extent. The air was cool, even at noon; while the water was cold. The beach is fine and so hard as to make a driveway undented by wheel or hoof. A 1600 foot wharf, where immense quantities of fish are caught runs out to meet deep-sea vessels. The

---

[3]   A trucker is a small vegetable farmer who raises a crop to take to market.

[4]   The Society for the Prevention of Cruelty to Animals (SPCA) was first founded in England in 1824 and was organized in the United States in 1866.

[5]   A slang term for Chinese.

[6]   A derogatory slur used to refer to Chinese workers.

[7]   A Chinese temple.

town runs two miles along shore and has one thousand people. Here annually the Chatauqua Society[8] of California meets. The session was just beginning on our arrival. Long Beach had been a "dry" town, but the saloon element was now on top sufficiently to order a new election to change the charter. It has Electric Lights and Water Works. Near here an attempt is being made to harness the Ocean with a system of floats which, rising and falling with the tide, work pumps which force fresh water in a reservoir. This acts on turbine wheels whose power is capable of running the cars at Los Angeles and its electric light plant also. This fresh water—salt would hurt the pumps and water wheels—is used over and over by the tide-driven pumps. Shore lots at Long Beach are worth $40 a foot. The omnipresent street-sprinkler keeps down the dust on the main streets; on others a coating of straw is applied which answers a good purpose. Our friend met us as he promised, and assuring us he had no axe to grind in the way of selling lots, and that our progress was purely a friendly move as far as he was concerned, took us a seven-mile drive along the "sounding shore." Through palm lined streets we went and by the most luxuriant flower-decked lawns. A whale caught some time since still raised a sensation in this quiet town, and much post mortem money for the railroads, which ran excursions from all points. It was sixty feet long and was patriotically kept until the adjacent citizens were driven from their homes, when it was quietly buried—except its bones—the obsequies costing $200. The frame was then being set up in a huge shed. The catching of this whale was an event, and Long Beach people will mark time by "the year we caught the Whale." We could not thank our friend Baker enough for his kindness in the excursion he gave us, and giving him farewell passed on to new scenes. . . .

Other fruits are grown around Riverside. Prunes, olives and English walnuts are much cultivated, and for the last two years lemons have been successful. Different sections are specially adapted for special vegetation. In Orange County is a soil famous for its celery. It is so spongy that the horses who work it are shod with broad, wooden shoes to keep them from being swamped in the soil. The growth of celery from this tract is phenomenal. Near Riverside is a plantation of 6000 acres, owned by an English company, on which they are growing Caniagre, or Tan Plant, which they pretend will take the place of oak-bark for tanning leather and do its work more quickly. Wise men say it bears the same relation to the oak or hemlock that the "Wine Plant," of unhappy memory, did to the grape. This valley is full of enthusiasts, often failing; ever hopeful. The production of fruit and vegetables

---

[8] Chatauqua societies became popular in the late nineteenth century, and they featured visits by speakers around the country.

is enormous; for drought and excessive rains are never feared; but the trouble is to find a market. There are no near-by cities, like Philadelphia, New York and Baltimore to take the surplus, so at great expense they rush their products long distances to find sale; the expenses of freight and commission leaving the farmers small margin.

The road back from San Bernardino was the same I traveled in 1858. Shall I draw those odious comparisons again? I cannot help doing so! Now rushing up the valley in crowded steam-cars; then I was on a solitary "march to the sea," near ninety miles away. Where now are tract after tract of orchard and vineyard, town after town and cities of ten thousand people, then stretched sixty miles of chapparal and pasture-lands, relieved by the small towns of San Bernardino, San Gabriel and El Monte, and a few ranches. Here unbounded hospitality was once granted strangers, but its abuse by Americans had soured the Mexican ranch owners, and they got scant courtesy. Till the "gringo" came the valley was a scene of pastoral content, and the ox-cart of wood and leather, the wooden plow and brush harrow, the tomales, tortillas and chile-con-carne were all that high and low cared for in implements and diet. All were natural horsemen and their skill and accoutrements were marvels!

. . . . We saw a curiosity on the beach at Santa Monica in the likeness of two bathing machines. Readers of Dickens have known them as belongings of English watering places; but they seemed as incongruous here as a Chinaman driving a horse. They are houses, swung low on two wheels, in which squeamish people take a ride in the water, under the propulsion of quiet sea-horses; and quiet they must be or they might soon make mer-men and mer-maids of their fares in the un-wadeable depths of the sounding sea.

On our way back we saw the "stubble" of a crop peculiar to Southern California. Both coal and wood are dear here, so it pays to raise trees. The Australian Gum,[9] being the fastest growing, is most planted and the stumps of a woods of this I saw. An acre, four years from setting out, yielded forty cords, and as wood brings $8 a cord, the profit can be counted up. This yield was told me by a fellow passenger, but I rather doubted the story. . . .

On the 22d of July I visited the oil district of West Los Angeles, two miles away over the hills. The derricks stood close together—300 to 400 in a territory one-fourth of a mile wide and a mile long. They average 30 barrels of oil a day, worth $1.25 per barrel. It is only fit for fuel or gas. The wells run from 100 to 1000 feet deep and while the above product was claimed, the pumpage did not show it. By a system of cables and cranks, the slack being taken up by heavy weights, ten or twelve wells were pumped with one

---

[9] Another name for eucalyptus.

engine. The soil is full of asphaltum, which oozes from the soil. It is a dirty place; this oil field, and I willingly left it to look at West Lake Park with its pretty lake and its surrounding of palms and flowers.

2 Theodore Roosevelt, from *Ranch Life and the Hunting-Trail*, 1888[7]

Theodore Roosevelt's (1858–1919) experiences as a hunter and cattle rancher in the West shaped his views of land preservation when he became president, following the assassination of William McKinley on September 14, 1901. Roosevelt's life as a "ranchman" in the Dakota Badlands lasted only two years, from 1884 to 1886, and during the winter after he moved back to the East, a storm killed most of his cattle. His subsequent trips to the West were primarily for hunting. By living, for a time, in an environment that required physical exertion and that provided first-hand observation of the negative effects of human exploitation of natural areas, Roosevelt gained a more complete perspective on the threats to the majestic natural legacy of which Americans were stewards.

Roosevelt's experiences in the West had much to with his subsequent policies as president. At the urging of Gifford Pinchot, a forester and adviser to the president, Roosevelt placed over 200 million acres of land under federal control. The president and Pinchot were not opposed to what they considered scientific management, or responsible use, of these lands, but they wanted to keep private developers from wholesale destruction of valuable forests, plains, and mineral resources.

Chapter III: The Home Ranch

The home ranch lies on both sides of the Little Missouri, the nearest ranchman above me being about twelve, and the nearest below me about ten, miles distant. The general course of the stream here is northerly, but, while flowing through my ranch, it takes a great westerly reach of some three miles, walled in, as always, between chains of steep, high bluffs half a mile or more apart. The stream twists down through the valley in long sweeps, leaving oval wooded bottoms, first on one side and then on the other; and in an open glade among the thick-growing timber stands the long, low house of hewn logs.

[7] (New York: The Century Co., 1888), pp. 25–36.

Just in front of the ranch veranda is a line of old cotton woods that shade it during the fierce heats of summer, rendering it always cool and pleasant. But a few feet beyond these trees comes the cut-off bank of the river, through whose broad, sandy bed the shallow stream winds as if lost, except when a freshet fills it from brim to brim with foaming yellow water. The bluffs that wall in the river-valley curve back in semicircles, rising from its alluvial bottom generally as abrupt cliffs, but often as steep, grassy slopes that lead up to great level plateaus; and the line is broken every mile or two by the entrance of a coulee, or dry creek, whose head branches may be twenty miles back. Above us, where the river comes round the bend, the valley is very narrow, and the high buttes bounding it rise, sheer and barren, into scalped hill-peaks and naked knife-blade ridges. The other buildings stand in the same open glade with the ranch house, the dense growth of cotton-woods and matted, thorny underbrush making a wall all about, through which we have chopped our wagon roads and trodden out our own bridle-paths. The cattle have now trampled down this brush a little, but deer still lie in it, only a couple of hundred yards from the house; and from the door sometimes in the evening one can see them peer out into the open, or make their way down, timidly and cautiously, to drink at the river. The stable, sheds, and other outbuildings, with the hayricks[10] and the pens for such cattle as we bring in during winter, are near the house; the patch of fenced garden land is on the edge of the woods; and near the middle of the glade stands the high, circular horse-corral, with a snubbing-post in the center, and a wing built out from one side of the gate entrance, so that the saddle-band can be driven in without trouble. As it is very hard to work cattle where there is much brush, the larger cow-corral is some four miles off on an open bottom.

A ranchman's life is certainly a very pleasant one, albeit generally varied with plenty of hardship and anxiety. Although occasionally he passes days of severe toil,—for example, if he goes on the round-up he works as hard as any of his men,—yet he no longer has to undergo the monotonous drudgery attendant upon the tasks of the cowboy or of the apprentice in the business. His fare is simple; but, if he chooses, it is good enough. Many ranches are provided with nothing at all but salt pork, canned goods, and bread; indeed, it is a curious fact that in traveling through the cow country it is often impossible to get any milk or butter; but this is only because the owners or managers are too lazy to take enough trouble to insure their own comfort. We ourselves always keep up two or three cows, choosing such as are natu-rally tame, and so we invariably have plenty of milk and, when there is time

[10]   Haystack.

for churning, a good deal of butter. We also keep hens, which, in spite of the damaging inroads of hawks, bob-cats, and foxes, supply us with eggs, and in time of need, when our rifles have failed to keep us in game, with stewed, roast, or fried chicken also. From our garden we get potatoes, and unless drought, frost, or grasshoppers interfere (which they do about every second year), other vegetables as well. For fresh meat we depend chiefly upon our prowess as hunters.

During much of the time we are away on the different round-ups, that "wheeled house," the great four-horse wagon, being then our home; but when at the ranch our routine of life is always much the same, save during the excessively bitter weather of midwinter, when there is little to do except to hunt, if the days are fine enough. We breakfast early—before dawn when the nights have grown long, and rarely later than sunrise, even in midsummer. Perhaps before this meal, certainly the instant it is over, the man whose duty it is rides off to hunt up and drive in the saddle-band. Each of us has his own string of horses, eight or ten in number, and the whole band usually split up into two or three companies. In addition to the scattered groups of the saddle-band, our six or eight mares, with their colts, keep by themselves, and are rarely bothered by us, as no cowboy ever rides anything but horses, because mares give great trouble where all the animals have to be herded together. Once every two or three days somebody rides round and finds out where each of these smaller bands is, but the man who goes out in the morning merely gathers one bunch. He drives these into the corral, the other men (who have been lolling idly about the house or stable, fixing their saddles or doing any odd job) coming out with their ropes as soon as they hear the patter of the unshod hoofs and the shouts of the cowboy driver. Going into the corral, and standing near the center, each of us picks out some one of his own string from among the animals that are trotting and running in a compact mass round the circle; and after one or more trials, according to his skill, ropes it and leads it out. When all have caught their horses the rest are again turned loose, together with those that have been kept up overnight. Some horses soon get tame and do not need to be roped; my pet cutting pony, little Muley, and good old Manitou, my companion in so many hunting trips, will neither of them stay with the rest of their fellows that are jamming and jostling each other as they rush round in the dust of the corral, but they very sensibly walk up and stand quietly with the men in the middle, by the snubbing-post. Both are great pets, Manitou in particular; the wise old fellow being very fond of bread and sometimes coming up of his own accord to the ranch house and even putting his head into the door to beg for it.

Once saddled, the men ride off on their different tasks; for almost everything is done in the saddle, except that in winter we cut our firewood and quarry our coal—both on the ranch,—and in summer attend to the garden and put up what wild hay we need.

If any horses have strayed, one or two of the men will be sent off to look for them; for hunting lost horses is one of the commonest and most irksome of our duties. Every outfit always has certain of its horses at large; and if they remain out long enough they become as wild and wary as deer and have to be regularly surrounded and run down. On one occasion, when three of mine had been running loose for a couple of months, we had to follow at full speed for at least fifteen miles before exhausting them enough to enable us to get some control over them and head them towards a corral.

. . .

A ranchman's work is, of course, free from much of the sameness attendant upon that of a mere cowboy. One day he will ride out with his men among the cattle, or after strayed horses; the next he may hunt, so as to keep the ranch in meat; then he can make the tour of his outlying camps; or, again, may join one of the round-ups for a week or two, perhaps keeping with it the entire time it is working. On occasions he will have a good deal of spare time on his hands, which, if he chooses, he can spend in reading or writing. If he cares for books, there will be many a worn volume in the primitive little sitting-room, with its log walls and huge fire-place; but after a hard day's work a man will not read much, but will rock to and fro in the flickering firelight, talking sleepily over his success in the day's chase and the difficulty he has had with the cattle; or else may simply lie stretched at full length on the elk-hides and wolf-skins in front of the hearthstone, listening in drowsy silence to the roar and crackle of the blazing logs and to the moaning of the wind outside.

3   María Amparo Ruiz de Burton, from *The Squatter and the Don* (1885)[11]

María Amparo Ruiz de Burton (1832–1895) was the first known novelist of Mexican American heritage to write fiction in English. She published two novels, this second one under the pen name C. Loyal. Born in Baja California, she moved to California in 1849, and married Henry Stanton Burton, an American army officer. Ruiz de Burton's life paralleled the

11   (San Francisco, 1885), pp. 366–79.

annexation of Mexican territory by the United States after the Mexican War, so she was in a unique position to observe the cultural and political blending and tensions of these two cultures. Both of her novels are based on the premise that Mexican landowners in California were essentially white elites who were the victims of American racism and corruption. She spent the final years of her life in widowhood, fighting to retain ownership of her California ranch, which she eventually lost.

In 1851, the US government had declared all Mexican land grants in US territory part of the public domain, unless an owner could establish legal title. As a result, these lands were opened up to settlement by American squatters, which accounts for the title of Ruiz de Burton's second novel. In Ruiz de Burton's analysis, both the squatters and the elite Mexican American landowners were victims of the greedy railroad owners and the corrupt politicians who yielded to their demands.

CHAPTER XXXV. The Fashion of Justice in San Diego.

But has the Judge no moral responsibility in this? *Has he the right to impose upon the community* a man so self-debased and noxious? If the Judge were to withdraw his support Peter would collapse like a pricked gas-bag, to be swept off into the gutter. But the Judge is the genii, *"the Slave of the Ring"* and his power keeps the little gas-bag afloat, soaring as high as it is in the nature of little gas-bags to soar. The Judge keeping in his hand the check-string, kindly preventing him from going to destruction.

With characteristic coarseness, amounting to inhumanity, Peter Roper and Gasbang decided to throw down their masks, and reveal their fraud in *"jumping"* Mr. Mechlin's house. They came to this decision about ten days after Mr. Mechlin's death.

Gabriel had returned that same day from San Francisco, where he had accompanied the remains of his father-in-law, and deposited them in a vault to await until Mrs. Mechlin should be able to travel, when she, with all the family, would go East.

Mr. Lawrence Mechlin had also arrived. He started from New York on the day of his brother's death, two hours after receiving George's telegram conveying the terrible news. He reached San Francisco on the night before the steamer for San Diego sailed. Thus he and George came together.

The Deputy Sheriff presented himself to announce to Mrs. Mechlin that her furniture left at her country house had been taken out by order of Peter Roper, and put on the road about two miles from the house. As Mrs. Mechlin was too ill to see any one, excepting the members of her family, the Sheriff made his statement to George, in the presence of his uncle and Gabriel, just arrived.

The proceedings seemed so atrocious that at first no one could understand the Sheriff.

"Do you mean to say that Peter Roper claims to own our house, and because he is the owner, has taken out the furniture and left it lying on the road?" asked George.

"Yes; that's what I was told to say," the Sheriff replied.

"But why? How is he the owner of our house?"

"Because he and Gasbang bought it from Hogsden, who located a claim there after you abandoned the place."

The trick was infamous. George and Gabriel saw through it. There was nothing to do but to bring a suit in ejectment to get rid of them, but in the meantime they would hold possession (perhaps for years), and that was what they wanted, to get the property into litigation.

Gabriel went to state the matter to the lawyer who had attended to Mr. Mechlin's law business, and he corroborated their opinion, that there was no other course to pursue but to file a complaint in ejectment to dispossess the thieves.

"Is there no quicker way to obtain redress ?" George asked.

"No, sir," the lawyer answered; "as the deed is done by Peter Roper and John Gasbang, the Judge will decide in their favor, and you will have to appeal."

"But this is atrocious," Mr. Lawrence Mechlin said; "Do you mean to say that people's houses can be taken like that in this country?"

"Not generally; but Peter Roper might, if there is the ghost of a pretext, and if there is a dishonest servant, like Hogsden, left in charge, who will steal and help to steal; then, you see, the thing is easy enough, as long as the Judge befriends trespassers. But the Supreme Court will put things to right again. That is to say, if the Judge's findings are not a string of falsehoods which will utterly mislead the Supreme Court."

This property, Mr. Mechlin had repeatedly said, he intended should be a homestead for his wife, so the suit in ejectment was brought in her name. She at the same time filing a petition for a homestead before the Probate Court, and asking that Gabriel Alamar be appointed administrator of her husband's estate.

All this would, of course, involve the property in tedious legal proceedings, there being the probate matters, beside the suit in ejectment to litigate in the District Court. The attorney employed in the case advised George to have a deed executed by Dona Josefa, conveying the property to Mrs. Mechlin, as it had been agreed before the death of their husbands that it should be done. Dona Josefa cheerfully assented, remembering that Don Mariano had said to her:

"If I should die before I get my land patented, the first thing you must do is to make a conveyance of his place to Mr. Mechlin."

The shock caused by his father's death when that of Don Mariano was yet so recent, acted most injuriously upon George's health. It made him feverish, inflaming his wound again very painfully, as the ball had never been extracted; now it chafed the wound and gave him as much pain as before.

Mrs. Mechlin, Dona Josefa and Mercedes were also in their beds, suffering with nervous prostration and night fevers. It seemed impossible that people could be more bereaved and disheartened than these ladies, and yet exist. Mr. Lawrence Mechlin saw that George must have skillful medical attendance without delay, and wanted his own doctor to take him under his care. So he and Gabriel arranged all business and other matters in order that George should go East. It was heart-rending to Elvira—the mere thought of leaving her mother and sister sick, and all the family in such distress—but she must go with her husband. Gabriel would attend to the lawsuits. He had powers of attorney from George and Mrs. Mechlin, and was the administrator.

The answer to Mrs. Mechlin's complaint was a masterpiece of unblushing effrontery that plainly showed it had originated in a brain where brazen falsehoods and other indecencies thrived like water-reptiles growing huge and luxuriating in slimy swamps. The characteristic document ran in the following manner:

In the District Court of the of the County of San Diego, State of California.
Beatrice Mechlin, Plaintiff,
v.
Peter Roper, John Gasbang, and Charles Hogsden, *Defendants.*

And now come the defendants, Peter Roper, John Gasbang and Charles Hogsden, and for answer to plaintiff's complaint, on file herein, they and each of them say:

That they deny that in the year of 1873, or at any other time before or after that date, James Mechlin was owner of the premises described in this complaint; deny that the said James Mechlin ever purchased from William Mathews the aforesaid property or any part thereof, or paid any money or any other valuable consideration; deny that the said Mechlin ever built a house, or planted trees, or resided on the said property himself, with his family, or by agent or servant occupied said premises; deny that respondent, Charles Hogsden, was ever put in charge of the aforesaid premises or any part thereof, as the agent, or servant, or tenant of the said James Mechlin; deny that the said James Mechlin ever was in the possession of the said premises, but on the contrary, these defendants allege that if James Mechlin had any kind of possession, it was as a naked trespasser, and his title to said property was at all times disputed and contested by other parties.

These defendants allege that defendant Charles Hogsden was the rightful owner of the said premises; that defendants Peter Roper and John Gasbang are the innocent purchasers of the legal and equitable title, and are now in actual and lawful possession of the said premises, having paid a just and fair price to the rightful owner, Charles Hogsden. These defendants further allege, that the plaintiff Beatrice Mechlin wrongfully, unlawfully, fraudulently and maliciously, and for the purpose of cheating and defrauding the aforesaid innocent purchasers, Peter Roper and John Gasbang, out of their rights in said property, entered into a fraudulent conspiracy with one Josefa Alamar and one Gabriel Alamar, wherein it was agreed by and between them that said Josefa Alamar, as executrix of the estate of Mariano Alamar, and purporting to carry out the wishes and instructions of her deceased husband, the said Mariano Alamar, would execute a deed of sale or a confirmatory deed of said property.

And these defendants aver, that in pursuance of the fraudulent conspiracy aforesaid, the said Josefa did execute a fraudulent deed of sale to the said Beatrice Mechlin, for the purpose of cheating and defrauding these innocent purchasers," etc.

This string of prevarications ran on for about twenty pages more, repeating, *ad nauseam*, the same falsehoods with all legal alliteration and more than legal license.

Gabriel was left to attend this suit and other matters, and with grief, which was too profound for description and too heart-rending almost for human endurance, the two loving families separated.

Elvira must leave her beloved mother in her sad bereavement; Lizzie must see hers go to perform the painful duty of accompanying the remains of a beloved husband.

In sorrow and silent tears the Alamar family returned to their country house the day after the Mechlins left.

Mrs. Mechlin's suit in ejectment against the "*innocent* purchasers," Peter and John, was, as a matter of course, decided in favor of these *innocents* of Judge Gryllus Lawlack. The Judge knew, as well as any one else, that the allegations of these men were brazen falsehoods strung together for the purpose of robbery. Nevertheless, his Honor Lawlack made his rulings, and set down his findings, all to suit the robbers. Among the findings that his Honor had the hardihood to write down, were these: That "James Mechlin had never possessed the premises in question; had never lived there in person or by proxy, and had never made any improvements, etc." And these premeditated falsehoods went to the Supreme Court. The case was, of course, reversed and remanded for new trial, but with additional misstatements it was again decided by Judge Lawlack in favor of his friends. Thus, in fact, the Supreme Court was *reversed by Judge Gryllus Lawlack*. The case was the second time remanded by the Supreme Court, but in a new trial it was *again* decided in favor of Peter and John. This being the same as "reversing the Supreme Court," but Lawlack laughs at this, saying that the Supreme Court decides according to their opinions, and he (Lawlack) does the same.

As for Peter Roper, he made no concealment of there being a *private bargain* between himself and Judge Gryllus Lawlack. Peter to render political or other services, Gryllus to reward them with judicial ones.

At a political meeting a friend of Roper (a lawyer in the pay of the monopoly), urged him to make a speech in favor of the railroad. Peter declined, saying that as Gryllus Lawlack wanted to run again for the Judgeship, and knew how anti-monopolist San Diego County was, it would hurt the Judge politically to have him (Peter Roper) speak for the monopoly, as everybody knew that he (Peter) was the principal support of the Judge, and exponent of his principles.

"And," concluded Peter, "if I speak for the monopoly the Judge will grant a rehearing in a suit I am opposing, and will not decide my case as I want. That is understood between us."

This is the fashion of dispensing justice in San Diego, just as Peter bargains for.

But this order of things (or rather disorder) could not have been possible if the Texas Pacific Railroad had not been strangled, as San Diego would not then be the poor, crippled and dwarfed little city that she now is. In this unfortunate condition it is that she submits to the scandalous debaucheries of judicial favorites; debaucheries and violations of common justice, social decorum, of individual rights; debaucheries tolerated because the local power sanctions with his encouragement such proceedings.

If San Diego had been permitted to grow, to have a population, her administration of the laws would have been in other hands, and outrages like breaking into the Mechlin house could not have occurred. The voters of the county would not then have elected a Judge that could reward such vandalism, by allowing the thieves to keep the stolen premises. Now, however, without a railroad, San Diego is at the bottom of a bag, the mouth of which Mr. Huntington[12] has closed and drawn the strings tight.

---

[12]   Collis P. Huntingdon (1821–1900), railroad magnate, helped to build the Central Pacific Railroad in California. He later completed the Chesapeake and Ohio system and became one of the most important entrepreneurs in railroad history.

4 Workingmen's Party, An Address from the Workingmen of San Francisco to Their Brothers throughout the Pacific Coast, 1878[13]

In 1876, 22,000 Chinese immigrants arrived in California, fueling public support for anti-Asian diatribes by labor leader Denis Kearney (1847–1907) and the California Workingmen's party. In July 1877, anti-Chinese labor riots broke out along the docks in San Francisco, as workers tried to keep ships loaded with Chinese immigrants from landing in the port. By September of that year, Kearney and other labor leaders had organized the Workingmen's party of California, in order to consolidate the political power of labor and to publicize the plight of the 15,000 unemployed laborers in San Francisco. Kearney was not above threatening violence against corrupt politicians and the railroads, which delighted his supporters in the labor movement. In late 1877, Kearney was arrested and spent two weeks in prison for inciting violence, but as soon as he was released, he returned to his verbal attacks on politicians. In January 1878, the Workingmen's party held its first convention, and the party exerted some measure of political power in the state during 1878 and 1879. In this address, the party attacked Chinese as cheap workers who threatened the standard of living of native-born Americans.

In spite of Kearney's pugnacious rants, he pushed for labor reforms that were, in large part, eventually adopted: the eight-hour workday, a state public school system, and antimonopoly laws. At the time, however, business leaders and mainstream politicians considered Kearney and his supporters to be dangerous radicals.

Our moneyed men have ruled us for the past thirty years. Under the flag of the slaveholder they hoped to destroy our liberty. Failing in that, they have rallied under the banner of the millionaire, the banker and the land monopolist, the railroad king and the false politician, to effect their purpose.

We have permitted them to become immensely rich against all sound republican policy, and they have turned upon us to sting us to death. They have seized upon the government by bribery and corruption. They have made speculation and public robbery a science. They have loaded the nation, the state, the county, and the city with debt. They have stolen the public lands. They have grasped all to themselves, and by their unprincipled greed

[13]   Denis Kearney, President, and H.L. Knight, Secretary, "Appeal from California. The Chinese Invasion. Workingmen's Address," *Indianapolis Times*, February 28, 1878.

brought a crisis of unparalleled distress on forty millions of people, who have natural resources to feed, clothe and shelter the whole human race.

Such misgovernment, such mismanagement, may challenge the whole world for intense stupidity, and would put to shame the darkest tyranny of the barbarous past.

We, here in California, feel it as well as you. We feel that the day and hour has come for the Workingmen of America to depose capital and put Labor in the Presidential chair, in the Senate and Congress, in the State House, and on the Judicial Bench. We are with you in this work. Workingmen must form a party of their own, take charge of the government, dispose gilded fraud, and put honest toil in power.

In our golden state all these evils have been intensified. Land monopoly has seized upon all the best soil in this fair land. A few men own from ten thousand to two hundred thousand acres each. The poor Laborer can find no resting place, save on the barren mountain, or in the trackless desert. Money monopoly has reached its grandest proportions. Here, in San Francisco, the palace of the millionaire looms up above the hovel of the starving poor with as wide a contrast as anywhere on earth.

To add to our misery and despair, a bloated aristocracy has sent to China—the greatest and oldest despotism in the world—for a cheap working slave. It rakes the slums of Asia to find the meanest slave on earth—the Chinese coolie—and imports him here to meet the free American in the Labor market, and still further widen the breach between the rich and the poor, still further to degrade white Labor.

These cheap slaves fill every place. Their dress is scant and cheap. Their food is rice from China. They hedge twenty in a room, ten by ten. They are w[h]ipped curs, abject in docility, mean, contemptible and obedient in all things. They have no wives, children or dependents.

They are imported by companies, controlled as serfs, worked like slaves, and at last go back to China with all their earnings. They are in every place, they seem to have no sex. Boys work, girls work; it is all alike to them.

The father of a family is met by them at every turn. Would he get work for himself? Ah! A stout Chinaman does it cheaper. Will he get a place for his oldest boy? He can not. His girl? Why, the Chinaman is in her place too! Every door is closed. He can only go to crime or suicide, his wife and daughter to prostitution, and his boys to hoodlumism and the penitentiary.

Do not believe those who call us savages, rioters, incendiaries, and outlaws. We seek our ends calmly, rationally, at the ballot box. So far good order has marked all our proceedings. But, we know how false, how inhuman, our adversaries are. We know that if gold, if fraud, if force can defeat us, they will all be used. And we have resolved that they shall not defeat us.

We shall arm. We shall meet fraud and falsehood with defiance, and force with force, if need be.

We are men, and propose to live like men in this free land, without the contamination of slave labor, or die like men, if need be, in asserting the rights of our race, our country, and our families.

California must be all American or all Chinese. We are resolved that it shall be American, and are prepared to make it so. May we not rely upon your sympathy and assistance?

With great respect for the Workingman's Party of California.

Denis Kearney, President
H.L Knight, Secretary

Discussion Questions: Chapter 2

1   Compare the views of immigrants presented by Kenderdine, Ruiz de Burton, and Kearney.
2   How did Roosevelt's experiences in the West shape his views on land conservation? How were his experiences different from those of the average cattle rancher?
3   According to Kenderdine, what changes were taking place in California?

Chapter 3   Native Americans

1 Zitkala-Sa, Native Americans and White Attempts to Assimilate, from "The School Days of an Indian Girl," 1900[1]

At the end of the nineteenth century, with the end of the Indian wars in the West, a new effort began seeking to assimilate American Indians into the dominant white culture. In 1887, the Dawes Act (named for Senator Henry L. Dawes of Massachusetts) provided that tribal lands would be broken up into individually held allotments. Ultimately, however, the Dawes Act helped to erode tribal unity and integrity. Indian landowners, who could sell their holdings after 25 years, gave away their lands at cheap prices. Over two-thirds of the 90 million acres under the Dawes Act fell out of Indian ownership. In addition, a widespread effort was made by reservation authorities and missionary groups to assimilate through Indian boarding schools that eradicated Indian culture and taught white ways.

Zitkala-Sa, a name which means "Red Bird" (1876–1938), was born a Lakota Sioux in South Dakota and lived on the Missouri River, on the Pine Ridge Reservation. At age 12 she was sent to White's Manual Institute, in Wabash, Indiana, a Quaker boarding school run for Indians. Later Zitkala-Sa was educated at Earlham College, a Quaker college in Indiana. During the Gilded Age and Progressive Era, Indian schooling emphasized

[1] "The School Days of an Indian Girl," *Atlantic Monthly* 85 (1900).

The Gilded Age and Progressive Era: A Documentary Reader, First Edition.
Edited by William A. Link and Susannah J. Link.
© 2012 Blackwell Publishing Ltd. Published 2012 by Blackwell Publishing Ltd.

assimilation – transforming Indian children culturally into white people and eradicating Indian culture. In this document, Zitkala-Sa describes her move to the boarding school and the impact of her experiences.

I

THE LAND OF RED APPLES

There were eight in our party of bronzed children who were going East with the missionaries. Among us were three young braves, two tall girls, and we three little ones, Judéwin, Thowin, and I.

We had been very impatient to start on our journey to the Red Apple Country, which, we were told, lay a little beyond the great circular horizon of the Western prairie. Under a sky of rosy apples we dreamt of roaming as freely and happily as we had chased the cloud shadows on the Dakota plains. We had anticipated much pleasure from a ride on the iron horse, but the throngs of staring palefaces disturbed and troubled us.

On the train, fair women, with tottering babies on each arm, stopped their haste and scrutinized the children of absent mothers. Large men, with heavy bundles in their hands, halted near by, and riveted their glassy blue eyes upon us.

I sank deep into the corner of my seat, for I resented being watched. Directly in front of me, children who were no larger than I hung themselves upon the backs of their seats, with their bold white faces toward me. Sometimes they took their forefingers out of their mouths and pointed at my moccasined feet. Their mothers, instead of reproving such rude curiosity, looked closely at me, and attracted their children's further notice to my blanket. This embarrassed me, and kept me constantly on the verge of tears.

I sat perfectly still, with my eyes downcast, daring only now and then to shoot long glances around me. Chancing to turn to the window at my side, I was quite breathless upon seeing one familiar object. It was the telegraph pole which strode by at short paces. Very near my mother's dwelling, along the edge of a road thickly bordered with wild sunflowers, some poles like these had been planted by white men. Often I had stopped, on my way down the road, to hold my ear against the pole, and, hearing its low moaning, I used to wonder what the paleface had done to hurt it. Now I sat watching for each pole that glided by to be the last one.

In this way I had forgotten my uncomfortable surroundings, when I heard one of my comrades call out my name. I saw the missionary standing very near, tossing candies and gums into our midst. This amused us all, and we tried to see who could catch the most of the sweetmeats. The missionary's generous distribution of candies was impressed upon my memory by a disastrous result which followed. I had caught more than my share of candies and gums, and soon after our arrival at the school I had a chance to disgrace myself, which, I am ashamed to say, I did.

Though we rode several days inside of the iron horse, I do not recall a single thing about our luncheons.

It was night when we reached the school grounds. The lights from the windows of the large buildings fell upon some of the icicled trees that stood beneath them. We were led toward an open door, where the brightness of the lights within flooded out over the heads of the excited palefaces who blocked the way. My body trembled more from fear than from the snow I trod upon.

Entering the house, I stood close against the wall. The strong glaring light in the large whitewashed room dazzled my eyes. The noisy hurrying of hard shoes upon a bare wooden floor increased the whirring in my ears. My only safety seemed to be in keeping next to the wall. As I was wondering in which direction to escape from all this confusion, two warm hands grasped me firmly, and in the same moment I was tossed high in midair. A rosy-cheeked paleface woman caught me in her arms. I was both frightened and insulted by such trifling. I stared into her eyes, wishing her to let me stand on my own feet, but she jumped me up and down with increasing enthusiasm. My mother had never made a plaything of her wee daughter. Remembering this I began to cry aloud.

They misunderstood the cause of my tears, and placed me at a white table loaded with food. There our party were united again. As I did not hush my crying, one of the older ones whispered to me, "Wait until you are alone in the night."

It was very little I could swallow besides my sobs, that evening.

"Oh, I want my mother and my brother Dawee! I want to go to my aunt!" I pleaded; but the ears of the palefaces could not hear me.

From the table we were taken along an upward incline of wooden boxes, which I learned afterward to call a stairway. At the top was a quiet hall, dimly lighted. Many narrow beds were in one straight line down the entire length of the wall. In them lay sleeping brown faces, which peeped just out of the coverings. I was tucked into bed with one of the tall girls, because she talked to me in my mother tongue and seemed to soothe me.

I had arrived in the wonderful land of rosy skies, but I was not happy, as I had thought I should be. My long travel and the bewildering sights had exhausted me. I fell asleep, heaving deep, tired sobs. My tears were left to dry themselves in streaks, because neither my aunt nor my mother was near to wipe them away.

2 Chief Joseph, Selected Statements and Speeches by the Nez Percé Chief, 1877–79[2]

Chief Joseph (ca.1840–1904), honoring the words of his dying father, refused to sign a treaty turning Nez Percé lands in Idaho over to the Americans, and joined with other non-signing tribes in the region who resisted their removal to reservations. After a series of confrontations with American settlers and soldiers, the allied tribes fled toward Canada, but were stopped short of the border by the troops of Colonel Nelson Miles. This clash resulted in the deaths of several key Indian leaders, and Chief Joseph finally surrendered.

The remaining Nez Percé were relocated to Montana, Kansas, and eventually to Indian Territory in Oklahoma. Many, however, succumbed to epidemic diseases. Chief Joseph campaigned to return to the Northwest, and, in 1885, the remaining band of 286 Nez Percé moved to several northwestern reservations. Joseph has become a strong symbol of the Native Americans' long struggle for justice.

The first white men of your people who came to our country were named Lewis and Clark. They brought many things which our people had never seen. They talked straight and our people gave them a great feast as proof that their hearts were friendly. They made presents to our chiefs and our people made presents to them. We had a great many horses of which we gave them what they needed, and they gave us guns and tobacco in return. All the Nez Percé made friends with Lewis and Clark and agreed to let them pass through their country and never to make war on white men. This promise the Nez Percé have never broken.

II

For a short time we lived quietly. But this could not last. White men had found gold in the mountains around the land of the Winding Water. They stole a great many horses from us and we could not get them back because we were Indians. The white men told lies for each other. They drove off a great many of our cattle. Some white men branded our young cattle so they could claim them. We had no friends who would plead our cause before the law councils. It seemed to me that some of the white men in Wallowa were doing these things on purpose to get up a war. They knew we were not

---

[2]   Chester Anders Fee, *Chief Joseph: The Biography of a Great Indian* (New York: Wilson-Erickson, 1936) (http://www.pbs.org/weta/thewest/resources/archives/six/jospeak.htm).

strong enough to fight them. I labored hard to avoid trouble and bloodshed. We gave up some of our country to the white men, thinking that then we could have peace. We were mistaken. The white men would not let us alone. We could have avenged our wrongs many times, but we did not. Whenever the Government has asked for help against other Indians we have never refused. When the white men were few and we were strong we could have killed them off, but the Nez Percé wishes to live at peace.

On account of the treaty made by the other bands of the Nez Percé the white man claimed my lands. We were troubled with white men crowding over the line. Some of them were good men, and we lived on peaceful terms with them, but they were not all good. Nearly every year the agent came over from Lapwai and ordered us to the reservation. We always replied that we were satisfied to live in Wallowa. We were careful to refuse the presents or annuities which he offered.

Through all the years since the white man came to Wallowa we have been threatened and taunted by them and the treaty Nez Percé. They have given us no rest. We have had a few good friends among the white men, and they have always advised my people to bear these taunts without fighting. Our young men are quick tempered and I have had great trouble in keeping them from doing rash things. I have carried a heavy load on my back ever since I was a boy. I learned then that we were but few while the white men were many, and that we could not hold our own with them. We were like deer. They were like grizzly bears. We had a small country. Their country was large. We were contented to let things remain as the Great Spirit Chief made them. They were not; and would change the mountains and rivers if they did not suit them.

III

[At his surrender in the Bear Paw Mountains, 1877]

Tell General Howard that I know his heart. What he told me before I have in my heart. I am tired of fighting. Our chiefs are killed. Looking Glass is dead, Tu-hul-hil-sote is dead. The old men are all dead. It is the young men who now say yes or no. He who led the young men [Joseph's brother Alikut] is dead. It is cold and we have no blankets. The little children are freezing to death. My people—some of them have run away to the hills and have no blankets and no food. No one knows where they are—perhaps freezing to death. I want to have time to look for my children and see how many of them I can find. Maybe I shall find them among the dead. Hear me, my chiefs, my heart is sick and sad. From where the sun now stands I will fight no more against the white man.

IV

[On a visit to Washington, DC, 1879]

At last I was granted permission to come to Washington and bring my friend Yellow Bull and our interpreter with me. I am glad I came. I have shaken hands with a good many friends, but there are some things I want to know which no one seems able to explain. I cannot understand how the Government sends a man out to fight us, as it did General Miles, and then breaks his word. Such a government has something wrong about it. I cannot understand why so many chiefs are allowed to talk so many different ways, and promise so many different things. I have seen the Great Father Chief [President Hayes]; the Next Great Chief [Secretary of the Interior]; the Commissioner Chief; the Law Chief; and many other law chiefs [Congressmen] and they all say they are my friends, and that I shall have justice, but while all their mouths talk right I do not understand why nothing is done for my people. I have heard talk and talk but nothing is done. Good words do not last long unless they amount to something. Words do not pay for my dead people. They do not pay for my country now overrun by white men. They do not protect my father's grave. They do not pay for my horses and cattle. Good words do not give me back my children. Good words will not make good the promise of your war chief, General Miles. Good words will not give my people a home where they can live in peace and take care of themselves. I am tired of talk that comes to nothing. It makes my heart sick when I remember all the good words and all the broken promises. There has been too much talking by men who had no right to talk. Too many misinterpretations have been made; too many misunderstandings have come up between the white men and the Indians. If the white man wants to live in peace with the Indian he can live in peace. There need be no trouble. Treat all men alike. Give them the same laws. Give them all an even chance to live and grow. All men were made by the same Great Spirit Chief. They are all brothers. The earth is the mother of all people, and all people should have equal rights upon it. You might as well expect all rivers to run backward as that any man who was born a free man should be contented penned up and denied liberty to go where he pleases. If you tie a horse to a stake, do you expect he will grow fat? If you pen an Indian up on a small spot of earth and compel him to stay there, he will not be contented nor will he grow and prosper. I have asked some of the Great White Chiefs where they get their authority to say to the Indian that he shall stay in one place, while he sees white men going where they please. They cannot tell me.

I only ask of the Government to be treated as all other men are treated. If I cannot go to my own home, let me have a home in a country where my people will not die so fast. I would like to go to Bitter Root Valley. There my people would be happy; where they are now they are dying. Three have died since I left my camp to come to Washington.

When I think of our condition, my heart is heavy. I see men of my own race treated as outlaws and driven from country to country, or shot down like animals.

I know that my race must change. We cannot hold our own with the white men as we are. We only ask an even chance to live as other men live. We ask to be recognized as men. We ask that the same law shall work alike on all men. If an Indian breaks the law, punish him by the law. If a white man breaks the law, punish him also.

Let me be a free man, free to travel, free to stop, free to work, free to trade where I choose, free to choose my own teachers, free to follow the religion of my fathers, free to talk, think and act for myself—and I will obey every law or submit to the penalty.

Whenever the white man treats the Indian as they treat each other then we shall have no more wars. We shall be all alike—brothers of one father and mother, with one sky above us and one country around us and one government for all. Then the Great Spirit Chief who rules above will smile upon this land and send rain to wash out the bloody spots made by brothers' hands upon the face of the earth. For this time the Indian race is waiting and praying. I hope no more groans of wounded men and women will ever go to the ear of the Great Spirit Chief above, and that all people may be one people.

Hin-mah-too-yah-lat-kekht has spoken for his people.

3 Lakota Accounts of the Massacre at Wounded Knee, 1896[3]

The massacre of Lakota Indians by the US Army took place on December 29, 1890, and was a reaction against the Ghost Dance, which was part of a new religious fervor among Native Americans that called for a rejection of attempts by whites to force Indians to assimilate and for a return to Native American culture. Sitting Bull had been killed two weeks earlier while resisting arrest, and another Lakota leader, Big Foot, led his followers toward Pine Ridge Reservation. They were met by US cavalry and were led to Wounded Knee Creek to be disarmed. As they were surrounded by the

[3] James Mooney, "The Ghost-dance Religion and the Sioux Outbreak of 1890," *14th Annual Report of the Bureau of American Ethnology to the Secretary of the Smithsonian Institution, 1892–93*, Part 2 (Washington: Government Printing Office, 1896), pp. 884–6.

*Seventh Cavalry, the Lakota resisted, and fighting broke out. When the
Indians tried to run, the soldiers opened fire on them with artillery, and over
200 Lakota were killed, including women and children.*

*After this confrontation, the US Army forced an end to the Ghost Dance.
Wounded Knee became a symbol of American injustice toward Native
Americans and was the site of a protest by the American Indian Movement
in 1973.*

TURNING HAWK, Pine Ridge (Mr. Cook, interpreter). Mr. Commissioner,
my purpose to-day is to tell you what I know of the condition of affairs at
the agency where I live. A certain falsehood came to our agency from the
west which had the effect of a fire upon the Indians, and when this certain
fire came upon our people those who had farsightedness and could see into
the matter made up their minds to stand up against it and fight it. The
reason we took this hostile attitude to this fire was because we believed that
you yourself would not be in favor of this particular mischief-making thing;
but just as we expected, the people in authority did not like this thing and
we were quietly told that we must give up or have nothing to do with this
certain movement. Though this is the advice from our good friends in the
east, there were, of course, many silly young men who were longing to
become identified with the movement, although they knew that there was
nothing absolutely bad, nor did they know there was anything absolutely
good, in connection with the movement.

In the course of time we heard that the soldiers were moving toward the
scene of trouble. After awhile some of the soldiers finally reached our
place and we heard that a number of them also reached our friends at
Rosebud. Of course, when a large body of soldiers is moving toward a
certain direction they inspire a more or less amount of awe, and it is
natural that the women and children who see this large moving mass are
made afraid of it and be put in a condition to make them run away. At
first we thought the Pine Ridge and Rosebud were the only two agencies
where soldiers were sent, but finally we heard that the other agencies
fared likewise. We heard and saw that about half our friends at Rosebud
agency, from fear at seeing the soldiers, began the move of running away
from their agency toward ours (Pine Ridge), and when they had gotten
inside of our reservation they there learned that right ahead of them at
our agency was another large crowd of soldiers, and while the soldiers
were there, there was constantly a great deal of false rumor flying back
and forth. The special rumor I have in mind is the threat that the soldiers

had come there to disarm the Indians entirely and to take away all their horses from them. That was the oft-repeated story.

So constantly repeated was this story that our friends from Rosebud, instead of going to Pine Ridge, the place of their destination, veered off and went to some other direction toward the "Bad Lands." We did not know definitely how many, but understood there were 300 lodges of them, about 1,700 people. Eagle Pipe, Turning Bear, High Hawk, Short Bull, Lance, No Flesh, Pine Bird, Crow Dog, Two Strike, and White Horse were the leaders.

Well, the people after veering off in this way, many of them who believe in peace and order at our agency, were very anxious that some influence should be brought upon these people. In addition to our love of peace we remembered that many of these people were related to us by blood. So we sent out peace commissioners to the people who were thus running away from their agency.

I understood at the time that they were simply going away from fear because of so many soldiers. So constant was the word of these good men from Pine Ridge agency that finally they succeeded in getting away half of the party from Rosebud, from the place where they took refuge, and finally were brought to the agency at Pine Ridge. Young-Man-Afraid-of-his-Horses, Little Wound, Fast Thunder, Louis Shangreau, John Grass, Jack Red Cloud, and myself were some of these peace-makers.

The remnant of the party from Rosebud not taken to the agency finally reached the wilds of the Bad Lands. Seeing that we had succeeded so well, once more we sent to the same party in the Bad Lands and succeeded in bringing these very Indians out of the depths of the Bad Lands and were being brought toward the agency. When we were about a day's journey from our agency we heard that a certain party of Indians (Big Foot's band) from the Cheyenne River agency was coming toward Pine Ridge in flight.

CAPTAIN SWORD. Those who actually went off of the Cheyenne River agency probably number 303, and there were a few from the Standing Rock reserve with them, but as to their number I do not know. There were a number of Ogalallas, old men and several school boys, coming back with that very same party, and one of the very seriously wounded boys was a member of the Ogalalla boarding school at Pine Ridge agency. He was not on the warpath, but was simply returning home to his agency and to his school after a summer visit to relatives on the Cheyenne river.

TURNING HAWK. When we heard that these people were coming toward our agency we also heard this. These people were coming toward Pine Ridge agency, and when they were almost on the agency they were met by the soldiers and surrounded and finally taken to the Wounded Knee creek, and there at a given time their guns were demanded. When they had delivered them up, the men were separated from their families, from the tipis, and taken to a certain spot. When the guns were thus taken and the men thus separated, there was a crazy man, a young man of very bad influence and in fact a nobody, among that bunch of Indians fired his gun, and of course the firing of a gun must have been the breaking of a military rule of some sort, because immediately the soldiers returned fire and indiscriminate killing followed.

SPOTTED HORSE. This man shot an officer in the army; the first shot killed this officer. I was a voluntary scout at that encounter and I saw exactly what was done, and that was what I noticed; that the first shot killed an officer. As soon as this shot was fired the Indians immediately began drawing their knives, and they were exhorted from all sides to desist, but this was not obeyed. Consequently the firing began immediately on the part of the soldiers.

TURNING HAWK. All the men who were in a bunch were killed right there, and those who escaped that first fire got into the ravine, and as they went along up the ravine for a long distance they were pursued on both sides by the soldiers and shot down, as the dead bodies showed afterwards. The women were standing off at a different place from where the men were stationed, and when the firing began, those of the men who escaped the first onslaught went in one direction up the ravine, and then the women, who were bunched together at another place, went entirely in a different direction through an open field, and the women fared the same fate as the men who went up the deep ravine.

AMERICAN HORSE. The men were separated, as has already been said, from the women, and they were surrounded by the soldiers. Then came next the village of the Indians and that was entirely surrounded by the soldiers also. When the firing began, of course the people who were standing immediately around the young man who fired the first shot were killed right together, and then they turned their guns, Hotchkill guns, etc., upon the women who were in the lodges standing there under a flag of truce, and of course as soon as they were fired upon they fled, the men fleeing in one direction and the women running in two different directions. So that there were three general directions in which they took flight.

There was a woman with an infant in her arms who was killed as she almost touched the flag of truce, and the women and children of course were strewn all along the circular village until they were dispatched. Right near the flag of truce a mother was shot down with her infant; the child not knowing that its mother was dead was still nursing, and that especially was a very sad sight. The women as they were fleeing with their babes were killed together, shot right through, and the women who were very heavy with child were also killed. All the Indians fled in these three directions, and after most all of them had been killed a cry was made that all those who were not killed or wounded should come forth and they would be safe. Little boys who were not wounded came out of their places of refuge, and as soon as they came in sight a number of soldiers surrounded them and butchered them there.

Of course we all feel very sad about this affair. I stood very loyal to the government all through those troublesome days, and believing so much in the government and being so loyal to it, my disappointment was very strong, and I have come to Washington with a very great blame on my heart. Of course it would have been all right if only the men were killed; we would feel almost grateful for it. But the fact of the killing of the women, and more especially the killing of the young boys and girls who are to go to make up the future strength of the Indian people, is the saddest part of the whole affair and we feel it very sorely.

I was not there at the time before the burial of the bodies, but I did go there with some of the police and the Indian doctor and a great many of the people, men from the agency, and we went through the battlefield and saw where the bodies were from the track of the blood.

TURNING HAWK. I had just reached the point where I said that the women were killed. We heard, besides the killing of the men, of the onslaught also made upon the women and children, and they were treated as roughly and indiscriminately as the men and boys were.

Of course this affair brought a great deal of distress upon all the people, but especially upon the minds of those who stood loyal to the government and who did all that they were able to do in the matter of bringing about peace. They especially have suffered much distress and are very much hurt at heart. These peace-makers continued on in their good work, but there were a great many fickle young men who were ready to be moved by the change in the events there, and consequently, in spite of the great fire that was brought upon all, they were ready to assume any hostile attitude. These young men got themselves in readiness and went in the direction of the scene of battle so they might be of service there. They got there and finally exchanged shots with the soldiers. This party of young men was made up from Rosebud, Ogalalla (Pine Ridge), and members of any other agencies that happened to be there at the time. While this was going on in the neighborhood of Wounded Knee—the Indians and soldiers exchanging shots—the agency, our home, was also fired into by the Indians. Matters went on in this strain until the evening came on, and then the Indians went off down by White Clay creek. When the agency was fired upon by the Indians from the hillside, of course the shots were returned by the Indian police who were guarding the agency buildings.

Although fighting seemed to have been in the air, yet those who believed in peace were still constant at their work. Young-Man-Afraid-of-his-Horses, who had been on a visit to some other agency in the north or northwest, returned, and immediately went out to the people living about White Clay creek, on the border of the Bad Lands, and brought his people out. He succeeded in obtaining the consent of the people to come out of their place of refuge and return to the agency. Thus the remaining portion of the Indians who started from Rosebud were brought back into the agency. Mr. Commissioner, during the days of the great whirlwind out there, those good men tried to hold up a counteracting power, and that was "Peace." We have now come to realize that peace has prevailed and won the day. While we were engaged in bringing about peace our property was left behind, of course, and most of us have lost everything, even down to the matter of guns with which to kill ducks, rabbits, etc, shotguns, and guns of that order. When Young-Man-Afraid brought the people in and their guns were asked for, both men who were called hostile and men who stood loyal to the government delivered up their guns.

4 Photographs and Images from Buffalo Bill's Wild West Show, 1896–99

William Frederick Cody (1846–1917) was a former soldier, a bison hunter, and the founder of a show that glorified the sharpshooters and Indian fighters of the Old West. He acquired his nickname by killing nearly 5,000 buffalo (American bison) in eight months during the late 1860s. His "Wild West" show featured legendary figures from the early days of American settlement of the West: Wild Bill Hickok, Annie Oakley, Sitting Bull, and George Custer (portrayed by Cody himself). The traveling show, which he and a partner started in Nebraska in 1883, coincided with the decline of the Old West: the herds of bison were decimated, the Native American tribes were massacred or were herded onto reservations, barbed-wire fences and railroads crisscrossed the territory, and exploitation of the area's mineral resources began in earnest. Despite the themes of his show, Cody was actually a defender of Native American rights and a proponent of conservation measures for bison and other wild animals of the Plains.

Figure 3.1   Sharpshooter Annie Oakley – "famous rifle shot and holder of the Police Gazette championship medal," *ca.*1899.
Source: Image © Library of Congress, Prints and Photographs Division. Photograph by Richard K. Fox.

Figure 3.2   Wild Bill Hickok, January 16, 1952, from a photograph taken earlier by Brown Brothers, New York.
Source: Library of Congress, Prints & Photographs Division, NYWT&S Collection.

Figure 3.3   "Buffalo Bill's Wild West and Congress of Rough Riders of the World – wild rivalries of savage, barbarous and civilized races."
Source: Library of Congress Prints and Photographs Division.

Discussion Questions: Chapter 3

1   Discuss the various perspectives of Native Americans and their relationship with whites that are presented in the Zitkala-Sa, Chief Joseph, Wounded Knee, and Buffalo Bill documents.

2   How did the opinions about the West presented by Chief Joseph and Buffalo Bill differ?

Part II   Industrial Society

Chapter 4   Big Business

1 Andrew Carnegie, "The Gospel of Wealth," 1889[1]

Andrew Carnegie (1835–1919) was one of the most successful entrepreneurs of his day. An emigrant from Scotland, he worked for the Pennsylvania Railroad and then moved into the iron and steel industry, eventually founding the Carnegie Steel Company, in Pittsburgh. By the 1880s, Carnegie had become one of the wealthiest steel producers in the United States, and his fortune was worth hundreds of millions of dollars. In this document, Carnegie proposed a unique vision of philanthropy. Like Carnegie, there were other Americans who had created fantastic private fortunes during the Gilded Age – and their fortunes were much too large to spend on themselves.

Carnegie advocated a new philosophy of giving – that the new wealth created by the Industrial Revolution be plowed back into philanthropy. Addressing his fellow class of the great wealthy, Carnegie urged the distribution of wealth – by enriched big businessmen. By his death in 1919, Carnegie was largely successful in giving his money away to various philanthropies that supported education and the construction of new libraries across the United States.

---

[1] Andrew Carnegie, "Wealth," *North American Review* 148, no. 391 (June 1889): 653, 657–62.

The Gilded Age and Progressive Era: A Documentary Reader, First Edition.
Edited by William A. Link and Susannah J. Link.
© 2012 Blackwell Publishing Ltd. Published 2012 by Blackwell Publishing Ltd.

The problem of our age is the administration of wealth, so that the ties of brotherhood may still bind together the rich and poor in harmonious relationship. The conditions of human life have not only been changed, but revolutionized, within the past few hundred years. In former days there was little difference between the dwelling, dress, food, and environment of the chief and those of his retainers. . . . The contrast between the palace of the millionaire and the cottage of the laborer with us to-day measures the change which has come with civilization.

This change, however, is not to be deplored, but welcomed as highly beneficial. It is well, nay, essential for the progress of the race, that the houses of some should be homes for all that is highest and best in literature and the arts, and for all the refinements of civilization, rather than that none should be so. Much better this great irregularity than universal squalor. Without wealth there can be no Maecenas.[2] The "good old times" were not good old times. Neither master nor servant was as well situated then as to-day. A relapse to old conditions would be disastrous to both-not the least so to him who serves—and would sweep away civilization with it. . . .

. . .

We start, then, with a condition of affairs under which the best interests of the race are promoted, but which inevitably gives wealth to the few. Thus far, accepting conditions as they exist, the situation can be surveyed and pronounced good. The question then arises—and, if the foregoing be correct, it is the only question with which we have to deal—What is the proper mode of administering wealth after the laws upon which civilization is founded have thrown it into the hands of the few? And it is of this great question that I believe I offer the true solution. It will be understood that fortunes are here spoken of, not moderate sums saved by many years of effort, the returns from which are required for the comfortable maintenance and education of families. This is not wealth, but only competence, which it should be the aim of all to acquire.

There are but three modes in which surplus wealth can be disposed of. It can be left to the families of the decedents; or it can be bequeathed for public purposes; or, finally, it can be administered during their lives by its possessors. Under the first and second modes most of the wealth of the world that has reached the few has hitherto been applied. Let us in turn consider each of these modes. The first is the most injudicious. In monarchial countries,

---

[2]   Gaius Cilnius Maecenas (70–8 BCE) was a supporter of Roman Emperor Octavian. He was also a major patron of the arts, and his name came to represent private support for the arts.

the estates and the greatest portion of the wealth are left to the first son, that the vanity of the parent may be gratified by the thought that his name and title are to descend to succeeding generations unimpaired. The condition of this class in Europe today teaches the futility of such hopes or ambitions. The successors have become impoverished through their follies or from the fall in the value of land. . . . Why should men leave great fortunes to their children? If this is done from affection, is it not misguided affection? Observation teaches that, generally speaking, it is not well for the children that they should be so burdened. Neither is it well for the state. Beyond providing for the wife and daughters moderate sources of income, and very moderate allowances indeed, if any, for the sons, men may well hesitate, for it is no longer questionable that great sums bequeathed oftener work more for the injury than for the good of the recipients. Wise men will soon conclude that, for the best interests of the members of their families and of the state, such bequests are an improper use of their means.

. . .

As to the second mode, that of leaving wealth at death for public uses, it may be said that this is only a means for the disposal of wealth, provided a man is content to wait until he is dead before it becomes of much good in the world. . . . The cases are not few in which the real object sought by the testator is not attained, nor are they few in which his real wishes are thwarted. . . .

The growing disposition to tax more and more heavily large estates left at death is a cheering indication of the growth of a salutary change in public opinion. . . . Of all forms of taxation, this seems the wisest. Men who continue hoarding great sums all their lives, the proper use of which for public ends would work good to the community, should be made to feel that the community, in the form of the state, cannot thus be deprived of its proper share. By taxing estates heavily at death, the state marks its condemnation of the selfish millionaire's unworthy life.

. . . This policy would work powerfully to induce the rich man to attend to the administration of wealth during his life, which is the end that society should always have in view, as being that by far most fruitful for the people. . . .

There remains, then, only one mode of using great fortunes: but in this way we have the true antidote for the temporary unequal distribution of wealth, the reconciliation of the rich and the poor—a reign of harmony—another ideal, differing, indeed from that of the Communist in requiring only the further evolution of existing conditions, not the total overthrow of our civilization. It is founded upon the present most intense individualism, and the race is prepared to put it in practice by degrees whenever it pleases. Under its sway we shall have an ideal state, in which the surplus wealth of the few will become, in the best sense, the property of the many, because administered for the common good, and this wealth, passing through the hands of the few, can be made a much more potent force for the elevation of our race than if it had been distributed in small sums to the people themselves. Even the poorest can be made to see this, and to agree that great sums gathered by some of their fellow-citizens and spent for public purposes, from which the masses reap the principal benefit, are more valuable to them than if scattered among them through the course of many years in trifling amounts.

. . .

This, then, is held to be the duty of the man of Wealth: First, to set an example of modest, unostentatious living, shunning display or extravagance; to provide moderately for the legitimate wants of those dependent upon him; and after doing so to consider all surplus revenues which come to him simply as trust funds, which he is called upon to administer, and strictly bound as a matter of duty to administer in the manner which, in his judgment, is best calculated to produce the most beneficial result for the community—the man of wealth thus becoming the sole agent and trustee for his poorer brethren, bringing to their service his superior wisdom, experience, and ability to administer—doing for them better than they would or could do for themselves.

2 Herbert Spencer, "The Coming Slavery," 1884[3]

Herbert Spencer (1820–1903) was a British journalist and social theorist who coined the term "survival of the fittest" in applying Charles Darwin's evolutionary theories to human social interaction and whose ideas had an important influence upon Gilded Age American social thought. Andrew Carnegie and William Graham Sumner, among other business leaders of the late nineteenth century, used Spencer's theory to justify ruthless capitalism.

The following excerpt is from a series of four essays that Spencer wrote in 1884 to expand on and confirm some of the predictions he had made in an article he wrote in 1860. Spencer's views on the plight of the poor, presented

[3] *Popular Science Monthly* XXIV (April 1884): 721–2.

here, clearly shocked those who believed that government and private wealth
could be used to improve conditions in society.

---

[2] THE COMING SLAVERY

The kinship of pity to love is shown among other ways in this, that it idealizes its object. Sympathy with one in suffering suppresses, for the time being, remembrance of his transgressions. The feeling which vents itself in "poor fellow!" on seeing one in agony, excludes the thought of "bad fellow," which might at another time arise. Naturally, then, if the wretched are unknown or but vaguely known, all the demerits they may have are ignored; and thus it happens that when, as just now, the miseries of the poor are depicted, they are thought of as the miseries of the deserving poor, instead of being thought of, as in large measure they should be, as the miseries of the undeserving poor. Those whose hardships are set forth in pamphlets and proclaimed in sermons and speeches which echo throughout society, are assumed to be all worthy souls, grievously wronged; and none of them are thought of as bearing the penalties of their own misdeeds.

On hailing a cab in a London street, it is surprising how frequently the door is officiously opened by one who expects to get something for his trouble. The surprise lessens after counting the many loungers about tavern-doors, or after observing the quickness with which a street-performance, or procession, draws from neighbouring slums and stable-yards a group of idlers. Seeing how numerous they are in every small area, it becomes manifest that tens of thousands of such swarm through London. "They have no work," you say. Say rather that they either refuse work or quickly turn themselves out of it. They are simply good-for-nothings, who in one way or other live on the good-for-somethings—vagrants and sots, criminals and those on the way to crime, youths who are burdens on hard-worked parents, men who appropriate the wages of their wives, fellows who share the gains of prostitutes; and then, less visible and less numerous, there is a corresponding class of women.

Is it natural that happiness should be the lot of such? or is it natural that they should bring unhappiness on themselves and those connected with them? Is it not manifest that there must exist in our midst an immense amount of misery which is a normal result of misconduct, and ought not to be dissociated from it? There is a notion, always more or less prevalent and just now vociferously expressed, that all social suffering is removable, and that it is the duty of somebody or other to remove it. Both these beliefs are false. To separate pain from ill-doing is to fight against the constitution of things, and will be followed by far more pain. Saving men from the natural penalties of dissolute living, eventually necessitates the infliction of artificial penalties in solitary cells, on tread-wheels, and by the lash. I suppose a dictum, on which the current creed and the creed of science are at one, may be considered to have as high an authority as can be found. Well, the command "if any would not work neither should he eat," is simply a Christian enunciation of that universal law of Nature under which life has reached its present height—the law that a creature not energetic enough to maintain itself must die: the sole difference being that the law which in the one case is to be artificially enforced, is, in the other case, a natural necessity. And yet this particular tenet of their religion which science so manifestly justifies, is the one which Christians seem least inclined to accept. The current assumption is that there should be no suffering, and that society is to blame for that which exists.

3   Henry Demarest Lloyd, "The Lords of Industry," 1884[4]

Henry Demarest Lloyd (1847–1903) was one of the original muckrakers, a group of journalists in the late nineteenth and early twentieth centuries who exposed corrupt politicians and monopolistic business practices. In 1881, he wrote an exposé of the railroads and Standard Oil Company that ran in the Atlantic Monthly. *In 1885, he left the* Tribune *and devoted himself to pursuing his interest in public welfare, traveling to various countries around the world and writing about their social welfare policies. His most important book,* Wealth against Commonwealth *(1894), was a 500-page critique of monopolies, especially Standard Oil. His faith in democracy was diminished when the book failed to spark a public outcry against monopolistic business practices. His experiences with populist and progressive politics were also disappointing, and he spent the last years of his life supporting socialism, which seemed to him the best hope for opposing monopoly power and obtaining rights for workers.*

The following article details the trend toward monopoly in a large number of essential industries in the United States. The excerpt presented here focuses on the coal industry.

Adam Smith said in 1776: "People of the same trade hardly meet together even for merriment and diversion but the conversation ends in a conspiracy against the public, or in some contrivance to raise prices." The expansive

---

[4]   *North American Review* 138 (January/June 1884): 535–53.

ferment of the New Industry, coming with the newscience, the new land, and the new liberties of our era, broke up these "conspiracies," and for a century we have heard nothing of them; but the race to overrun is being succeeded by the struggle to divide, and combinations are re-appearing on all sides. This any one may see from the reports of the proceedings of the conventions and meetings of innumerable associations of manufacturers and dealers and even producers, which are being held almost constantly. They all do something to raise prices, or hold them up, and they wind up with banquets for which we pay.

. . .

Last July Messrs. Vanderbilt, Sloan,[5] and one or two others out of several hundred owners of coal lands and coal railroads, met in the pleasant shadows of Saratoga to make "a binding arrangement for the control of the coal trade." . . . . The gratuitous warmth of summer suggested to these men the need the public would have of artificial heat, at artificial prices, the coming winter. It was agreed to fix prices, and to prevent the production of too much of the raw material of warmth, by suspensions of mining. In anticipation of the arrival of the cold wave from Manitoba, a cold wave was sent out all over the United States, from their parlors in New York, in an order for halftime work by the miners during the first three months of this year, and for an increase of prices. These are the means this combination uses to keep down wages—the price of men, and keep up the price of coal—the wages of capital. Prices of coal in the West are fixed by the Western Anthracite Coal Association, controlled entirely by the large railroads and mine-owners of Pennsylvania. This association regulates the price west of Buffalo and Pittsburgh and in Canada. Our annual consumption of anthracite is now between 31,000,000 and 32,000,000 tons. The West takes between 5,000,000 and 6,000,000 tons. The companies which compose the combination mine, transport, and sell their own coal. They are obliterating other mine-owners and the retailer. The Chicago and New York dealer has almost nothing to say about what he shall pay or what he shall charge, or what his profits shall be. The great companies do not let the little men make too much. Year by year the coal retailers are sinking into the status of mere agents of the combination, with as little freedom as the consumer.

There was an investigation of the coal combination by the Pennsylvania legislature in 1871, the testimony taken in which showed, as summarized in

[5] Railroad industrialist William Henry Vanderbilt (1821–1885) and Pennsylvania coal magnate Samuel Sloan (1817–1907).

"The Nation," then the leading antimonopoly paper in the United States, that when, after a thirty-days' strike by the men, a number of private coal-mine owners acceded to their terms and wished to reopen their mines and send coal again to market, the railroads, by which alone they could get to market, raised their freights, as their men were still on strike, to three times the previous figures. These great corporations had determined not to yield to their men, and as they were mine-owners and coal sellers as well as carriers, they refused to take coal for their competitors. The latter, if they could have got transportation, would have given their own men employment and supplied the people of the country with coal. This would have compelled the great companies either to make terms with their workmen, or to let these other mine-owners take the trade. Instead of doing so, they used their power over the only available means of transportation to dictate the terms upon which every other employer should deal with his men, by preventing him from sending his products to market so long as he granted his men better terms than those laid down by the company. The result was that the price of coal was doubled, rising to $12 a ton; the resumption by the private mine-owners was stopped; and they, the workmen and the Consumer, were all delivered over to the tender mercies of the six great companies.

The coal combination was again investigated by the New York legislature in 1878, after the combination had raised the prices of coal in New York to double what they had been. The legislature found that private mine-operators who were not burdened like the great companies with extravagant and often corrupt purchases of coal lands, heavily watered stock, and disadvantageous contracts, forced on them by interested directors, and who have only to pay the actual cost of producing the coal, "can afford to sell at a much less price than the railroad coal-producing companies, and would do so if they could get transportation from the mines to the market." This is denied them by the great companies. "The private operators," says the report, "either find themselves entirely excluded from the benefits of transportation by reason of the high freights, or find it for their interest to make contracts with the railroads, by which they will not sell to others, and so the railroads have and will keep the control, of the supply of the private operators." To those who will not make such contracts, rates are fixed excluding them from the market, with the result, usually, of forcing them to sell their property to the lords of the pool. "The combination," the committee declared, "can limit the supply, and thereby create such a demand and price as they may deem advisable." The committee found that coal could be laid down on the dock in New York, after paying all charges, for an average of $3.20 a ton. It was at that time retailing in the city for $4.90 to $5.25 a ton. "The purposes of the combination are solely to advance the price of coal, and it has been successful to the amount of seventy-five cents to one dollar a ton. Its further advance is only a question whether the combination can continue to repress the production." An advance of only twenty-five cents a ton would on 32,000,000 tons be $8,000,000 a year, which is not a bad thing—for the combination.

. . .

One of the sights which this coal side of our civilization has to show is the presence of herds of little children of all ages, from six years upward, at work in the coal breakers, toiling in dirt, and air thick with carbon dust, from dawn to dark, of every day in the week except Sunday. These coal breakers are the only schools they know. A letter from the coal regions in the Philadelphia "Press" declares that "there are no schools in the world where more evil is learned or more innocence destroyed than in the breakers. It is shocking to watch the vile practices indulged in by these children, to hear the frightful oaths they use, to see their total disregard for religion and humanity." In the upper part of Luzerne county, out of 22,000 inhabitants 3000 are children, between six and fifteen years of age, at work in this way. "There is always a restlessness among the miners," an officer of one of the New York companies said, "when we are working them on half time." The latest news from the region of the coal combination is that the miners are so dissatisfied with the condition in which they are kept, by the suspension of work and the importation of competing Hungarian laborers in droves, that they are forming a combination of their own, a revival of the old Miners and Laborers' Association, which was broken up by the labor troubles of 1874 and 1875.

Combination is busy in those soft-coal districts, whose production is so large that it must be sent to competitive markets. A pool has just been formed covering the annual product of 6,000,000 tons of the mines of Ohio. Indiana and Illinois are to be brought in, and it is planned to extend it to all the bituminous coal districts that compete with each other. The appearance of Mr. Vanderbilt, last December, in the Clearfield district, of Pennsylvania, at the head of a company capitalized for $5,000,000, was the first entry of a metropolitan mind into this field. Mr. Vanderbilt's role is to be that of producer, carrier, dealer, and consumer, all in one. Until he came, the district was occupied by a number of small companies and small operators, as used to be the case in the anthracite field in the old days. But the man who works himself, with his sons, in a small mine, cutting perhaps from twenty to forty tons a day, cannot expect to survive the approach of the Manhattan capitalist. The small Clearfield producers, looking at the fate of their kind in the anthracite country, greeted Mr. Vanderbilt's arrival with the question, "What is to become of us?" "If the small operator," said one of the great man's lieutenants, "goes to the wall, that is his misfortune, not our fault."

. . .

We have given competition its own way, and have found that we are not good enough or wise enough to be trusted with this power of ruining ourselves in the attempt to ruin others. Free competition could be let run only in a community where every one had learned to say and act "I am the state." We have had an era of material inventions. We now need a renaissance of moral inventions, contrivances to tap the vast currents of moral magnetism flowing uncaught over the face of society. Morals and values rise and fall together. If our combinations have no morals, they can have no values. If the tendency to combination is irresistible, control of it is imperative. Monopoly and antimonopoly, odious as these words have become to the literary ear, represent the two great tendencies of our time: monopoly, the tendency to combination; anti-monopoly, the demand for social control of it. As the man is bent toward business or patriotism, he will negotiate combinations or agitate for laws to regulate them. The first is capitalistic, the second is social. The first, industrial; the second, moral. The first promotes wealth; the second, citizenship. These combinations are not to be waved away as fresh pictures of folly or total depravity. There is something in them deeper than that. The Aryan has proved by the experience of thousands of years that he can travel. "But travel," Emerson says, "is the fool's paradise." We must now prove that we can stay at home, and stand it as well as the Chinese have done. Future Puritans cannot emigrate from Southampton to Plymouth Rock. They can only sail from righteousness to righteousness. Our young men can no longer go west; they must go up or down. Not new land, but new virtue must be the outlet for the future. Our halt at the shores of the Pacific is a much more serious affair than that which brought our ancestors to a pause before the barriers of the Atlantic, and compelled them to practice living together for a few hundred years. We cannot hereafter, as in the past, recover freedom by going to the prairies; we must find it in the society of the good. In the presence of great combinations, in all departments of life, the moralist and patriot have work to do of a significance never before approached during the itinerant phases of our civilization. It may be that the coming age of combination will issue in a nobler and fuller liberty for the individual than has yet been seen, but that consummation will be possible, not in a day of competitive trade, but in one of competitive morals.

4 US Supreme Court, *Slaughterhouse Cases*, 1873[6]

The US Supreme Court's decision in the Slaughterhouse Cases, *resolved in April 1873, represents the Court's first interpretation of the Fourteenth Amendment to the US Constitution, ratified in 1868. In 1869, the Louisiana state legislature granted the Crescent City Livestock Landing & Slaughterhouse Company exclusive rights to slaughter animals in New Orleans. While the state of Louisiana viewed this measure as a way to centralize the slaughterhouse industry and improve health and safety standards, local butchers argued that the new law, which prohibited independent slaughterhouses from operating in New Orleans, created a monopoly and violated the "privileges or immunities" of US citizenship conferred by the Fourteenth Amendment.*

After state courts upheld the law, butchers appealed to the US Supreme Court in 1873. In a five-to-four decision, the Court ruled the Louisiana law constitutional, arguing that the Fourteenth Amendment only protected the rights of federal, not state citizenship. This narrow reading of the Fourteenth Amendment constitutes an important decision in early civil rights legislation and marked a significant limitation over civil protections provided in the Reconstruction amendments.

. . . . Mr. Justice MILLER, now, April 14th, 1873, delivered the opinion of the court.

These cases are brought here by writs of error to the Supreme Court of the State of Louisiana. They arise out of the efforts of the butchers of New Orleans to resist the Crescent City Livestock Landing and Slaughter-House Company in the exercise of certain powers conferred by the charter which created it, and which was granted by the legislature of that State.

The cases named on a preceding page, with others which have been brought here and dismissed by agreement, were all decided by the Supreme Court of Louisiana in favor of the Slaughter-House Company, as we shall hereafter call it for the sake of brevity, and these writs are brought to reverse those decisions.

The records were filed in this court in 1870, and were argued before it at length on a motion made by plaintiffs in error for an order in the nature of an injunction or supersedeas, pending the action of the court on the merits. The opinion on that motion is reported in 77 U. S. 10 Wallace 273. . . .

The statute thus assailed as unconstitutional was passed March 8th, 1869, and is entitled "An act to protect the health of the city of New Orleans, to

[6]   83 U.S. 36 (1873).

locate the stock landings and slaughterhouses, and to incorporate the Crescent City Livestock Landing and Slaughter-House Company."

The first section forbids the landing or slaughtering of animals whose flesh is intended for food within the city of New Orleans and other parishes and boundaries named and defined, or the keeping or establishing any slaughterhouses or abattoirs within those limits except by the corporation thereby created, which is also limited to certain places afterwards mentioned. Suitable penalties are enacted for violations of this prohibition.

The second section designates the corporators, gives the name to the corporation, and confers on it the usual corporate powers.

The third and fourth sections authorize the company to establish and erect within certain territorial limits, therein defined, one or more stockyards, stock landings, and slaughterhouses, and impose upon it the duty of erecting, on or before the first day of June, 1869, one grand slaughterhouse of sufficient capacity for slaughtering five hundred animals per day.

It declares that the company, after it shall have prepared all the necessary buildings, yards, and other conveniences for that purpose, shall have the sole and exclusive privilege of conducting and carrying on the livestock landing and slaughterhouse business within the limits and privilege granted by the act, and that all such animals shall be landed at the stock landings and slaughtered at the slaughterhouses of the company, and nowhere else. Penalties are enacted for infractions of this provision, and prices fixed for the maximum charges of the company for each steamboat and for each animal landed.

Section five orders the closing up of all other stock landings and slaughterhouses after the first day of June, in the parishes of Orleans, Jefferson, and St. Bernard, and makes it the duty of the company to permit any person to slaughter animals in their slaughterhouses under a heavy penalty for each refusal. Another section fixes a limit to the charges to be made by the company for each animal so slaughtered in their building, and another provides for an inspection of all animals intended to be so slaughtered by an officer appointed by the governor of the State for that purpose.

These are the principal features of the statute, and are all that have any bearing upon the questions to be decided by us.

. . .

The institution of African slavery, as it existed in about half the States of the Union, and the contests pervading the public mind for many years between those who desired its curtailment and ultimate extinction and those who desired additional safeguards for its security and perpetuation, culminated in the effort, on the part of most of the States in which slavery existed, to separate from the Federal government and to resist its authority. This constituted the war of the rebellion, and whatever auxiliary causes may have contributed to bring about this war, undoubtedly the overshadowing and efficient cause was African slavery.

In that struggle, slavery, as a legalized social relation, perished. It perished as a necessity of the bitterness and force of the conflict. When the armies of freedom found themselves upon the soil of slavery, they could do nothing less than free the poor victims whose enforced servitude was the foundation of the quarrel. And when hard-pressed in the contest, these men (for they proved themselves men in that terrible crisis) offered their services and were accepted by thousands to aid in suppressing the unlawful rebellion, slavery was at an end wherever the Federal government succeeded in that purpose. The proclamation of President Lincoln expressed an accomplished fact as to a large portion of the insurrectionary districts when he declared slavery abolished in them all. But the war being over, those who had succeeded in reestablishing the authority of the Federal government were not content to permit this great act of emancipation to rest on the actual results of the contest or the proclamation of the Executive, both of which might have been questioned in after times, and they determined to place this main and most valuable result in the Constitution of the restored Union as one of its fundamental articles. Hence, the thirteenth article of amendment of that instrument.

. . .

Before we proceed to examine more critically the provisions of this amendment, on which the plaintiffs in error rely, let us complete and dismiss the history of the recent amendments, as that history relates to the general purpose which pervades them all. A few years' experience satisfied the thoughtful men who had been the authors of the other two amendments that, notwithstanding the restraints of those articles on the States and the laws passed under the additional powers granted to Congress, these were inadequate for the protection of life, liberty, and property, without which freedom to the slave was no boon. They were in all those States denied the right of suffrage. The laws were administered by the white man alone. It was urged that a race of men distinctively marked, as was the negro, living in the midst of another and dominant race, could never be fully secured in their person and their property without the right of suffrage. . . .

The first section of the fourteenth article to which our attention is more specially invited opens with a definition of citizenship—not only citizenship of the United States, but citizenship of the States. No such definition was previously found in the Constitution, nor had any attempt been made to define it by act of Congress. It had been the occasion of much discussion in the courts, by the executive departments, and in the public journals. It had been said by eminent judges that no man was a citizen of the United States except as he was a citizen of one of the States composing the Union. Those, therefore, who had been born and resided always in the District of Columbia or in the Territories, though within the United States, were not citizens. Whether this proposition was sound or not had never been judicially decided. But it had been held by this court, in the celebrated *Dred Scott* case, only a few years before the outbreak of the civil war, that a man of African descent, whether a slave or not, was not and could not be a citizen of a State or of the United States. This decision, while it met the condemnation of some of the ablest statesmen and constitutional lawyers of the country, had never been overruled, and if was to be accepted as a constitutional limitation of the right of citizenship, then all the negro race who had recently been made freemen were still not only not citizens, but were incapable of becoming so by anything short of an amendment to the Constitution.

To remove this difficulty primarily, and to establish clear and comprehensive definition of citizenship which should declare what should constitute citizenship of the United States and also citizenship of a State, the first clause of the first section was framed. . . . It declares that persons may be citizens of the United States without regard to their citizenship of a particular State, and it overturns the *Dred Scott* decision by making all persons born within the United States and subject to its jurisdiction citizens of the United States. That its main purpose was to establish the citizenship of the negro can admit of no doubt. . . .

The next observation is more important in view of the arguments of counsel in the present case. It is that the distinction between citizenship of the United States and citizenship of a State is clearly recognized and established.

Not only may a man be a citizen of the United States without being a citizen of a State, but an important element is necessary to convert the former into the latter. He must reside within the State to make him a citizen of it, but it is only necessary that he should be born or naturalized in the United States to be a citizen of the Union.

It is quite clear, then, that there is a citizenship of the United States, and a citizenship of a State, which are distinct from each other, and which depend upon different characteristics or circumstances in the individual.

We think this distinction and its explicit recognition in this amendment of great weight in this argument, because the next paragraph of this same section, which is the one mainly relied on by the plaintiffs in error, speaks only of privileges and immunities of citizens of the United States, and does not speak of those of citizens of the several States. The argument, however, in favor of the plaintiffs rests wholly on the assumption that the citizenship is the same, and the privileges and immunities guaranteed by the clause are the same.

The language is, "No State shall make or enforce any law which shall abridge the privileges or immunities of citizens of *the United States*." It is a little remarkable, if this clause was intended as a protection to the citizen of a State against the legislative power of his own State, that the word citizen of the State should be left out when it is so carefully used, and used in contradistinction to citizens of the United States in the very sentence which precedes it. It is too clear for argument that the change in phraseology was adopted understandingly and, with a purpose.

Of the privileges and immunities of the citizen of the United States, and of the privileges and immunities of the citizen of the State, and what they respectively are, we will presently consider; but we wish to state here that it is only the former which are placed by this clause under the protection of the Federal Constitution, and that the latter, whatever they may be, are not intended to have any additional protection by this paragraph of the amendment.

If, then, there is a difference between the privileges and immunities belonging to a citizen of the United States as such and those belonging to the citizen of the State as such, the latter must rest for their security and protection where they have heretofore rested, for they are not embraced by this paragraph of the amendment.

. . .

With the exception of these and a few other restrictions, the entire domain of the privileges and immunities of citizens of the States, as above defined, lay within the constitutional and legislative power of the States, and without that of the Federal government. Was it the purpose of the fourteenth amendment, by the simple declaration that no State should make or enforce any law which shall abridge the privileges and immunities of citizens of the United States, to transfer the security and protection of all the civil rights which we have mentioned, from the States to the Federal government? And where it is declared that Congress Shall have the power to enforce that article, was it intended to bring within the power of Congress the entire domain of civil rights heretofore belonging exclusively to the States?

All this and more must follow if the proposition of the plaintiffs in error be sound. For not only are these rights subject to the control of Congress whenever, in its discretion, any of them are supposed to be abridged by State legislation, but that body may also pass laws in advance, limiting and restricting the exercise of legislative power by the States, in their most ordinary and usual functions, as in its judgment it may think proper on all such subjects. And still further, such a construction followed by the reversal of the judgments of the Supreme Court of Louisiana in these cases, would constitute this court a perpetual censor upon all legislation of the States, on the civil rights of their own citizens, with authority to nullify such as it did not approve as consistent with those rights, as they existed at the time of the adoption of this amendment. The argument, we admit, is not always the most conclusive which is drawn from the consequences urged against the adoption of a particular construction of an instrument. But when, as in the case before us, these consequences are so serious, so far-reaching and pervading, so great a departure from the structure and spirit of our institutions; when the effect is to fetter and degrade the State governments by subjecting them to the control of Congress in the exercise of powers heretofore universally conceded to them of the most ordinary and fundamental character; when, in fact, it radically changes the whole theory of the relations of the State and Federal governments to each other and of both these governments to the people, the argument has a force that is irresistible in the absence of language which expresses such a purpose too clearly to admit of doubt.

We are convinced that no such results were intended by the Congress which proposed these amendments, nor by the legislatures of the States which ratified them.

. . .

In the light of the history of these amendments, and the pervading purpose of them, which we have already discussed, it is not difficult to give a meaning to this clause. The existence of laws in the States where the newly emancipated negroes resided, which discriminated with gross injustice and hardship against them as a class, was the evil to be remedied by this clause, and by it such laws are forbidden.

If, however, the States did not conform their laws to its requirements, then by the fifth section of the article of amendment Congress was authorized to enforce it by suitable legislation. We doubt very much whether any action of a State not directed by way of discrimination against the negroes as a class, or on account of their race, will ever be held to come within the purview of this provision. It is so clearly a provision for that race and that emergency that a strong case would be necessary for its application to any other. But as it is a State that is to be dealt with, and not alone the validity of its laws, we may safely leave that matter until Congress shall have exercised its power, or some case of State oppression, by denial of equal justice in its courts, shall have claimed a decision at our hands. We find no such case in the one before us, and do not deem it necessary to go over the argument again, as it may have relation to this particular clause of the amendment.

. . .

We do not see in those amendments any purpose to destroy the main features of the general system. Under the pressure of all the excited feeling growing out of the war, our statesmen have still believed that the existence of the State with powers for domestic and local government, including the regulation of civil rights the rights of person and of property was essential to the perfect working of our complex form of government, though they have thought proper to impose additional limitations on the States, and to confer additional power on that of the Nation.

But whatever fluctuations may be seen in the history of public opinion on this subject during the period of our national existence, we think it will be found that this court, so far as its functions required, has always held with a steady and an even hand the balance between State and Federal power, and we trust that such may continue to be the history of its relation to that subject so long as it shall have duties to perform which demand of it a construction of the Constitution or of any of its parts.

The judgments of the Supreme Court of Louisiana in these cases are AFFIRMED.

5 Frederick Winslow Taylor, from *The Principles of Scientific Management*, 1911[7]

The rise of big business ushered in efforts to manage labor more efficiently and productively, and an entire "science" of labor management emerged by the end of the nineteenth century. These efforts focused on limiting the power of labor unions, increasing work loads, and expanding supervision and control of parts of the work process.

Perhaps the best known of the advocates of scientific management was Frederick Winslow Taylor (1856–1915). Born in Philadelphia, he was accepted at Harvard University, but instead went into industry, working his way up the ladder for the Midvale Steel Company and becoming its chief engineer. In 1881, he introduced time-and-motion studies that sought to

[7] *The Principles of Scientific Management* (New York: Harper & Brothers, 1911).

study the work process in order to make it more efficient. He is best known for his Principles of Scientific Management *(1911) – from which the following extract is taken – which became a sort of bible for the modern scientific management movement in industry.*

It would seem to be so self-evident that maximum prosperity for the employer, coupled with maximum prosperity for the employé ought to be the two leading objects of management, that even to state this fact should be unnecessary. And yet there is no question that, throughout the industrial world, a large part of the organization of employers, as well as employés, is for war rather than for peace, and that perhaps the majority on either side do not believe that it is possible so to arrange their mutual relations that their interests become identical.

The majority of these men believe that the fundamental interests of employés and employers are necessarily antagonistic. Scientific management, on the contrary, has for its very foundation the firm conviction that the true interests of the two are one and the same; that prosperity for the employer cannot exist through a long term of years unless it is accompanied by prosperity for the employé and *vice versa;* and that it is possible to give the workman what he most wants—high wages—and the employer what he wants—a low labor cost—for his manufactures.

It is hoped that some at least of those who do not sympathize with each of these objects may be led to modify their views; that some employers, whose attitude toward their workmen has been that of trying to get the largest amount of work out of them for the smallest possible wages, may be led to see that a more liberal policy toward their men will pay them better; and that some of those workmen who begrudge a fair and even a large profit to their employers, and who feel that all of the fruits of their labor should belong to them, and that those for whom they work and the capital invested in the business are entitled to little or nothing, may be led to modify these views.

No one can be found who will deny that in the case of any single individual the greatest prosperity can exist only when that individual has reached his highest state of efficiency; that is, when he is turning out his largest daily output.

. . .

If the above reasoning is correct, it follows that the most important object of both the workmen and the management should be the training and development of each individual in the establishment, so that he can do (at his fastest pace and with the. maximum of efficiency) the highest class of work for which his natural abilities fit him.

These principles appear to be so self-evident that many men may think it almost childish to state them. Let us, however, turn to the facts, as they actually exist in this country and in England. The English and American peoples are the greatest sportsmen in the world. Whenever an American workman plays baseball, or an English workman plays cricket, it is safe to say that he strains every nerve to secure victory for his side. He does his very best to make the largest possible number of runs. The universal sentiment is so strong that any man who fails to give out all there is in him in sport is branded as a "quitter," and treated with contempt by those who are around him.

When the same workman returns to work on the following day, instead of using every effort to turn out the largest possible amount of work, in a majority of the cases this man deliberately plans to do as little as he safely can—to turn out far less work than he is well able to do—in many instances to do not more than one-third to one-half of a proper day's work. And in fact if he were to do his best to turn out his largest possible day's work, he would be abused by his fellow-workers for so doing, even more than if he had proved himself a "quitter" in sport. Underworking, that is, deliberately working slowly so as to avoid doing a full day's work, "soldiering," as it is called in this country, "hanging it out," as it is called in England, "ca canae," as it is called in Scotland, is almost universal in industrial establishments, and prevails also to a large extent in the building trades; and the writer asserts without fear of contradiction that this constitutes the greatest evil with which the working-people of both England and America are now afflicted.

It will be shown later in this paper that doing away with slow working and "soldiering" in all its forms and so arranging the relations between employer and employé that each workman will work to his very best advantage and at his best speed, accompanied by the intimate cooperation with the management and the help (which the workman should receive) from the management, would result on the average in nearly doubling the output of each man and each machine. What other reforms, among those which are being discussed by these two nations, could do as much toward promoting prosperity, toward the diminution of poverty, and the alleviation of suffering? America and England have been recently agitated over such subjects as the tariff, the control of the large corporations on the one hand, and of hereditary power on the other hand, and over various more or less socialistic proposals for taxation, etc. On these subjects both peoples have been profoundly stirred, and yet hardly a voice has been raised to call attention to this vastly greater and more important subject of "soldiering," which directly and powerfully affects the wages, the prosperity, and the life of almost every working-man, and also quite as much the prosperity of every industrial establishment in the nation.

The elimination of "soldiering" and of the several causes of slow working would so lower the cost of production that both our home and foreign markets would be greatly enlarged, and we could compete on more than even terms with our rivals. It would remove one of the fundamental causes for dull times, for lack of employment, and for poverty, and therefore would have a more permanent and far-reaching effect upon these misfortunes than any of the curative remedies that are now being used to soften their consequences. It would insure higher wages and make shorter working hours and better working and home conditions possible.

Why is it, then, in the face of the self-evident fact that maximum prosperity can exist only as the result of the determined effort of each workman to turn out each day his largest possible day's work, that the great majority of our men are deliberately doing just the opposite, and that even when the men have the best of intentions their work is in most cases far from efficient?

There are three causes for this condition, which may be briefly summarized as:

First. The fallacy, which has from time immemorial been almost universal among workmen, that a material increase in the output of each man or each machine in the trade would result in the end in throwing a large number of men out of work.

Second. The defective systems of management which are in common use, and which make it necessary for each workman to soldier, or work slowly, in order that he may protect his own best interests.

Third. The inefficient rule-of-thumb methods, which are still almost universal in all trades, and in practising which our workmen waste a large part of their effort.

This paper will attempt to show the enormous gains which would result from the substitution by our workmen of scientific for rule-of-thumb methods.

To explain a little more fully these three causes:

First. The great majority of workmen still believe that if they were to work at their best speed they would be doing a great injustice to the whole trade by throwing a lot of men out of work, and yet the history of the development of each trade shows that each improvement, whether it be the invention of a new machine or the introduction of a better method, which results in increasing the productive capacity of the men in the trade and cheapening the costs, instead of throwing men out of work make in the end work for more men.

The cheapening of any article in common use almost immediately results in a largely increased demand for that article. Take the case of shoes, for instance. The introduction of machinery for doing every element of the work which was formerly done by hand has resulted in making shoes at a fraction of their former labor cost, and in selling them so cheap that now almost every man, woman, and child in the working-classes buys one or two pairs of shoes per year, and wears shoes all the time, whereas formerly each workman bought perhaps one pair of shoes every five years, and went barefoot most of the time, wearing shoes only as a luxury or as a matter of the sternest necessity. In spite of the enormously increased output of shoes per workman, which has come with shoe machinery, the demand for shoes has so increased that there are relatively more men working in the shoe industry now than ever before.

The workmen in almost every trade have before them an object lesson of this kind, and yet, because they are ignorant of the history of their own trade even, they still firmly believe, as their fathers did before them, that it is against their best interests for each man to turn out each day as much work as possible.

Under this fallacious idea a large proportion of the workmen of both countries each day deliberately work slowly so as to curtail the output. Almost every labor union has made, or is contemplating making, rules which have for their object curtailing the output of their members, and those men who have the greatest influence with the working-people, the labor leaders as well as many people with philanthropic feelings who are helping them, are daily spreading this fallacy and at the same time telling them that they are overworked.

A great deal has been and is being constantly said about "sweat-shop" work and conditions. The writer has great sympathy with those who are overworked, but on the whole a greater sympathy for those who are *under paid*. For every individual, however, who is overworked, there are a hundred who intentionally underwork—greatly underwork—every day of their lives, and who for this reason deliberately aid in establishing those conditions which in the end inevitably result in low wages. And yet hardly a single voice is being raised in an endeavor to correct this evil.

As engineers and managers, we are more intimately acquainted with these facts than any other class in the community, and are therefore best fitted to lead in a movement to combat this fallacious idea by educating not only the workmen but the whole of the country as to the true facts. And yet we are practically doing nothing in this direction, and are leaving this field entirely in the hands of the labor agitators (many of whom are misinformed and misguided), and of sentimentalists who are ignorant as to actual working conditions.

Second. As to the second cause for soldiering—the relations which exist between employers and employés under almost all of the systems of management which are in common use—it is impossible in a few words to make it clear to one not familiar with this problem why it is that the *ignorance of employers* as to the proper time in which work of various kinds should be done makes it for the interest of the workman to "soldier."

. . .

According to scientific laws, the management must take over and perform much of the work which is now left to the men; almost every act of the workman should be preceded by one or more preparatory acts of the management which enable him to do his work better and quicker than he otherwise could. And each man should daily be taught by and receive the most friendly help from those who are over him, instead of being, at the one extreme, driven or coerced by his bosses, and at the other left to his own unaided devices.

This close, intimate, personal cooperation between the management and the men is of the essence of modern scientific or task management.

It will be shown by a series of practical illustrations that, through this friendly cooperation, namely, through sharing equally in every day's burden, all of the great obstacles (above described) to obtaining the maximum output for each man and each machine in the establishment are swept away. The 30 per cent. to 100 per cent. increase in wages which the workmen are able to earn beyond what they receive under the old type of management, coupled with the daily intimate shoulder to shoulder contact with the management, entirely removes all cause for soldiering. And in a few years, under this system, the workmen have before them the object lesson of seeing that a great increase in the output per man results in giving employment to more men, instead of throwing men out of work, thus completely eradicating the fallacy that a larger output for each man will throw other men out of work.

It is the writer's judgment, then, that while much can be done and should be done by writing and talking toward educating not only workmen, but all classes in the community, as to the importance of obtaining the maximum output of each man and each machine, it is only through the adoption of modern scientific management that this great problem can be finally solved. Probably most of the readers of this paper will say that all of this is mere theory. On the contrary, the theory, or philosophy, of scientific management is just beginning to be understood, whereas the management itself has been a gradual evolution, extending over a period of nearly thirty years. And during this time the employés of one company after another, including a large range and diversity of industries, have gradually changed from the ordinary to the scientific type of management. At least 50,000 workmen in the United States are now employed under this system; and they are receiving from 30 per cent. to 100 per cent. higher wages daily than are paid to men of similar caliber with whom they are surrounded, while the companies employing them are more prosperous than ever before. In these companies the output, per man and per machine, has on an average been doubled. During all these years there has never been a single strike among the men working under this system. In place of the suspicious watchfulness and the more or less open warfare which characterizes the ordinary types of management, there is universally friendly cooperation between the management and the men.

6 Russell Conwell, from *Acres of Diamonds*, 1915[8]

Russell Conwell (1843–1925) was a Baptist minister who founded what is now known as the Gordon-Conwell Theological Seminary in Massachusetts. After rescuing a failing Baptist church in Boston, he was called to Grace Baptist Church, a struggling congregation in Philadelphia. The church grew and prospered under his leadership, and Temple University grew out of a church school started in the basement of the new church building, known as Baptist Temple. Although driven by contemporary goals of material success, he was also a philanthropist, whose profits from the lecture circuit were used to pay for the education of thousands of young men. In particular, the following lecture was among his most popular, and he delivered it more than 6,000 times.

The story that the Arab guide told Conwell was about a man, Ali Hafed, who sold his farm and went all over the world looking for diamonds, which he never found, and he ended his life by throwing himself into the ocean. However, the man who bought his farm found a diamond shining in the river that ran through the property, and on the instructions of the priest who had originally told Ali Hafed about the value of diamonds, he dug up the farm and discovered the greatest diamond mine in the world.

When going down the Tigris and Euphrates rivers many years ago with a party of English travelers I found myself under the direction of an old Arab guide whom we hired up at Baghdad, and I have often thought how that guide resembled our barbers in certain mental characteristics. He thought

[8] Russell H. Conwell, *Acres of Diamonds* (New York: Harper & Row, 1915), pp. 3, 8–21, 50, 58–9.

that it was not only his duty to guide us down those rivers, and do what he was paid for doing, but to entertain us with stories curious and weird, ancient and modern, strange and familiar. Many of them I have forgotten, and I am glad I have, but there is one I shall never forget.

. . .

Those Arab guides have morals to their stories, although they are not always moral. As he swung his hat, he said to me, "Had Ali Hafed remained at home and dug in his own cellar, or underneath his own wheat fields or in his own garden, instead of wretchedness, starvation, and death by suicide in a strange land, he would have had 'acres of diamonds.' For every acre of that old farm, yes, every shovelful, afterward revealed gems which since have decorated the crowns of monarchs."

When he had added the moral of his story I saw why he reserved it for "his particular friends." But I did not tell him that I could see it. It was that mean old Arab's way of going around a thing like a lawyer, to say indirectly what he did not dare say directly, that "in his private opinion there was a certain young man then traveling down the Tigris River that might better be at home in America." I did not tell him I could see that, but I told it to him quick, and I think I will tell it to you.

I told him of a man out in California in 1847, who owned a ranch. He heard they had discovered gold in southern California, and so with a passion for gold he sold his ranch to Colonel Sutter, and away he went, never to come back. Colonel Sutter put a mill upon a stream that ran through that ranch, and one day his little girl brought some wet sand from the raceway into their home and sifted it through her fingers before the fire, and in that falling sand a visitor saw the first shining scales of real gold that were ever discovered in California. The man who had owned that ranch wanted gold, and he could have secured it for the mere taking. Indeed, thirty-eight millions of dollars has been taken out of a very few acres since then.

About eight years ago I delivered this lecture in a city that stands on that farm, and they told me that a one-third owner for years and years had been getting one hundred and twenty dollars in gold every fifteen minutes, sleeping or waking, without taxation. You and I would enjoy an income like that—if we didn't have to pay an income tax.

But a better illustration really than that occurred here in our town of Pennsylvania. If there is anything I enjoy above another on the platform, it is to get one of these German audiences in Pennsylvania, and fire that at them, and I enjoy it tonight. There was a man living in Pennsylvania, not unlike some Pennsylvanians you have seen, who owned a farm, and he did with that farm just what I should do with a farm if I owned one in

Pennsylvania—he sold it. But before he sold it he decided to secure employment collecting coal-oil for his cousin, who was in the business in Canada, where they first discovered oil on this continent. They dipped it from the running streams at that early time. So this Pennsylvania farmer wrote to his cousin asking for employment. You see, friends, this farmer was not altogether a foolish man. No, he was not. He did not leave his farm until he had something else to do. Of all the simpletons the stars shine on I don't know of a worse one than the man who leaves one job before he has gotten another. That has especial reference to my profession, and has no reference whatever to a man seeking a divorce. When he wrote to his cousin for employment, his cousin replied, "I cannot engage you because you know nothing about the oil business." Well, then the old farmer said, "I will know," and with most commendable zeal (characteristic of the students of Temple University) he sat himself at the study of the whole subject. He began away back at the second day of God's creation when this world was covered thick and deep with that rich vegetation which since has turned to the primitive beds of coal. He studied the subject until he found that the drainings really of those rich beds of coal furnished the coal-oil that was worth pumping, and then he found how it came up with the living springs. He studied until he knew what it looked like, smelled like, tasted like, and how to refine it. Now said he in his letter to his cousin, "I understand the oil business." His cousin answered, "All right, come on."

So he sold his farm, according to the county record, for $833 (even money, "no cents"). He had scarcely gone from that place before the man who purchased the spot went out to arrange for the watering of the cattle. He found the previous owner had gone out years before and put a plank across the brook back of the barn, edgewise into the surface of the water just a few inches. The purpose of that plank at that sharp angle across the brook was to throw over to the other bank a dreadful-looking scum through which the cattle would not put their noses. But with that plank there to throw it all over to one side, the cattle would drink below, and thus that man who had gone to Canada had been himself damming back for twenty-three years a flood of coal-oil which the state geologists of Pennsylvania declared to us ten years later was even then worth a hundred millions of dollars to our state, a thousand millions of dollars. The man who owned that territory on which the city of Titusville now stands, and those Pleasantville valleys, had studied the subject from the second day of God's creation clear down to the present time. He studied it until he knew all about it, and yet he is said to have sold the whole of it for $833, and again I say, "no sense."

But I need another illustration. I found it in Massachusetts, and I am sorry I did because that is the state I came from. This young man in Massachusetts furnishes just another phase of my thought. He went to Yale College and studied mines and mining, and became such an adept as a mining engineer that he was employed by the authorities of the university to train students who were behind their classes. During his senior year he earned $15 a week for doing that work. When he graduated they raised his pay from $15 to $45 a week, and offered him a professorship, as soon as they did he went right home to his mother. If they had raised that boy's pay from $14 to $15.60 he would have stayed and been proud of the place, but when they put it up to $45 at one leap, he said, "Mother, I won't work for $45 a week. The idea of a man with a brain like mine working for $45 a week! Let's go out to California and stake out gold-mines and silver-mines, and be immensely rich." Said his mother, "Now, Charlie, it is just as well to be happy as it is to be rich." "Yes," said Charlie, "But it is just as well to be rich and happy too." And they were both right about it. As he was an only son and she a widow, of course he had his way. They always do.

They sold out in Massachusetts, and instead of going to California they went to Wisconsin, where he went into the employ of the superior Copper Mining Company at $15 a week again, but with the proviso in his contract that he should have an interest in any mines he should discover for the company. I don't believe he ever discovered a mine, and if I am looking in the face of any stockholder of that copper company you wish he had discovered something or other. I have friends who are not here because they could not afford a ticket, who did have stock in that company at the time this young man was employed there. This young man went out there and I have not heard a word from him. I don't know what became of him, and I don't know whether he found any mines or not, but I don't believe he ever did.

But I do know the other end of the line. He had scarcely gotten the other end of the old homestead before the succeeding owner went out to dig potatoes. The potatoes were already growing in the ground when he bought the farm, and as the old farmer was bringing in a basket of potatoes it hugged very tight between the ends of the stone fence. You know in Massachusetts our farms are nearly all stone wall. There you are obliged to be very economical of front gateways in order to have some place to put the stone. When that basket hugged so tight he set it down on the ground, and then dragged on one side, and pulled on the other side, and as he was dragging that basket though this farmer noticed in the upper and outer corner of that stone wall, right next the gate, a block of native silver eight inches square. That professor of mines, mining, and mineralogy who knew so much about the subject that he would not work for $45 a week, when he sold that homestead in Massachusetts sat right on that silver to make the bargain. He was born on that homestead, was brought up there, and had gone back and forth rubbing the stone with his sleeve until it reflected his countenance, and seemed to say, "Here is a hundred thousand dollars right down here just for the taking." But he would not take it. It was in a home in Newburyport, Massachusetts, and there was no silver there, all away off— well, I don't know were, and he did not, but somewhere else, and he was a professor of mineralogy.

My friends, that mistake is very universally made, and why should we even smile at him. I often wonder what has become of him. I do not know at all, but I will tell you what I "guess" as a Yankee. I guess that he sits out there by his fireside to-night with his friends gathered around him, and he is saying to them something like this: "Do you know that man Conwell who lives in Philadelphia?" "Oh yes, I have heard of him." "Do you know of that man Jones that lives in Philadelphia?" "Yes, I have heard of him, too."

Then he begins to laugh, and shakes his sides, and says to his friends, "Well, they have done just the same thing I did, precisely"—and that spoils the whole joke, for you and I have done the same thing he did, and while we sit here and laugh at him he has a better right to sit out there and laugh at us. I know I have made the same mistakes, but, of course, that does not make any difference, because we don't expect the same man to preach and practice, too.

As I come here to-night and look around this audience I am seeing again what through these fifty years I have continually seen—men that are making precisely that same mistake. I often wish I could see the younger people, and would that the Academy had been filled to-night with our high school scholars and our grammar-school scholars, that I could have them to talk to. While I would have preferred such an audience as that, because they are most susceptible, as they have not gotten into any custom that they cannot break, they have not met with any failures as we have; and while I could perhaps do such an audience as that more good than I can do grown-up people, yet I will do the best I can with the material I have. I say to you that you have "acres of diamonds" in Philadelphia right where you now live. "Oh," but you will say, "you cannot know much about your city if you think there are any 'acres of diamonds' here."

I was greatly interested in that account in the newspaper of the young man who found that diamond in North Carolina. It was one of the purest diamonds that has ever been discovered, and it has several predecessors near the same locality. I went to a distinguished professor in mineralogy and asked him where he thought those diamonds came from. The professor secured the map of the geologic formations of our continent, and traced it. He said it went either through the underlying carboniferous strata adapted for such production, westward through Ohio and the Mississippi, or in more probability came eastward through Virginia and up the shore of the Atlantic Ocean. It is a fact that the diamonds were there, for they have been discovered and sold; and that they were carried down there during the drift period, from some northern locality. Now who can say but some person going down with his drill in Philadelphia will find some trace of a diamond-mine yet down here? Oh, friends! You cannot say that you are not over one of the greatest diamond-mines in the world, for such a diamond as that only comes from the most profitable mines that are found on earth.

But it serves to simply to illustrate my thought, which I emphasize by saying if you do not have the actual diamond-mines literally you have all that they would be good for to you. Because now that the Queen of England has given the greatest compliment ever conferred upon American woman for her attire because she did not appear with any jewels at all at the late reception in England, it has almost done away with the use of diamonds anyhow. All you would care for would be the few you would wear if you wish to be modest, and the rest of you would sell for money.

Now then, I say again that the opportunity to get rich, to attain unto great wealth, is here in Philadelphia now, within the reach of almost every man and woman who hears me speak to-night, and I mean just what I say. I have not come to this platform even under these circumstances to recite something to you. I have come to tell you what in God's sight I believe to be the truth, and if the years of life have been of any value to me in the attainment of common sense, I know I am right; that the men and women sitting here, who found it difficult perhaps to buy a ticket to this lecture or gathering to-night, have within their reach "acres of diamonds," opportunities to get largely wealthy. There never was a place on earth more adapted than the city of Philadelphia to-day, and never in the history of the world did a poor man without capital have such an opportunity to get rich quickly and honestly as he has now in our city. I say it is the truth, and I want you to accept it as such; for if you think I have come to simply recite something, then I would better not be here. I have no time to waste in any such talk, but to say the things I believe, and unless some of you get richer for what I am saying to-night my time is wasted.

I say that you ought to get rich, and it is our duty to get rich. How many of my pious brethren say to me, "Do you, a Christian minister, spend your time going up and down the country advising young people to get rich, to get money?" "Yes, of course I do." They say, "Isn't that awful! Why don't you preach the gospel instead of preaching about man's making money?" "Because to make money honestly is to preach the gospel." That is the reason. The men who get rich may be the most honest men you find in the community. "Oh," but says some young man here to-night, "I have been told all my life that if a person has money he is very dishonest and dishonorable and mean and contemptible."

My friend, that is the reason why you have none, because you have that idea of people. The foundation of your faith is altogether false. Let me say here clearly, and say it briefly, though subject to discussion which I have not time for here, ninety-eight out of one hundred of the rich men of America are honest. That is why they are rich. That is why they carry on great enterprises and find plenty of people to work with them. It is because they are honest men.

Says another young man, "I hear sometimes of men that get millions of dollars dishonestly." Yes, of course you do, and so do I. But they are so rare a thing in fact that the newspapers talk about them all the time as a matter of news until you get the idea that all the other rich men got rich dishonestly.

My friend, you take and drive me—if you furnish the auto—out into the suburbs of Philadelphia, and introduce me to the people who own their homes around this great city, those beautiful homes with gardens and flowers, those magnificent homes so lovely in their art, and I will introduce you to the very best people in character as well as in enterprise in our city, and you know I will. A man is not really a true man until he owns his own home, and they that own their homes are made more honorable and honest and pure, true and economical and careful, by owning the home.

For a man to have money, even in large sum, is not an inconsistent thing. We preach against covetousness, and you know we do, in the pulpit, and oftentimes preach against it so long and use the terms about "filthy lucre" so extremely that Christians get the idea that when we stand in the pulpit we believe it is wicked for any man to have money—until the collection-basket goes around, and then we almost swear at the people because they don't give more money. Oh, the inconsistency of such doctrines as that!

Money is power, and you ought to be reasonably ambitious to have it. You ought because you can do more good with it than you could without it. Money printed your Bible, money builds your churches, money sends your missionaries, and money pays your preachers, and you would not have many of them, either, if you did not pay them. I am always willing that my church should raise my salary, because the church that pays the largest salary always raises it the easiest. You never knew an exception to it in your life. The man who gets the largest salary can do the most good with the power that is furnished to him. Of course he can if his spirit be right to use it for what it is given to him.

I say, then, you ought to have money. If you can honestly attain unto riches in Philadelphia, it is our Christian and godly duty to do so. It is an awful mistake of these pious people to think you must be awfully poor in order to be pious.

Some men say, "Don't you sympathize with the poor people?" Of course I do, or else I would not have been lecturing these years. I wont give in but what I sympathize with the poor, but the number of poor who are to be with is very small. To sympathize with a man whom God has punished for his sins, thus to help him when God would still continue a just punishment, is to do wrong, no doubt about it, and we do that more than we help those who are deserving. While we should sympathize with God's poor—that is, those who cannot help themselves—let us remember that is not a poor person in the United States who was not made poor by his own shortcomings, or by the shortcomings of some one else. It is all wrong to be poor, anyhow. Let us give in to that argument and pass that to one side.

. . .

Arise, you millions of Philadelphians, trust in God and man, and believe in the great opportunities that are right here—not over in New York or Boston, but here—for business, for everything that is worth living for on earth. There was never an opportunity greater. Let us talk up our won city.

. . .

Oh, I learned the lesson then that I will never forget so long as the tongue of the bell of time continues to swing for me. Greatness consists not in the holding of some future office, but really consists in doing great deeds with little means and the accomplishment of vast purposes from the private ranks of life. To be great at all one must be great here, now, in Philadelphia. He who can give to this city better streets and better sidewalks, better schools and more colleges, more happiness and more civilization, more of God, he will be great anywhere. Let every man or woman here, if you never hear me again, remember this, that if you wish to be great at all, you must begin where you are and what you are, in Philadelphia, now. He that can give to his city any blessing, he who can be a good citizen while he lives here, he that can make better homes, he that can be a blessing whether he works in the shop or sits behind the counter or keeps house, whatever be his life, he who would be great anywhere must first be great in his own Philadelphia.

Discussion Questions: Chapter 4

1 How do Carnegie and Spencer agree or disagree in their views of social classes and social conflict?

2 How does Lloyd portray big business in the Gilded Age? What evidence does he provide of collusion and unfair practices? What is the impact of monopoly control on labor and working conditions?

3 What is Carnegie's view of wealth – how it was produced and how it should be spent?

4 "If the tendency to combination is irresistible," wrote Lloyd, "control of it is imperative." What did he mean by this statement?

5 How did the justices arrive at their strict interpretation of the Fourteenth Amendment in the *Slaughterhouse Cases?*

6 According to Taylor, what factors kept workers from reaching their potential for productivity?

7 In what ways were the economic theories of Lloyd and Conwell similar to or different from each other?

Chapter 5   Gilded Age Society

1 Thorstein Veblen, from *The Theory of the Leisure Class*, 1899[1]

Thorstein Veblen (1857–1929) was an American political economist known for his criticism of capitalism and the inventor of the phrase "conspicuous consumption," which describes ostentatious displays of wealth. Like other contemporaries during the Gilded Age, Veblen offered a critique of industrial capitalism and its impact on society.

The following excerpt is from his best-known work, The Theory of the Leisure Class, *which argues that the leisure class in society serves as an incentive for the working class. This theory differs from Marxism, because, according to Veblen, the working class does not try to overthrow the leisure class. The main conflict in economics, he argued, occurred between entrepreneurs, who simply manipulated financial systems, and engineers and industrialists, who actually produced goods and provided stability in the economy. During his academic career, Veblen taught at the University of Chicago, Stanford University, and the University of Wisconsin. He helped found the New School for Social Research in New York.*

---

[1] Thorstein Veblen, *The Theory of the Leisure Class* (New York: Macmillan, 1899).

The Gilded Age and Progressive Era: A Documentary Reader, First Edition.
Edited by William A. Link and Susannah J. Link.
© 2012 Blackwell Publishing Ltd. Published 2012 by Blackwell Publishing Ltd.

Chapter Four: Conspicuous Consumption

. . .

Conspicuous consumption of valuable goods is a means of reputability to the gentleman of leisure. As wealth accumulates on his hands, his own unaided effort will not avail to sufficiently put his opulence in evidence by this method. The aid of friends and competitors is therefore brought in by resorting to the giving of valuable presents and expensive feasts and entertainments. Presents and feasts had probably another origin than that of naive ostentation, but they required their utility for this purpose very early, and they have retained that character to the present; so that their utility in this respect has now long been the substantial ground on which these usages rest. Costly entertainments, such as the potlatch or the ball, are peculiarly adapted to serve this end. The competitor with whom the entertainer wishes to institute a comparison is, by this method, made to serve as a means to the end. He consumes vicariously for his host at the same time that he is witness to the consumption of that excess of good things which his host is unable to dispose of single-handed, and he is also made to witness his host's facility in etiquette.

. . .

As wealth accumulates, the leisure class develops further in function and structure, and there arises a differentiation within the class. There is a more or less elaborate system of rank and grades. This differentiation is furthered by the inheritance of wealth and the consequent inheritance of gentility. With the inheritance of gentility goes the inheritance of obligatory leisure; and gentility of a sufficient potency to entail a life of leisure may be inherited without the complement of wealth required to maintain a dignified leisure. Gentle blood may be transmitted without goods enough to afford a reputably free consumption at one's ease. Hence results a class of impecunious gentlemen of leisure, incidentally referred to already. These half-caste gentlemen of leisure fall into a system of hierarchical gradations. Those who stand near the higher and the highest grades of the wealthy leisure class, in point of birth, or in point of wealth, or both, outrank the remoter-born and the pecuniarily weaker. These lower grades, especially the impecunious, or marginal, gentlemen of leisure, affiliate themselves by a system of dependence or fealty to the great ones; by so doing they gain an increment of repute, or of the means with which to lead a life of leisure, from their patron. They become his courtiers or retainers, servants; and being fed and countenanced by their patron they are indices of his rank and vicarious consumers of his superfluous wealth. Many of these affiliated gentlemen of leisure are at the same time lesser men of substance in their own right; so that some of them are scarcely at all, others only partially, to be rated as vicarious consumers. So many of them, however, as make up the retainer and hangers-on of the patron may be classed as vicarious consumers without qualification. Many of these again, and also many of the other aristocracy of less degree, have in turn attached to their persons a more or less comprehensive group of vicarious consumers in the persons of their wives and children, their servants, retainers, etc.

. . .

And here occurs a curious inversion. It is a fact of common observance that in this lower middle class there is no pretense of leisure on the part of the head of the household. Through force of circumstances it has fallen into disuse. But the middle-class wife still carries on the business of vicarious leisure, for the good name of the household and its master. In descending the social scale in any modern industrial community, the primary fact—the conspicuous leisure of the master of the household—disappears at a relatively high point. The head of the middle-class household has been reduced by economic circumstances to turn his hand to gaining a livelihood by occupations which often partake largely of the character of industry, as in the case of the ordinary business man of today. But the derivative fact—the vicarious leisure and consumption rendered by the wife, and the auxiliary vicarious performance of leisure by menials—remains in vogue as a conventionality which the demands of reputability will not suffer to be slighted. It is by no means an uncommon spectacle to find a man applying himself to work with the utmost assiduity, in order that his wife may in due form render for him that degree of vicarious leisure which the common sense of the time demands.

The leisure rendered by the wife in such cases is, of course, not a simple manifestation of idleness or indolence. It almost invariably occurs disguised under some form of work or household duties or social amenities, which prove on analysis to serve little or no ulterior end beyond showing that she does not occupy herself with anything that is gainful or that is of substantial use. As has already been noticed under the head of manners, the greater part of the customary round of domestic cares to which the middle-class housewife gives her time and effort is of this character. Not that the results of her attention to household matters, of a decorative and mundificatory character, are not pleasing to the sense of men trained in middle-class proprieties; but the taste to which these effects of household adornment and tidiness appeal is a taste which has been formed under the selective guidance of a canon of propriety that demands just these evidences of wasted effort. The effects are pleasing to us chiefly because we have been taught to find them pleasing.

There goes into these domestic duties much solicitude for a proper combination of form and color, and for other ends that are to be classed as aesthetic in the proper sense of the term; and it is not denied that effects having some substantial aesthetic value are sometimes attained. Pretty much all that is here insisted on is that, as regards these amenities of life, the housewife's efforts are under the guidance of traditions that have been shaped by the law of conspicuously wasteful expenditure of time and substance. If beauty or comfort is achieved—and it is a more or less fortuitous circumstance if they are—they must be achieved by means and methods that commend themselves to the great economic law of wasted effort. The more reputable, "presentable" portion of middle-class household paraphernalia are, on the one hand, items of conspicuous consumption, and on the other hand, apparatus for putting in evidence the vicarious leisure rendered by the housewife.

. . .

The modern organization of industry works in the same direction also by another line. The exigencies of the modern industrial system frequently place individuals and households in juxtaposition between whom there is little contact in any other sense than that of juxtaposition. One's neighbors, mechanically speaking, often are socially not one's neighbors, or even acquaintances; and still their transient good opinion has a high degree of utility. The only practicable means of impressing one's pecuniary ability on these unsympathetic observers of one's everyday life is an unremitting demonstration of ability to pay. In the modern community there is also a more frequent attendance at large gatherings of people to whom one's everyday life is unknown; in such places as churches, theaters, ballrooms, hotels, parks, shops, and the like. In order to impress these transient observers, and to retain one's self-complacency under their observation, the signature of one's pecuniary strength should be written in characters which he who runs may read. It is evident, therefore, that the present trend of the development is in the direction of heightening the utility of conspicuous consumption as compared with leisure.

. . .

Consumption becomes a larger element in the standard of living in the city than in the country. Among the country population its place is to some extent taken by savings and home comforts known through the medium of neighborhood gossip sufficiently to serve the like general purpose of Pecuniary repute. These home comforts and the leisure indulged in—where the indulgence is found—are of course also in great part to be classed as items of conspicuous consumption; and much the same is to be said of the savings. The smaller amount of the savings laid by by the artisan class is no doubt due, in some measure, to the fact that in the case of the artisan the savings are a less effective means of advertisement, relative to the environment in which he is placed, than are the savings of the people living on farms and in the small villages. Among the latter, everybody's affairs, especially everybody's pecuniary status, are known to everybody else. Considered by itself simply—taken in the first degree—this added provocation to which the artisan and the urban laboring classes are exposed may not very seriously decrease the amount of savings; but in its cumulative action, through raising the standard of decent expenditure, its deterrent effect on the tendency to save cannot but be very great.

. . .

The early ascendency of leisure as a means of reputability is traceable to the archaic distinction between noble and ignoble employments. Leisure is honorable and becomes imperative partly because it shows exemption from ignoble labor. The archaic differentiation into noble and ignoble classes is based on an invidious distinction between employments as honorific or debasing; and this traditional distinction grows into an imperative canon of decency during the early quasi-peaceable stage. Its ascendency is furthered by the fact that leisure is still fully as effective an evidence of wealth as consumption. Indeed, so effective is it in the relatively small and stable human environment to which the individual is exposed at that cultural stage, that, with the aid of the archaic tradition which deprecates all productive labor, it gives rise to a large impecunious leisure class, and it even tends to limit the production of the community's industry to the subsistence minimum. This extreme inhibition of industry is avoided because slave labor, working under a compulsion more vigorous than that of reputability, is forced to turn out a product in excess of the subsistence minimum of the working class. The subsequent relative decline in the use of conspicuous leisure as a basis of repute is due partly to an increasing relative effectiveness of consumption as an evidence of wealth; but in part it is traceable to another force, alien, and in some degree antagonistic, to the usage of conspicuous waste.

. . .

The use of the term "waste" is in one respect an unfortunate one. As used in the speech of everyday life the word carries an undertone of deprecation. It is here used for want of a better term that will adequately describe the same range of motives and of phenomena, and it is not to be taken in an odious sense, as implying an illegitimate expenditure of human products or of human life. In the view of economic theory the expenditure in question is no more and no less legitimate than any other expenditure. It is here called "waste" because this expenditure does not serve human life or human well-being on the whole, not because it is waste or misdirection of effort or expenditure as viewed from the standpoint of the individual consumer who chooses it. If he chooses it, that disposes of the question of its relative utility to him, as compared with other forms of consumption that would not be deprecated on account of their wastefulness. Whatever form of expenditure the consumer chooses, or whatever end he seeks in making his choice, has utility to him by virtue of his preference. As seen from the point of view of the individual consumer, the question of wastefulness does not arise within the scope of economic theory proper. The use of the word "waste" as a technical term, therefore, implies no deprecation of the motives or of the ends sought by the consumer under this canon of conspicuous waste.

But it is, on other grounds, worth noting that the term "waste" in the language of everyday life implies deprecation of what is characterized as wasteful. This common-sense implication is itself an outcropping of the instinct of workmanship. The popular reprobation of waste goes to say that in order to be at peace with himself the common man must be able to see in any and all human effort and human enjoyment an enhancement of life and well-being on the whole. In order to meet with unqualified approval, any economic fact must approve itself under the test of impersonal usefulness—usefulness as seen from the point of view of the generically human. Relative or competitive advantage of one individual in comparison with another does not satisfy the economic conscience, and therefore competitive expenditure has not the approval of this conscience.

. . .

It is obviously not necessary that a given object of expenditure should be exclusively wasteful in order to come in under the category of conspicuous waste. An article may be useful and wasteful both, and its utility to the consumer may be made up of use and waste in the most varying proportions. Consumable goods, and even productive goods, generally show the two elements in combination, as constituents of their utility; although, in a general way, the element of waste tends to predominate in articles of consumption, while the contrary is true of articles designed for productive use. Even in articles which appear at first glance to serve for pure ostentation only, it is always possible to detect the presence of some, at least ostensible, useful purpose; and on the other hand, even in special machinery and tools contrived for some particular industrial process, as well as in the rudest appliances of human industry, the traces of conspicuous waste, or at least of the habit of ostentation, usually become evident on a close scrutiny. It would be hazardous to assert that a useful purpose is ever absent from the utility of any article or of any service, however obviously its prime purpose and chief element is conspicuous waste; and it would be only less hazardous to assert of any primarily useful product that the element of waste is in no way concerned in its value, immediately or remotely.

2 Charlotte Perkins Gilman, from "The Yellow Wall-Paper," 1892[2]

Born in Hartford, Connecticut, Charlotte Perkins Gilman (1860–1935) grew up in poverty – her father abandoned the family – and she lived with relatives. An aspiring artist, she attended the Rhode Island School of Design. Not long after her marriage to fellow artist Charles Walter Stetson and the birth of a daughter, Katharine Beecher Stetson, in 1885, Gilman suffered from depression and a nervous breakdown. Rejecting the diagnosis of her psychological problems, in 1888 Gilman separated from her husband (she remarried in 1900, to George Houghton Gilman) and became a feminist and supporter of women's rights in labor and voting.

The following excerpt is from Gilman's best-known writing, "The Yellow Wall-Paper." The most important themes in her feminist writings were woman suffrage and the need for women's economic independence. Her book, Women and Economics *(1898), provided a major exposition of her theories. She argued that women should give up their role as housewives and take advantage of jobs available through industry and the professions. In her view, housekeeping and childrearing were jobs better left to trained and paid workers. Gilman (1860–1935) was the great-granddaughter of Lyman Beecher and the grandniece of Henry Ward Beecher and Harriet Beecher Stowe. She was an advocate of the right to die, and when she learned that she had incurable breast cancer, she committed suicide with chloroform rather than succumbing to the disease itself.*

It is very seldom that mere ordinary people like John and myself secure ancestral halls for the summer.

A colonial mansion, a hereditary estate, I would say a haunted house, and reach the height of romantic felicity, — but that would be asking too much of fate!

Still I will proudly declare that there is something queer about it.

---

[2] Charlotte Perkins Stetson [Gilman], "The Yellow Wall-Paper," *The New England Magazine* V (January 1892): 647–56.

Else, why should it be let so cheaply? And why have stood so long un- tenanted?

John laughs at me, of course, but one expects that in marriage.

John is practical in the extreme. He has no patience with faith, an intense horror of superstition, and he scoffs openly at any talk of things not to be felt and seen and put down in figures.

John is a physician, and perhaps — (I would not say it to a living soul, of course, but this is dead paper and a great relief to my mind) — perhaps that is one reason I do not get well faster.

You see, he does not believe I am sick!

And what can one do?

If a physician of high standing, and one's own husband, assures friends and relatives that there is really nothing the matter with one but temporary nervous depression, — a slight hysterical tendency, — what is one to do?

My brother is also a physician, and also of high standing, and he says the same thing.

So I take phosphates or phosphites, — whichever it is, — and tonics, and journeys, and air, and exercise, and am absolutely forbidden to "work" until I am well again.

Personally I disagree with their ideas.

Personally I believe that congenial work, with excitement and change, would do me good.

But what is one to do?

I did write for a while in spite of them; but it does exhaust me a good deal — having to be so sly about it, or else meet with heavy opposition.

I sometimes fancy that in my condition if I had less opposition and more society and stimulus — but John says the very worst thing I can do is to think about my condition, and I confess it always makes me feel bad.

So I will let it alone and talk about the house.

The most beautiful place! It is quite alone, standing well back from the road, quite three miles from the village. It makes me think of English places that you read about, for there are hedges and walls and gates that lock, and lots of separate little houses for the gardeners and people.

There is a delicious garden! I never saw such a garden — large and shady, full of box-bordered paths, and lined with long grape-covered arbors with seats under them.

There were greenhouses, too, but they are all broken now.

There was some legal trouble, I believe, something about the heirs and co-heirs; anyhow, the place has been empty for years.

That spoils my ghostliness, I am afraid; but I don't care — there is something strange about the house — I can feel it.

I even said so to John one moonlight evening, but he said what I felt was a draught, and shut the window.

I get unreasonably angry with John sometimes. I'm sure I never used to be so sensitive. I think it is due to this nervous condition.

But John says if I feel so I shall neglect proper self-control; so I take pains to control myself, — before him, at least, — and that makes me very tired.

I don't like our room a bit. I wanted one downstairs that opened on the piazza and had roses all over the window, and such pretty, old-fashioned chintz hangings! but John would not hear of it.

He said there was only one window and not room for two beds, and no near room for him if he took another.

He is very careful and loving, and hardly lets me stir without special direction.

I have a schedule prescription for each hour in the day; he takes all care from me, and so I feel basely ungrateful not to value it more.

He said we came here solely on my account, that I was to have perfect rest and all the air I could get. "Your exercise depends on your strength, my dear," said he, "and your food somewhat on your appetite; but air you can absorb all the time." So we took the nursery, at the top of the house.

It is a big, airy room, the whole floor nearly, with windows that look all ways, and air and sunshine galore. It was nursery first and then playground and gymnasium, I should judge; for the windows are barred for little children, and there are rings and things in the walls.

The paint and paper look as if a boys' school had used it. It is stripped off — the paper — in great patches all around the head of my bed, about as far as I can reach, and in a great place on the other side of the room low down. I never saw a worse paper in my life.

One of those sprawling flamboyant patterns committing every artistic sin.

It is dull enough to confuse the eye in following, pronounced enough to constantly irritate, and provoke study, and when you follow the lame, uncertain curves for a little distance they suddenly commit suicide — plunge off at outrageous angles, destroy themselves in unheard-of contradictions.

The color is repellant, almost revolting; a smouldering, unclean yellow, strangely faded by the slow-turning sunlight.

It is a dull yet lurid orange in some places, a sickly sulphur tint in others.

No wonder the children hated it! I should hate it myself if I had to live in this room long.

There comes John, and I must put this away, — he hates to have me write a word.

We have been here two weeks, and I haven't felt like writing before, since that first day.

I am sitting by the window now, up in this atrocious nursery, and there is nothing to hinder my writing as much as I please, save lack of strength.

John is away all day, and even some nights when his cases are serious.

I am glad my case is not serious!

But these nervous troubles are dreadfully depressing.

John does not know how much I really suffer. He knows there is no reason to suffer, and that satisfies him.

Of course it is only nervousness. It does weigh on me so not to do my duty in any way!

I meant to be such a help to John, such a real rest and comfort, and here I am a comparative burden already!

Nobody would believe what an effort it is to do what little I am able — to dress and entertain, and order things.

It is fortunate Mary is so good with the baby. Such a dear baby!

And yet I cannot be with him, it makes me so nervous.

I suppose John never was nervous in his life. He laughs at me so about this wall paper!

At first he meant to repaper the room, but afterwards he said that I was letting it get the better of me, and that nothing was worse for a nervous patient than to give way to such fancies.

He said that after the wall paper was changed it would be the heavy bedstead, and then the barred windows, and then that gate at the head of the stairs, and so on.

"You know the place is doing you good," he said, "and really, dear, I don't care to renovate the house just for a three months' rental."

"Then do let us go downstairs," I said, "there are such pretty rooms there."

. . .

I wish I could get well faster.

But I must not think about that. This paper looks to me as if it knew what a vicious influence it had!

There is a recurrent spot where the pattern lolls like a broken neck and two bulbous eyes stare at you upside-down.

I got positively angry with the impertinence of it and the everlastingness. Up and down and sideways they crawl, and those absurd, unblinking eyes are everywhere. There is one place where two breadths didn't match, and the eyes go all up and down the line, one a little higher than the other.

I never saw so much expression in an inanimate thing before, and we all know how much expression they have! I used to lie awake as a child and get more entertainment and terror out of blank walls and plain furniture than most children could find in a toy-store.

I remember what a kindly wink the knobs of our big old bureau used to have, and there was one chair that always seemed like a strong friend.

I used to feel that if any of the other things looked too fierce I could always hop into that chair and be safe.

The furniture in this room is no worse than inharmonious, however, for we had to bring it all from downstairs. I suppose when this was used as a playroom they had to take the nursery things out, and no wonder! I never saw such ravages as the children have made here.

The wall paper, as I said before, is torn off in spots, and it sticketh closer than a brother — they must have had perseverance as well as hatred.

Then the floor is scratched and gouged and splintered, the plaster itself is dug out here and there, and this great heavy bed, which is all we found in the room, looks as if it had been through the wars.

But I don't mind it a bit — only the paper.

There comes John's sister. Such a dear girl as she is, and so careful of me! I must not let her find me writing.

She is a perfect, an enthusiastic housekeeper, and hopes for no better profession. I verily believe she thinks it is the writing which made me sick!

But I can write when she is out, and see her a long way off from these windows.

There is one that commands the road, a lovely, shaded, winding road, and one that just looks off over the country. A lovely country, too, full of great elms and velvet meadows.

This wall paper has a kind of sub-pattern in a different shade, a particularly irritating one, for you can only see it in certain lights, and not clearly then.

But in the places where it isn't faded, and where the sun is just so, I can see a strange, provoking, formless sort of figure, that seems to sulk about behind that silly and conspicuous front design.

There's sister on the stairs!

Well, the Fourth of July is over! The people are all gone and I am tired out. John thought it might do me good to see a little company, so we just had mother and Nellie and the children down for a week.

Of course I didn't do a thing. Jennie sees to everything now.

But it tired me all the same.

John says if I don't pick up faster he shall send me to Weir Mitchell[3] in the fall.

But I don't want to go there at all. I had a friend who was in his hands once, and she says he is just like John and my brother, only more so!

Besides, it is such an undertaking to go so far.

I don't feel as if it was worth while to turn my hand over for anything, and I'm getting dreadfully fretful and querulous.

I cry at nothing, and cry most of the time.

Of course I don't when John is here, or anybody else, but when I am alone.

---

[3] Samuel Weir Mitchell (1829–1914), a leading American neurologist and specialist in treating women's nervous diseases through a rest cure. He worked as Gilman's physician during her recuperation from her nervous collapse.

And I am alone a good deal just now. John is kept in town very often by serious cases, and Jennie is good and lets me alone when I want her to.

So I walk a little in the garden or down that lovely lane, sit on the porch under the roses, and lie down up here a good deal.

I'm getting really fond of the room in spite of the wall paper. Perhaps because of the wall paper.

It dwells in my mind so!

3 Henry George, from *Progress and Poverty*, 1879[4]

Henry George (1839–1897) was a self-educated political economist who wrote Progress and Poverty *(1879) while he was a printer in San Francisco. He became an advocate of a single-tax system after watching San Francisco grow from a village to a thriving metropolis and seeing the subsequent development of both wealthy and poor classes within the city. Like many other Gilded Age social commentators, George was appalled at the expanding gap between rich and poor. His solution for industrial social divisions was the single tax, which would impose a tax on the value of land. The single tax, for George and his followers, would serve as a vehicle for the redistribution of wealth.*

In the words of his granddaughter, the choreographer Agnes George deMille, written in 1979: "His ideas stand: he who makes should have; he who saves should enjoy; what the community produces belongs to the community for communal uses; and God's earth, all of it, is the right of the people who inhabit the earth." Unlike socialists and communists, George believed in the right to private property, but only for those who earned that property. He regarded as detrimental to society the ability of corporations and wealthy individuals to control public and natural resources, as well as the domination of the marketplace by monopolies. Progress and Poverty *was fantastically popular: soon after its publication, it had sold three million copies, and over the next decade the book was outsold only by the Bible. Across the country, Single Tax clubs came into existence in support of George's ideas, and a number of Single Tax communities, such as Fairhope, Alabama, were founded in support of his solution to social problems.*

Chapter 26
The Injustice of Private Property in Land

Justice is fundamental to the human mind, though often warped by superstition, habit, and selfishness. When I propose to abolish private property in land, the first question to be asked is that of justice. Only what

---

[4] *Progress and Poverty: An Inquiry into the Cause of Industrial Depressions, and of Increase of Want with Increase of Wealth* (San Francisco: W.M. Hinton & Co., 1879).

is just can be wise; only what is right will endure. I bow to this demand and accept this test. If private property in land is just, then what I propose is false. If private property in land is unjust, then my remedy is true.

What constitutes the rightful basis of property? What allows someone to justly say, "This is mine!"? Is it not, primarily, the right of a person to one's own self? To the use of one's own powers? To enjoy the fruits of one's own labor? Each person is a definite, coherent, independent whole. Each particular pair of hands obeys a particular brain and is related to a particular body. And this alone justifies individual ownership.

As each person belongs to himself or herself, so labor belongs to the individual when put in concrete form. For this reason, what someone makes or produces belongs to that person—even against the claim of the whole world. It is that person's property, to use or enjoy, give or exchange, or even destroy. No one else can rightfully claim it. And this right to the exclusive possession and enjoyment wrongs no one else. Thus, there is a clear and indisputable title to everything produced by human exertion. It descends from the original producer, in whom it is vested by natural law.

The pen that I write with is justly mine. No other human being can rightfully lay claim to it, for in me is the title of the producers who made it. It has become mine because it was transferred to me by the stationer, to whom it was transferred by the importer, who obtained the exclusive right to it by transfer from the manufacturer. By the same process of purchase, the manufacturer acquired the vested rights of those who dug the material from the ground and shaped it into a pen.

Thus, my exclusive right of ownership in the pen springs from the natural right of individuals to the use of their own faculties—the source from which all ideas of exclusive ownership arise. It is not only the original source, it is the only source.

Nature acknowledges no ownership or control existing in humans, except the results of labor. Is there any other way to affect material things except by exerting the power of one's own faculties? All people exist in nature on equal footing and have equal rights. Nature recognizes no claim but labor—and without respect to who claims it. When a pirate ship spreads its sails, wind fills them; as it would those of a missionary. Fish will bite whether the line leads to a good child who goes to Sunday school or a bad one playing truant. The sun shines and the rain falls on the just and unjust alike.

The laws of nature are the decrees of the Creator. They recognize no right but labor. As nature gives only to labor, the exertion of labor in production is the only title to exclusive possession.

This right of ownership springing from labor excludes the possibility of any other right of ownership. A person is rightfully entitled to the product of his or her labor (or the labor of someone else from whom the right has been received).

It is production that gives the producer the right to exclusive possession and enjoyment. If so, there can be no right to exclusive possession of anything that is not the product of labor. Therefore, private property in land is wrong.

The right to the product of labor cannot be enjoyed without the right to free use of the opportunities offered by nature. To admit a right to property in nature is to deny the right of property as the product of labor. When non-producers can claim a portion of the wealth created by producers—as rent—then the right of producers to the fruits of their labor is denied to that extent.

There is no escape from this position. To affirm that someone can rightfully claim exclusive ownership of his or her own labor—when embodied in material things—is to deny that any one can rightfully claim exclusive ownership in land. Property in land is a claim having no justification in nature—it is a claim founded in the way societies are organized.

What keeps us from recognizing the injustice of private property in land? By habit, we include all things made subject to ownership in one category—which we call "property." The only distinctions are drawn by lawyers, who distinguish only personal property from real estate—things movable from things immovable. The real and natural distinction, however, is between the product of labor and the free offerings of nature. In the terms of political economy, between wealth and land. To class them together is to confuse all thought regarding justice or injustice, right or wrong.

A house and the lot on which it stands are classed together by lawyers as real estate. Yet in nature and relations they differ widely. One is produced by human labor (wealth). The other is a part of nature (land).

The essential characteristic of wealth is that it embodies labor. It is brought into being by human exertion. Its existence or nonexistence, its increase or decrease, depends on humans. The essential characteristic of land is that it does not embody labor. It exists irrespective of human exertion, and irrespective of people. It is the field, or environment, in which people find themselves; the storehouse from which their needs must be supplied; the raw material on which—and the forces with which—they can act.

The moment this distinction is recognized, we see that the sanction natural justice gives to one kind of property is denied to the other. The rightfulness of property that is the product of labor implies the wrongfulness of the individual ownership of land. The recognition of the former places all people upon equal terms, and gives them the due reward of their labor. Whereas the recognition of the latter is to deny the equal rights of people. It allows those who do not work to take the natural reward of those who do.

Whatever may be said for the institution of private property in land, it clearly cannot be defended on the grounds of justice.

The equal right of all people to the use of land is as clear as their equal right to breathe the air—a right proclaimed by the very fact of their existence. We cannot suppose that some people have a right to be in this world and others do not. If we are all here by permission of the Creator, we are all here with an equal title to the bounty of nature.

This is a right that is natural and inalienable. It is a right that vests in every human being who enters the world. During each person's stay in the world it can be limited only by the equal rights of others. If all people living were to unite to grant away their equal rights, they could not grant away the rights of those who follow them. Have we made the earth, that we should determine the rights of those who come after us? No matter how long the claim, nor how many pieces of paper are issued, there is no right that natural justice recognizes to give one person possession of land that is not equally the right of all other people. The smallest infant born in the most squalid room of the most miserable tenement acquires, at the moment of birth, a right to land equal to millionaires. And that child is robbed if that right is denied.

4 Photographs of Gilded Age Mansions[5]

One of the most visible manifestations of the Gilded Age's great wealth – and its ostentatious display – were the large mansions constructed by the very rich. The sudden rise to wealth by new families such as the Vanderbilts, Rockefellers, and Astors created a large disposable income that was used to acquire art from around the world and to construct fantastically large homes. During the late nineteenth century, Newport, Rhode Island became a summer center for the Gilded Age rich, many of whom migrated from New York City seasonally and maintained an elaborate social life. Perhaps the most elaborate of the Gilded Age mansions was Biltmore, located near Asheville, North Carolina, with 250 rooms, 34 bedrooms, and 43 bathrooms in four acres of floor space. Completed in 1895, Biltmore was designed and built for George Vanderbilt by the architect Richard Morris Hunt – who was also architect of eight Newport mansions – with the grounds of the 125,000-acre estate designed by the leading American landscape architect, Frederick Law Olmsted.

---

5   http://www.corbis.com/BettMann100/Archive/BettmannArchive.asp.

Figure 5.1 The Biltmore Estate, Asheville, NC.
Source: Photo Bettmann/Corbis.

Figure 5.2 The Breakers, Vanderbilt mansion, Newport, RI.
Source: Bettmann/Corbis, photo T.H. Lindsey.

5 Hubert Howe Bancroft, The Woman's Building, from *The Book of the Fair*, 1893[6]

The Columbian Exposition of 1893, also known as the Chicago World's Fair, celebrated the four-hundredth anniversary of Columbus's expedition to the New World. The exposition attracted over 27 million people, far exceeding previous world's fairs. The fair displayed a variety of scientific, technological, and cultural wonders, becoming in many senses a symbol of the United States as an emerging world power.

As Hubert Howe Bancroft (1832–1918) points out, one of the most notable things about the Chicago World's Fair was the scope of the woman's department. In particular, a spectacular Woman's Building, designed by Sophia G. Hayden, stood as the central hub for female exhibits and activity. The building constituted an impressive example of neoclassical architecture, and an emblem of women's progress and future advancement.

Among the features which distinguish the Columbian from all former international expositions are the scope and character of its Woman's department; and among the most pleasing exhibits of that department is the building which contains them. For the first time in World's Fair annals, as I have said, a special edifice has been devoted to the purposes of that department, or rather to a portion of its purposes, for, side by side, not only in the great temples of industry, but in state and foreign pavilions, are specimens of male and female workmanship. For the first time also has been designed by a woman a structure fashioned for such uses.

In the plan of this building we have the result of a national competition, but of competition only among women, the choice being made from a large number of designs, not a few of which were of unquestionable merit. The successful candidate was Sophia G. Hayden, a graduate of the architectural school of the Massachusetts Institute of Technology; and in the evolution of her scheme she has presented a neat and artistic solution of one of the most difficult problems of the Fair. In this building must be contained, not only a general and retrospective display of woman's work, whether in our own or foreign lands, but space must be provided for the exhibits of charitable and reformatory organizations, for a library, and assembly-room, for parlors, committee rooms, and administration and other purposes. All this must be

[6] Hubert Howe Bancroft, *The Book of the Fair* (Chicago and San Francisco: The Bancroft Co., 1893).

accomplished in a space 400 feet long by half that width, adjacent to the Midway plaisance and the Horticultural Hall. . . .

In style the building is modelled after that of the Italian renaissance, with the facades of the first story fashioned in the form of an Italian arcade, and surrounded with a portico, the roof of which serves as a balcony for the second story. The colonnade of the upper story is suggestive of the Corinthian order, and between the columns are windowed spaces, adapted to the comparatively small dimensions of the chambers within. The principal entrance is in the form of a triple arched pavilion, flanked by a surface of solid wall, with double pilasters, above it an open colonnade of the same design as those on either side, and with the pediment richly decorated in bas-relief. In front the corner pavilions are similarly treated, as also are the side entrances, but without pediments, and with rows of pilasters in place of colonnades. Over the side entrances is a third or attic story, opening at the main roof on gardens, around which is a screen of pilasters. From the central pavilion spacious stairways lead to a terrace a few feet above the water, where a landing is built on the northern arm of the lagoon.

In the interior is a central hall opening into a rotunda, with decorated skylight, unencumbered by columns, and of sufficient altitude to admit the light from rows of clear-story windows. On both floors this open space is surrounded with open arcades, those on the upper story serving as galleries, and resembling somewhat the corridors of an Italian courtyard. The interior plan displays the most careful economy of space in providing for suites of connected apartments, differing in size but for the most part of almost domestic proportions, and with due regard to lighting, circulation, and communication. The appearance of the building is in harmony with the conditions from which its design was evolved, suggesting rather the lyric features of the Art Palace than the heroic aspect of the larger temples of industry and science, and with a grace of expression worthy of its uses and its artificer.

For the decorative as for the structural scheme of the building designs were invited among women qualified for such work throughout the United States, and after eager and close competition the prize was awarded to Alice Rideout, of San Francisco, by whom were modelled the compositions on the main pediment and the symbolical groups of the roof-gardens. All the groups are more or less typical of the part that woman has played in the history of the world, of what has been, is, and will be her sphere of duty and influence. The mural paintings, with other ornamental features, as the carved wainscotings, screens, and balustrades, the tapestries and panels were also contributed by women, while from many of the states came offers of cabinet woods, marble and other materials in quantities larger than could be accepted, though to some was granted as a privilege the right of furnishing and decorating their own apartments and interior decorations.

On the roof are winged groups typical of feminine characteristics and virtues, all in choices symbolism, one of the central figures representing the spirituality of woman, and at its feet a pelican, emblem of love and sacrifice. In the same group charity stands side by side with virtue, and sacrifice is further symbolized by a nun, placing her jewels on the altar. In another group is the genius of civilization, with the bird of wisdom at her feet; on the right a student, and on the left a woman groping in intellectual darkness but struggling after light. These and others, together with the figures on the pediment, typical of literature and art, of charity, beneficence, and home are from the hand of the San Francisco sculptress. On the frieze is a figure of youth, and on the panels of the entrance-ways are represented the occupations of women. . . . From the corridors which surround the court, on the second floor, open the various parlors, exhibition rooms, and assembly chambers. The northern end of the main hall is decorated in gold and white, its windows of stained glass adding to the effect. The central window was furnished by Massachusetts, and symbolizes the part which that commonwealth has played in the advancement of woman. It is flanked by two smaller ones, presented by the women of Chelsea and Boston. The walls are covered with portraits of some of the more prominent personages in the cause of education, reform, and philanthropy. A large space is occupied by a picture of Burdett-Coutts, with models of some of her institutions, and other illustrations of her labors. The figure of Fredericka Bremer is the most prominent in the Swedish gallery. France, Norway, and the United States have also their niches of fame filled by such women as Lucretia Mott and Harriet Beecher Stowe. . . . . .

The 1st of May, the opening day of the Columbian Exposition, was also the time appointed for the dedication of the Woman's edifice, though the latter was completed long before that date, and as I have said was the first one finished of all the department buildings. The ceremonies were held in the court of honor, the hall of the rotunda; at two o'clock the doors were opened, and a few minutes later every chair was occupied, with many hundreds crowding the passage ways, and many thousands who could find neither seats nor standing room. On the platform, in front of which the Spanish colors, flanked by those of other powers, drooped from the gallery overhead, were the Lady Managers and their invited guests, among whom the presence of some of the most prominent women of the time, including Lady Aberdeen, the duchess of Sutherland, the countess of Craven, the duchess of Veragua, the Russian princess Schalovsky, and the Swedish baroness Thomburg-Rappe, with a goodly representation from our own and other lands, attested the world wide interest in the Woman's department. . . .

As with the Woman's building so with the exhibits by women, they form of themselves a unique and distinctive feature of the Exposition, such as never before was presented to the world, such as never before was attempted. Not as at the international fairs held in London, in Paris, and Vienna, have these collective specimens of woman's industry and art been cast into such nooks and corners as might be spared by the several departments. For the first time they were housed in a home of their own, in one of the most beautiful homes among all these palatial groups, or in the larger buildings were arrayed in open competition with the workmanship of men. At the Philadelphia Exposition, it is true, and also at the Cotton Centenary Exposition held a few years later at New Orleans, there were comprehensive exhibits of woman's work that more than merited the attention they received; but here we have not a mere adjunct of the Fair but an integral and most interesting portion of it, one recognized by the national legislature, approved by the commission constituted by that legislature, and with the earnest and cordial support, not only of our own but of European nations, whose titled dames, even those of royal blood, did not disdain to serve on committees acting in cooperation with the Board of Lady Managers. . . .

If in the United States the number of bread-winners is smaller than among European nations, it is because there is less need for them to earn their bread, though many do so from choice, or for what Burns has described as the glorious privilege of being independent. On the other hand there is no country in the world where the avocations of women are so diversified or so largely represented in commercial and professional circles. According to recent data there are nearly 3,000,000 women and girls who are self-supporting, many of them contributing to the support of others, and with at least an equal number who provide in part for their own maintenance. Of these more than 14,000 are at the head of business firms or conduct a business of their own, and 26,000 are employed as clerks and book-keepers. Of school-teachers there are 155,000; of teachers of music and professional musicians, 13,000; of physicians and surgeons 2,400, and of chemists and pharmacists nearly 2,000. Of journalists there are 600, of authors known to fame about half that number, while more than 200 are practising lawyers or architects. But most remarkable of all is the number engaged in farming, planting, and stock-raising, in which pursuits no less than 59,000 women are represented. Such is the part that woman plays in the great workshop of our western republic, as, with the lapse of years, she rises slowly but surely toward the higher plane of her destiny.

One by one the disqualifications of women have been laid aside, their legal rights asserted, and acknowledged, so that in many of the states they share nearly all the political privileges and civic duties pertaining to citizenship.

In Wyoming, Washington, and Utah women may vote and serve on juries; in Kansas there are municipalities where the office of mayor has been filled by women; in Pennsylvania they may be appointed masters in equity, and in New York, Massachusetts, Connecticut, and in several of the western states as notaries public, commissioners of deeds, administrators, and executors. By the general government they may be commissioned as post-mistresses, army surgeons, captains of steamboats, and even as United States marshals. With some exceptions, our leading universities have not been slow to recognize the claims of women to such opportunities for higher and special branches of education as are accorded to men. At many of the law schools, the schools of medicine, surgery, dentistry, music, and the fine arts, women are trained and graduated, on department only closing its doors against them, and that is the department of theology. Thus, it will be seen that women can no longer be excluded on the ground of mental inferiority, and those who would advocate such exclusion must do so on other grounds. . .

Of all the lessons of the Exposition there are none that will be longer remembered than those which the Woman's department has taught us, and to none is more credit due than to the Board of Lady Managers, forming, with its associated boards, an organization of women for the common benefit of woman-kind such as has never before existed in the history of the world. Theirs was the hardest task of all, and never perhaps was success more hardly won; never were the barriers of prejudice and apathy more difficult to overcome. From oriental countries especially came most discouraging reports; for there were neither schools nor women with intelligence equal to the work. Many European countries were at first indifferent though later responding nobly to the invitation. Says the president of the Board: "We travelled together a hitherto untrodden path; we were subjected to tedious delays; and overshadowed with dark clouds which threatened disaster to our enterprise. We were obliged to march with peace offerings in our hands, lest hostile motives should be ascribed to us. When our invitations were sent to foreign lands, the commissioners already appointed generally smiled doubtfully, and explained that their women were doing nothing; that they would not feel inclined to help us, and in many cases stated that it was not the custom of their country for women to take part in any public effort."

But to the women of every land, to women who have near at heart the cause of their sex, who would not merely live a life of ease without a thought for their less fortunate sisters, personal letters were addressed soliciting their cooperation, and with most favorable results. Then it was that what had been merely a hope began to assume reality, and, continues the president, "our burdens were greatly lightened by the spontaneous sympathy and aid which have reached us from women in every part of the world, and which have proved an added incentive and inspiration." When first the Womans' building was designed, the managers were somewhat doubtful as to filling its space with creditable exhibits; but long before it was opened applications were made for four or five times the available room, thus permitting a selection of the choices and most attractive specimens of female work. Most fitting it is that the best of these specimens, including the Woman's library, should find a permanent home in a memorial building, there to serve as a nucleus for still more valuable collections.

Discussion Questions: Chapter 5

1 What are Veblen's ideas about a "social good"? How does he define this?
2 What are Veblen's views on social classes and social conflict?
3 From reading Gilman's piece, what can you tell about the social environment against which she was reacting?
4 On what basis would Henry George disapprove of the Gilded Age mansions pictured in document 5.4?
5 What did the Columbian Exposition show observers about changes in opportunities for women?

Chapter 6   Working People

1 Stephen Crane, "In the Depths of a Coal Mine," 1894[1]

*Stephen Crane (1871–1900) was born in Newark, New Jersey, and grew up
with his widowed mother and 13 siblings in Asbury Park. He dropped out of
college and moved to New York City after his mother died, working as
freelance writer and a stringer for various New York newspapers. During the
early 1890s, while he was writing his most famous novel,* The Red Badge of
Courage, *he also wrote a number of poems and short stories, one of which is
the story presented below. Crane and an artist were sent by McClure's
Magazine to Scranton, Pennsylvania, to do a story on coal miners and the
dangers they faced. He was reportedly unhappy with the severe cuts the
editors made in his story before it was published, saying that they were
whitewashing the unhealthy and dangerous conditions in the mines.*

The "breakers" squatted upon the hillsides and in the valley like enormous
preying monsters, eating of the sunshine, the grass, the green leaves. The
smoke from their nostrils had ravaged the air of coolness and fragrance. All
that remained of vegetation looked dark, miserable, half-strangled. Along the
summit line of the mountain a few unhappy trees were etched upon the
clouds. Overhead stretched a sky of imperial blue, incredibly far away from
the sombre land.

[1] *McClure's Magazine* III (August 1894): 195–209.

The Gilded Age and Progressive Era: A Documentary Reader, First Edition.
Edited by William A. Link and Susannah J. Link.
© 2012 Blackwell Publishing Ltd. Published 2012 by Blackwell Publishing Ltd.

We approached the colliery over paths of coal dust that wound among the switches. A "breaker" loomed above us, a huge and towering frame of blackened wood. It ended in a little curious peak, and upon its sides there was a profusion of windows appearing at strange and unexpected points. Through occasional doors one could see the flash of whirring machinery. Men with wondrously blackened faces and garments came forth from it. The sole glitter upon their persons was at their hats, where the little tin lamps were carried. They went stolidly along, some swinging lunch-pails carelessly; but the marks upon them of their forbidding and mystic calling fascinated our new eyes until they passed from sight. They were symbols of a grim, strange war that was being waged in the sunless depths of the earth.

Around a huge central building clustered other and lower ones, sheds, engine-houses, machine-shops, offices. Railroad tracks extended in web-like ways. Upon them stood files of begrimed coal cars. Other huge structures similar to the one near us, upreared their uncouth heads upon the hills of the surrounding country. From each a mighty hill of culm extended. Upon these tremendous heaps of waste from the mines, mules and cars appeared like toys. Down in the valley, upon the railroads, long trains crawled painfully southward, where a low-hanging gray cloud, with a few projecting spires and chimneys, indicated a town.

Car after car came from a shed beneath which lay hidden the mouth of the shaft. They were dragged, creaking, up an inclined cable road to the top of the "breaker."

At the top of the "breaker," laborers were dumping the coal into chutes. The huge lumps slid slowly on their journey down through the building, from which they were to emerge in classified fragments. Great teeth on revolving cylinders caught them and chewed them. At places there were grates that bid each size go into its proper chute. The dust lay inches deep on every motionless thing, and clouds of it made the air dark as from a violent tempest. A mighty gnashing sound filled the ears. With terrible appetite this huge and hideous monster sat imperturbably munching coal, grinding its mammoth jaws with unearthly and monotonous uproar.

In a large room sat the little slate-pickers. The floor slanted at an angle of forty-five degrees, and the coal, having been masticated by the great teeth, was streaming sluggishly in long iron troughs. The boys sat straddling these troughs, and as the mass moved slowly, they grabbed deftly at the pieces of slate therein. There were five or six of them, one above another, over each trough. The coal is expected to be fairly pure after it passes the final boy. The howling machinery was above them. High up, dim figures moved about in the dust clouds.

. . .

The slate-pickers all through this region are yet at the spanking period. One continually wonders about their mothers, and if there are any school-houses. But as for them, they are not concerned. When they get time off, they go out on the culm heap and play baseball, or fight with boys from other "breakers" or among themselves, according to the opportunities. And before them always is the hope of one day getting to be door-boys down in the mines; and, later, mule-boys; and yet later, laborers and help-ers. Finally, when they have grown to be great big men, they may become miners, real miners, and go down and get "squeezed," or perhaps escape to a shattered old man's estate with a mere "miner's asthma." They are very ambitious.

Meanwhile they live in a place of infernal dins. The crash and thunder of the machinery is like the roar of an immense cataract. The room shrieks and blares and bellows. Clouds of dust blur the air until the windows shine pal-lidly afar off. All the structure is a-tremble from the heavy sweep and circle of the ponderous mechanism. Down in the midst of it sit these tiny urchins, where they earn fifty-five cents a day each. They breathe this atmosphere until their lungs grow heavy and sick with it. They have this clamor in their ears until it is wonderful that they have any hoodlum valor remaining. But they are uncowed; they continue to swagger. And at the top of the "breaker" laborers can always be seen dumping the roaring coal down the wide, vora-cious maw of the creature.

Over in front of a little tool-house a man smoking a pipe sat on a bench. "Yes," he said, "I'll take yeh down if yeh like." He led us by little cinder paths to the shed over the shaft of the mine. A gigantic fan-wheel near by was twirling swiftly. It created cool air for the miners, who on the lowest vein of this mine were some eleven hundred and fifty feet below the surface. As we stood silently waiting for the elevator we had opportunity to gaze at the mouth of the shaft. The walls were of granite blocks, slimy, moss-grown, dripping with water. Below was a curtain of ink-like blackness. It was like the opening of an old well, sinister from tales of crimes.

The black, greasy cables began to run swiftly. We stood staring at them and wondering. Then of a sudden the elevator appeared and stopped with a crash. It was a plain wooden platform. Upon two sides iron bars ran up to support a stout metal roof. The men upon it, as it came into view, were like apparitions from the center of the earth.

A moment later we marched aboard, armed with little lights, feeble and gasping in the daylight. There was an instant's creak of machinery, and then the landscape, that had been framed for us by the door-posts of the shed, disappeared in a flash. We were dropping with extraordinary swiftness straight into the earth. It was a plunge, a fall. The flames of the little lamps fluttered and flew and struggled like tied birds to release themselves from the wicks. "Hang on," bawled our guide above the tumult.

The dead black walls slid swiftly by. They were a swirling dark chaos on which the mind tried vainly to locate some coherent thing, some intelligible spot. One could only hold fast to the iron bars and listen to the roar of this implacable descent. When the faculty of balance is lost, the mind becomes a confusion. The will fought a great battle to comprehend something during this fall, but one might as well have been tumbling among the stars. The only thing was to await revelation. It was a journey that held a threat of endlessness.

Then suddenly the dropping platform slackened its speed. It began to descend slowly and with caution. At last, with a crash and a jar, it stopped. Before us stretched an inscrutable darkness, a soundless place of tangible loneliness. Into the nostrils came a subtly strong odor of powder-smoke, oil, wet earth. The alarmed lungs began to lengthen their respirations.

Our guide strode abruptly into the gloom. His lamp flared shades of yellow and orange upon the walls of a tunnel that led away from the foot of the shaft. Little points of coal caught the light and shone like diamonds. Before us there was always the curtain of an impenetrable night. We walked on with no sound save the crunch of our feet upon the coal-dust of the floor. The sense of an abiding danger in the roof was always upon our foreheads. It expressed to us all the unmeasured, deadly tons above us, as if the roof were a superlative might that regarded with the supreme calmness of almighty power. . . . Sometimes we were obliged to bend low to avoid it. Always our hands rebelled vaguely from touching it, refusing to affront this gigantic mass.

All at once, far ahead, shone a little flame, blurred and difficult of location. It was a tiny, indefinite thing, like a wisp-light. We seemed to be looking at it through a great fog. Presently there were two of them. They began to move to and fro and dance before us.

After a time we came upon two men crouching where the roof of the passage came near to meeting the floor. If the picture could have been brought to where it would have had the opposition and the contrast of the glorious summer-time earth, it would have been a grim and ghastly thing. The garments of the men were no more sable than their faces, and when they turned their heads to regard our tramping party, their eyeballs and teeth shone white as bleached bones. It was like the grinning of two skulls there in the shadows. The tiny lamps in their hats made a trembling light that left weirdly shrouded the movements of their limbs and bodies. We might have been confronting terrible spectres.

...

From this tunnel of our first mine we went with our guide to the foot of the main shaft. Here we were in the most important passage of a mine, the main gangway. The wonder of these avenues is the noise — the crash and clatter of machinery as the elevator speeds upward with the loaded cars and drops thunderingly with the empty ones. The place resounds with the shouts of mule-boys, and there can always be heard the noise of approaching coal-cars, beginning in mild rumbles and then swelling down upon one in a tempest of sound. In the air is the slow painful throb of the pumps working at the water which collects in the depths. There is booming and banging and crashing, until one wonders why the tremendous walls are not wrenched by the force of this uproar. And up and down the tunnel there is a riot of lights, little orange points flickering and flashing. Miners stride in swift and sombre procession. But the meaning of it all is in the deep bass rattle of a blast in some hidden part of the mine. It is war. It is the most savage part of all in the endless battle between man and nature. These miners are grimly in the van. They have carried the war into places where nature has the strength of a million giants. Sometimes their enemy becomes exasperated and snuffs out ten, twenty, thirty lives. Usually she remains calm, and takes one at a time with method and precision. She need not hurry. She possesses eternity. After a blast, the smoke, faintly luminous, silvery, floats silently through the adjacent tunnels.

In our first mine we speedily lost all ideas of time, direction, distance. The whole thing was an extraordinary, black puzzle. We were impelled to admire the guide because he knew all the tangled passages. He led us through little tunnels three and four feet wide and with roofs that sometimes made us crawl. At other times we were in avenues twenty feet wide, where double rows of tracks extended. There were stretches of great darkness, majestic silences. The three hundred miners were distributed into all sorts of crevices and corners of the labyrinth, toiling in this city of endless night. At different points one could hear the roar of traffic about the foot of the main shaft, to which flowed all the commerce of the place.

We were made aware of distances later by our guide, who would occasionally stop to tell us our position by naming a point of the familiar geography of the surface. "Do you remember that rolling-mill yeh passed coming up? Well, you're right under it." "You're under th' depot now." The length of these distances struck us with amazement when we reached the surface. Near Scranton one can really proceed for miles, in the black streets of the mines.

2 Walter A. Wyckoff, from *The Workers: An Experiment in Social Reality*, 1899[2]

Walter A. Wyckoff (1865–1908) graduated from Princeton University in 1888 and enrolled at Princeton Theological Seminary. Taking a year off to travel in Europe, he received a degree from Princeton Seminary in 1891. His original intention was to become a minister, and he entered Princeton Theological Seminary, but, deciding that he needed more worldly experience, he set out on a trip across the country, working as a day-laborer, and reached San Francisco in 1893. He then traveled across the country, living as a hobo in order to experience poverty.

Traveling around the world, he returned to Princeton in 1894 as a graduate student. While at Princeton, he was both a student and a colleague of future president Woodrow Wilson. In 1895, he was appointed a lecturer in sociology. With a focus on poverty, Wycoff taught at his alma mater for 13 years. The following excerpt is from a book about this cross-country trip, which was originally published in serial form in Scribner's Magazine.

Chapter III: Finding Steady Work

. . . Blue Island Avenue, Chicago, Ill., December 22, 1891

That night when Clark and I reached the head of the staircase which descends to the basement of the station-house we found the way blocked by men. We thought at first that a prisoner was being booked, but a second glance revealed the fact that the door of iron grating was wide open. With his back against it stood an officer. The lodgers were passing him in slow order, and, as they filed by, the policeman held each in sharp examination for a moment. Soon I could see him clearly. He stood, obstructing the exit from the stairs, a straight, massive figure well on to two hundred and fifty pounds. A side-view was toward us, and I took delight in the clean-shaven face with the well-chiselled Grecian profile, the eye deep-set and widening to the upward lift of the lashes, and the dark, abundant hair rising in short, crisp curls from under the pressure of his cap-rim.

He was putting the men through a catechism respecting their nationalities, their homes and occupations, and their motives in coming to Chicago. Beside him stood two men, the elder a man past middle life, of sober, dignified appearance, and with an air of philosophical interest in what he saw. The younger was a callow youth, just grown to manhood, and he may have been the other's son. They were out "slumming," evidently, and the

² (New York: Charles Scribner's Sons, 1899), pp. 86–99.

officer had been detailed as their guide. Their purpose may have been a good one, but the boy's face, as I watched it, seemed to me to show plainly the marks of an un-wholesome curiosity. And certainly as they stood there in well-dressed, well-fed comfort, eying at leisure, as though it were exhibited for their diversion, this company of homeless, ragged, needful men, there was to my mind a deliberate insult in the attitude sharper than the sting of a blow in the face. I thought at first that I might be alone in feeling this, until I heard a man behind me say, as the cause of the delay became clear to him:

"Who is them jays, and what business have they inspectin' us?"

On the step below me was as good a vagrant type as the slowly moving line on the staircase disclosed. I could not see his face, but I could guess at its effect from the dark, bristling, unkempt beard that sprouted in tangled, wiry masses from his cheeks and throat, and the heavy, cohering hair that lay long and thick about his ears and on his neck. There was an unnatural corpulence about the figure, the reality of which was belied by the lean, sharp lines that appeared beneath a bulging collar and in the emaciated arms that were red, and raw, and almost bare below the elbows, where the ragged sleeves hung in fraying ribbons.

The obesity was purely artificial. The tramp had on three flannel shirts, at least, besides several heavy waistcoats and two pairs of trousers and as many coats, with a possibility of there being three. The outer garments were quaint mosaics of patches, positively ingenious in their interlacing adherence to one another and in their rude preservation of original outlines of dress. From him came the pungent reek of bad whiskey and stale tobacco.

It was as though the man stood clothed in outward and visible signs of unseen realities, enveloped in the rigid habit of his own wrong-doing, draped in the mystery of inherited tendencies, and cloaked in the stern facts of a hard environment. And yet, as beneath the filthy outer covering there was a human being, so under these veiling, unseen vestures was a man, a living soul created by the Almighty.

I could hear him muttering gruffly to himself as he slowly descended to his turn at the foot of the steps.

"Well, Weary, where are you from? A hobo from Hoboville, I guess," and the officer's voice rang strong and clear up the staircase to the dim landing, where stood the waiting line of men.

The two shimmers[3] laughed aloud. "From Maine," said the tramp. The voice came hoarse and thin and broken-winded from a throat eaten out by disease.

---

[3]   Slang for hobo.

"Well, you're a rare one, if you're a Yankee. But what brought you to Chicago?"

"Lookin' for work at the World's Fair."

"You lie, you lazy loafer. The last thing you're looking for is work. You all tell that World's Fair lie. There's been as many of you in Chicago every winter for the last ten years as there is this winter."

The man was stung.

"I've as good a right here as you," he said.

"You have, have you!" cried the officer in quick rejoinder, but with no loss of temper. "Look at me, you filthy hobo," he added, drawing himself to his full, imposing height. "I'm a police officer. I've held my job for eleven years, and got my promotions. I'm earning eighty dollars a month, do you see? Now go down there where you belong," and he pointed imperiously to the far end of the corridor.

My turn came next.

"Here's another whiskers," announced the officer in explanation to his charges; "same kind, only younger and newer to the business." And then to me, "Where are you from?" he said.

I replied with some inanity in mock German.

"Oh, he's a Dutchman. We get a few of them. But they're mostly older men, and kind of moody, and they tramp alone a good bit. Can't you talk English?"

I said something in very bad French. "Oh, I guess he's a Frenchy. That's very uncommon—"

I interrupted his information with a line from Virgil, spoken with an inflection of inquiry.

"He may be a Dago, or a—ah," he hesitated. I broke in with a sentence in Greek.

"Or a Russian," concluded the officer.

I thought that I could mystify him finally, and so I pronounced a verse from Genesis in Hebrew. But he was equal to the emergence.

"I've got it," he exclaimed, with a note of exultation; "he's a Sheeny!4" And free to go I walked down the corridor, feeling that I had come rather badly out of that encounter.

None of us, I think, resented much the action of the officer. The policemen understand us perfectly, and in a certain broad, human sense we know them for our friends. I have been much impressed with this quality of natural bonhomie in the relation of the police officers to the vagrant and criminal classes. It seems to be the outcome of sturdy common sense and genuine

4 Slang for a Jew.

knowledge and human sympathy. It would be difficult, I fancy, seriously to deceive an average officer of good experience. He may not know his man personally in every case, but he knows his type, and he takes his measure with admirable accuracy. He is not far misled by either his virtue or his vice. He knows him for a human being, even if he be a vagrant or a criminal, and he has come by practical experience to a fair acquaintance with human limitations in these spheres of life.

The sympathy of which I have spoken is conspicuously innocent of sentimentality. It comes from a saner source, and is of a hardier fibre. Unfortunately it lays open a way of corruption to corrupt men on the force, but it is the basis, too, of high practical efficiency in the difficult task of locating crime and keeping it within control. And it has another value little suspected, perhaps. I have met more than one working-man at work who owed his job to the friendly aid of a policeman, who had singled him out from the ranks of the unemployed as being worthy of his help. And this sort of timely succor is bounded, I judge, only by the limits of opportunity. Certainly I shall never forget the kindness of an officer who had evidently grown familiar with me on the streets, and who to my great surprise stopped me suddenly one day with the question:

"Ain't yous got a job yet?"

" No," I said, as I stood looking up in deep admiration of his height and breadth and ruddy, wholesome face and generous Irish brogue.

"Well, that is hard luck," he went on. "There isn't many jobs ever at this season of the year, but just yous come around this way now and again, and I'll tell yous, if I hears of anything."

That was only a day or two before I found work, and when I had a chance to tell him of my success, his pleasure seemed as genuine as my own.

. . .

I had made frequent inquiries of the men whom I met, and it was from one of these that I learned that the time was Sunday afternoon; but none of them knew the place nor seemed to take the smallest interest in the matter. I thought that a policeman might be able to put me on the track of the meeting, if he chose, but then I feared that there were even chances that he would "run me in" as a revolutionary, upon hearing my request. I concluded that if I should be so fortunate as to find the place, it would be by some happy chance; and that if I gained admission, it would be by a happier one, due largely to my rough appearance.

I pictured this rude hall thronged with men, grizzled, bearded men, with eyes aflame and hair dishevelled, listening in high excitement to leaders whose inflammatory speeches lashed them into fury against all established order. Curiosity kindled to liveliest interest under the free play of imagination. In my eagerness I grew bolder. Repeatedly I stopped workingmen upon the street, and asked to be directed. No one knew, until I chanced upon a man who had a vague suspicion that the Socialists met in a hall over a saloon somewhere in West Lake Street.

I crossed the river and passed under the dark-steel framework of the elevated railway. The snow was falling through the still, sooty air in heavy flakes, which clung to every exposed surface, and turned the street-slime into a dark, granular slush. It seemed to be a region of warehouses and cheap shops, but chiefly of saloons; scarcely a soul was to be seen on the pavements; and brooding over the long, deserted street was the decorous quiet of Sunday.

I quickened my pace to overtake three men in front of me. Before I caught up with them they disappeared through a door which opened on the pavement. It was that of a saloon. The shades were drawn, and the place, like all the others of its kind, had every appearance of being closed for the day. I tried the door, and, finding it unlocked, followed the men inside. They had already mingled in a group of workingmen who sat about a large stove in the far corner of the bar-room, drinking beer and talking quietly.

They did not notice me until the one of whom I inquired appealed to the others for some knowledge of the question. Then there was a moment of passing the inquiry from one to another, until a good-looking young workman spoke up.

"Why, I know," he said; "I've just come from there. It's over in Waverley Hall, corner of Lake and Clark." "Will you help me to get into the meeting?" I asked. "I am a stranger here, and I should very much like to go."

"There ain't no trouble," he responded; "you just go up two flights of steps from the street, and walk right in."

3   Image from the *National Police Gazette*, 1879

Founded in 1845 and in existence until it went bankrupt in 1932, the National Police Gazette *became a popular tabloid with a wide circulation with themes of sensationalism, both in fact and fiction. Its subjects included crime, but the magazine extended well beyond this into stories about the Wild West, theater, and heavyweight boxing. The* Police Gazette *appealed especially to working-class audiences, and its stories about urban America. Its themes emphasized struggles with authority, people on the margins, and the fantastic and often lurid world of Gilded Age urban America. Prominently featured were women: sometimes victims, but often assertive.*

Figure 6.1   "Boozy female shoppers – A disgraceful scene on Fourteenth Street during the holiday season – the result of refreshment rooms in fashionable stores." From the US *National Police Gazette*, 1887. The caption claims that female shoppers at department stores had to be pulled from refreshment rooms and sent home after becoming drunk.
Source: Getty Figures/Hulton Archive.

4 Edward Eggleston, Hardshell Preacher, from *The Hoosier Schoolmaster*, 1871[5]

> *Edward Eggleston (1837–1902) published his famous* The Hoosier Schoolmaster *in 1871, which includes the following description of religious life in rural Indiana. Growing up in southern Indiana, Eggleston became a*

Methodist minister at age 19. In 1866, he became involved in journalism,
and in 1870 moved to Brooklyn to edit the periodical The Independent. *After*
the publication of The Hoosier Schoolmaster, *which first appeared in a*
14-part magazine serialization, was published in three languages, Eggleston
became a novelist with a wide following.

The Hoosier Schoolmaster is largely autobiographical. It describes life in
southern Indiana, near the town of Vevray. Although Eggleston himself was
not a rural schoolteacher, he vividly describes the challenges of teaching in a
one-room schoolhouse. Much of the book describes other aspects of life in
the rural Midwest, and in this passage he examines the life of a Hardshell
Baptist, a variety of conservative Baptist who sought to preserve original
versions of Christianity in worship and belief.

"They's preachin' down to Bethel Meetin'-house to-day," said the Squire at
breakfast. Twenty years In the West could not cure Squire Hawkins of saying "to" for "at." "I rather guess as how the old man Bosaw will give pertick-
eler fits to our folks to-day." For Squire Hawkins, having been expelled from
the "Hardshell" church of which Mr. Bosaw was pastor, for the grave offense
of joining a temperance society, had become a member of the "Reformers,"
the very respectable people who now call themselves "Disciples," but whom
the profane will persist in calling "Campbellites." They had a church in the
village of Clifty, three miles away.

I know that explanations are always abominable to story readers, as
they are to story writers, but as so many of my readers have never had the
inestimable privilege of sitting under the gospel as it is ministered in
enlightened neighborhoods like Flat Creek, I find myself under the necessity—need-cessity the Rev. Mr. Bosaw would call it—of rising to explain.
Some people think the "Hardshells" a myth, and some sensitive Baptist
people at the East resent all allusion to them. But the "Hardshell Baptists,"
or, as they are otherwise called, the "Whisky Baptists," and the "Forty-gal-
lon Baptists," exist in all the old Western and South-western States. They
call themselves "Anti-means Baptists" from their Antinomian tenets. Their
confession of faith is a caricature of Calvinism, and is expressed by their
preachers about as follows: "Ef you're elected, you'll be saved; ef you a'n't,
you'll be damned. God'll take keer of his elect. It's a sin to run Sunday-
schools, or temp'rince s'cieties, or to send missionaries. You let God's business alone. What is to be will be, and you can't hender it." This writer has
attended a Sunday-school, the superintendent of which was solemnly
arraigned and expelled from the Hardshell Church for "meddling with
God's business" by holding a Sunday-school. Of course the Hardshells
are prodigiously illiterate, and often vicious. Some of their preachers are

notorious drunkards. They sing their sermons out sometimes for three hours at a stretch.

Ralph found that he was to ride the "clay-bank mare," the only one of the horses that would "carry double," and that consequently he would have to take Miss Hawkins behind him. If it had been Hannah instead, Ralph might not have objected to this "young Lochinvar" mode of riding with a lady on "the croup," but Martha Hawkins was another affair. He had only this consolation; his keeping the company of Miss Hawkins might serve to disarm the resentment of Bud. At all events, he had no choice. What designs the Squire had in this arrangement he could not tell; but the clay-bank mare carried him to meeting on that December morning, with Martha Hawkins behind. And as Miss Hawkins was not used to this mode of locomotion, she was in a state of delightful fright every time the horse sank to the knees in the soft, yellow Flat Creek clay.

"We don't go to church so at the East," she said. "The mud isn't so deep at the East. When I was to Bosting—" but Ralph never heard what happened when she was to Bosting, for just as she said Bosting the mare put her foot into a deep hole molded by the foot of the Squire's horse, and already full of muddy water.

As the mare's foot went twelve inches down into this track, the muddy water spurted higher than Miss Hawkins's head, and mottled her dress with golden spots of clay. She gave a little shriek, and declared that she had never "seen it so at the East."

The journey seemed a little long to Ralph, who found that the subjects upon which he and Miss Hawkins could converse were few; but Miss Martha was determined to keep things going, and once, when the conversation had died out entirely, she made a desperate effort to renew it by remarking, as they met a man on horseback, "That horse switches his tail just as they do at the East. When I was to Bosting I saw horses switch their tails just that way."

What surprised Ralph was to see that Flat Creek went to meeting. Everybody was there—the Meanses, the Joneses, the Bantas, and all the rest. Everybody on Flat Creek seemed to be there, except the old wooden-legged basket-maker. His family was represented by Shocky, who had come, doubtless, to get a glimpse of Hannah, not to hear Mr. Bosaw preach. In fact, few were thinking of the religious service. They went to church as a common resort to hear the news, and to find out what was the current sensation.

On this particular morning there seemed to be some unusual excitement. Ralph perceived it as he rode up. An excited crowd, even though it be at a church-door on Sunday morning, can not conceal its agitation. Ralph deposited Miss Hawkins on the stile, and then got down himself, and paid her the closest attention to the door. This attention was for Bud's benefit. But Bud only stood with his hands in his pockets, scowling worse than ever. Ralph did not go in at the door. It was not the Flat Creek custom. The men gossiped outside, while the women chatted within. Whatever may have been the cause of the excitement, Ralph could not get at it. When he entered a little knot of people they became embarrassed, the group dissolved, and its component parts joined other companies. What had the current of conversation to do with him? He overheard Pete Jones saying that the blamed old wooden leg was in it anyhow. He'd been seen goin' home at two in the mornin'. And he could name somebody else ef he choosed. But it was best to clean out one at a time. And just then there was a murmur: "Meetin's took up." And the masculine element filled the empty half of the "hewed-log" church.

When Ralph saw Hannah looking utterly dejected, his heart smote him, and the great struggle set in again. Had it not been for the thought of the other battle, and the comforting presence of the Helper, I fear Bud's interests would have fared badly. But Ralph, with the spirit of a martyr, resolved to wait until he knew what the result of Bud's suit should be, and whether, indeed, the young Goliath had prior claims, as he evidently thought he had. He turned hopefully to the sermon, determined to pick up any crumbs of comfort that might fall from Mr. Bosaw's meager table.

In reporting a single specimen passage of Mr. Bosaw's sermon, I shall not take the liberty which Thucydides and other ancient historians did, of making the sermon and putting it into the hero's mouth, but shall give that which can be vouched for.

"You see, my respective hearers," he began—but alas! I can never picture to you the rich red nose, the see sawing gestures, the nasal resonance, the sniffle, the melancholy minor key, and all that. "My respective hearers-ah, you see-ah as how-ah as my tex'-ah says that the ox-ah knoweth his owner-ah, and-ah the ass-ah his master's crib-ah. A-h-h! Now, my respective hearers-ah, they're a mighty sight of resemblance-ah atwext men-ah and oxen-ah" [Ralph could not help reflecting that there was a mighty sight of resemblance between some men and asses. But the preacher did not see this analogy. It lay too close to him], "bekase-ah, you see, men-ah is mighty like oxen-ah. Fer they's a tremengious defference-ah atwixt defferent oxen-ah, jest as thar is atwext defferent men-ah; fer the ox knoweth-ah his owner-ah, and the ass-ah, his master's crib-ah. Now, my respective hearers-ah" [the preacher's voice here grew mellow, and the succeeding sentences were in the most pathetic and lugubrious tones], "you all know-ah that your humble speaker-ah has got-ah jest the best yoke of steers-ah in this township-ah." [Here Betsey Short shook the floor with a suppressed titter.] "They a'n't no sech steers as them air two of mine-ah in this whole kedentry-ah. Them crack oxen over at Clifty-ah ha'n't a patchin' to mine-ah. Fer the ox knoweth his owner-ah and the ass-ah his master's crib-ah.

"Now, my respective hearers-ah, they's a right smart sight of defference-ah atwext them air two oxen-ah, jest like they is atwext defferent men-ah. Fer-ah" [here the speaker grew earnest, and sawed the air, from this to the close, in a most frightful way], "fer-ah, you see-ah, when I go out-ah in the mornin'-ah to yoke-ah up-ah them air steers-ah, and I says-ah, 'Wo, Berry-ah! *Wo, Berry-ah!* WO, BERRY-AH', why Berry-ah jest stands stock still-ah and don't hardly breathe-ah while I put on the yoke-ah, and put in the bow-ah, and put in the key-ah, fer, my brethering-ah and sistering-ah, the ox knoweth his owner-ah, and the ass-ah his master's crib-ah. Hal-le-lu-ger-ah!

"But-ah, my hearers-ah, but-ah when I stand at t'other eend of the yoke-ah, and say, 'Come, Buck-ah! *Come, Buck-ah!* COME, BUCK-AH! COME, BUCK-AH!' why what do you think-ah? Buck-ah, that ornery ole Buck-ah, 'stid of comin' right along-ah and puttin' his neck under-ah, acts jest like some men-ah what is fools-ah. Buck-ah jest kinder sorter stands off-ah, and kinder sorter puts his head down-ah this 'ere way-ah, and kinder looks mad-ah, and says, Boo-*oo*-OO-OO-ah!"

Alas! Hartsook found no spiritual edification there, and he was in no mood to be amused. And so, while the sermon drew on through two dreary hours, he forgot the preacher in noticing a bright green lizard which, having taken up its winter quarters behind the tin candlestick that hung just back of the preacher's head, had been deceived by the genial warmth coming from the great box-stove, and now ran out two or three feet from his shelter, looking down upon the red-nosed preacher in a most confidential and amusing manner. Sometimes he would retreat behind the candlestick, which was not twelve inches from the preacher's head, and then rush out again. At each reappearance Betsey Short would stuff her handkerchief into her mouth and shake in a most distressing way. Shocky wondered what the lizard was winking at the preacher about. And Miss Martha thought that it reminded her of a lizard that she see at the East, the time she was to Bosting, in a jar of alcohol in the Natural History Rooms. The Squire was not disappointed in his anticipation that Mr. Bosaw would attack his denomination with some fury. In fact, the old preacher outdid himself in his violent indignation at "these people that follow Campbell-ah, that thinks-ah that obejience-ah will save 'em-ah and that belongs-ah to temp'rince societies-ah and Sunday-schools-ah, and them air things-ah, that's not ortherized in the Bible-ah, but comes of the devil-ah, and takes folks as belongs to 'em to hell-ah."

As they came out the door Ralph rallied enough to remark: "He did attack your people, Squire."

"Oh, yes," said the Squire. "Didn't you see the Sarpent inspirin' him?"

But the long, long hours were ended and Ralph got on the clay-bank mare and rode up alongside the stile whence Miss Martha mounted. And as he went away with a heavy heart, he overheard Pete Jones call out to somebody: "We'll tend to his case & Christmas." Christmas was two days off.

And Miss Martha remarked with much trepidation that poor Pearson would have to leave. She'd always been afraid that would be the end of it. It reminded her of something she heard at the East, the time she was down to Bosting.

5 Leon Ray Livingston, Tramping in America, 1910[6]

In Gilded Age America, tramping by so-called "hobos" became increasingly common. Part of a migratory, marginal population, tramps were common to cities, moving often by foot or, increasingly, by hopping the rails to their destinations. The existence of tramps provided evidence of the persistence of poverty during the industrial age.

Leon Ray Livingston (1872–1944), one of the best-known tramps in late nineteenth-century America, was known as the "King of the Hoboes." He began riding the rails at age 11, and eventually traveled nearly 500,000 miles during his lifetime. His nickname became "A No. 1," which he wrote on walls and boxcars to show where he had been. Livingston chose the tramping life for adventure and discovery, rather than poverty, and he wrote about his experiences in several books. In this account, he describes life as a hobo, and how people on the margins lived in industrial America.

Without a single idea which way to turn I left San Francisco. I caught a train going towards Los Angeles, intending to put as many miles between myself and home as possible. After two days out I made the acquaintance of two neat looking young fellows bound for the same city. That evening, while we were riding in a box car, they grabbed me from behind, and tied my hands and feet. After that they took every cent I had, my hat, shoes and the suit of clothes I had on. Then they tried to throw me out of the door while the train was running fast. I begged them for my life, as only one could who is about to be killed, and they took pity on me. They gagged me by stuffing a red handkerchief into my mouth, and then dragging me into a corner left me helpless, while they jumped from the car at the next stopping place.

[6] Leon Ray Livingston, *Life and Adventures of A-No 1* (Cambridge Springs, PA: A-No. 1 Publishing Co., 1910), pp. 60–74.

There I lay until two o'clock in the afternoon of the next day, when a railroad man, who by chance happened to look into the car, discovered me and cut the cords which bound me. I told him what had happened, but he told me to keep quiet about it, as I could never get the fellows convicted. "Furthermore," he added, "if we could catch them, you would have to wait here three or four months, until the next trial, and possibly they would lock you all into one and the same filthy cell together, so you better keep quiet."

After this experience I became even more careful, and hardly ever spoke to and never again traveled with tramps. The railroad man gave me a suit of greasy old overalls and arvold cap, and thus equipped I started for Los Angeles. I was in the Mojave Desert and unable to beg even a pair of shoes.

Upon reaching Bakersfield, Cal., early one morning I saw a tramp at a camp-fire, and went over to warm myself a little. "Kid," said the tramp, "what have you done with your shoes?" I told him I had been held up, and he gave me a good pointer.

"I will put you wise, Kid," he said, "if you will give me the booze they hand you." I promised to do so, and he continued: "The county jail is a 'boodle proposition,' and say, Kid, you get yourself pinched and they will do the square thing by you."

Acting upon his advice, I approached the first deputy sheriff I saw and begged for my breakfast. He asked me how I would like to be arrested. I blinked my eyes and told him I was next, and willing to take the chance. He took me to the jail, and gave me a nice warm breakfast, made out some papers and then took me to the judge's office. The judge, a white haired, solemn looking rascal sentenced me to a fine of thirty dollars and thirty days in jail for vagrancy. The deputy took me back to jail and locked me in a cell. I commenced to feel uneasy, and thought maybe I had fallen into a trap again.

An hour passed away that seemed ages, then the deputy returned and after cautioning me not to speak, he took me to a shoe store where he bought me a pair of nice shoes, then on the way back to the jail he gave me a dollar and a big bottle of whiskey, and told me to hustle out of town by side streets and alleys as quickly as possible, and not to forget to call again some other time. I was overjoyed, for I now had shoes and a dollar besides. I hustled back to the camp and delivered the booze to the tramp who had told me what to do.

"Well", he asked, not satisfied with the booze alone, "didn't they hand you any dough?" I denied having received money. "We big ones," he continued, "usually get a five dollar note, but they are getting scared, as some of us have been pinched too often."

I asked him why the officials did this, and he explained it as follows: "Ah, Kid, you aint wise at all. They have these boodle jails all over the United

States. It's graft, Kid, don't you see? They fined you thirty dollars and thirty days; you can't pay the thirty dollars, but the sheriff gets one dollar a day for every day you are supposed to be locked up; the judge, five dollars for your sentence; the lawyer, five dollars for your conviction; the clerk, five dollars for your commitment, and the deputysheriff five dollars for arresting you, so you see it is all graft. None of them receive a regular salary, so an officer has to steal all the fees he can to make a living."

. . .

I knew after listening to his explanation of this graft-jail, that the man was of a more superior intelligence than the average tramp, and thinking that perhaps I could get some valuable information, I sat down to the camp-fire.

After he had taken several hearty pulls out of the bottle I had delivered, he remarked: "Kid, if I were in your hide, I would beat it 'hot foot' off the road, for we older ones know there is no stopping once you get a good start." I assured him that I would take the very first job offered, and he patted me on my shoulder and said:

"That is right, Kid, make a man out of yourself before it is too late."

To change the subject, I asked if all jails were as easy as this one? "Ah, no Kid, this one is an exception. You see, not many tramps have lately travelled up and down this fine, so they have to 'double up tramps' to draw enough money out of the county treasury to meet their grocery bills or go to work the same as other folks do. Where many tramps pass along they give sentences from ten to sixty, with an average of thirty days, the only difference between these two methods is, that the first gang of grafters steals outright, while the other gang has an actual expense of perhaps five cents a day feeding ' slops' to the tramps, so you see there is no difference in the game, only that the 'honest' grafters pay cash to the tramps, while the crooked bunch feeds them a similar amount gradually, and usually mistreat their poor victims besides; but you see the latter style of grafting is the safest, as it is done under the pretense of lawful punishment."

Here I asked: "If those thirty days imprisonment did not reform some of the tramps?" This innocent inquiry roused his ire. "Nixie Kid," he retorted, "Reform? None of such wise talk from a little 'Gunsel' (young boy) like you. Reform a fellow by locking him up for thirty days and never speak one word of encouragement to him all this time; never give him advice for his future good? No, none of that, but on the contrary, turn him out after his time is up, lousy as a cuckoo; almost certain to be infected with some dangerous disease; hungry as a starved wolf; ragged and filthy to the very limit; without a cent, without a job or friendly lift of any kind, and branded an ex-convict in the eyes of society. Do you call this reforming him? Nixie, Kid, instead of reform they stamp indelibly upon his mind the words of the avenger from the Genesis of the Holy Bible: 'An eye for an eye and a tooth for a tooth,' and instill a lasting hate against those who countenance such humbug, under the guise of antiquated laws, and with a vengeance he spreads the Vermin and diseases to repay society for his incarceration." And he added: "Many a case of tuberculosis in wealthy families can be directly traced back to a tramp who had been imprisoned in an unsanitary jail."

Here I interrupted him again by asking if he thought the "rock-pile" and other kindred punishments would prevent tramping? "Nixie, Kid," he replied, "there is absolutely no cure for tramping except a tramp quits himself in disgust. Some folks," he continued, "come to tramping just as natural as others to hunting elephants and lions; playing golf, racing horses or automobiles; swimming, hunting, preaching, fishing, go crazy on baseball and prize fighting, smoking and chewing tobacco, dipping snuff and enjoy these and thousands of other strange notions to the limit, each of which would cause the 'tired feeling' if not disgust in a different set of people, who in turn have other faults of their own, and let me tell you, Kid," he added with emphasis, "it's another queer fact that one fellow always spots the other fellow's faults, fibs and fancies and overlooks that he is demented on one or more subjects himself. And about the rock-pile and farm-colonies being reformatory and a detriment, I guess not my lad. For scores of years down in the Southern States they have sentenced tramps and 'out-of works' to months and even years at the most dangerous and hardest labor under revolting conditions, in coal mines, farms and lumber camps owned by wealthy individuals or corporations who permit their superintendents to mistreat these poor 'American' slaves with such beastly inhumanity that the United States Government has put many of the inhumane taskmasters for long terms into federal penitentiaries, where their fellow convicts plague them into committing suicide or if half a chance offers itself, beat them to death. Despite this wanton cruelty to human beings there are more tramps than ever known before in the Southern States, and what is worse is the fact, where formerly only three per cent, of the tramps were of Southern parentage, now 90 per cent, of these form the tramp element 'down in Dixie.'"

Here I interrupted him by asking if there was not some remedy to curb or stop tramping? He quickly replied: "You bet there is, Kid, and a remedy so absolutely cheap that it never will be advocated by grafters and those loathsome wretches, who make a living collecting money under the pretense of assisting and reforming tramps, as there is no money to be made in its application. And, Kid," he continued, "do you know that the special agents of the railroads, the 'railroad cops' as we call them, have applied this remedy for more than a score of years and have prevented thousands of lively kids becoming tramps, and a burden upon the communities in one form or another? Yes," he continued, earnestly speaking, when he noted an incredulous expression flitting across my face, as Frenchy had preached to me daily that the railroad police were the tramps' sworn enemies, "the railroad cops are the only real friends the tramps have, and not until you become an habitual tramp will you realize this fact, for they apply the only sano and effective remedy to stop tramping, and at least reduce the numbers of wanderers to the minimum by tackling the problem by its root, and not like all others do, at its tail end. Just wait, my boy until I have another 'pull' out of this 'old reliable' before I put you wise."

While he handled the whiskey bottle, I waited anxiously for him to resume his lecture, for had he not said he knew a cheap, sane and effective manner to stop or at least reduce the tramp horde? This seemed strange to me, for that it is the public's money these other reformers are after, is easily proven by the fact that in one place tramps are "hunted" and arrested, while perhaps a mile farther, or towards the end of the month in the same place, they are not molested.

. . .

After a pause and several hearty drinks out of the bottle he commenced again: "There is another source of tramp supply that could be closed up without trouble and expense to anyone for the lasting benefit of all humanity. It would prevent at least 75 per cent of tramps from becoming tramps; in fact it would close the biggest source that makes the lowest class of tramps and bums out of grown-up people, and these are the 'dives' and 'hang-out' saloons in the slums of all the larger cities. Look at me, my lad," he rose showing his superb physique, "I used to be a mechanic earning over $5.00 a day, and now I am a tramp and a 'Distillery Tramp' at that, because booze and the tramping 'Wanderlust' have both claimed me. Do you know, my boy, how I managed to fall down this low? Listen and I will tell you. I used to drink many a glass of beer in certain saloons on South Clark Street in old Chicago. I never would have thought in those days that I would be just as low as those filthy hanging around those slums. . . . I didn't have much money so was drifted down to the free lunch counters of my favorite saloons and there came in close contact with those sodden bums who made their way easier through life than I thought I did, and had no strikes to contend with.

I struck up an acquaintanceship with one of the cleanest, who himself had been a good mechanic in his day. I watched how he turned the trick, imitated him and forgot my honest trade for the life of a saloon sod. When summer with its hot days made things unpleasant in those slums, I followed the others out on 'the road', and now I am a 'Distillery Tramp' for the rest of my life, because while away from booze and the city I feel more like a human being. Laughing, are you, kid?" he hotly remarked when he noticed me smiling at the strange story of how, he became a tramp. "Kid, you don't realize yet what this strange something, the 'Wanderlust' means until it holds you so tight you cannot break away." I became strangely silent and thought of my poor mother at home, and the promise I had made to quit the "road."

He continued, "I always travel alone my lad, but if the officers would chase away gangs of 'Distillery Tramps 'hanging around stock-yards or thickets close to towns and cities often for weeks, as fast as they spot them, they would do another long step towards the elimination of the tramp, as the camp-fire bums draw all the loafers and truants for miles around to their hangouts and give the kids their practical initiation into the mysteries of tramp life."

.... What sort of a tramp is the 'Scenery Tramp' you mentioned as being the third and last tramp class?" I questioned the tramp.

"Well, Kid," he replied, "I call a 'Scenery Tramp' a confirmed rover, who is so absolutely restless, that even offers of a good home, easy employment at large wages, or any other inducement have no attraction for him, as he craves only for a constant change of scenery. He always acts as if someone was hunting him, misses meals and sleep to reach a destination, and no sooner arrives there, than he is off for the next one. Many a 'Scenery Tramp' is born with a touch of the 'Wanderlust.' His parents, perchance having had prenatal intentions to change their home to some other locality, etc., and if these parents, while their restless kids are young, would have them enlist in the U. S. Navy, many a fine lad, instead of being a restless drummer, circus follower or tramp, would be a good sailor, wearing the beautiful uniform of Uncle Sam's proud navy."

"How can you stop the 'Scenery Tramp?'" I inquired.

"Well, Kid," he replied, "he is a 'goner,' and as long as he keeps on the move and harms no one, let him wander, as he is a confirmed victim of the 'Wanderlust,' and money spent on him in any shape or form is absolutely wasted, as 75 per cent, of them are the grown-up 'Kid Tramps' who were permitted to run away from home."

Here I asked him about the yeggmen. "Say, Gunsel," he retorted, "them guys are not tramps at all, they are gun toters, a real tramp loves his liberty too well and has no excuse anyhow to carry a gun; so, my lad, when you hear of these yeggmen throwing tramps naked off moving trains after taking

their 'duds' (clothes) from them, you know what 'good' tramps they are."
And he added: "I did wish that every tramping or camping tough-looking
gun-toter would be sent to the penitentiary for life, as this would put a
mighty sudden stop to postoffice, box-car, depot and bank robberies and
prevent many wanton murders of citizens as well as tramps."

He took another drink out of the bottle, emptying it and after he smashed
it with a curse against the rails he finished: "I have known these railroad
cops to feed many a poor fellow they picked up trespassing, and even give
them lifts on the sly to leave town without walking their feet sore, and they
always discriminate between the man in search of employment, the harmless
tramp" and the tough, never molesting the first, helping to move on the
second and making things unpleasant for the third class, because they receive
regular salaries from their companies and do not benefit financially by adding unnecessary burdens upon the communities as for instance these grafters
in this 'Burg' do right here in broad daylight."

The campfire had almost died down during the tramp's recitation, and
while he went to forage for some material to rekindle the fire, I took the
chance to leave him. I resolved then and there to accept the very first chance
offered to go to work and thus escape the drama he had portrayed, and he
had said was in store for all those who follow "The Call of the Road."

6   Upton Sinclair, from *The Jungle*, 1906[7]

*Upton Sinclair's The Jungle, published as a novel in 1906, highlights the
harsh conditions of the American meatpacking industry in the early
twentieth century. The novel portrays the industry as corrupt and aims to
elicit sympathy for the working class and American Socialist movement by
illuminating the cruel living and working conditions of factory workers.
Sinclair describes the industry in such gruesome detail, in fact, that several
early publishers rejected the novel as too shocking. When the work was
finally published in full in 1906, however, it not only proved an instant
financial success, but also had a considerable social impact. The American
public's outrage at the unsanitary conditions in meatpacking factories
facilitated the establishment of federal standards for meat inspection, and the
passage of the Pure Food and Drug Act in 1906.*

*The Jungle is situated in the stockyards of Chicago, and the main
characters include Jurgis Rudkus, who migrated from Lithuania in search of
work. Jurgis's story is one of disappointment and betrayal, however, as the*

---

[7]   Upton Sinclair, *The Jungle* (New York: Doubleday, Page, & Co., 1906), pp. 75–85.

system, as Sinclair portrayed, was exploitative and oppressive. In Chapter 7, an excerpt from which is given here, Jurgis plans marriage but confronts the reality of the harsh urban–industrial environment.

Jurgis and Ona were very much in love; they had waited a long time—it was now well into the second year, and Jurgis judged everything by the criterion of its helping or hindering their union. All his thoughts were there; he accepted the family because it was a part of Ona. . . .

The cost of the wedding feast would, of course, be returned to them; but the problem was to raise it even temporarily. . . . Ona began thinking of seeking employment herself, saying that if she had even ordinarily good luck, she might be able to take two months off the time. They were just beginning to adjust themselves to this necessity, when out of the clear sky there fell a thunderbolt upon them—a calamity that scattered all their hopes to the four winds.

About a block away from them there lived another Lithuanian family, consisting of an elderly widow and one grown son; their name was Majauszkis, and our friends struck up an acquaintance with them before long. One evening they came over for a visit, and naturally the first subject upon which the conversation turned was the neighborhood and its history; and then Grandmother Majauszkiene, as the old lady was called, proceeded to recite to them a string of horrors that fairly froze their blood. She was a wrinkled-up and wizened personage—she must have been eighty—and as she mumbled the grim story through her toothless gums, she seemed a very old witch to them. Grandmother Majauszkiene had lived in the midst of misfortune so long that it had come to be her element, and she talked about starvation, sickness, and death as other people might about weddings and holidays.

The thing came gradually. In the first place as to the house they had bought, it was not new at all, as they had supposed; it was about fifteen years old, and there was nothing new upon it but the paint, which was so bad that it needed to be put on new every year or two. The house was one of a whole row that was built by a company which existed to make money by swindling poor people. The family had paid fifteen hundred dollars for it, and it had not cost the builders five hundred, when it was new. Grandmother Majauszkiene knew that because her son belonged to a political organization with a contractor who put up exactly such houses. They used the very flimsiest and cheapest material; they built the houses a dozen at a time, and they cared about nothing at all except the outside shine. The family could take her word as to the trouble they would have, for she had been through it all—she and her son had bought their house in exactly the same way. They had fooled the company, however, for her son was a skilled man, who made as high as a hundred dollars a month, and as he had had sense enough not to marry, they had been able to pay for the house.

Grandmother Majauszkiene saw that her friends were puzzled at this remark; they did not quite see how paying for the house was "fooling the company." Evidently they were very inexperienced. Cheap as the houses were, they were sold with the idea that the people who bought them would not be able to pay for them. When they failed—if it were only by a single month—they would lose the house and all that they had paid on it, and then the company would sell it over again. And did they often get a chance to do that? Dieve! (Grandmother Majauszkiene raised her hands.) They did it— how often no one could say, but certainly more than half of the time. They might ask any one who knew anything at all about Packingtown as to that; she had been living here ever since this house was built, and she could tell them all about it. And had it ever been sold before? Susimilkie! Why, since it had been built, no less than four families that their informant could name had tried to buy it and failed. She would tell them a little about it.

The first family had been Germans. The families had all been of different nationalities—there had been a representative of several races that had displaced each other in the stockyards. Grandmother Majauszkiene had come to America with her son at a time when so far as she knew there was only one other Lithuanian family in the district; the workers had all been Germans then—skilled cattle butchers that the packers had brought from abroad to start the business. Afterward, as cheaper labor had come, these Germans had moved away. The next were the Irish—there had been six or eight years when Packingtown had been a regular Irish city. There were a few colonies of them still here, enough to run all the unions and the police force and get all the graft; but most of those who were working in the packing houses had gone away at the next drop in wages—after the big strike. The Bohemians had come then, and after them the Poles. People said that old man Durham himself was responsible for these immigrations; he had sworn that he would fix the people of Packingtown so that they would never again call a strike on him, and so he had sent his agents into every city and village in Europe to spread the tale of the chances of work and high wages at the stockyards. The people had come in hordes; and old Durham had squeezed them tighter and tighter, speeding them up and grinding them to pieces and sending for new ones. The Poles, who had come by tens of thousands, had been driven to the wall by the Lithuanians, and now the Lithuanians were giving way to the Slovaks. Who there was poorer and more miserable than the Slovaks, Grandmother Majauszkiene had no idea, but the packers would find them, never fear. It was easy to bring them, for wages were really much higher, and it was only when it was too late that the poor people found out that everything else was higher too. They were like rats in a trap, that was the truth; and more of them were piling in every day. By and by they would have their revenge, though, for the thing was getting beyond human endurance, and the people would rise and murder the packers. Grandmother Majauszkiene was a socialist, or some such strange thing; another son of hers was working in the mines of Siberia, and the old lady herself had made speeches in her time—which made her seem all the more terrible to her present auditors.

They called her back to the story of the house. The German family had been a good sort. To be sure there had been a great many of them, which was a common failing in Packingtown; but they had worked hard, and the father had been a steady man, and they had a good deal more than half paid for the house. But he had been killed in an elevator accident in Durham's.

Then there had come the Irish, and there had been lots of them, too; the husband drank and beat the children—the neighbors could hear them shrieking any night. They were behind with their rent all the time, but the company was good to them; there was some politics back of that, Grandmother Majauszkiene could not say just what, but the Laffertys had belonged to the "War Whoop League," which was a sort of political club of all the thugs and rowdies in the district; and if you belonged to that, you could never be arrested for anything. Once upon a time old Lafferty had been caught with a gang that had stolen cows from several of the poor people of the neighborhood and butchered them in an old shanty back of the yards and sold them. He had been in jail only three days for it, and had come out laughing, and had not even lost his place in the packing house. He had gone all to ruin with the drink, however, and lost his power; one of his sons, who was a good man, had kept him and the family up for a year or two, but then he had got sick with consumption. . .

To come back to the house again, it was the woman of the next family that had died. That was after they had been there nearly four years, and this woman had had twins regularly every year—and there had been more than you could count when they moved in. After she died the man would go to work all day and leave them to shift for themselves—the neighbors would help them now and then, for they would almost freeze to death. At the end there were three days that they were alone, before it was found out that the father was dead. He was a "floorsman" at Jones's, and a wounded steer had broken loose and mashed him against a pillar. Then the children had been taken away, and the company had sold the house that very same week to a party of emigrants.

So this grim old woman went on with her tale of horrors. How much of it was exaggeration—who could tell? It was only too plausible. There was that about consumption, for instance. They knew nothing about consumption whatever, except that it made people cough; and for two weeks they had been worrying about a coughing-spell of Antanas. It seemed to shake him all over, and it never stopped; you could see a red stain wherever he had spit upon the floor.

And yet all these things were as nothing to what came a little later. They had begun to question the old lady as to why one family had been unable to pay, trying to show her by figures that it ought to have been possible; and Grandmother Majauszkiene had disputed their figures—"You say twelve dollars a month; but that does not include the interest."

Then they stared at her. "Interest!" they cried.

"Interest on the money you still owe," she answered.

"But we don't have to pay any interest!" they exclaimed, three or four at once. "We only have to pay twelve dollars each month."

And for this she laughed at them. "You are like all the rest," she said; "they trick you and eat you alive. They never sell the houses without interest. Get your deed, and see."

Then, with a horrible sinking of the heart, Teta Elzbieta unlocked her bureau and brought out the paper that had already caused them so many agonies. Now they sat round, scarcely breathing, while the old lady, who could read English, ran over it. "Yes," she said, finally, "here it is, of course: 'With interest thereon monthly, at the rate of seven per cent per annum.'"

And there followed a dead silence. "What does that mean?" asked Jurgis finally, almost in a whisper.

"That means," replied the other, "that you have to pay them seven dollars next month, as well as the twelve dollars."

Then again there was not a sound. It was sickening, like a nightmare, in which suddenly something gives way beneath you, and you feel yourself sinking, sinking, down into bottomless abysses. As if in a flash of lightning they saw themselves—victims of a relentless fate, cornered, trapped, in the grip of destruction. All the fair structure of their hopes came crashing about their ears.—And all the time the old woman was going on talking. They wished that she would be still; her voice sounded like the croaking of some dismal raven. Jurgis sat with his hands clenched and beads of perspiration on his forehead, and there was a great lump in Ona's throat, choking her. Then suddenly Teta Elzbieta broke the silence with a wail, and Marija began to wring her hands and sob, "Ai! Ai! Beda man!"

. . . And meantime, because they were young, and hope is not to be stifled before its time, Jurgis and Ona were again calculating; for they had discovered that the wages of Stanislovas would a little more than pay the interest, which left them just about as they had been before! It would be but fair to them to say that the little boy was delighted with his work, and at the idea of earning a lot of money; and also that the two were very much in love with each other.

Discussion Questions: Chapter 6

1   What was the impact of industrialization on American workers?
2   What were the characteristics of working-class culture in the industrializing United States?
3   How did work life differ in the accounts by Crane, Wyckoff, and Eggleston?
4   In Sinclair's view, what problems did the working class face in early twentieth-century American cities?

Chapter 7 Immigrants in the Industrial Age

1 Abraham Cahan, "The Russian Jew in America," 1898[1]

*Abraham Cahan (1860–1951) was a distinguished Jewish journalist and
fiction writer who immigrated from Russia in 1882 and settled in the Lower
East Side of Manhattan. He served as an important voice for Jewish
immigrants in their struggles to become acclimated to their new lives in
America. Between 1903 and 1946, Cahan was editor of the* Jewish Daily
Forward, *a newspaper that he transformed into a nationally influential
publication. As Cahan became more Americanized, his political radicalism
grew more pragmatic.*

*Cahan was influential in the development of Jewish trade unions and in
the use of Yiddish to explain life in America to immigrants and to help
preserve Old World Jewish culture. One of his novels,* Yekl, *presents the
story of a Russian Jewish immigrant who becomes Americanized and
ultimately regrets abandoning his native culture. Cahan's descriptive writing
about life in the Jewish ghetto is among the best in that genre. In the article
that follows, Cahan talks about the plight of the Russian Jew in America.*

[1] *Atlantic Monthly* 82 (July 1898): 128–39.

The Gilded Age and Progressive Era: A Documentary Reader, First Edition.
Edited by William A. Link and Susannah J. Link.
© 2012 Blackwell Publishing Ltd. Published 2012 by Blackwell Publishing Ltd.

Before 1882 the emigration of Russian Jews to America was restricted to the provinces lying about the Niemen and the Dwina, notably to the government of Souvalki, where economical conditions caused Catholic peasants as well as Jewish tradesmen and artisans to go elsewhere "in search of bread." Some of these Lithuanian and Polish Jews sought their fortune in the southern districts of the empire, where their brethren enjoyed a high average of prosperity, while the more venturesome crossed the frontier to embark for the New World. Among the Jews of the south (Ukraine and New Russia) and of the central provinces (Great Russia) self-expatriation was an unknown thing. But with the breaking out of the epidemic of anti-Jewish riots, which rendered thousands of well-to-do families homeless and penniless, Hebrew immigration to this country underwent an abrupt change in character as well as in volume.

Not only did the government of Alexander III blink at the atrocities and practically encourage them, but it even sent a series of measures in their wake which had the effect of depriving new multitudes of "stepchildren" of their means of livelihood, and of dislodging thousands of families from their long-established homes. The cry "To America!" was taken up by city after city and hamlet after hamlet, till its fascinating echo reached every synagogue in the empire. Many left because they had been driven from their homes, and these were joined by many others who, while affected neither by the outbursts of mob violence nor by the new restrictions, succumbed to the contagious example of their co-religionists and to a general sense of insecurity and of wounded race pride. The efflux which had hitherto been sporadic suddenly became epidemic. The prosperous and the cultivated—an element formerly rare among the Jewish arrivals at New York—came to form a respectable minority in nearly every company of immigrants which, thanks to the assistance of the Hebrew communities of western Europe and of this country, the steamships brought from the domains of the Czar. The Jewish college student, whose faith barred him from the educational institutions of the empire, sought these shores in order to complete his studies, and many a graduated physician, chemist, dentist, architect, and artist came here to take up the profession from which he was interdicted at his birthplace.

Sixteen years have elapsed. The Jewish population in the United States has grown from a quarter of a million to about one million. Scarcely a large American town but has some Russo-Jewish names in its directory, with an educated Russian-speaking minority forming a colony within a Yiddish-speaking colony, while cities like New York, Chicago, Philadelphia, and Boston have each a Ghetto rivaling in extent of population the largest Jewish cities in Russia, Austria, and Roumania. The number of Jewish residents in Manhattan Borough is estimated at two hundred and fifty thousand, making it the largest centre of Hebrew population in the world. The Russian tongue, which twenty years ago was as little used in this country as Persian, has been added to the list of languages spoken by an appreciable portion of the polyglot immigrant population.

. . .

The cry raised by the Russian anti-Semites against the backwardness of the Jew in adopting the tongue and the manners of his birthplace, in the same breath in which they urge the government to close the doors of its schools to subjects of the Hebrew faith, reminds one of the hypocritical miser who kept his gate guarded by ferocious dogs, and then reproached his destitute neighbor with holding himself aloof. . . .

Nor does the tailor or peddler who hires these tutors, as a rule, content him- self with an elementary knowledge of the language of his new home. I know many Jewish workmen who before they came here knew not a word of Russian,[2] and were ignorant of any book except the Scriptures, or perhaps the Talmud, but whose range of English reading places them on a level with the average college-bred American. The grammar schools of the Jewish quarter are overcrowded with children of immigrants, who, for progress and deportment, are rated with the very best in the city. At least 500 of 1677 students at the New York City College, where tuition and books are free, are Jewish boys from the East Side. The poor laborer who will pinch himself to keep his child at college, rather than send him to a factory that he may contribute to the family's income, is another type peculiar to the Ghetto.

The innumerable Yiddish publications with which the quarter is flooded are also a potent civilizing and Americanizing agency. The Russian Jews of New York, Philadelphia, and Chicago have within the last fifteen years created a vast periodical literature which furnishes intellectual food not only to themselves, but also to their brethren in Europe. A feverish literary activity unknown among the Jews in Russia, Roumania, and Austria, but which has arisen here among the immigrants from those countries, educates thousands of ignorant tailors and peddlers, lifts their intelligence, facilitates their study of English, and opens to them the doors of the English library. The five million Jews living under the Czar had not a single Yiddish daily paper even when the government allowed such publications, while their fellow countrymen and co-religionists who have taken up their abode in America publish six dailies (five in New York and one in Chicago), not to mention

[2]   Most likely, they knew only Yiddish.

the countless Yiddish weeklies and monthlies, and the pamphlets and books which to-day make New York the largest Yiddish book market in the world.

. . .

I have visited the houses of many American workingmen, in New England and elsewhere, as well as the residences of their Jewish shopmates, and I have found scarcely a point of difference. The squalor of the typical tenement house of the Ghetto is far more objectionable and offensive to the people who are doomed to live in it than to those who undertake slumming expeditions as a fad, and is entirely due to the same economical conditions which are responsible for the lack of cleanliness in the homes of such poor workingmen as are classed among the most desirable contribution to the population. The houses of the poor Irish laborers who dwell on the outskirts of the great New York Ghetto (and they are not worse than the houses occupied by the poor Irish families of the West Side) are not better, in point of cleanliness, than the residences of their Jewish neighbors. . . .

Is the Russian Jew responsible for the sweating system? He did not bring it with him. He found it already developed here. In its varied forms it exists in other industries as well as in the tailoring trades. But far from resigning himself to his burden the Jewish tailor is ever struggling to shake it from his shoulder. Nor are his efforts futile. In many instances the sweat-shop system has been abolished or its curse mitigated. The sweating system and its political ally the ward heeler are accountable for ninety-nine per cent of whatever vice may be found in the Ghetto, and the Jewish tailor is slowly but surely emancipating himself from both. . . . The anti-Semitic assertion that the Jew as a rule avoids productive labor, which is pure calumny so far as the Jews of Russia, Austria, and Roumania are concerned, would certainly be out of place in this country, where at least eighty per cent of all Jewish immigrants are among the most diligent wage-earners. As to the remainder, it includes, besides a large army of poor peddlers, thousands of such business men as news-dealers and rag-men, whose occupations are scarcely less productive or more agreeable than manual labor. More than ninety per cent of all the news-stands and news-routes in the city of New York are now in the hands of Russian Jews, and most of the rag-peddlers of New England are persons of the same nationality.

Farming settlements of Jews have not been very successful in this country. There are some Jews in Connecticut, in New Jersey, and in the Western states who derive a livelihood from agriculture, but the majority of the Jewish immigrants who took to tilling the soil in the eighties have been compelled to sell or to abandon their farms, and to join the urban population.

But how many American farmers have met with a similar fate! This experience is part of the same great economic question, and it does not seem to have any direct bearing on the peculiar inclinations or disinclinations of the Hebrew race. It may not be generally known that in southern Russia there are hundreds of flourishing farms which are owned and worked by Jews, although, owing to their legal disabilities, the titles are fictitiously held by Christians. Hundreds of Russian and Polish Jews have been more or less successful in business, and the names of several of them are to be found on the signs along Broadway, but the richest is hardly worth a quarter of a million.

As to the educated Jewish immigrants, the college-bred men and women who constitute the professional class and the intellectual aristocracy of the Ghetto, judged by the standard of the slum district, they are prosperous.

. . .

Only from three to five per cent of the vacancies in the Russian universities and gymnasiums[3] are now open to applicants of the Mosaic faith. As a consequence, the various university towns of Germany, Switzerland, Belgium, France, and Austria have each a colony of Russo-Jewish pilgrims of learning. The impecunious student, however, finds a university course in those countries inaccessible. Much more favorable in this respect is the United States, where students from among the Jewish immigrants find it possible to sustain themselves during their college course by some occupation; and this advantage has to some extent made this country the Mecca of that class of young men. It is not, however, always the educated young men, the graduates of Russian gymnasiums, from whom the Russian members at the American colleges are recruited. Not to speak of the hundreds of immigrant boys and girls who reach the New York City College or the Normal College by way of the grammar schools of the Ghetto, there are in the colleges of New York, Philadelphia, Chicago, and Boston, as well as among the professional men of the Jewish colonies, not a few former peddlers or workmen who received their first lessons in the rudimentary branches of education within the walls of an American tenement house. . . . Altogether there are in New York alone about one hundred and fifty Russian physicians, about five hundred druggists and drug clerks, some twenty lawyers, from thirty to forty dentists, and several representatives of each of the other professions.

---

3 Similar to American high schools.

The Russian-speaking population is represented also in the colleges for women. There are scores of educated Russian girls in the sweat-shops, and their life is one of direst misery, of overwork in the shop, and of privations at home.

Politically the Jewish quarter is among the most promising districts in the metropolis. The influence of the vote-buyer, which is the blight of every poor neighborhood in the city, becomes in the Ghetto smaller and smaller. . . . The ward heeler is as active in the Ghetto as elsewhere. Aided by an army of workers, which is largely made up of the lowest dregs of the neighborhood, he knocks, on election day, at the door of every tenement house apartment, while on the street the vote market goes on in open daylight as freely as it did before there was a Parkhurst[4] to wage war against a guilty police organization. This statement is true of every destitute district, and the Jewish quarter is no exception to the rule. As was revealed by the Lexow committee, some of the leading district "bosses" in the great city, including a civil justice, owe their power to the political cooperation of criminals and women of the street. Unfortunately this is also the case with the Jewish neighborhood, where every wretch living on the profits of vice, almost without exception, is a member of some political club and an active worker for one of the two machines, and where, during the campaign, every disreputable house is turned into an electioneering centre. . . .

The immigration reformers' dread of foreign socialism is scarcely consistent with his classification of the various nationalities who immigrate in large numbers. To judge from the overwhelming social-democratic vote in Germany, a large proportion of the Germans who come to our ports are socialists, and yet they are placed at the very top of the list of desirable immigrants. Moreover, with some twenty states of the Union officially recognizing the Socialist Labor Party and printing its ballots, a crusade against the doctrine by the government would be a self-contradiction. Nor is it true that socialism is a foreign importation. The two socialist aldermen in the country (at Paterson, New Jersey, and Haverhill, Massachusetts) were elected by American workingmen; the new socialist organization called the Social Democracy is largely composed of Americans, and makes converts among the native elements of the working class.

The Jewish immigrants, at all events, bring no socialism with them; and if it is true that the socialist following among Jewish workingmen is considerable and is growing, they owe it to the economic conditions which surround them here and to the influence of the American socialist with whom they come in contact. Like other socialists, they look to the ballot-box for the changes which they advocate. It is the Jewish socialist who leads the neighborhood in

[4]   Charles H. Parkhurst, a notable New York City reformer.

its fight against the political and moral turpitude which the politician spreads in the tenement houses. The Jewish immigrants look upon the United States as their country, and now that it is engaged in war they do not shirk their duty. They have contributed three times their quota of volunteers to the army, and they had their representatives among the first martyrs of the campaign, two of the brave American sailors who were wounded at Cardenas and Cienfuegos being the sons of Hebrew immigrants.

The Russian Jew brings with him the quaint customs of a religion full of poetry and of the sources of good citizenship. The orthodox synagogue is not merely a house of prayer; it is an intellectual centre, a mutual aid society, a fountain of self-denying altruism, and a literary club, no less than a place of worship. The study-rooms of the hundreds of synagogues, where the good old people of the Ghetto come to read and discuss "words of law" as well as the events of the day, are crowded every evening in the week with poor street peddlers, and with those gray-haired, misunderstood sweat-shop hands of whom the public hears every time a tailor strike is declared. So few are the joys which this world has to spare for these over- worked, enfeebled victims of the inferno of modern times that their religion is to many of them the only thing which makes life worth living. In the fervor of prayer or the abandon of religious study they forget the grinding poverty of their homes. Between the walls of the synagogue, on the top floor of some ramshackle tenement house, they sing beautiful melodies, some of them composed in the caves and forests of Spain, where the wandering people worshiped the God of their fathers at the risk of their lives; and these and the sighs and sobs of the Days of Awe, the thrill that passes through the heart-broken talith-covered congregation when the shoffar blows, the mirth which fills the house of God and the tenement homes upon the Rejoicing of the Law, the tearful greetings and humbled peace-makings on Atonement Eve, the mysterious light of the Chanuccah candles, the gifts and charities of Purim, the joys and kingly solemnities of Passover, all these pervade the atmosphere of the Ghetto with a beauty and a charm without which the life of its older residents would often be one of unrelieved misery.

2   Treaty Regulating Immigration from China, 1880[5]

Between the 1850s and 1870s, anti-Chinese tensions in California resulted in the passage of a number of state restrictions on Chinese immigration, but the federal government overturned much of this legislation, arguing that the

---

[5] Treaty (1880) and congressional act (1882).

anti-Chinese discrimination violated the Burlingame–Seward Treaty of 1868. By 1879, however, opponents of Chinese immigration achieved passage of federal restrictions on Chinese immigration in Congress, but the bill was vetoed by President Rutherford B. Hayes. In an attempt to satisfy western demands for total Chinese exclusion from the United States, Hayes agreed to renegotiate the treaty with China. James B. Angell (1829–1916), the diplomat appointed to this task, achieved restrictions on, but not total exclusion of, Chinese immigration under the following Angell Treaty.

Congress passed the Chinese Exclusion Act in 1882, which suspended Chinese immigration for ten years and required Chinese who left the country and wanted to return to carry a certificate of identification. This legislation was the first broad immigration restriction imposed by the US government. These restrictions were made permanent ten years later, and this legislation represented the beginning of a long period of broad US immigration restriction from many parts of the world, lasting until 1965 with the passage of the Immigration and Nationality Act, which overturned the national-origins restrictions of the Immigration Act of 1924 and significantly raised the overall immigration quotas.

I

Treaty Regulating Chinese Immigration into the United States (concluded November 17, 1880, proclaimed October 5, 1881)[6]

Whereas the Government of the United States, because of the constantly increasing immigration of Chinese laborers to the territory of the United States, and the embarrassments consequent upon such immigration, now desires to negotiate a modification of the existing Treaties which shall not be in direct contravention of their spirit:

Article I. Whenever in the opinion of the Government of the United States, the coming of Chinese laborers to the United States, or their residence therein, affects or threatens to affect the interests of that country, or to endanger the good order of the said country or of any locality within the territory thereof, the Government of China agrees that the Government of the United States may regulate, limit, or suspend such coming or residence, but may not absolutely prohibit it. The limitation or suspension shall be reasonable and shall apply only to Chinese who may go to the United States as laborers, other classes not being included in the limitations. Legislation taken in regard to Chinese laborers will be of such a character only as is

---

[6]   Freeman Snow, ed., *Treaties and Topics in American Diplomacy* (Boston: Boston Book Co., 1894), pp. 163–6.

necessary to enforce the regulation, limitation or suspension of immigration, and immigrants shall not be subject to personal maltreatment or abuse.

Article II. Chinese subjects, whether proceeding to the United States as teachers, students, merchants, or from curiosity, together with their body and household servants, and Chinese Laborers who are now in the United States, shall be allowed to go and come of their own free will and accord, and shall be accorded all the rights, privileges, immunities and exemptions which are accorded to the citizens and subjects of the most favored nation."

Article III. If Chinese laborers, or Chinese of any other class, now either permanently or temporarily residing in the territory of the United States, meet with ill treatment at the hands of any other persons, the Government of the United States will exert all its power to devise measures for their protection and to secure to them the same rights, privileges, immunities and exemptions as may be enjoyed by the citizens or subjects of the most favored nation, and to which they are entitled by treaty.

Article IV. The high contracting Powers having agreed upon the foregoing articles, whenever the Government of the United States shall adopt legislative measures in accordance therewith, such measures will be communicated to the Government of China. If the measures as enacted are found to work hardship upon the subjects of China, the Chinese Minister at Washington may bring the matter to the notice of the Secretary of State of the United States, who will consider the subject with him; and the Chinese Foreign Office may also bring the matter to the notice of the United States Minister at Peking and consider the subject with him, to the end that mutual and unqualified benefit may result.

II

LAWS RELATING TO THE ADMISSION OF CHINESE PROVIDING FOR THE ENFORCEMENT OF THE EXCLUSION TREATY WITH CHINA, May 6, 1882; Amended July 5, 1884[7]

WHEREAS, in the opinion of the Government of the United States the coming of Chinese laborers to this country endangers the good order of certain localities within the territory thereof: Therefore,

---

[7]   *Treaty, Laws, and Rules Governing Admission of Chinese: Rules of May 1, 1917* (Washington, DC: Government Printing Office, 1917), pp. 6–10.

Sec 2. . . . Be it enacted by the Senate and House of Representatives of the United States of America in Congress assembled, That from and after the passage of this act, and until the expiration of ten years next after the passage of this act, the coming of Chinese laborers to the United States be, and the same is hereby suspended, and during such suspension it shall not be lawful for any Chinese laborer to come from any foreign port or place, or having so come to remain within the United States.

Section two of said act is hereby amended so as to read as follows:

. . .

SEC. 14. That hereafter no State court or court of the United States shall admit Chinese to citizenship; and all laws in conflict with this act are hereby repealed.

PROHIBITING THE COMING OF CHINESE PERSONS INTO THE UNITED STATES AND PROVIDING FOR REGISTRATION OF RESIDENT LABORERS[8]

[Act of May 5, 1892 (27 Stat. L., 25)]

. . .

SEC. 2. That any Chinese person or person of Chinese descent, when convicted and adjudged under any of said laws to be not lawfully entitled to be or remain in the United States, shall be removed from the United States to China, unless he or they shall make it appear to the justice, judge, or commissioner before whom he or they are tried that he or they are subjects or citizens of some other country, in which case he or they shall be removed from the United States to such country: Provided, That in any case where such other country of which such Chinese person shall claim to be a citizen or subject shall demand any tax as a condition of the removal of such person to that country, he or she shall be removed to China.

SEC. 3. That any Chinese person or person of Chinese descent arrested under the provisions of this act or the acts hereby extended shall be adjudged to be unlawfully within the United States unless such person shall establish, by affirmative proof to the satisfaction of such justice, judge, or commissioner, his lawful right to remain. . . .

---

[8]   *Treaty, Laws, and Rules Governing Admission of Chinese*, pp. 13–16.

3 Samuel Bryan, "Mexican Americans and Southwestern Growth," 1912[9]

Two forces explain the origins of Mexican immigration to the United States in the late nineteenth and early twentieth centuries. The spread of American capitalism into the southwestern region acquired by the United States following the Mexican War transformed that region. A number of factors contributed to this economic activity, among them the rise of mining, ranching, and large-scale agriculture in the region. Contributing to the rise of these industries were the completion of the transcontinental railroad, the application of new technology to mining, and the Newlands Reclamation Act of 1902, which provided federal money for agricultural irrigation projects. These developments created a demand for a large low-paid labor force. Because the United States had acquired the northern half of Mexico in the Treaty of Guadalupe Hidalgo at the end of the Mexican War, there were already a large number of Mexican Americans living in the new territory.

Because the Newlands Act also specifically outlawed the use of "Mongolian" (i.e., Chinese) labor on its irrigation projects, the stage was set for an increasing demand for Mexican labor. A second interpretation focuses on the destabilizing effect on Mexico of the Mexican Revolution of 1910. The revolution created upheaval in Mexican society and in its economy and pushed Mexicans out of the country to seek stability and employment. Between 1910 and 1921, more than 1,500,000 Mexicans came to the United States looking for work, significantly increasing the existing Mexican American population and creating the social and economic network that became the basis for waves of immigrants from Mexico through the twentieth century and into the twenty-first.

In the following article, Samuel Bryan, an economist at Stanford University, supported the first theory, which emphasized the "pull" effects of the American economy rather than the "push" of problems in Mexico. However, at the time of the article's publication, the complete effect of the Mexican Revolution had not yet been felt in the United States.

Comparatively few people in the United States have any conception of the extent to which Mexicans are entering this country each year, of their geographical distribution, or of their relative importance in the various industries in which they are employed after their arrival. Nor are the social problems resulting from the influx of Mexicans fully appreciated by many persons who are not acquainted with the situation at first hand. This is

[9]   *The Survey* XXVIII (September 1912): 726–30.

primarily because the attention of students of the race problem has been focused upon the more important development of European and eastern Asiatic immigration to the eastern states, and upon Chinese, Japanese, and East Indian immigration to the Pacific coast. Other factors in diverting attention from Mexican immigration have been the relatively non-competitive character of their employment in certain parts of the country, and the lack of adequate data with regard to their numbers.

Previous to 1900 the influx of Mexicans was comparatively unimportant. It was confined almost exclusively to those portions of Texas, New Mexico, Arizona, and California which are near the boundary line between Mexico and the United States. Since these states were formerly Mexican territory and have always possessed a considerable Mexican population, a limited migration back and forth across the border was a perfectly natural result of the existing blood relationship. During the period from 1880 to 1900 the Mexican-born population of these border states increased from 66,312 to 99,969—a gain of 33,657 in twenty years. This increase was not sufficient to keep pace with the growth of the total population of the states. Since 1900, however, there has been a rapid increase in the volume of Mexican immigration, and also some change in its geographical distribution, with the result that distinct social and economic problems have arisen.

Until 1908 the officials of the Bureau of Immigration who were stationed upon the Mexican border concerned themselves chiefly with the examination of Japanese and Syrians who sought to enter this country by the way of Mexico. Since that time some effort has been made to secure data with regard to immigrants of Mexican birth, but the results obtained are so obviously incomplete as to be of little value. In 1908 it was estimated that from 60,000 to 100,000 Mexicans entered the United States each year. This estimate, however, should be modified by the well known fact that each year a considerable number of Mexicans return to Mexico. Approximately 50 per cent of those Mexicans who find employment as section hands upon the railroads claim the free transportation back to El Paso which is furnished by the railroad companies to those who have been in their employ six months or a year. Making allowance for this fact, it would be conservative to place the yearly accretion of population by Mexican immigration at from 5,000 to 70,000. It is probable, therefore, that the Mexican-born population of the United States has trebled since the census of 1900 was taken.

This rapid increase within the last decade has resulted from the expansion of industry both in Mexico and in the United States. In this country the industrial development of the Southwest has opened up wider fields of employment for unskilled laborers in transportation, agriculture, mining, and smelting. A similar expansion in northern Mexico has drawn many

Mexican laborers from the farms of other sections of the country farther removed from the border, and it is an easy matter to go from the mines and section gangs of northern Mexico to the more remunerative employment to be had in similar industries of the southwestern United States. Thus the movement from the more remote districts of Mexico to the newly developed industries of the North has become largely a stage in a more general movement to the United States. Entrance into this country is not difficult, for employment agencies in normal times have stood ready to advance board, lodging, and transportation to a place where work was to be had, and the immigration officials have usually deemed no Mexican likely to become a public charge so long as this was the case. This was especially true before 1908. Thus many penniless Mexicans who would be rejected at an eastern port have been admitted without question on the Mexican border.

The employment agencies are well organized and supply a large number of immigrants to the various railroad companies operating in the Southwest, and to employers in other industries. The more important agencies are located at El Paso, Texas. One of the larger companies supplied from there no fewer than 6,474 Mexican laborers to four railroad companies during the period between January and September, 1907. During eight months falling in the latter half of 1907 and the early part of 1908, six employment agencies operating in El Paso supplied 16,479 Mexicans to the various railroad companies, or an average of 2,060 per month. These supply companies have been in existence from one to five years and report a fairly constant business during that time.

The profits in the business are derived primarily from supplying board to the laborers *en route* to their place of employment, and from the sale of food and merchandise to them while at work. Charges for such services and sales are deducted in favor of the employment agencies by the employers from the first wages earned by the men. In addition an employment fee of $1.00 per man is ordinarily charged. In cases of desertion before enough money has been earned to offset the debts due the agencies, the loss is borne by the latter. The supply companies use such losses to justify the higher prices charged, at the commissary stores, which in some instances are admittedly fixed at from 5 to 10 per cent in excess of the ordinary retail rates.

Transportation to points where laborers are needed is furnished by the railroad companies, and also, as a rule, by other industrial concerns which secure Mexicans in considerable numbers from the employment agencies. The railroad companies agree further to return the men to the Mexican border free of charge after they have worked six months (on the Santa Fe) or a year (on the Southern Pacific). Since most of the Mexican immigrants expect to return to Mexico, and since they are too improvident to save enough from their earnings to pay for their transportation back to the border, this offer is very attractive to them, and enables the railroad companies to hold their employees of this race at lower wages than are customary in other industries of the same locality. Some Mexicans, however, do desert railroad work when especially attractive employment offers elsewhere, as for example in the harvest fields of Kansas and Oklahoma, or the sugar-beet fields of southern California.

Most of the Mexican immigrants have at one time been employed as railroad laborers. At present they are used chiefly as section hands and as members of construction gangs, but a number are also to be found working as common-laborers about the shops and powerhouses. Although a considerable number are employed as helpers, few have risen above unskilled labor in any branch of the railroad service. As section hands on the two more important systems they were paid a uniform wage of $1 per day from their first employment in 1902 until 1909, except for a period of about one year previous to the financial stringency of 1907, when they were paid $1.25 per day. In 1909 the wages of all Mexican section hands employed upon the Santa Fe lines were again raised to $1.25 per day. The significant feature is, however, that as a general rule they have earned less than the members of any other race similarly-employed. For example, of 2,455 Mexican section hands from whom data were secured by the Immigration Commission in 1908 and 1909, 2,111, or 85.9 per cent, were earning less than $1.25 per day, while the majority of the Greeks, Italians, and Japanese earned more than $1.25 and a considerable number more than $1.50 per day.

In the arid regions of the border states where they have always been employed and where the majority of them still live, the Mexicans come into little direct competition with other races, and no problems of importance result from their presence. But within the last decade their area of employment has expanded greatly. They are now used as section hands as far east as Chicago and as far north as Wyoming. Moreover, they are now employed to a considerable extent in the coal mines of Colorado and New Mexico, in the ore mines of Colorado and Arizona, in the smelters of Arizona, in the cement factories of Colorado and California, in the beet-sugar industry of the last mentioned states, and in fruit growing and canning in California. In these localities they have at many points come into direct competition with other races, and their low stand-ards have acted as a check upon the progress of the more assertive of these.

Where they are employed in other industries, the same wage discrimination against them as was noted in the case of railroad employees is generally apparent where the work is done on an hour basis, but no discrimination exists in the matter of rates for piece-work. As piece-workers in the fruit canneries and in the sugar-beet industry the proverbial sluggishness of the Mexicans prevents them from earning as much as the members of other races. In the citrus fruit industry their treatment varies with the locality. In some instances they are paid the same as the "whites"—in others the same as the Japanese, according to the class with which they share the field of employment. The data gathered by the Immigration Commission show that although the earnings of Mexicans employed in the other industries are somewhat higher than those of the Mexican section hands, they are with few exceptions noticeably lower than the earnings of Japanese, Italians, and members of the various Slavic races who are similarly employed. This is true in the case of smelting, ore mining, coal mining, and sugar refining. Specific instances of the use of Mexicans to curb the demands of other races are found in the sugar-beet industry of central California, where they were introduced for the purpose of showing the Japanese laborers that they were not indispensable, and in the same industry in Colorado, where they were used in a similar way against the German-Russians. Moreover, Mexicans have been employed as strike-breakers in the coal mines of Colorado and New Mexico, and in one instance in the shops of one important railroad system.

Socially and politically the presence of large numbers of Mexicans in this country gives rise to serious problems. The reports of the Immigration Commission show that they lack ambition, are to a very large extent illiterate in their native language, are slow to learn English, and in most cases show no political interest. In some instances, however, they have been organized to serve the purposes of political bosses, as for example in Phoenix, Arizona. Although more of them are married and have their families with them than is the case among the south European immigrants, they are unsettled as a class, move readily from place to place, and do not acquire or lease land to any extent. But their most unfavorable characteristic is their inclination to form colonies and live in a clannish manner. Wherever a considerable group of Mexicans are employed, they live together, if possible, and associate very little with members of other races. In the mining towns and other small industrial communities they live ordinarily in rude adobe huts outside of the town limits. As section hands they of course live as the members of the other races have done, in freight cars fitted with windows and bunks, or in rough shacks along the line of the railroad. In the cities their colonization has become a menace. The unwholesome conditions of the Mexican quarter in El Paso, Tex., have been described with photographic illustrations in previous articles in The Survey. In Los Angeles the housing problem centers largely in the cleaning up or demolition of the Mexican "house courts," which have become the breeding ground of disease and crime, and which have now attracted a considerable population of immigrants of other races. It is estimated that approximately 2,000 Mexicans are living in these "house courts." Some 15,000 persons of this race are residents of Los Angeles and vicinity. Conditions of life among the immigrants of the city, which are moulded to a certain extent by Mexican standards, have been materially improved by the work of the Los Angeles Housing Commission, upon which Johanna Von Wagner has served as an expert social worker. However, the Mexican quarter continues to offer a serious social problem to the community.

As is to be expected under the circumstances, the proportion of criminals and paupers among the Mexicans is noticeably greater than among the other foreign-born or among the natives. In Los Angeles County, California, the Mexicans comprised 11.4 per cent of the total number of persons bound over for felonies in 1907. In 1908 and 1909 the percentages were 12.6 and 13.4 respectively. During the year ending July 1, 1908, the chief of police of Los Angeles estimates that approximately 20,000 police cases were handled, in 2,357 or 8 per cent of which Mexicans were the defendants. In Arizona, where the proportion of Mexicans to the total population is greater than in Los Angeles, a correspondingly large proportion of the inmates of the various penal institutions are of this race. In 1908, 24.2 per cent of the prisoners in the jail at Tucson, Ariz., were Mexicans, while in the Pima county jail they comprised 62 per cent of the inmates. The territorial prison reported in the same year that 61 per cent of those incarcerated were Mexicans. In both Arizona and California the offenses for which they were committed were in the large majority of cases traceable to gambling or excessive drinking. Most of the serious trouble with Mexicans, however, arises from quarrels among themselves which interfere very little with the white population.

In the matter of poor relief, Mexican families were concerned in 11.7 per cent of the cases dealt with by the Associated Charities of Los Angeles in 1908. The proportion has increased since that time, and in 1910 it was estimated that Mexicans comprised fully one-third of those given relief from this source. The county authorities had charge of approximately 3,000 individuals in 1908, of whom about one-third were Mexicans. The proportion of Mexicans among those dependent upon the County Board of Charities has continued about the same, for in the month of November, 1910, which was said to be typical of that year, 30.1 per cent of the applications for aid were made by members of that race.

In conclusion it should be recognized that although the Mexicans have proved to be efficient laborers in certain industries, and have afforded a cheap and elastic labor supply for the southwestern United States, the evils to the community at large which their presence in large numbers almost invariably brings may more than overbalance their desirable qualities. Their low standards of living and of morals, their illiteracy, their utter lack of proper political interest, the retarding effect of their employment upon the wage scale of the more progressive races, and finally their tendency to colonize in urban centers, with evil results, combine to stamp them as a rather undesirable class of residents.

4 Jacob Riis, Photographs from *How the Other Half Lives*, 1890[10]

Jacob Riis (1849–1914) was born in Denmark and in 1870 immigrated to the United States. After several years of struggling to find steady work, he was hired to work for a news bureau and a small Brooklyn newspaper before employment as a police reporter by the New York Tribune *in 1877. Using his first-hand knowledge of poverty to communicate his belief that the poor were the victims and not the creators of their fate, he turned to photojournalism as his medium. As one of the first photographers to use flash powder, he was able to take photographs of night scenes and the interiors of homes and factories in order to show vividly the living and working conditions of New York's poor. In 1889, Scribner's Magazine published an important piece by Riis on city life, and the piece was expanded in 1890 into a full-length book entitled* How the Other Half Lives.

Until the end of his life, Riis continued to lecture and write about the conditions of America's poor. He had to counter the prevailing opinion that poverty was caused by individual moral weakness. In his opinion, his role as a reformer was to inform middle- and upper-class citizens about the problems of the poor and then to explain that it was the responsibility of these wealthier members of the community to support charities and municipal actions that would improve the lives of those living in poverty.

---

[10] *How the Other Half Lives* (New York: Charles Scribner's Sons, 1890).

Figure 7.1   Hester Street, New York, 1890. From Jacob A. Riis, *How the Other Half Lives*, 1890 (New York: Dover Publications, 1971), p. 84.
Source: Photograph by Jacob A. Riis, Library of Congress, Prints and Photographs Division.

Figure 7.2   Sweatshop in Ludlow Street Tenement, New York, 1889. From Jacob A. Riis, *How the Other Half Lives*, 1890 (New York: Dover Publications, 1971), p. 96.
Source: Photograph by Jacob A. Riis, Library of Congress, Prints and Photographs Division.

5   Theodore Roosevelt, Hyphenated Americanism, 1915[11]

From the 1890s until the early 1920s, the term "hyphenated American" was used as a derogatory description of immigrant Americans who retained strong loyalties to their native countries, particularly Irish-Americans and German-Americans during World War I. Both Theodore Roosevelt and Woodrow Wilson applied this term to those they believed did not have as their primary goal the best interests of the American republic.

---

[11]   October 12, 1915, address to the Knights of Columbus, Carnegie Hall, New York City.

The following speech, delivered to the Irish-American, Catholic group Knights of Columbus, has been used up to the present day by conservative and nativist Americans who disagree with growing multiculturalism, ethnic identity, and immigration in American society. Historians have disagreed over the intent of Roosevelt's speech and have used it to justify nationalism and anti-immigrant sentiments, as well as to confirm the view that Roosevelt was a racist who opposed immigration to the United States by non-Europeans, particularly Asians.

There is no room in this country for hyphenated Americanism. When I refer to hyphenated Americans, I do not refer to naturalized Americans. Some of the very best Americans I have ever known were naturalized Americans, Americans born abroad. But a hyphenated American is not an American at all. This is just as true of the man who puts "native" before the hyphen as of the man who puts German or Irish or English or French before the hyphen. Americanism is a matter of the spirit and of the soul. Our allegiance must be purely to the United States. We must unsparingly condemn any man who holds any other allegiance. But if he is heartily and singly loyal to this Republic, then no matter where he was born, he is just as good an American as any one else.

The one absolutely certain way of bringing this nation to ruin, of preventing all possibility of its continuing to be a nation at all, would be to permit it to become a tangle of squabbling nationalities, an intricate knot of German-Americans, Irish-Americans, English-Americans, French-Americans, Scandinavian-Americans or Italian-Americans, each preserving its separate nationality, each at heart feeling more sympathy with Europeans of that nationality, than with the other citizens of the American Republic. The men who do not become Americans and nothing else are hyphenated Americans; and there ought to be no room for them in this country. The man who calls himself an American citizen and who yet shows by his actions that he is primarily the citizen of a foreign land, plays a thoroughly mischievous part in the life of our body politic. He has no place here; and the sooner he returns to the land to which he feels his real heart-allegiance, the better it will be for every good American. There is no such thing as a hyphenated American who is a good American. The only man who is a good American is the man who is an American and nothing else.

For an American citizen to vote as a German-American, an Irish-American, or an English-American, is to be a traitor to American institutions; and those hyphenated Americans who terrorize American politicians by threats of the foreign vote are engaged in treason to the American Republic.

Americanization

The foreign-born population of this country must be an Americanized population—no other kind can fight the battles of America either in war or peace. It must talk the language of its native-born fellow-citizens, it must possess American citizenship and American ideals. It must stand firm by its oath of allegiance in word and deed and must show that in very fact it has renounced allegiance to every prince, potentate, or foreign government. It must be maintained on an American standard of living so as to prevent labor disturbances in important plants and at critical times. None of these objects can be secured as long as we have immigrant colonies, ghettos, and immigrant sections, and above all they cannot be assured so long as we consider the immigrant only as an industrial asset. The immigrant must not be allowed to drift or to be put at the mercy of the exploiter. Our object is not to imitate one of the older racial types, but to maintain a new American type and then to secure loyalty to this type. We cannot secure such loyalty unless we make this a country where men shall feel that they have justice and also where they shall feel that they are required to perform the duties imposed upon them. The policy of "Let alone" which we have hitherto pursued is thoroughly vicious from two stand-points. By this policy we have permitted the immigrants, and too often the native-born laborers as well, to suffer injustice. Moreover, by this policy we have failed to impress upon the immigrant and upon the native-born as well that they are expected to do justice as well as to receive justice, that they are expected to be heartily and actively and single-mindedly loyal to the flag no less than to benefit by living under it.

We cannot afford to continue to use hundreds of thousands of immigrants merely as industrial assets while they remain social outcasts and menaces any more than fifty years ago we could afford to keep the black man merely as an industrial asset and not as a human being. We cannot afford to build a big industrial plant and herd men and women about it without care for their welfare. We cannot afford to permit squalid overcrowding or the kind of living system which makes impossible the decencies and necessities of life. We cannot afford the low wage rates and the merely seasonal industries which mean the sacrifice of both individual and family life and morals to the industrial machinery. We cannot afford to leave American mines, munitions plants, and general resources in the hands of alien workmen, alien to America and even likely to be made hostile to America by machinations such as have recently been provided in the case of the two foreign embassies in Washington. We cannot afford to run the risk of having in time of war men working on our railways or working in our munition plants who would in the name of duty to their own foreign countries bring destruction to us. Recent events have shown us that incitements to sabotage and strikes are in the view of at least two of the great foreign powers of Europe within their definition of neutral practices. What would be done to us in the name of war if these things are done to us in the name of neutrality?

One America

All of us, no matter from what land our parents came, no matter in what way we may severally worship our Creator, must stand shoulder to shoulder in a united America for the elimination of race and religious prejudice. We must stand for a reign of equal justice to both big and small. We must insist on the maintenance of the American standard of living. We must stand for an adequate national control which shall secure a better training of our young men in time of peace, both for the work of peace and for the work of war. We must direct every national resource, material and spiritual, to the task not of shirking difficulties, but of training our people to overcome difficulties. Our aim must be, not to make life easy and soft, not to soften soul and body, but to fit us in virile fashion to do a great work for all mankind. This great work can only be done by a mighty democracy, with these qualities of soul, guided by those qualities of mind, which will both make it refuse to do injustice to any other nation, and also enable it to hold its own against aggression by any other nation. In our relations with the outside world, we must abhor wrongdoing, and disdain to commit it, and we must no less disdain the baseness of spirit which lamely submits to wrongdoing. Finally and most important of all, we must strive for the establishment within our own borders of that stern and lofty standard of personal and public neutrality which shall guarantee to each man his rights, and which shall insist in return upon the full performance by each man of his duties both to his neighbor and to the great nation whose flag must symbolize in the future as it has symbolized in the past the highest hopes of all mankind.

6 The Emergence of Reform Judaism, 1883 and 1885[12]

In the late nineteenth century, Reform Judaism became a way for Jews to acculturate to the prevailing Christian culture. In German, Reform Jews changed traditional practices of worship and belief by adopting innovations such as the music of cantors, changing the practice of the Sabbath, and mixing the seating of males and females. In some instances, they also abandoned circumcision, removed Hebrew from the liturgy, and altered bar mitzvah practices. Reform Judaism proved especially popular in the United States after the middle of the nineteenth century, and over 90 percent of Jewish congregations were Reformed by 1880.

In one of the earliest statements of Reform faith and practice, the Pittsburgh Conference brought together Reform rabbis from around the United States. Among the most important of the leaders of this movement was Isaac Mayer Wise (1819–1900), who immigrated to the United States from Bohemia and spent 46 years as rabbi of the Lodge Street Synagogue in Cincinnati, Ohio.

Declaration of Principles, 1885 Pittsburgh Conference

Convening at the call of Kaufmann Kohler of New York, Reform rabbis from around the United States met from November 16 through November 19, 1885 with Isaac Mayer Wise presiding. The meeting was declared the continuation of the Philadelphia Conference of 1869, which was the continuation of the German Conference of 1841 to 1846. The rabbis adopted the following seminal text:

1. We recognize in every religion an attempt to grasp the Infinite, and in every mode, source or book of revelation held sacred in any religious system the consciousness of the indwelling of God in man. We hold that Judaism presents the highest conception of the God-idea as taught in our Holy Scriptures and developed and spiritualized by the Jewish teachers, in accordance with the moral and philosophical progress of their respective ages. We maintain that Judaism preserved and defended midst continual struggles and trials and under enforced isolation, this God-idea as the central religious truth for the human race.

12   http://people.ucalgary.ca/~elsegal/363_Transp/PittsburgPlatform.html; Isaac Mayer Wise, *Judaism and Christianity: Their Agreements and Disagreements* (Cincinnati, OH: Block & Co., 1883), pp. 3–9.

2. We recognize in the Bible the record of the consecration of the Jewish people to its mission as the priest of the one God, and value it as the most potent instrument of religious and moral instruction. We hold that the modern discoveries of scientific researches in the domain of nature and history are not antagonistic to the doctrines of Judaism, the Bible reflecting the primitive ideas of its own age, and at times clothing its conception of divine Providence and Justice dealing with men in miraculous narratives.

3. We recognize in the Mosaic legislation a system of training the Jewish people for its mission during its national life in Palestine, and today we accept as binding only its moral laws, and maintain only such ceremonies as elevate and sanctify our lives, but reject all such as are not adapted to the views and habits of modern civilization.

4. We hold that all such Mosaic and rabbinical laws as regulate diet, priestly purity, and dress originated in ages and under the influence of ideas entirely foreign to our present mental and spiritual state. They fail to impress the modern Jew with a spirit of priestly holiness; their observance in our days is apt rather to obstruct than to further modern spiritual elevation.

5. We recognize, in the modern era of universal culture of heart and intellect, the approaching of the realization of Israel s great Messianic hope for the establishment of the kingdom of truth, justice, and peace among all men. We consider ourselves no longer a nation, but a religious community, and therefore expect neither a return to Palestine, nor a sacrificial worship under the sons of Aaron, nor the restoration of any of the laws concerning the Jewish state.

6. We recognize in Judaism a progressive religion, ever striving to be in accord with the postulates of reason. We are convinced of the utmost necessity of preserving the historical identity with our great past. Christianity and Islam, being daughter religions of Judaism, we appreciate their providential mission, to aid in the spreading of monotheistic and moral truth. We acknowledge that the spirit of broad humanity of our age is our ally in the fulfillment of our mission, and therefore we extend the hand of fellowship to all who cooperate with us in the establishment of the reign of truth and righteousness among men.

7. We reassert the doctrine of Judaism that the soul is immortal, grounding the belief on the divine nature of human spirit, which forever finds bliss in righteousness and misery in wickedness. We reject as ideas not rooted in Judaism, the beliefs both in bodily resurrection and in Gehenna and Eden (Hell and Paradise) as abodes for everlasting punishment and reward.

8. In full accordance with the spirit of the Mosaic legislation, which strives to regulate the relations between rich and poor, we deem it our duty to participate in the great task of modern times, to solve, on the basis of justice and righteousness, the problems presented by the contrasts and evils of the present organization of society.

Isaac Mayer Wise, *Judaism and Christianity* (1883)

The true religious belief, commonly called faith, must rest upon that conviction that our ideas of the objects of religion, like God, Providence, immortality, etc., are truthful representations of those objects in reality. This state of the mind can be reached by the reasoning process only.

This is the standpoint, ladies and gentlemen, which prompts us to reason on the religious beliefs which we or others may entertain. . . . This impresses us with the solemn lesson: Fear not the progress of science, dread not the discoveries of philosophy, be not terrified even by the necessity of advancing through error to truth, for truth is deathless, as God said to Moses, "This is my name forever, and this is my memorial from generation to generation"; and truth only can be the mother of true religion, while falsehood and fiction, however useful they may appear for the time being, are invariably the progenitors of degrading superstition and fanaticism. Be not alarmed if cherished beliefs examined under the light of free thought appear untenable, for there is no salvation in self delusion, as there is none in the *Fata Morgana* for the traveler in the wilderness. Truth redeems. Truth is the prince of peace. We seek truth. If priests maintain salvation comes by faith, the uninquired and thoughtless faith, the belief in dogmas, because they are absurd, they can not prove it, as none has returned from the realms of eternity to furnish them with the evidence. It is demonstrable, however, that truth redeems, it is demonstrable by the peace and good-will, the prosperity and happiness which it brings to man on earth.

 . . . .Thank Heaven we are in America, and in Cincinnati, where free thought and free speech are the birthright of every law-abiding person. Speech and arguments govern the community, and personal liberty is esteemed as man's most precious boon. Thank Heaven that we live in an age and a country in which bigotry and fanaticism are subjected to the scepter of justice and reason, and have learned the art of moderation. Now and here, it is possible to discuss fairly any important subject, and none is more important than religion, which is after all the motive power of individual volitions, and the character of the generality. Now and here it is proper to compare and review Judaism and Christianity, their agreements and disagreements, at the electric light of reason; to criticise and expose errors with the apparatus of logic; to praise and recommend, whatever may be found praiseworthy and recommendable, without prejudice or fanaticism ; to reconcile and unite, wherever conciliation is admissible and unification possible; to attack error and advance truth without malice, scorn or any unnecessary offense; to contribute a man's share to the dominion of peace and good will by a mutual better understanding of our intentions, aims and objects.

Whoever is afraid of the two-edged sword of truth and the cold steel of logic, is not expected to listen to these lectures. We say the two-edged sword, and mean what we say; for we will have to cut into both Judaism and Christianity, as there are old sores in each system which must be cut, now or later, and will be cut and healed by the world's steady progress, whether we recognize them or not. Whatever can not stand the rigid application of reason is doomed to perish. Whatever is in the way of the unity and fraternity of the human family will be overthrown. Whatever is unkind, uncharitable, ungenerous, intolerant, illiberal or unfree can not last much longer in our country. . . .

It would be in its place here to give definitions of Judaism and Christianity, and I would gladly do so if anybody could define those generic terms to the satisfaction of the majority of their votaries. That which is in a continuous state of evolution can not be fixed or limited by any definition. Judaism always was in a state of evolution, as must be evident to any observer of large periods thereof. The Judaism from and after Moses was not the same as the Judaism from and after Samuel and David; nor was the Judaism of the first Hebrew Common wealth identical with that of the second Commonwealth; so before and after the close of the Talmud; before and after the casuists had written; before and after the Spanish school, and so on to our days, Judaism changed.

The same precisely is the case with Christianity. From and after Jesus and the original Apostles; from and after Paul of Tarsus; from and after John the Evangelist; from and after the Council of Nice, the establishment of the Roman and Greek Churches; from and after the Councils and scholasts of the Middle Ages; from and after the Reformation—and so on to our days, Christianity changed and changes yet, so that every now and then a new sect springs into existence. You can not define that which admits of no definition, to cover the whole subject. At this very moment, take the past out of the consideration, it is impossible to furnish an adequate definition of either Judaism or Christianity. You send down to Longworth Street, where a small congregation of Russian orthodox Jews meet, and ask of that body, as of our friends over yonder in Lodge Street, a definition of Judaism. They let you have it to the best of their knowledge, and you read it to any of our temple congregations here, or in St. Louis, Chicago or New York, or elsewhere, and you will be frankly told that is not Judaism. Go across the street to the Roman Catholic prelate, or there to the Unitarian pastor; ask our German pastors, and then our Puritan preachers, to define Christianity for you; then compare notes, and you will find that none has given you an exact definition of Christianity, because none could do it to the satisfaction of all. There must be something wrong in all those systems, something not in harmony with reason and logic, or else the definitions must be identical, as every scientist could tell what is geometry, what is chemistry, what is physics, and so on with all the sciences. Therefore, I will not now define what is Judaism or what is Christianity. I must first investigate the elements essential to either, and then define.

In some of those essential elements Judaism and Christianity agree, are almost identical; in others, however, they differ. We will review first the "agreements," as one of my excellent friends once advised me. He said: "If you should ever feel compelled to quarrel with any neighbor about some disputed point, begin with the attempt of ascertaining in what points you agree; that matter settled, then speak of the disputed point, and in nine cases out of ten you will be astonished to discover that you did not essentially disagree at all.

Discussion Questions: Chapter 7

1   How did immigrants adapt to American society? How did different groups, such as Jews and Italians, deal with the new cultural environment and with the hostility of native-born Americans?
2   What was Teddy Roosevelt's view of immigrants?
3   According to Wise, what challenges faced Jews and Christians in America?

Part III   Social Conflict

Chapter 8   Populism

1 Annie L. Diggs, "The Women in the Alliance Movement," 1892[1]

*When both agricultural conditions and prices declined in the years following
the Civil War, farmers in the South and on the Great Plains began to organize
to promote cooperative warehouses for their crops and to protest monopolies
by the railroads and financial institutions. Starting in Texas, the Farmers'
Alliance quickly spread throughout the South and north into Kansas and
Nebraska. Women were encouraged to become actively involved in the
movement.*

*In her role as a writer and activist from Kansas, Annie L. Diggs
(1848–1916) supported both women's rights and the Populist movement. She
toured the country in 1892 to promote the platform of the national Populist
(People's) party. Heavily involved in the civic life of Kansas, she became
president of both the Kansas Women's Free Silver League and Kansas Equal
Suffrage Association, was appointed Kansas State Librarian, and was elected
president of the Kansas Press Women. In 1882, Diggs and her husband
began publishing the* Kansas Liberal, *a newspaper dedicated to criticizing the
power of the wealthy and supporting a fair chance for farmers and working
people to succeed. Along with her fellow Populist orator, Mary Lease, Diggs
proved that women could be influential political activists.*

*Woman suffrage was an important component of the Populist platform, as
reformers realized that farmers would achieve political power only if women*

---

[1]   *The Arena* 6 (July 1892): 161–79.

The Gilded Age and Progressive Era: A Documentary Reader, First Edition.
Edited by William A. Link and Susannah J. Link.
© 2012 Blackwell Publishing Ltd. Published 2012 by Blackwell Publishing Ltd.

could vote as well. Kansas defeated a woman suffrage referendum in 1894,
but finally granted women full suffrage in 1912.

The women prominent in the great farmer manifesto of this present time were long preparing for their part; not consciously, not by any manner of means even divining that there would be a part to play. In the many thousands of isolated farm homes the early morning, the noonday and the evening-time work went on with a dreary monotony which resulted in that startling report of the physicians that American farms were recruiting stations from whence more women went to insane asylums than from any other walk in life.

Farm life for women is a treadmill. The eternal climb must be kept -up though the altitude never heightens. For more than a quarter of a century these churning, washing, ironing, baking, darning, sewing, cooking, scrubbing, drudging women, whose toilsome, dreary lives were unrelieved by the slight incident or by-play of town life, felt that their treadmills slipped cogs. Climb as they would, they slipped—down two steps while they climbed one. They were not keeping pace with the women of the towns and cities. The industry which once led in the march toward independence and prosperity, was steadily falling behind as to remuneration. Something was wrong.

The Grange came on—a most noble order, of untold service and solace to erstwhile cheerless lives. Pathetic the heart-hunger for the beauty side of life. The Grange blossomed forth in "Floras" and "Pomonas."[2] There was a season of sociability, with much good cookery, enchanting Jellies, ethereal angel cakes, and flower-decked tables. There was much burnishing of bright-witted women—not always listeners, often essayists. Sometimes, indeed, leaders of discussion and earnest talk about middlemen, the home market, the railroad problem, and such other matters as would have shed light on the cause of the farmer's declining prosperity had not wary politicians sniffed danger, and, under specious pretence of "keeping out politics lest it kill the Grange," tabooed free speech and thus adroitly injected the fatalest of policies. The Grange is dead. Long live the Grange born again—the Alliance! This time not to be frightened out of politics or choked of utterance; born this time to do far more than talk—to vote.

The Granger sisters through the intervening years, climbing laboriously, patiently, felt their treadmill cogs a slipping three steps down to one step up. Reincarnate in the Alliance the whilom[3] Floras and Pomonas became

---

[2] Pomona was the Roman goddess of plenty; Flora the Roman goddess of flowers and spring.
[3] Archaic word for "formerly."

secretaries and lecturers. The worn and weary treadmillers are anxious, troubled. They have no heart for poetry or play. Life is work unremitting. There is no time for ransacking of heathen mythologies for fashions with which to trig out modern goddesses. Instead of mythologic lore, they read "Seven Financial Conspiracies," "Looking Backward," "Progress and Poverty." Alas! of this last word they know much and fear more—fear for their children's future. These once frolicking Floras and playful Pomonas turn with all the fierceness of the primal mother-nature to protect their younglings from devouring, devastating plutocracy.

Politics for the farmer had been recreation, relaxation, or even exhilaration, according to the varying degree of his interest, or of honor flatteringly bestowed by town committeemen upon a "solid yeoman" at caucus or convention. The flush of pride over being selected to make a nominating speech, or the sense of importance consequent upon being placed on a resolution committee to acquiesce in the prepared document conveniently at hand— these high honors lightened much muddy plowing and hot harvest work.

But the farmers' wives participated in no such ecstacies. Hence for them no blinding party ties. And therefore when investigation turned on the light, the women spoke right out in meeting, demanding explanation for the non-appearance of the home market for the farm products, which their good husbands had been prophesying and promising would follow the upbuilding of protected industries. These women in the Alliance, grown apt in keeping close accounts from long economy, cast eyes over the long account of promises of officials managing public business, and said, "Promise and performance do not balance." "Of what value are convention honors, or even elected eloquence in national Capitol, if homelessness must be our children's heritage?"

Carlyle's Menads,[4] hungrier than American women are as yet, penetrated the French Assembly "to the shamefulest interruption of public speaking" with cries of, "*Du pain! pas tant de longs discours!*" Our Alliance women spake the same in English: "Bread! not so much discoursing! less eloquence and more justice!"

Strangely enough, the women of the South, where women, and men's thought about women, are most conservative, were first to go into the Alliance, and in many instances were most clear of thought and vigorous of speech. Though never venturing upon the platform, they contributed much to the inspiration and tenacity of the Alliance.

In several states, notably Texas, Georgia, Michigan, California, Colorado, and Nebraska, women have been useful and prominent in the farmer

---

[4] English historian Thomas Carlyle, in his *The French Revolution* (1837), describes the Menads, a group that helped storm the Bastille and launch the French Revolution.

movement, which indeed is now widened and blended with the cause of labor other than that of the farm.

Kansas, however, furnished by far the largest quota of Active, aggressive women, inasmuch as Kansas was the theatre where the initial act of the great labor drama was played. This drama, which, please God, must not grow into tragedy, is fully set on the world stage, and the curtain will never ring down nor the lights be turned off, until there be ushered in the eternal era of justice to the men and women who toil.

The great political victory of the people of Kansas would not have been won without the help of the women of the Alliance. Women who never dreamed of becoming public speakers grew eloquent in their zeal and fervor. Farmers' wives and daughters rose earlier and worked later to gain time to cook the picnic dinners, to paint the mottoes on the banners, to practice with the glee clubs, to march in procession. Josh Billings' saying that "wimmin is everywhere," was literally true in that wonderful picnicking, speech-making Alliance summer of 1890.

Kansas politics was no longer "dirty pool." That marvelous campaign was a great thrilling crusade. It was religious to the core. Instinctively the women knew that the salvation of their homes, and more even, the salvation of the republic, depended upon the outcome of that test struggle. Every word, every thought, every act, was a prayer for victory, and for the triumph of light. Victory was compelled to come.

Narrow ignoramuses long ago stumbled upon the truth. "The home is woman's sphere." Ignoramus said, "Women should cook and gossip, and rock cradles, and darn socks"—merely these and nothing more. Whereas the whole truth is, women should watch and work in all things which shape and mould the home, whether "money," "land" or "transportation." So now Alliance women look at politics and trace the swift relation to the home—their special sphere. They say, "Our homes are threatened by the dirty pool. The pool must go."

Before this question of the salvation of the imperiled homes of the nation, all other questions, whether of "prohibition" or "suffrage," pale into relative inconsequence. For where shall temperance or high thought of franchise be taught the children, by whose breath the world is saved, if sacred hearth fires shall go out? The overtopping, all-embracing moral question of the age is this for which the Alliance came. Upon such great ethical foundation is the labor movement of to-day building itself. How could women do otherwise than be in and of it?

Easily first among the Kansas women who rose to prominence, as a platform speaker for the political party which grew out of the Alliance, is Mrs. Mary E. Lease.

An Irishwoman by birth, Mrs. Lease is typically fervid, impulsive, and heroic. All the hatred of oppression and scorn of oppressors, which every true son and daughter of Erin feels, found vent in Mrs. Lease's public utterances as she denounced the greedy governing class which has grown rich and powerful at the expense of the impoverished and helpless multitude.

Mrs. Lease came to America when quite a little girl. Her father went into the Union army and died at Andersonville. She was educated a Catholic, but thought herself out of that communion, and is now not over-weighted with reverence for the clergy of any sect. She not infrequently rouses their ire by her stinging taunts as to their divergence from the path marked out by their professed Master, whose first concern was for the poor and needy.

Mrs. Lease's home is at Wichita, Kan. Her husband is a pharmacist. Her children are exceptionally bright and lovely. Her eldest son, grown to young manhood, bids fair to follow his distinguished mother on the platform.

A most trying experience of farm life on a Western claim taught Mrs. Lease the inside story of the farmers' declining prosperity. Turning from unprofitable farming, she began the study of law, in which she was engaged when the Union Labor campaign of 1888 claimed her services as a speaker. During this campaign she only gained a local notoriety. Further study, larger opportunity, and the bugle call of the Alliance movement roused her latent powers, and in the campaign of 1890 she made speeches so full of fiery eloquence, of righteous wrath, and fierce denunciation of the oppressors and betrayers of the people, that she became the delight of the people of the new party, and the detestation of the followers of the old. Seldom, if ever, was a woman so vilified and so misrepresented by malignant newspaper attacks. A woman of other quality would have sunk under the avalanche. She was quite competent to cope with all that was visited upon her. Indeed, the abuse did her much service. The people but loved her the more for the enemies she made.

Her career on the public platform since that memorable campaign has been one of uninterrupted and unparalleled success. Her chiefest distinguishing gift is her powerful voice; deep and resonant, its effect is startling and controlling. Her speeches are philippics. She hurls sentences as Jove hurled thunderbolts. Her personal appearance upon the platform is most commanding. She is tall and stately in bearing, well meriting the title bestowed upon her at St. Louis by General Weaver, when he introduced her to a wildly welcoming audience as "Our Queen Mary." Queen of women orators she truly is. She has the characteristic combination which marks the beautiful Irishwoman, of black hair, fair complexion, and blue eyes,—sad blue eyes that seem to see and feel the weight and woe of all the world.

Her style and subject matter of discourse are distinctively hers. She is neither classifiable nor comparable. Her torrent of speech is made up of terse, strong sentences. These she launches with resistless force at the defenceless head of whatever may be the objective point of her attack. Hers a nature which compels rather than persuades.

Already the story of the wondrous part she has played in the people's struggle for justice has reached other countries than our own.

Mrs. Lease will be constantly engaged in speaking for the People's Party through the coming summer and fall.

In the to-be-written history of this great epoch, Mrs. Mary E. Lease will have a most conspicuous place.[5]

. . .

Consider this Kansas record, oh supercilious sneerer at "strong-minded" women. Most of these women have opened their mouths and spake before many people; they have sat in counsel with bodies of men, among whom were their husbands and sons. And oh, Ultima Thule[6] of "un-womanliness," they have voted actually cast ballot, thereby saying in quietest of human way that virtue shall dethrone vice in municipal government. All these heretical things have they done, and yet are womanliest, gentlest of women, the best of homekeepers, the loyalest of wives, the carefulest of mothers.

What answer to this, oh, most bombastic cavilers—you who would shield woman from the demoralizing ballot? What answer, most ridiculous of theorists, who tremble lest any sort of man-made laws be mightier than nature's laws, who writhe lest statutes should change the loving, loyal mother-nature of woman? . . . .

Thus splendidly do the *facts* about women in politics refute the frivolous *theories* of timorous or hostile objectors. The women. Prominent as active, responsible factors in the political arena are those who are characterized by strong common sense, high ideals, and lofty patriotism. When such as these cast ballot throughout the nation,

> Then shall their voice of sovereign choice
> Swell the deep bass of duty done,
> And strike the key of time to be
> When God and man shall speak as one."

[5]   In addition to her profile of Mary Lease, Diggs goes on to profile numerous other women who were active in the Farmers' Alliance.

[6]   Among medieval cartographers, Ultima Thule was a region beyond the known borders of the world.

2 The Omaha Platform: Launching the Populist Party, 1892[7]

Populism, one of the largest mass movements in American history, expressed the fundamental discontent that farmers and rural people had with industrial and big business in the Gilded Age. Founded in Lampasas County, Texas, in 1876, the Farmers' Alliance grew as a largely local organization protecting the interests of farmers and ranchers. During the 1880s, it expanded its appeal into the cotton-growing regions of the South and Midwest, promising to represent agricultural interests against the power of railroads and industrialists. The Alliance attracted members by promising "cooperation" from its members through Alliance-run stores and cooperatives, but inevitably the organization became drawn into politics. In particular, the Alliance championed the adoption of a federally-run subtreasury system, which would extend credit to farmers based on their future crops – a system which was designed to overcome the chronic debt problems in rural America.

Between 1889 and 1892, a debate raged between those in the Alliance favoring a nonpolitical stance, and those pushing for the creation of an organized third party. Frustrated in its encounters with the two-party system, some of the Alliance members favored an independent third party that would strike an alliance with labor unions and the urban working class. Meeting in Omaha, Nebraska, in July 1892, the Peoples' party nominated a slate of candidates for the presidential election during the following November. Its party platform announced Populist principles and remains one of the more important documents in American political history.

NATIONAL PEOPLE'S PARTY PLATFORM

Assembled upon the 116th anniversary of the Declaration of Independence, the People's Party of America, in their first national convention, invoking upon their action the blessing of Almighty God, put forth in the name and on behalf of the people of this country, the following preamble and declaration of principles:

PREAMBLE

The conditions which surround us best justify our co-operation; we meet in the midst of a nation brought to the verge of moral, political, and material ruin. Corruption dominates the ballot-box, the Legislatures, the Congress, and touches even the ermine of the bench. The people are demoralized; most

---

[7] John D. Hicks, *The Populist Revolt: A History of the Farmers' Alliance and the People's Party* (Minneapolis: University of Minnesota Press, 1931), Appendix F, pp. 439–44.

of the States have been compelled to isolate the voters at the polling places to prevent universal intimidation and bribery. The newspapers are largely subsidized or muzzled, public opinion silenced, business prostrated, homes covered with mortgages, labor impoverished, and the land concentrating in the hands of capitalists. The urban workmen are denied the right to organize for self-protection, imported pauperized labor beats down their wages, a hireling standing army, unrecognized by our laws, is established to shoot them down, and they are rapidly degenerating into European conditions. The fruits of the toil of millions are boldly stolen to build up colossal fortunes for a few, unprecedented in the history of mankind; and the possessors of those, in turn, despise the republic and endanger liberty. From the same prolific womb of governmental injustice we breed the two great classes—tramps and millionaires.

The national power to create money is appropriated to enrich bondholders; a vast public debt payable in legal tender currency has been funded into gold-bearing bonds, thereby adding millions to the burdens of the people. Silver, which has been accepted as coin since the dawn of history, has been demonetized to add to the purchasing power of gold by decreasing the value of all forms of property as well as human labor, and the supply of currency is purposely abridged to fatten usurers, bankrupt enterprise, and enslave industry. A vast conspiracy against mankind has been organized on two continents, and it is rapidly taking possession of the world. If not met and overthrown at once it forebodes terrible social convulsions, the destruction of civilization, or the establishment of an absolute despotism.

We have witnessed for more than a quarter of a century the struggles of the two great political parties for power and plunder, while grievous wrongs have been inflicted upon the suffering people. We charge that the controlling influences dominating both these parties have permitted the existing dreadful conditions to develop without serious effort to prevent or restrain them. Neither do they now promise us any substantial reform. They have agreed together to ignore, in the coming campaign, every issue but one. They propose to drown the outcries of a plundered people with the uproar of a sham battle over the tariff, so that capitalists, corporations, national banks, rings, trusts, watered stock, the demonetization of silver and the oppressions of the usurers may all be lost sight of. They propose to sacrifice our homes, lives, and children on the altar of mammon; to destroy the multitude in order to secure corruption funds from the millionaires.

Assembled on the anniversary of the birthday of the nation, and filled with the spirit of the grand general and chief who established our independence, we seek to restore the government of the Republic to the hands of "the plain people," with which class it originated. We assert our purposes to be identical with the purposes of the National Constitution; to form a more perfect union and establish justice, insure domestic tranquillity, provide for the common defence, promote the general welfare, and secure the blessings of liberty for ourselves and our posterity.

We declare that this Republic can only endure as a free government while built upon the love of the whole people for each other and for the nation; that it cannot be pinned together by bayonets; that the civil war is over, and that every passion and resentment which grew out of it must die with it, and that we must be in fact, as we are in name, one united brotherhood of free men.

Our country finds itself confronted by conditions for which there is no precedent in the history of the world; our annual agricultural productions amount to billions of dollars in value, which must, within a few weeks or months, be exchanged for billions of dollars' worth of commodities consumed in their production; the existing currency supply is wholly inadequate to make this exchange; the results are falling prices, the formation of combines and rings, the impoverishment of the producing class. We pledge ourselves that if given power we will labor to correct these evils by wise and reasonable legislation, in accordance with the terms of our platform.

We believe that the power of government—in other words, of the people—should be expanded (as in the case of the postal service) as rapidly and as far as the good sense of an intelligent people and the teachings of experience shall justify, to the end that oppression, injustice, and poverty shall eventually cease in the land.

While our sympathies as a party of reform are naturally upon the side of every proposition which will tend to make men intelligent, virtuous, and temperate, we nevertheless regard these questions, important as they are, as secondary to the great issues now pressing for solution, and upon which not only our individual prosperity but the very existence of free institutions depend; and we ask all men to first help us to determine whether we are to have a republic to administer before we differ as to the conditions upon which it is to be administered, believing that the forces of reform this day organized will never cease to move forward until every wrong is remedied and equal rights and equal privileges securely established for all the men and women of this country.

PLATFORM

We declare, therefore—

First.—That the union of the labor forces of the United States this day consummated shall be permanent and perpetual; may its spirit enter into all hearts for the salvation of the Republic and the uplifting of mankind.

Second.—Wealth belongs to him who creates it, and every dollar taken from industry without an equivalent is robbery. "If any will not work, neither shall he eat." The interests of rural and civic labor are the same; their enemies are identical.

Third.—We believe that the time has come when the railroad corporations will either own the people or the people must own the railroads, and should the government enter upon the work of owning and managing all railroads, we should favor an amendment to the Constitution by which all persons engaged in the government service shall be placed under a civil-service regulation of the most rigid character, so as to prevent the increase of the power of the national administration by the use of such additional government employees.

FINANCE.—We demand a national currency, safe, sound, and flexible, issued by the general government only, a full legal tender for all debts, public and private, and that without the use of banking corporations, a just, equitable, and efficient means of distribution direct to the people, at a tax not to exceed 2 per cent. per annum, to be provided as set forth in the sub-treasury plan of the Farmers' Alliance, or a better system; also by payments in discharge of its obligations for public improvements.

1.   We demand free and unlimited coinage of silver and gold at the present legal ratio of 16 to 1.
2.   We demand that the amount of circulating medium be speedily increased to not less than $50 per capita.
3.   We demand a graduated income tax.
4.   We believe that the money of the country should be kept as much as possible in the hands of the people, and hence we demand that all State and national revenues shall be limited to the necessary expenses of the government, economically and honestly administered.
5.   We demand that postal savings banks be established by the government for the safe deposit of the earnings of the people and to facilitate exchange.

TRANSPORTATION—Transportation being a means of exchange and a public necessity, the government should own and operate the railroads in the interest of the people. The telegraph, telephone, like the post-office system, being a necessity for the transmission of news, should be owned and operated by the government in the interest of the people.

LAND.—The land, including all the natural sources of wealth, is the heritage of the people, and should not be monopolized for speculative purposes, and alien ownership of land should be prohibited. All land now held by railroads and other corporations in excess of their actual needs, and all lands now owned by aliens should be reclaimed by the government and held for actual settlers only.

EXPRESSION OF SENTIMENTS

Your Committee on Platform and Resolutions beg leave unanimously to report the following:

Whereas, Other questions have been presented for our consideration, we hereby submit the following, not as a part of the Platform of the People's Party, but as resolutions expressive of the sentiment of this Convention.

1. RESOLVED, That we demand a free ballot and a fair count in all elections and pledge ourselves to secure it to every legal voter without Federal Intervention, through the adoption by the States of the unperverted Australian or secret ballot system.
2. RESOLVED, That the revenue derived from a graduated income tax should be applied to the reduction of the burden of taxation now levied upon the domestic industries of this country.
3. RESOLVED, That we pledge our support to fair and liberal pensions to ex-Union soldiers and sailors.
4. RESOLVED, That we condemn the fallacy of protecting American labor under the present system, which opens our ports to the pauper and criminal classes of the world and crowds out our wage-earners; and we denounce the present ineffective laws against contract labor, and demand the further restriction of undesirable emigration.
5. RESOLVED, That we cordially sympathize with the efforts of organized workingmen to shorten the hours of labor, and demand a rigid enforcement of the existing eight-hour law on Government work, and ask that a penalty clause be added to the said law.
6. RESOLVED, That we regard the maintenance of a large standing army of mercenaries, known as the Pinkerton system, as a menace to our liberties, and we demand its abolition. . . .
7. RESOLVED, That we commend to the favorable consideration of the people and the reform press the legislative system known as the initiative and referendum.
8. RESOLVED, That we favor a constitutional provision limiting the office of President and Vice-President to one term, and providing for the election of Senators of the United States by a direct vote of the people.
9. RESOLVED, That we oppose any subsidy or national aid to any private corporation for any purpose.

10.   RESOLVED, That this convention sympathizes with the Knights of Labor and their righteous contest with the tyrannical combine of clothing manufacturers of Rochester, and declare it to be a duty of all who hate tyranny and oppression to refuse to purchase the goods made by the said manufacturers, or to patronize any merchants who sell such goods.

3 Thomas E. Watson, "The Negro Question in the South," 1892[8]

Thomas E. Watson (1856–1922) was a controversial politician and lawyer from Georgia who served as a state legislator and as both a US congressman and senator. He was nominated by the Populist party as its vice-presidential candidate in 1896. Influential in Georgia politics, he is remembered for his support of agrarian and egalitarian causes in his early career, but as a demagogue and racist at the peak of it. As an opponent of the new industrial forces controlling the direction of the New South economy, Watson rose to political power through the Farmers' Alliance of Georgia, although he was never a formal member. As such, he was opposed by promoters of New South industrialization, such as Henry W. Grady, editor of the Atlanta Constitution. *Realizing that the African American vote had become essential for political power, he supported policies designed to curry favor with black voters: elimination of the convict-lease system, state-funded public education, and economic policies favoring poor farmers and sharecroppers, both black and white. As a congressman, Watson promoted an Alliance agenda, but was only successful in achieving free rural mail delivery.*

The following article by Watson reflects the complicated nature of race in southern politics. Watson clearly supported interracial political cooperation at this time, but opposed a racially integrated society. His support for black political power ended once he no longer served in elected office. By the early twentieth century, Watson favored disfranchisement of blacks, as well as racial segregation.

The Negro Question in the South has been for nearly thirty years a source of danger, discord, and bloodshed. It is an ever-present irritant and menace.

Several millions of slaves were told that they were the prime cause of the civil war; that their emancipation was the result of the triumph of the North over the South; that the ballot was placed in their hands as a weapon of defence against their former interns; that the war-won political equality of the black man with the white, must be asserted promptly and aggressively, under the leadership of adventurers who had swooped down upon the conquered section in the wake of the Union armies.

[8]   *The Arena* 6 (October 1892): 540–50.

No one, who wishes to be fair, can fail to see that, in such a condition of things, strife between the freedman and his former owner was inevitable. In the clashing of interests and of feelings, bitterness was born. The black man was kept in a continual fever of suspicion that we meant to put him back into slavery. In the assertion of his recently acquired privileges, he was led to believe that the best proof of his being on the right side of any issue was that his old master was on the other. When this was the case, he felt easy in his mind. But if, by any chance, he found that he was voting the same ticket with his former owner, he at once became reflective and suspicious. In the irritable temper of the times, a whispered warning from a Northern "carpet-bagger," having no justification in rhyme or reason, outweighed with him a carload of sound argument and earnest expostulation from the man whom he had known all his life; who had hunted with him through every swamp and wooded upland for miles around; who had wrestled and run foot-races with him in the "Negro quarters" on many a Saturday afternoon; who had fished with him at every "hole" in the creek; and who had played a thousand games of "marble" with him under the cool shade of the giant oaks which, in those days, sheltered a home they had both loved. . . .

Now consider: here were two distinct races dwelling together, with political equality established between them by law. They lived in the same section; won their livelihood by the same pursuits; cultivated adjoining fields on the same terms; enjoyed together the bounties of a generous climate; suffered together the rigors of cruelly unjust laws; spoke the same language; bought and sold in the same markets; classified themselves into churches under the same denominational teachings; neither race antagonizing the other in any branch of industry; each absolutely dependent on the other in all the avenues of labor and employment; and yet, instead of being allies, as every dictate of reason and prudence and self-interest and justice said they should be, they were kept apart, in dangerous hostility, that the sordid aims of partisan politics might be served!

So completely has this scheme succeeded that the Southern black man almost instinctively supports any measure the Southern white man condemns, while the latter almost universally antagonizes any proposition suggested by a Northern Republican. We have, then, a solid South as opposed to a solid North; and in the South itself, a solid black vote against the solid white. . . .

II

. . .

It is safe to say that the present status of hostility between the races can only be sustained at the most imminent risk to both. It is leading by logical necessity to results which the imagination shrinks from contemplating. And the horrors of such a future can only be averted by honest attempts at a solution of the question which will be just to both races and beneficial to both.

Having given this subject much anxious thought, my opinion is that the future happiness of the two races will never be assured until the political motives which drive them asunder, into two distinct and hostile factions, can be removed. There must be a new policy inaugurated, whose purpose is to allay the passions and prejudices of race conflicts and which makes its appeal to the sober sense and honest judgment of the citizen regardless of his color.

To the success of this policy two things are indispensable—a common necessity acting upon both races, and a common benefit assured to both— Without injury or humiliation to either.

Then, again, outsiders must let us alone. We must work out our own salvation. In no other way can it be done. Suggestions of Federal interference with our elections postpone the settlement and render our task the more difficult. Like all free people, we love home rule, and resent foreign compulsion of any sort. The Northern leader who really desires to see a better state of things in the South, puts his finger on the hands of the clock and forces them backward every time he intermeddles with the question. This is the literal truth; and the sooner it is well understood, the sooner we can accomplish our purpose. . . .

As long as there was no choice, except as between the Democrats and the Republicans, the situation of the two races was bound to be one of antagonism. The Republican Party represented everything which was hateful to the whites; the Democratic Party, everything which was hateful to the blacks.

Therefore a new party was absolutely necessary. It has come, and it is doing its work with marvelous rapidity.

Why does a Southern Democrat leave his party and come to ours?

Because his industrial condition is pitiably bad; because he struggles against a system of laws which have almost filled him with despair; because he is told that he is without clothing because he produces too much cotton, and without food because corn is too plentiful; because he sees everybody growing rich off the products of labor except the laborer; because the millionaires who manage the Democratic Party have contemptuously ignored his plea for a redress of grievances and have nothing to say to him beyond the cheerful advice to "work harder and live closer."

Why has this man joined the PEOPLE's PARTY? Because the same grievances have been presented to the Republicans by the farmer of the West, and the millionaires who control that party have replied to the petition with the soothing counsel that the Republican farmer of the West should "work more and talk less."

Therefore, if he were confined to a choice between the two old parties, the question would merely be (on these issues) whether the pot were larger than the kettle—the color of both being precisely the same.

III

The key to the new political movement called the People's Party has been that the Democratic farmer was as ready to leave the Democratic ranks as the Republican farmer was to leave the Republican ranks. In exact proportion as the West received the assurance that the South was ready for a new party, it has moved.

In exact proportion to the proof we could bring that the West had broken Republican ties, the South has moved. Without a decided break in both sections, neither would move. With that decided break, both moved.

The very same principle governs the race question in the South. The two races can never act together permanently, harmoniously, beneficially, till each race demonstrates to the other a readiness to leave old party affiliations and to form new ones, based upon the profound conviction that, in acting together, both races are seeking new laws which will benefit both. On no other basis under heaven can the "Negro Question" be solved. . . .

V

The People's Party will settle the race question. First, by enacting the Australian ballot system. Second, by offering to white and black a rallying point which is free from the odium of former discords and strifes. Third, by presenting a platform immensely beneficial to both races and injurious to neither. Fourth, by making it to the interest of both races to act together for the success of the platform. Fifth, by making it to the interest of the colored man to have the same patriotic zeal for the welfare of the South that the whites possess.

Now to illustrate. Take two planks of the People's Party platform: that pledging a free ballot under the Australian system and that which demands a distribution of currency to the people upon pledges of land, cotton, etc.

The guaranty as to the vote will suit the black man better than the Republican platform, because the latter contemplates Federal interference, which will lead to collisions and bloodshed. The Democratic platform contains no comfort to the Negro, because, while it denounces the Republican programme, as usual, it promises nothing which can be specified. It is a generality which does not even possess the virtue of being "glittering."

The People's Party, however, not only condemns Federal interference with elections, but also distinctly commits itself to the method by which every citizen shall have his constitutional right to the free exercise of his electoral choice. We pledge ourselves to isolate the voter from all coercive influences and give him the free and fair exercise of his franchise under state laws.

Now couple this with the financial plank which promises equality in the distribution of the national currency, at low rates of interest.

The white tenant lives adjoining the colored tenant. Their houses are almost equally destitute of comforts. Their living is confined to bare necessities. They are equally burdened with heavy taxes. They pay the same high rent for gullied and impoverished land. They pay the same enormous prices for farm supplies. Christmas finds them both without any satisfactory return for a year's toil. Dull and heavy and unhappy, they both start the plows again when "New Year's" passes.

Now the People's Party says to these two men, "You are kept apart that you may be separately fleeced of your earnings. You are made to hate each other because upon that hatred is rested the keystone of the arch of financial despotism which enslaves you both. You are deceived and blinded that you may not see how this race antagonism perpetuates a monetary system which beggars both."

This is so obviously true it is no wonder both these unhappy laborers stop to listen. No wonder they begin to realize that no change of law can benefit the white tenant which does not benefit the black one likewise; that no system which now does injustice to one of them can fail to injure both. Their every material interest is identical. The moment this becomes a conviction, mere selfishness, the mere desire to better their conditions, escape onerous taxes, avoid usurious charges, lighten their rents, or change their precarious tenements into smiling, happy homes, will drive these two men together, just as their mutually inflamed prejudices now drive them apart.

Suppose these two men now to have become fully imbued with the idea that their material welfare depends upon the reforms we demand. Then they act together to secure them. Every white reformer finds it to the vital interest of his home, his family, his fortune, to see to it that the vote of the colored reformer is freely cast and fairly counted.

Then what? Every colored voter will be thereafter a subject of industrial education and political teaching.

Concede that in the final event, a colored man will vote where his material interests dictate that he should vote; concede that in the South the accident of color can make no possible difference in the interests of farmers, croppers, and laborers; concede that under full and fair discussion the people can be depended upon to ascertain where their interests lie—and we reach the conclusion that the Southern race question can be solved by the People's Party on the simple proposition that each race will be led by self interest to support that which benefits it, when so presented that neither is hindered by the bitter party antagonisms of the past.

Let the colored laborer realize that our platform gives him a better guaranty for political independence; for a fair return for his work; a better chance to buy a home and keep it; a better chance to educate his children and see them profitably employed; a better chance to have public life freed from race collisions; a better chance for every citizen to be considered as a citizen regardless of color in the making and enforcing of laws,—let all this be fully realized, and the race question at the South will have settled itself through the evolution of a political movement in which both whites and blacks recognize their surest way out of wretchedness into comfort and independence.

The illustration could be made quite as clearly from other planks in the People's Party platform. On questions of land, transportation and finance, especially, the welfare of the two races so clearly depends upon that which benefits either, that intelligent discussion would necessarily lead to just conclusions. Why should the colored man always be taught that the white man of his neighborhood hates him, while a Northern man, who taxes every rag on his back, loves him? Why should not my tenant come to regard me as his friend rather than the manufacturer who plunders us both? Why should we perpetuate a policy which drives the black man into the arms of the Northern politician?

Why should we always allow Northern and Eastern Democrats to enslave us forever by threats of the Force Bill?[9]

Let us draw the supposed teeth of this fabled dragon by founding our new policy upon justice—upon the simple but profound truth that, if the voice of passion can be hushed, the self interest of both races will drive them to act in concert. There never was a day during the last twenty years when the South could not have flung the money power into the dust by patiently teaching the Negro that we could not be wretched under any system which would not afflict him likewise; that we could not prosper under any law which would not also bring its blessings to him.

To the emasculated individual who cries "Negro supremacy!" there is little to be said. His cowardice shows him to be a degeneration from the race which has never yet feared any other race. Existing under such conditions as they now do in this country, there is no earthly chance for Negro domination,

---

[9]   Legislation, proposed but defeated in Congress in 1890, that would have provided greater federal protection of the Fifteenth Amendment and African American voting.

unless we are ready to admit that the colored man is our superior in will power, courage, and intellect.

Not being prepared to make any such admission in favor of any race the sun ever shone on, I have no words which can portray my contempt for the white men, Anglo-Saxons, who can knock their knees together, and through their chattering teeth and pale lips admit that they are afraid the Negroes will "dominate us."

The question of social equality does not enter into the calculation at all. That is a thing each citizen decides for himself. No statute ever yet drew the latch of the humblest home—or ever will. Each citizen regulates his own visiting list—and always will.

The conclusion, then, seems to me to be this: the crushing burdens which now oppress both races in the South will cause each to make an effort to cast them off.

They will see a similarity of cause and a similarity of remedy. They will recognize that each should help the other in the work of repealing bad laws and enacting good ones. They will become political allies, and neither can injure the other without weakening both. It will be to the interest of both that each should have justice. And on these broad lines of mutual interest, mutual forbearance, and mutual support the present will be made the stepping-stone to future peace and prosperity.

4 William Jennings Bryan, "Cross of Gold" Speech, 1896[10]

William Jennings Bryan (1860–1925) had a long political and legal career that included three presidential campaigns. He served as a congressman from Nebraska and was Woodrow Wilson's secretary of state. As the leading prosecutor in the Scopes trial in 1925, which tested whether or not evolution could be taught in Tennessee's public schools, he succeeded in obtaining a guilty verdict, but became associated with conservative Protestant fundamentalist anti-evolutionists and was the object of derision among educated Americans. By the turn of the twentieth century, Bryan had emerged as an outspoken anti-imperialist. He resigned as secretary of state after Wilson engaged in preparing the country for war in Europe.

Although Bryan was a popular and well-known orator, his political goals were too narrow to allow him to gain widespread support as a presidential candidate. In 1896, he appealed to rural audiences across the United States because of his fervent support for "free silver." In 1893, Congress had

[10] *Official Proceedings of the Democratic National Convention Held in Chicago, Illinois, July 7, 8, 9, 10, and 11, 1896* (Logansport, IN, 1896), pp. 226–34.

removed silver as a form of official currency and, like the rest of the
industrialized world, adopted gold as the single official monetary standard.
Those in favor of expanding the money supply by remonetizing silver during
the depression of the 1890s rallied around the slogan of "free silver," and this
became the central element of Bryan's presidential campaign. Free silver
attracted many adherents among Populists, and they nominated Bryan as a
"fusion" candidate in 1896. Even though Bryan failed to achieve the
majority of his political agenda, many of the ideas that he supported
eventually became reality: among them, woman suffrage, a graduated federal
income tax, prohibition of alcohol, and the popular election of US Senators.

Never before in the history of this country has there been witnessed such a contest as that through which we have passed. Never before in the history of American politics has a great issue been fought out as this issue has been by the voters themselves.

On the 4th of March, 1895, a few Democrats, most of them members of Congress, issued an address to the Democrats of the nation asserting that the money question was the paramount issue of the hour; asserting also the right of a majority of the Democratic Party to control the position of the party on this paramount issue; concluding with the request that all believers in free coinage of silver in the Democratic Party should organize and take charge of and control the policy of the Democratic Party. Three months later, at Memphis, an organization was perfected, and the silver Democrats went forth openly and boldly and courageously proclaiming their belief and declaring that if successful they would crystallize in a platform the declaration which they had made; and then began the conflict with a zeal approaching the zeal which inspired the crusaders who followed Peter the Hermit. Our silver Democrats went forth from victory unto victory, until they are assembled now, not to discuss, not to debate, but to enter up the judgment rendered by the plain people of this country.

But in this contest, brother has been arrayed against brother, and father against son. The warmest ties of love and acquaintance and association have been disregarded. Old leaders have been cast aside when they refused to give expression to the sentiments of those whom they would lead, and new leaders have sprung up to give direction to this cause of freedom. Thus has the contest been waged, and we have assembled here under as binding and solemn instructions as were ever fastened upon the representatives of a people. . . .

We stand here representing people who are the equals before the law of the largest cities in the state of Massachusetts. When you come before us and tell us that we shall disturb your business interests, we reply that you have disturbed our business interests by your action. We say to you that you have made too limited in its application the definition of a businessman. The man who is employed for wages is as much a businessman as his employer. The attorney in a country town is as much a businessman as the corporation counsel in a great metropolis. The merchant at the crossroads store is as much a businessman as the merchant of New York. The farmer who goes forth in the morning and toils all day, begins in the spring and toils all summer, and by the application of brain and muscle to the natural resources of this country creates wealth, is as much a businessman as the man who goes upon the Board of Trade and bets upon the price of grain. The miners who go 1,000 feet into the earth or climb 2,000 feet upon the cliffs and bring forth from their hiding places the precious metals to be poured in the channels of trade are as much businessmen as the few financial magnates who in a backroom corner the money of the world.

We come to speak for this broader class of businessmen. Ah, my friends, we say not one word against those who live upon the Atlantic Coast; but those hardy pioneers who braved all the dangers of the wilderness, who have made the desert to blossom as the rose—those pioneers away out there, rearing their children near to nature's heart, where they can mingle their voices with the voices of the birds—out there where they have erected schoolhouses for the education of their children and churches where they praise their Creator, and the cemeteries where sleep the ashes of their dead— are as deserving of the consideration of this party as any people in this country.

It is for these that we speak. We do not come as aggressors. Our war is not a war of conquest. We are fighting in the defense of our homes, our families, and posterity. We have petitioned, and our petitions have been scorned. We have entreated, and our entreaties have been disregarded. We have begged, and they have mocked when our calamity came.

We beg no longer; we entreat no more; we petition no more. We defy them!

. . . . We say in our platform that we believe that the right to coin money and issue money is a function of government. We believe it. We believe it is a part of sovereignty and can no more with safety be delegated to private individuals than can the power to make penal statutes or levy laws for taxation.

Mr. Jefferson,[11] who was once regarded as good Democratic authority, seems to have a different opinion from the gentleman who has addressed us on the part of the minority. Those who are opposed to this proposition tell us that the issue of paper money is a function of the bank and that the

---

[11]   Thomas Jefferson.

government ought to go out of the banking business. I stand with Jefferson rather than with them, and tell them, as he did, that the issue of money is a function of the government and that the banks should go out of the governing business.

They complain about the plank which declares against the life tenure in office. They have tried to strain it to mean that which it does not mean. What we oppose in that plank is the life tenure that is being built up in Washington which establishes an office-holding class and excludes from participation in the benefits the humbler members of our society. . . .

Let me call attention to two or three great things. The gentleman from New York says that he will propose an amendment providing that this change in our law shall not affect contracts which, according to the present laws, are made payable in gold. But if he means to say that we cannot change our monetary system without protecting those who have loaned money before the change was made, I want to ask him where, in law or in morals, he can find authority for not protecting the debtors when the act of 1873 was passed when he now insists that we must protect the creditor. He says he also wants to amend this platform so as to provide that if we fail to maintain the parity within a year that we will then suspend the coinage of silver. We reply that when we advocate a thing which we believe will be successful we are not compelled to raise a doubt as to our own sincerity by trying to show what we will do if we are wrong.

I ask him, if he will apply his logic to us, why he does not apply it to himself. He says that he wants this country to try to secure an international agreement. Why doesn't he tell us what he is going to do if they fail to secure an international agreement. There is more reason for him to do that than for us to expect to fail to maintain the parity. They have tried for thirty years— thirty years—to secure an international agreement, and those are waiting for it most patiently who don't want it at all.

Now, my friends, let me come to the great paramount issue. If they ask us here why it is we say more on the money question than we say upon the tariff question, I reply that if protection has slain its thousands the gold standard has slain its tens of thousands. If they ask us why we did not embody all these things in our platform which we believe, we reply to them that when we have restored the money of the Constitution, all other necessary reforms will be possible, and that until that is done there is no reform that can be accomplished.

Why is it that within three months such a change has come over the sentiments of the country? Three months ago, when it was confidently asserted that those who believed in the gold standard would frame our platforms and nominate our candidates, even the advocates of the gold standard did not think that we could elect a President; but they had good reasons for the suspicion, because there is scarcely a state here today asking for the gold standard that is not within the absolute control of the Republican Party.

But note the change. Mr. McKinley was nominated at St. Louis upon a platform that declared for the maintenance of the gold standard until it should be changed into bimetallism by an international agreement. Mr. McKinley was the most popular man among the Republicans; and everybody three months ago in the Republican Party prophesied his election. How is it today? Why, that man who used to boast that he looked like Napoleon, that man shudders today when he thinks that he was nominated on the anniversary of the Battle of Waterloo. Not only that, but as he listens he can hear with ever increasing distinctness the sound of the waves as they beat upon the lonely shores of St. Helena.[12]

Why this change? Ah, my friends, is not the change evident to anyone who will look at the matter? It is because no private character, however pure, no personal popularity, however great, can protect from the avenging wrath of an indignant people the man who will either declare that he is in favor of fastening the gold standard upon this people, or who is willing to surrender the right of self-government and place legislative control in the hands of foreign potentates and powers. . . .

We go forth confident that we shall win. Why? Because upon the paramount issue in this campaign there is not a spot of ground upon which the enemy will dare to challenge battle. Why, if they tell us that the gold standard is a good thing, we point to their platform and tell them that their platform pledges the party to get rid of a gold standard and substitute bimetallism. If the gold standard is a good thing, why try to get rid of it? If the gold standard, and I might call your attention to the fact that some of the very people who are in this convention today and who tell you that we ought to declare in favor of international bimetallism and thereby declare that the gold standard is wrong and that the principles of bimetallism are better— these very people four months ago were open and avowed advocates of the gold standard and telling us that we could not legislate two metals together even with all the world.

I want to suggest this truth, that if the gold standard is a good thing we ought to declare in favor of its retention and not in favor of abandoning it; and if the gold standard is a bad thing, why should we wait until some other nations are willing to help us to let it go?

---

[12]   After his defeat at Waterloo in 1815, Napoleon Bonaparte was exiled to the remote South Atlantic island of St Helena.

Here is the line of battle. We care not upon which issue they force the fight. We are prepared to meet them on either issue or on both. If they tell us that the gold standard is the standard of civilization, we reply to them that this, the most enlightened of all nations of the earth, has never declared for a gold standard, and both the parties this year are declaring against it. If the gold standard is the standard of civilization, why, my friends, should we not have it? So if they come to meet us on that, we can present the history of our nation. More than that, we can tell them this, that they will search the pages of history in vain to find a single instance in which the common people of any land ever declared themselves in favor of a gold standard. They can find where the holders of fixed investments have.

. . . . My friends, it is simply a question that we shall decide upon which side shall the Democratic Party fight. Upon the side of the idle holders of idle capital, or upon the side of the struggling masses? That is the question that the party must answer first; and then it must be answered by each individual hereafter. The sympathies of the Democratic Party, as described by the platform, are on the side of the struggling masses, who have ever been the foundation of the Democratic Party.

There are two ideas of government. There are those who believe that if you just legislate to make the well-to-do prosperous, that their prosperity will leak through on those below. The Democratic idea has been that if you legislate to make the masses prosperous their prosperity will find its way up and through every class that rests upon it.

You come to us and tell us that the great cities are in favor of the gold standard. I tell you that the great cities rest upon these broad and fertile prairies. Burn down your cities and leave our farms, and your cities will spring up again as if by magic. But destroy our farms and the grass will grow in the streets of every city in the country.

My friends, we shall declare that this nation is able to legislate for its own people on every question without waiting for the aid or consent of any other nation on earth, and upon that issue we expect to carry every single state in the Union.

I shall not slander the fair state of Massachusetts nor the state of New York by saying that when citizens are confronted with the proposition, "Is this nation able to attend to its own business?"—I will not slander either one by saying that the people of those states will declare our helpless impotency as a nation to attend to our own business. It is the issue of 1776 over again. Our ancestors, when but 3 million, had the courage to declare their political independence of every other nation upon earth. Shall we, their descendants, when we have grown to 70 million, declare that we are less independent than our forefathers? No, my friends, it will never be the judgment of this people. Therefore, we care not upon what lines the battle is fought. If they say bimetallism is good but we cannot have it till some nation helps us, we reply that, instead of having a gold standard because England has, we shall restore bimetallism, and then let England have bimetallism because the United States have.

If they dare to come out in the open field and defend the gold standard as a good thing, we shall fight them to the uttermost, having behind us the producing masses of the nation and the world. Having behind us the commercial interests and the laboring interests and all the toiling masses, we shall answer their demands for a gold standard by saying to them, you shall not press down upon the brow of labor this crown of thorns. You shall not crucify mankind upon a cross of gold.

Discussion Questions: Chapter 8

1   To what extent was the Farmers' Alliance dominated by men?
2   To what extent did the Populists favor governmental intervention?
3   How important was the factor of race in the rise of Populism? What view does Tom Watson present?

Chapter 9   The Coming of Jim Crow

1   Ida B. Wells, "Lynch Law in America," 1900[1]

Ida B. Wells (1862–1931) started her career as a crusader for social justice when, in 1884, she was forcibly removed from a Chesapeake & Ohio train after she refused to move from the ladies' car to the smoking and "Jim Crow" car. This incident occurred after the passage of the Civil Rights Act of 1875, which banned discrimination in public accommodations on the basis of race, and before the Supreme Court decision in 1896 in Plessy v. Ferguson, which legalized segregation on the basis of race. When Wells returned home to Memphis, she sued the railroad and won in the lower circuit court, but the decision was overturned by the Tennessee Supreme Court. At the time, Wells was a 25-year-old schoolteacher, and she made the decision to devote her life to defeating injustices against women and people of color. Her career in journalism began here, as African American and Christian newspapers sought her stories.

In 1892, three of her friends were lynched, and this tragic event led Wells to write investigative articles about lynching and caused her to move to Chicago, where the atmosphere was more receptive to her muckraking journalism. Lynching of black men reached epidemic proportions in the South during the 1890s and the first decade of the twentieth century, so Wells stayed busy. In addition to her anti-lynching crusade, she formed several women's and reform groups for African Americans in Chicago.

[1]   Ida B. Wells-Barnett, "Lynch Law in America," *The Arena* 23, no. 1 (January 1900): 15–24.

The Gilded Age and Progressive Era: A Documentary Reader, First Edition.
Edited by William A. Link and Susannah J. Link.
© 2012 Blackwell Publishing Ltd. Published 2012 by Blackwell Publishing Ltd.

As a supporter of woman suffrage, she participated in the famous march on Washington in 1913, which advocated universal suffrage. She also joined forces with W.E.B. Du Bois in the Niagara Movement and was a founder of the NAACP in 1909. In 1930, dissatisfied with the candidates running for the state legislature from Chicago, she decided to join the race and, although she did not win, became the first African American woman to run for public office in the United States.

Our country's national crime is *lynching*. It is not the creature of an hour, the sudden outburst of uncontrolled fury, or the unspeakable brutality of an insane mob. It represents the cool, calculating deliberation of intelligent people who openly avow that there is an "unwritten law" that justifies them in putting human beings to death without complaint under oath, without trial by jury, without opportunity to make defense, and without right of appeal. . . . The alleged menace of universal suffrage having been avoided by the absolute suppression of the negro vote, the spirit of mob murder should have been satisfied and the butchery of negroes should have ceased. But men, women, and children were the victims of murder by individuals and murder by mobs, just as they had been when killed at the demands of the "unwritten law" to prevent "negro domination." Negroes were killed for disputing over terms of contracts with their employers. If a few barns were burned some colored man was killed to stop it. If a colored man resented the imposition of a white man and the two came to blows, the colored man had to die, either at the hands of the white man then and there or later at the hands of a mob that speedily gathered. If he showed a spirit of courageous manhood he was hanged for his pains, and the killing was justified by the declaration that he was a "saucy nigger." Colored women have been murdered because they refused to tell the mobs where relatives could be found for "lynching bees." Boys of fourteen years have been lynched by white representatives of American civilization. In fact, for all kinds of offenses—and, for no offenses—from murders to misdemeanors, men and women are put to death without judge or jury; so that, although the political excuse was no longer necessary, the wholesale murder of human beings went on just the same. . . .

It is considered a sufficient excuse and reasonable justification to put a prisoner to death under this "unwritten law" for the frequently repeated charge that these lynching horrors are necessary to prevent crimes against women. The sentiment of the country has been appealed to, in describing the isolated condition of white families in thickly populated negro districts; and the charge is made that these homes are in as great danger as if they were surrounded by wild beasts. And the world has accepted this theory without let or hindrance. . . . No matter that our laws presume every man innocent until he is proved guilty; no matter that it leaves a certain class of individuals completely at the mercy of another class; no matter that it encourages those criminally disposed to blacken their faces and commit any crime in the calendar so long as they can throw suspicion on some negro, as is frequently done, and then lead a mob to take his life; no matter that mobs make a farce of the law and a mockery of justice; no matter that hundreds of boys are being hardened in crime and schooled in vice by the repetition of such scenes before their eyes—if a white woman declares herself insulted or assaulted, some life must pay the penalty, with all the horrors of the Spanish Inquisition and all the barbarism of the Middle Ages. The world looks on and says it is well.

Not only are two hundred men and women put to death annually, on the average, in this country by mobs, but these lives are taken with the greatest publicity. In many instances the leading citizens aid and abet by their presence when they do not participate, and the leading journals inflame the public mind to the lynching point with scare-head articles and offers of rewards. Whenever a burning is advertised to take place, the railroads run excursions, photographs are taken, and the same jubilee is indulged in that characterized the public hangings of one hundred years ago. There is, however, this difference: in those old days the multitude that stood by was permitted only to guy or jeer. The nineteenth century lynching mob cuts off ears, toes, and fingers, strips off flesh, and distributes portions of the body as souvenirs among the crowd. If the leaders of the mob are so minded, coal-oil is poured over the body and the victim is then roasted to death. This has been done in Texarkana and Paris, Tex., in Bardswell, Ky., and in Newman, Ga. In Paris the officers of the law delivered the prisoner to the mob. The mayor gave the school children a holiday and the railroads ran excursion trains so that the people might see a human being burned to death. In Texarkana, the year before, men and boys amused themselves by cutting off strips of flesh and thrusting knives into their helpless victim. At Newman, Ga., of the present year, the mob tried every conceivable torture to compel the victim to cry out and confess, before they set fire to the faggots that burned him. But their trouble was all in vain—he never uttered a cry, and they could not make him confess.

This condition of affairs were brutal enough and horrible enough if it were true that lynchings occurred only because of the commission of crimes against women—as is constantly declared by ministers, editors, lawyers, teachers, statesmen, and even by women themselves. It has been to the interest of those who did the lynching to blacken the good name of the helpless and defenseless victims of their hate. For this reason they publish at every possible opportunity this excuse for lynching, hoping thereby not only to palliate their own crime but at the same time to prove the negro a moral monster and unworthy of the respect and sympathy of the civilized world. But this alleged reason adds to the deliberate injustice of the mob's work. Instead of lynchings being caused by assaults upon women, the statistics show that not one-third of the victims of lynchings are even charged with such crimes. . . .

Quite a number of the one-third alleged cases of assault that have been personally investigated by the writer have shown that there was no foundation in fact for the charges; yet the claim is not made that there were no real culprits among them. The negro has been too long associated with the white man not to have copied his vices as well as his virtues. But the negro resents and utterly repudiates the efforts to blacken his good name by asserting that assaults upon women are peculiar to his race. The negro has suffered far more from the commission of this crime against the women of his race by white men than the white race has ever suffered through *his* crimes. Very scant notice is taken of the matter when this is the condition of affairs. What becomes a crime deserving capital punishment when the tables are turned is a matter of small moment when the negro woman is the accusing party. . . .

Our country should be placed speedily above the plane of confessing herself a failure at self-government. This cannot be until Americans of every section, of broadest patriotism and best and wisest citizenship, not only see the defect in our country's armor but take the necessary steps to remedy it. Although lynchings have steadily increased in number and barbarity during the last twenty years, there has been no single effort put forth by the many moral and philanthropic forces of the country to put a stop to this wholesale slaughter. Indeed, the silence and seeming condonation grow more marked as the years go by.

2 U.S. Supreme Court, *Plessy v. Ferguson*, 1896[2]

In 1890, Louisiana passed a law that required segregation by race on railroads. In response, Homer Plessy, a businessman in Baton Rouge who had only one African American grandparent and who did not consider himself black, decided, at the request of the New Orleans Committee of Citizens, to form a group of African American activists. The Committee of Citizens was dominated by the city's mixed-race population, who were most offended by the new segregation laws.

[2] *Plessy v. Ferguson*, 163 U.S. 537 (1896).

*Plessy, who was seven-eighths white in racial origin, was persuaded to
initiate a test case by getting himself arrested in the hope of overturning the
law. Appealing the case against the original trial judge all the way to the US
Supreme Court, Plessy lost in a ruling that established the doctrine of
"separate but equal," which then allowed southern states free rein in passing
"Jim Crow" segregation laws that applied to nearly all aspects of racial
interaction in the South.*

Mr. Justice BROWN,[3] after stating the facts in the foregoing language, delivered the opinion of the court. . . .

By the fourteenth amendment, all persons born or naturalized in the United States, and subject to the jurisdiction thereof, are made citizens of the United States and of the state wherein they reside; and the states are forbidden from making or enforcing any law which shall abridge the privileges or immunities of citizens of the United States, or shall deprive any person of life, liberty, or property without due process of law, or deny to any person within their jurisdiction the equal protection of the laws. . . .

While we think the enforced separation of the races, as applied to the internal commerce of the state, neither abridges the privileges or immunities of the colored man, deprives him of his property without due process of law, nor denies him the equal protection of the laws, within the meaning of the fourteenth amendment, we are not prepared to say that the conductor, in assigning passengers to the coaches according to their race, does not act at his peril, or that the provision of the second section of the act that denies to the passenger compensation in damages for a refusal to receive him into the coach in which he properly belongs is a valid exercise of the legislative power. Indeed, we understand it to be conceded by the state's attorney that such part of the act as exempts from liability the railway company and its officers is unconstitutional. The power to assign to a particular coach obviously implies the power to determine to which race the passenger belongs, as well as the power to determine who, under the laws of the particular state, is to be deemed a white, and who [is to be deemed] a colored, person. This question, though indicated in the brief of the plaintiff in error, does not properly arise upon the record in this case, since the only issue made is as to the unconstitutionality of the act, so far as it requires the railway to provide separate accommodations, and the conductor to assign passengers according to their race. . . .

---

[3] Henry Billings Brown (1836–1913), who served as associate justice of the Supreme Court from 1891 to 1906.

We consider the underlying fallacy of the plaintiff's argument to consist in the assumption that the enforced separation of the two races stamps the colored race with a badge of inferiority. If this be so, it is not by reason of anything found in the act, but solely because the colored race chooses to put that construction upon it. The argument necessarily assumes that if, as has been more than once the case, and is not unlikely to be so again, the colored race should become the dominant power in the state legislature, and should enact a law in precisely similar terms, it would thereby relegate the white race to an inferior position. We imagine that the white race, at least, would not acquiesce in this assumption. The argument also assumes that social prejudices may be overcome by legislation, and that equal rights cannot be secured to the negro except by an enforced commingling of the two races. We cannot accept this proposition. If the two races are to meet upon terms of social equality, it must be the result of natural affinities, a mutual appreciation of each other's merits, and a voluntary consent of individuals. . . . Legislation is powerless to eradicate racial instincts, or to abolish distinctions based upon physical differences, and the attempt to do so can only result in accentuating the difficulties of the present situation. . . . If one race be inferior to the other socially, the constitution of the United States cannot put them upon the same plane.

It is true that the question of the proportion of colored blood necessary to constitute a colored person, as distinguished from a white person, is one upon which there is a difference of opinion in the different states; some holding that any visible admixture of black blood stamps the person as belonging to the colored race. . . . But these are questions to be determined under the laws of each state, and are not properly put in issue in this case. Under the allegations of his petition, it may undoubtedly become a question of importance whether, under the laws of Louisiana, the petitioner belongs to the white or colored race.

The judgment of the court below is therefore affirmed.

Mr. Justice BREWER[4] did not hear the argument or participate in the decision of this case.

Mr. Justice HARLAN[5] dissenting.

By the Louisiana statute the validity of which is here involved, all railway companies (other than street-railroad companies) [that] carry passengers

---

[4]   David Josiah Brewer (1837–1910), who served as an associate justice on the Supreme Court from 1889 to 1909.
[5]   John Marshall Harlan was the only justice voting against the majority in the *Plessy* case. His dissent follows.

in that state are required to have separate but equal accommodations for white and colored persons, 'by providing two or more passenger coaches for each passenger train, or by dividing the passenger coaches by a partition so as to secure separate accommodations.' Under this statute, no colored person is permitted to occupy a seat in a coach assigned to white persons; nor any white person to occupy a seat in a coach assigned to colored persons. The managers of the railroad are not allowed to exercise any discretion in the premises, but are required to assign each passenger to some coach or compartment set apart for the exclusive use of his race. If a passenger insists upon going into a coach or compartment not set apart for persons of his race, he is subject to be fined, or to be imprisoned in the parish jail. Penalties are prescribed for the refusal or neglect of the officers, directors, conductors, and employees of railroad companies to comply with the provisions of the act.

Only nurses attending children of the other race are excepted from the operation of the statute. No exception is made of colored attendants traveling with adults. A white man is not permitted to have his colored servant with him in the same coach, even if his condition of health requires the constant personal assistance of such servant. If a colored maid insists upon riding in the same coach with a white woman whom she has been employed to serve, and who may need her personal attention while traveling, she is subject to be fined or imprisoned for such an exhibition of zeal in the discharge of duty.

While there may be in Louisiana persons of different races who are not citizens of the United States, the words in the act 'white and colored races' necessarily include all citizens of the United States of both races residing in that state. So that we have before us a state enactment that compels, under penalties, the separation of the two races in railroad passenger coaches, and makes it a crime for a citizen of either race to enter a coach that has been assigned to citizens of the other race.

Thus, the state regulates the use of a public highway by citizens of the United States solely upon the basis of race. However apparent the injustice of such legislation may be, we have only to consider whether it is consistent with the constitution of the United States.... But I deny that any legislative body or judicial tribunal may have regard to the race of citizens when the civil rights of those citizens are involved. Indeed, such legislation as that here in question is inconsistent not only with that equality of rights which pertains to citizenship, national and state, but with the personal liberty enjoyed by every one within the United States.

The thirteenth amendment does not permit the withholding or the deprivation of any right necessarily inhering in freedom. It not only struck down the institution of slavery as previously existing in the United States, but it prevents the imposition of any burdens or disabilities that constitute badges of slavery or servitude. It decreed universal civil freedom in this country. This court has so adjudged. But, that amendment having been found inadequate to the protection of the rights of those who had been in slavery, it was followed by the fourteenth amendment, which added greatly to the dignity and glory of American citizenship, and to the security of personal liberty, by declaring that "all persons born or naturalized in the United States, and subject to the jurisdiction thereof, are citizens of the United States and of the state wherein they reside," and that "no state shall make or enforce any law which shall abridge the privileges or immunities of citizens of the United States; nor shall any state deprive any person of life, liberty or property without due process of law, nor deny to any person within its jurisdiction the equal protection of the laws."

These two amendments, if enforced according to their true intent and meaning, will protect all the civil rights that pertain to freedom and citizenship. Finally, and to the end that no citizen should be denied, on account of his race, the privilege of participating in the political control of his country, it was declared by the fifteenth amendment that "the right of citizens of the United States to vote shall not be denied or abridged by the United States or by any state on account of race, color or previous condition of servitude."

The white race deems itself to be the dominant race in this country. And so it is, in prestige, in achievements, in education, in wealth, and in power. So, I doubt not, it will continue to be for all time, if it remains true to its great heritage, and holds fast to the principles of constitutional liberty. But in view of the constitution, in the eye of the law, there is in this country no superior, dominant, ruling class of citizens. There is no caste here. Our constitution is color-blind, and neither knows nor tolerates classes among citizens. In respect of civil rights, all citizens are equal before the law. The humblest is the peer of the most powerful. The law regards man as man, and takes no account of his surroundings or of his color when his civil rights as guarantied by the supreme law of the land are involved. It is therefore to be regretted that this high tribunal, the final expositor of the fundamental law of the land, has reached the conclusion that it is competent for a state to regulate the enjoyment by citizens of their civil rights solely upon the basis of race.

In my opinion, the judgment this day rendered will, in time, prove to be quite as pernicious as the decision made by this tribunal in the Dred Scott Case....

The present decision, it may well be apprehended, will not only stimulate aggressions, more or less brutal and irritating, upon the admitted rights of colored citizens, but will encourage the belief that it is possible, by means of state enactments, to defeat the beneficent purposes which the people of the United States had in view when they adopted the recent amendments of the constitution, by one of which the blacks of this country were made citizens of the United States and of the states in which they respectively reside, and whose privileges and immunities, as citizens, the states are forbidden to abridge. Sixty millions of whites are in no danger from the presence here of eight millions of blacks. The destinies of the two races, in this country, are indissolubly linked together, and the interests of both require that the common government of all shall not permit the seeds of race hate to be planted under the sanction of law. What can more certainly arouse race hate, what more certainly create and perpetuate a feeling of distrust between these races, than state enactments which, in fact, proceed on the ground that colored citizens are so inferior and degraded that they cannot be allowed to sit in public coaches occupied by white citizens? That, as all will admit, is the real meaning of such legislation as was enacted in Louisiana.

3 Booker T. Washington, The Atlanta Compromise, 1895[6]

Speaking before the Cotton States and International Exposition in Atlanta on September 18, 1895, Booker T. Washington (1856–1916) told his audience – which was mostly white – about a new formula for racial compromise in the age of segregation and white supremacy. His "Atlanta Compromise" address expressed Washington's philosophy of accommodation: that African Americans should become useful workers in agriculture and trades and not attempt to integrate into white society. In turn, he also expressed the hope that whites would hire black southerners instead of employing immigrants.

Setting aside their concerns that white southerners would oppose their invitation to Washington, the organizers of the exposition believed that his speech there would show the North that race relations were improving in the South. The speech was widely, but not unanimously, applauded by both blacks and whites. W.E.B. Du Bois, a civil rights activist who called for immediate integration, criticized what he regarded as Washington's cautious approach, because he believed that it kept blacks in a second-class position.

Mr. President and Gentlemen of the Board of Directors and Citizens:

One-third of the population of the South is of the Negro race. No enterprise seeking the material, civil, or moral welfare of this section can disregard this element of our population and reach the highest success. I but convey to you, Mr. President and Directors, the sentiment of the masses of

---

[6] Louis R. Harlan, ed., *The Booker T. Washington Papers*, III (Urbana: University of Illinois Press, 1974), pp. 583–87.

my race when I say that in no way have the value and manhood of the American Negro been more fittingly and generously recognized than by the managers of this magnificent Exposition at every stage of its progress. It is a recognition that will do more to cement the friendship of the two races than any occurrence since the dawn of our freedom.

Not only this, but the opportunity here afforded will awaken among us a new era of industrial progress. Ignorant and inexperienced, it is not strange that in the first years of our new life we began at the top instead of at the bottom; that a seat in Congress or the state legislature was more sought than real estate or industrial skill; that the political convention or stump speaking had more attractions than starting a dairy farm or truck garden.

A ship lost at sea for many days suddenly sighted a friendly vessel. From the mast of the unfortunate vessel was seen a signal, "Water, water; we die of thirst!" The answer from the friendly vessel at once came back, "Cast down your bucket where you are." A second time the signal, "Water, water; send us water!" ran up from the distressed vessel, and was answered, "Cast down your bucket where you are." And a third and fourth signal for water was answered, "Cast down your bucket where you are." The captain of the distressed vessel, at last heeding the injunction, cast down his bucket, and it came up full of fresh, sparkling water from the mouth of the Amazon River. To those of my race who depend on bettering their condition in a foreign land or who underestimate the importance of cultivating friendly relations with the Southern white man, who is their next-door neighbor, I would say: "Cast down your bucket where you are" — cast it down in making friends in every manly way of the people of all races by whom we are surrounded.

Cast it down in agriculture, mechanics, in commerce, in domestic service, and in the professions. And in this connection it is well to bear in mind that whatever other sins the South may be called to bear, when it comes to business, pure and simple, it is in the South that the Negro is given a man's chance in the commercial world, and in nothing is this Exposition more eloquent than in emphasizing this chance. Our greatest danger is that in the great leap from slavery to freedom we may overlook the fact that the masses of us are to live by the productions of our hands, and fail to keep in mind that we shall prosper in proportion as we learn to dignify and glorify common labour, and put brains and skill into the common occupations of life; shall prosper in proportion as we learn to draw the line between the superficial and the substantial, the ornamental gewgaws of life and the useful. No race can prosper till it learns that there is as much dignity in tilling a field as in writing a poem. It is at the bottom of life we must begin, and not at the top. Nor should we permit our grievances to overshadow our opportunities.

To those of the white race who look to the incoming of those of foreign birth and strange tongue and habits for the prosperity of the South, were I permitted

I would repeat what I say to my own race, "Cast down your bucket where you are." Cast it down among the eight millions of Negroes whose habits you know, whose fidelity and love you have tested in days when to have proved treacherous meant the ruin of your firesides. Cast down your bucket among these people who have, without strikes and labour wars, tilled your fields, cleared your forests, builded your railroads and cities, and brought forth treasures from the bowels of the earth, and helped make possible this magnificent representation of the progress of the South. Casting down your bucket among my people, helping and encouraging them as you are doing on these grounds, and to education of head, hand, and heart, you will find that they will buy your surplus land, make blossom the waste places in your fields, and run your factories. While doing this, you can be sure in the future, as in the past, that you and your families will be surrounded by the most patient, faithful, law-abiding, and unresentful people that the world has seen. As we have proved our loyalty to you in the past, in nursing your children, watching by the sick-bed of your mothers and fathers, and often following them with tear-dimmed eyes to their graves, so in the future, in our humble way, we shall stand by you with a devotion that no foreigner can approach, ready to lay down our lives, if need be, in defense of yours, interlacing our industrial, commercial, civil, and religious life with yours in a way that shall make the interests of both races one. In all things that are purely social we can be as separate as the fingers, yet one as the hand in all things essential to mutual progress.

There is no defense or security for any of us except in the highest intelligence and development of all. If anywhere there are efforts tending to curtail the fullest growth of the Negro, let these efforts be turned into stimulating, encouraging, and making him the most useful and intelligent citizen. Effort or means so invested will pay a thousand per cent interest. These efforts will be twice blessed—blessing him that gives and him that takes. There is no escape through law of man or God from the inevitable:

The laws of changeless justice bind Oppressor with oppressed;

And close as sin and suffering joined We march to fate abreast.... Nearly sixteen millions of hands will aid you in pulling the load upward, or they will pull against you the load downward. We shall constitute one-third and more of the ignorance and crime of the South, or one-third [of] its intelligence and progress; we shall contribute one-third to the business and industrial prosperity of the South, or we shall prove a veritable body of death, stagnating, depressing, retarding every effort to advance the body politic.

Gentlemen of the Exposition, as we present to you our humble effort at an exhibition of our progress, you must not expect overmuch. Starting thirty years ago with ownership here and there in a few quilts and pumpkins and chickens (gathered from miscellaneous sources), remember the path that has led from these to the inventions and production of agricultural implements, buggies, steam-engines, newspapers, books, statuary, carving, paintings, the management of drug stores and banks, has not been trodden without contact with thorns and thistles. While we take pride in what we exhibit as a result of our independent efforts, we do not for a moment forget that our part in this exhibition would fall far short of your expectations but for the constant help that has come to our educational life, not only from the Southern states, but especially from Northern philanthropists, who have made their gifts a constant stream of blessing and encouragement.

The wisest among my race understand that the agitation of questions of social equality is the extremest folly, and that progress in the enjoyment of all the privileges that will come to us must be the result of severe and constant struggle rather than of artificial forcing. No race that has anything to contribute to the markets of the world is long in any degree ostracized. It is important and right that all privileges of the law be ours, but it is vastly more important that we be prepared for the exercise of these privileges. The opportunity to earn a dollar in a factory just now is worth infinitely more than the opportunity to spend a dollar in an opera-house.

In conclusion, may I repeat that nothing in thirty years has given us more hope and encouragement, and drawn us so near to you of the white race, as this opportunity offered by the Exposition; and here bending, as it were, over the altar that represents the results of the struggles of your race and mine, both starting practically empty-handed three decades ago, I pledge that in your effort to work out the great and intricate problem which God has laid at the doors of the South, you shall have at all times the patient, sympathetic help of my race; only let this be constantly in mind, that, while from representations in these buildings of the product of field, of forest, of mine, of factory, letters, and art, much good will come, yet far above and beyond material benefits will be that higher good, that, let us pray God, will come, in a blotting out of sectional differences and racial animosities and suspicions, in a determination to administer absolute justice, in a willing obedience among all classes to the mandates of law. This, coupled with our material prosperity, will bring into our beloved South a new heaven and a new earth.

4 W.E.B. Du Bois, "Of Booker T. Washington and Others," from *The Souls of Black Folk*, 1903[7]

William Edward Burghardt Du Bois (1868–1963) was a civil rights activist, writer, and sociologist, who helped found the Niagara Movement and, in

[7]   Source: W.E.B. Du Bois, *The Souls of Black Folk* (Chicago, 1903), pp. 50–9.

1909, the National Association for the Advancement of Colored People
(NAACP). Born in Great Barrington, Massachusetts, Du Bois was educated
at Fisk University in Nashville in 1888, and then received a PhD from
Harvard University in 1895 – the first African American to receive a
doctorate from that institution. From 1910 to 1934, he edited the NAACP's
magazine, The Crisis.

    Du Bois's background, ideas, and approach to the race crisis differed
fundamentally from Booker T. Washington's. In one of his best-known works,
The Souls of Black Folk *(1903), Du Bois here outlined how he differed from*
Washington's gradualist and accommodationist approach to race relations.

Mr. Washington represents in Negro thought the old attitude of adjustment and submission; but adjustment at such a peculiar time as to make his programme unique. This is an age of unusual economic development, and Mr. Washington's programme naturally takes an economic cast, becoming a gospel of Work and Money to such an extent as apparently almost completely to overshadow the higher aims of life. Moreover, this is an age when the more advanced races are coming in closer contact with the less developed races, and the race-feeling is therefore intensified; and Mr. Washington's programme practically accepts the alleged inferiority of the Negro races. Again, in our own land, the reaction from the sentiment of war time has given impetus to race-prejudice against Negroes, and Mr. Washington withdraws many of the high demands of Negroes as men and American citizens. In other periods of intensified prejudice all the Negro's tendency to self-assertion has been called forth; at this period a policy of submission is advocated. In the history of nearly all other races and peoples the doctrine preached at such crises has been that manly self-respect is worth more than lands and houses, and that a people who voluntarily surrender such respect, or cease striving for it, are not worth civilizing.

    In answer to this, it has been claimed that the Negro can survive only through submission. Mr. Washington distinctly asks that black people give up, at least for the present, three things,—

    First, political power,

    Second, insistence on civil rights,

    Third, higher education of Negro youth, —and concentrate all their energies on industrial education, the accumulation of wealth, and the conciliation of the South. This policy has been courageously and insistently advocated for over fifteen years, and has been triumphant for perhaps ten years. As a result of this tender of the palm-branch, what has been the return? In these years there have occurred:

1. The disfranchisement of the Negro.
2. The legal creation of a distinct status of civil inferiority for the Negro.
3. The steady withdrawal of aid from institutions for the higher training of the Negro.

These movements are not, to be sure, direct results of Mr. Washington's teachings; but his propaganda has, without a shadow of doubt, helped their speedier accomplishment. The question then comes: Is it possible, and probable, that nine millions of men can make effective progress in economic lines if they are deprived of political rights, made a servile caste, and allowed only the most meagre chance for developing their exceptional men? If history and reason give any distinct answer to these questions, it is an emphatic No. And Mr. Washington thus faces the triple paradox of his career:

1. He is striving nobly to make Negro artisans business men and property-owners; but it is utterly impossible, under modern competitive methods, for workingmen and property-owners to defend their rights and exist without the right of suffrage.
2. He insists on thrift and self-respect, but at the same time counsels a silent submission to civic inferiority such as is bound to sap the manhood of any race in the long run.
3. He advocates common-school and industrial training, and depreciates institutions of higher learning; but neither the Negro common-schools, nor Tuskegee itself, could remain open a day were it not for teachers trained in Negro colleges, or trained by their graduates. . . .

The other class of Negroes who cannot agree with Mr. Washington has hitherto said little aloud. They deprecate the sight of scattered counsels, of internal disagreement; and especially they dislike making their just criticism of a useful and earnest man an excuse for a general discharge of venom from small-minded opponents. Nevertheless, the questions involved are so fundamental and serious that it is difficult to see how men . . . [of] this group can much longer be silent. Such men feel in conscience bound to ask of this nation three things.

1. The right to vote.
2. Civic equality.
3. The education of youth according to ability.

They acknowledge Mr. Washington's invaluable service in counselling patience and courtesy in such demands; they do not ask that ignorant black men vote when ignorant whites are debarred, or that any reasonable restrictions in the suffrage should not be applied; they know that the low social level or the mass of the race is responsible for much discrimination against it, but they also know, and the nation knows, that relentless color-prejudice is more often a cause than a result of the Negro's degradation; they seek the abatement of this relic of barbarism, and not its systematic encouragement and pampering by all agencies of social power from the Associated Press to the Church of Christ. They advocate, with Mr. Washington, a broad system of Negro common schools supplemented by thorough industrial training; but they are surprised that a man of Mr. Washington's insight cannot see that no such educational system ever has rested or can rest on any other basis than that of the well-equipped college and university, and they insist that there is a demand for a few such institutions throughout the South to train the best of the Negro youth as teachers, professional men, and leaders.

This group of men honor Mr. Washington for his attitude of conciliation toward the white South; they accept the "Atlanta Compromise" in its broadest interpretation; they recognize, with him, many signs of promise, many men of high purpose and fair judgment, in this section; they know that no easy task has been laid upon a region already tottering under heavy burdens. But, nevertheless, they insist that the way to truth and right lies in straightforward honesty, not in indiscriminate flattery; in praising those of the South who do well and criticizing uncompromisingly those who do ill; in taking advantage of the opportunities at hand and urging their fellows to do the same, but at the same time in remembering that only a firm adherence to their higher ideals and aspirations will ever keep those ideals within the realm of possibility. They do not expect that the free right to vote, to enjoy civic rights, and to be educated, will come in a moment; they do not expect to see the bias and prejudices of years disappear at the blast of a trumpet; but they are absolutely certain that the way for a people to gain their reasonable rights is not by voluntarily throwing them away and insisting that they do not want them; that the way for a people to gain respect is not by continually belittling and ridiculing themselves; that, on the contrary, Negroes must insist continually, in season and out of season, that voting is necessary to modern manhood, that color discrimination is barbarism, and that black boys need education as well as white boys. . . .

It is the duty of black men to judge the South discriminatingly. The present generation of Southerners are not responsible for the past, and they should not be blindly hated or blamed for it. Furthermore, to no class is the indiscriminate endorsement of the recent course of the South toward Negroes more nauseating than to the best thought of the South. The South is not "solid"; it is a land in the ferment of social change, wherein forces of all kinds are fighting for supremacy; and to praise the ill the South is to-day perpetrating is just as wrong as to condemn the good. Discriminating and broad-minded criticism is what the South needs,—needs it for the sake of her own white sons and daughters, and for the insurance of robust, healthy mental and moral development. . . .

[Booker T. Washington's] doctrine has tended to make the whites, North and South, shift the burden of the Negro problem to the Negro's shoulders and stand aside as critical and rather pessimistic spectators; when in fact the burden belongs to the nation, and the hands of none of us are clean if we bend not our energies to righting these great wrongs. . . .

The black men of America have a duty to perform, a duty stern and delicate,—a forward movement to oppose a part of the work of their greatest leader. So far as Mr. Washington preaches Thrift, Patience, and Industrial Training for the masses, we must hold up his hands and strive with him, rejoicing in his honors and glorying in the strength of this Joshua called of God and of man to lead the headless host. But so far as Mr. Washington apologizes for injustice, North or South, does not rightly value the privilege and duty of voting, belittles the emasculating effects of caste distinctions, and opposes the higher training and ambition of our brighter minds,—so far as he, the South, or the Nation, does this,—we must unceasingly and firmly oppose them. By every civilized and peaceful method we must strive for the rights which the world accords to men, clinging unwaveringly to those great words which the sons of the Fathers would fain forget: "We hold these truths to be self-evident: That all men are created equal; that they are endowed by their Creator with certain unalienable rights; that among these are life, liberty, and the pursuit of happiness."

5 Images from the North Carolina White Supremacy Campaign, 1898

The triumph of racism during the 1890s significantly shaped the political status and civil rights of African Americans. During Reconstruction, freed slaves had acquired, in principle, rights of citizenship and voting in the United States, according to the Thirteenth, Fourteenth, and Fifteenth Amendments. Those rights were seriously limited in practice, especially after anti-Reconstruction political parties asserted control in the South during the 1860s and 1870s. Still, there were pockets of black political power during the Gilded Age, especially in states such as North Carolina, where the Republican Party – which had championed black political rights during Reconstruction – remained competitive.

In North Carolina, Republicans shared control of the legislature in a coalition (or "fusion") with the Populists; in 1896, a Republican governor,

Daniel L. Russell, was elected. The Democrats struck back furiously with an all-out political attack that was based on appeals to race. In 1898, in elections to the state legislature, leading Democratic newspapers across the state conducted what they called a "White Supremacy campaign," which called on white voters to rally behind the Democratic cause. The campaign was inflamed especially around an editorial written by African American Alex Manly, who edited the Wilmington Daily Record. *Responding to an article defending lynching as a justifiable response to black rape, Manly asserted that consensual relations between white women and black men were not uncommon. In reaction to this break from the taboo against interracial sex between white women and black men, the Democratic press singled out Manly – and so-called "Negro Rule" in Wilmington, where black officeholders helped to run the city. As the election approached in November 1898, Wilmington whites launched a military coup d'état. Manly's* Daily Record *offices were burned, and black officeholders expelled from the city.*

Figure 9.1 "A Serious Question – How Long Will This Last?," image from North Carolina's White Supremacy Campaign, 1898, from H. Leon Prather, Sr., *We Have Taken a City: Wilmington Racial Massacre and Coup of 1898* (Cranbury, NJ, Associated University Presses), p. 64.
Source: Raleigh *News and Observer*, August 13, 1898, North Carolina Collection, University of North Carolina at Chapel Hill Library.

REMEMBER THE

These degenerate sons of the white race who control the republican machine in this county, or those whose positions made them influential in putting negro rule on the whites, will suffer the penalty of their responsibility for any disturbance consequent on the determination of the white men of this county to carry the election at any cost.

REMEMBER THE

Figure 9.2   Image from North Carolina's White Supremacy Campaign, 1898, from H. Leon Prather, Sr., *We Have Taken a City: Wilmington Racial Massacre and Coup of 1898* (Cranbury, NJ, Associated University Presses), p. 86.
Source: North Carolina Collection, University of North Carolina at Chapel Hill Library.

6 Mary Church Terrell, "What It Means to be Colored in the Capital of the United States," 1906[8]

Mary Church Terrell (1863–1954), born in Tennessee, was the daughter of slaves and one of the first African American women to earn a college degree, graduating from Oberlin College, Ohio, in 1884 and earning a master's degree there in 1888. She devoted much of her life to advancing the causes of civil rights and suffrage.

Terrell became a high-school teacher and principal in Washington, DC, and was appointed to the school board, the first black woman to hold such a position in the United States. A member of numerous important social and political organizations, such as the National American Woman Suffrage Association (NAWSA) and the National Association of Colored Women's Clubs (NACWC), she was also one of the founding members of the National

[8]   Delivered October 10, 1906, United Women's Club, Washington, DC (copy at http://gos.sbc.edu/t/terrell1.html).

Association for the Advancement of Colored People (NAACP). As late as
1950, Terrell started a successful effort to integrate restaurants in the District
of Columbia. She lived just long enough to witness the Supreme Court
decision in 1954 in Brown v. Board of Education, *which prohibited school*
segregation on the basis of race.

Washington, D.C., has been called "The Colored Man's Paradise." Whether this sobriquet was given to the national capital in bitter irony by a member of the handicapped race, as he reviewed some of his own persecutions and rebuffs, or whether it was given immediately after the war by an ex-slave-holder who for the first time in his life saw colored people walking about like free men, minus the overseer and his whip, history saith not. It is certain that it would be difficult to find a worse misnomer for Washington than "The Colored Man's Paradise" if so prosaic a consideration as veracity is to determine the appropriateness of a name.

For fifteen years I have resided in Washington, and while it was far from being a paradise for colored people when I first touched these shores it has been doing its level best ever since to make conditions for us intolerable. As a colored woman I might enter Washington any night, a stranger in a strange land, and walk miles without finding a place to lay my head. Unless I happened to know colored people who live here or ran across a chance acquaintance who could recommend a colored boarding-house to me, I should be obliged to spend the entire night wandering about. Indians, Chinamen, Filipinos, Japanese and representatives of any other dark race can find hotel accommodations, if they can pay for them. The colored man alone is thrust out of the hotels of the national capital like a leper.

As a colored woman I may walk from the Capitol to the White House, ravenously hungry and abundantly supplied with money with which to purchase a meal, without finding a single restaurant in which I would be permitted to take a morsel of food, if it was patronized by white people, unless I were willing to sit behind a screen. As a colored woman I cannot visit the tomb of the Father of this country, which owes its very existence to the love of freedom in the human heart and which stands for equal opportunity to all, without being forced to sit in the Jim Crow section of an electric car which starts from the very heart of the city–midway between the Capitol and the White House. If I refuse thus to be humiliated, I am cast into jail and forced to pay a fine for violating the Virginia laws. . . .

As a colored woman I may enter more than one white church in Washington without receiving that welcome which as a human being I have the right to expect in the sanctuary of God. . . .

Unless I am willing to engage in a few menial occupations, in which the pay for my services would be very poor, there is no way for me to earn an honest living, if I am not a trained nurse or a dressmaker or can secure a position as teacher in the public schools, which is exceedingly difficult to do. It matters not what my intellectual attainments may be or how great is the need of the services of a competent person, if I try to enter many of the numerous vocations in which my white sisters are allowed to engage, the door is shut in my face.

From one Washington theater I am excluded altogether. In the remainder certain seats are set aside for colored people, and it is almost impossible to secure others. . . .

With the exception of the Catholic University, there is not a single white college in the national capitol to which colored people are admitted. . . . A few years ago the Columbian Law School admitted colored students, but in deference to the Southern white students the authorities have decided to exclude them altogether.

Some time ago a young woman who had already attracted some attention in the literary world by her volume of short stories answered an advertisement which appeared in a Washington newspaper, which called for the services of a skilled stenographer and expert typewriter. . . . The applicants were requested to send specimens of their work and answer certain questions concerning their experience and their speed before they called in person. In reply to her application the young colored woman. . . received a letter from the firm stating that her references and experience were the most satisfactory that had been sent and requesting her to call. When she presented herself there was some doubt in the mind of the man to whom she was directed concerning her racial pedigree, so he asked her point-blank whether she was colored or white. When she confessed the truth the merchant expressed. . . deep regret that he could not avail himself of the services of so competent a person, but frankly admitted that employing a colored woman in his establishment in any except a menial position was simply out of the question. . . .

Not only can colored women secure no employment in the Washington stores, department and otherwise, except as menials, and such positions, of course, are few, but even as customers they are not infrequently treated with discourtesy both by the clerks and the proprietor himself. . . .

Although white and colored teachers are under the same Board of Education and the system for the children of both races is said to be uniform, prejudice against the colored teachers in the public schools is manifested in a variety of ways. From 1870 to 1900 there was a colored superintendent at the head of the colored schools. During all that time the directors of the cooking, sewing, physical culture, manual training, music and art departments were colored people. Six years ago a change was inaugurated. The colored superintendent was legislated out of office and the director-ships, without a single exception, were taken from colored teachers and given to the whites. . . .

Now, no matter how competent or superior the colored teachers in our public schools may be, they know that they can never rise to the height of a directorship, can never hope to be more than an assistant and receive the meager salary therefore, unless the present regime is radically changed. . . .

Strenuous efforts are being made to run Jim Crow cars in the national capital. . . . Representative Heflin, of Alabama, who introduced a bill pro-viding for Jim Crow street cars in the District of Columbia last winter, has just received a letter from the president of the East Brookland Citizens' Association "indorsing the movement for separate street cars and sincerely hoping that you will be successful in getting this enacted into a law as soon as possible." Brookland is a suburb of Washington.

The colored laborer's path to a decent livelihood is by no means smooth. Into some of the trades unions here he is admitted, while from others he is excluded altogether. By the union men this is denied, although I am person-ally acquainted with skilled workmen who tell me they are not admitted into the unions because they are colored. But even when they are allowed to join the unions they frequently derive little benefit, owing to certain tricks of the trade. When the word passes round that help is needed and colored laborers apply, they are often told by the union officials that they have secured all the men they needed, because the places are reserved for white men, until they have been provided with jobs, and colored men must remain idle, unless the supply of white men is too small. . . .

And so I might go on citing instance after instance to show the variety of ways in which our people are sacrificed on the altar of prejudice in the Capital of the United States and how almost insurmountable are the obstacles which block his path to success. . . .

It is impossible for any white person in the United States, no matter how sympathetic and broad, to realize what life would mean to him if his incentive to effort were suddenly snatched away. To the lack of incentive to effort, which is the awful shadow under which we live, may be traced the wreck and ruin of score of colored youth. And surely nowhere in the world do oppression and persecution based solely on the color of the skin appear more hateful and hideous than in the capital of the United States, because the chasm between the principles upon which this Government was founded, in which it still professes to believe, and those which are daily practiced under the protection of the flag, yawn so wide and deep.

Discussion Questions: Chapter 9

1   According to Wells, in what ways are legal standards unequally applied to blacks and whites?

2   How important was white racism in southern politics? How did white supremacy figure in the politics of the 1890s?

3   What were the implications of the Supreme Court's decision in *Plessy*? How did it shape public policy?

4   Was Booker T. Washington's approach in the Atlanta Compromise realistic or excessively accepting of white racism?

5   What were the basic elements of Du Bois's policy toward white supremacy, and how did they differ from Washington's approach?

Chapter 10   Labor Protest

1   Roger O'Mara, Testimony on Railroad Labor Strikes, 1878[1]

When railroad workers on the Baltimore and Ohio line struck for better wages in Martinsburg, West Virginia, in July 1877, the majority of newspaper editorials sided with the owners, arguing, as the New York Times *did on July 21, 1877, that, just as labor had a right to negotiate for a high wage, so, too, did owners of a business have the right to hire labor for as low a wage as possible. Arguing that the strike and the resulting protests were "simply a revolt against law and order," the* Times *equated the strikers' demands for better wages with a man demanding items from a grocer "at a certain price or have his head shot off." Overexpansion of the railroads following the Civil War and rampant speculation in railroad stocks contributed to an economic panic in 1873 and a severe depression for several years afterward. Unemployment rates rose, as wages fell.*

The strikes started on July 14, 1877, in West Virginia and spread to Pittsburgh and across the nation, accompanied by varying degrees of violence and little sympathy for the strikers, who were regarded by supporters of business as a dangerous threat to free enterprise and to economic and social stability. The strikes lasted 45 days and were stopped by local, state, and federal troops. In some cities, notably Chicago, the strikes

---

[1] *Report of the Committee to Investigate the Railroad Riots in July, 1877* (Harrisburg: Lane S. Hart, 1878).

The Gilded Age and Progressive Era: A Documentary Reader, First Edition.
Edited by William A. Link and Susannah J. Link.
© 2012 Blackwell Publishing Ltd. Published 2012 by Blackwell Publishing Ltd.

affected not only railroads but spread to other industries as well.
Working-class women who participated in the strikes were derided as
"Bohemian Amazons" in an attempt to make them seem unconventional and
masculine. Although the socialist Workingmen's party encouraged some of the
strikes in the West and played a prominent role in the more general industrial
strikes in Chicago and St Louis, socialists were unfairly blamed for planning
and leading the strikes. Workers argued that the American labor system verged
on slavery, with employers who claimed that if a worker refused to accept
lower wages, there was always someone else who would. In this document,
Roger O'Mara, Pittsburgh Chief of Detectives, testified on February 11, 1878,
to the committee appointed to investigate the railroad strikes.

A: I was out there (at the scene of disturbance) on Sunday morning early, along the line on Liberty Street. There was a good deal of trouble about the city, and we were gathering the police in and sending them out throughout the city. We were afraid that the mob would break into the gun shops. The excitement was so great that I thought they might attempt to break into places, and so I gathered the men up and sent them to different places.

Q: If the mayor had made a call for policemen on Thursday afternoon, how many men could he have raised?

A: I do not know. I have no idea.

Q: Would there have been any difficulty in raising any number of policemen, do you think?

A: There might have been some. That call was made through the Sunday papers, and a good many responded.

Q: How many officers and men does the night force consist of?

A: The whole force was one hundred and twenty men—nine of them were engaged in the station-houses, and ten of them watched lamps—patrolmen, detectives, and all. That was for the whole city.

Q: How many men were discharged from the day force?

A: One hundred and sixteen men were discharged. Our whole force consisted of two hundred and thirty-six men, all told. The appropriation ran out, and we had to knock the men off.

Q: What reason was given by the officer for not serving the warrants? He had them one night, had he not?

A: We did not get the houses all located. It seems they were out that night, and we could not get them served, and the next morning we were ordered not to serve them. The case was put into the hands of the sheriff on Friday, I think.

Q: While you had those warrants for the arrest of those ten men, could you not have arrested them?

A: I do not think, with the few men we could have got, that we could have arrested them out there, on account of those men out there. It might have made the thing worse if we had attempted to arrest them on the ground. I thought it was better to arrest them away from there.

Q: Did you attempt to locate them at their homes that night—you did not go to their homes?

A: No; we did not go to their homes, but we got information from the parties who made the information.

Q: Did you have any arrangement to watch those men?

A: From all accounts, the men seemed to be in the crowd. We had no one watching their houses that night, because we did not find out that night where they all lived.

Q: Did you not have men to watch these men or follow them around?

A: No sir, not to my knowledge.

Q: Were you present at any time during the destruction of the property of the railroad company by fire?

A: I was along the line Sunday morning, in Liberty street. I drove along with the mayor in a buggy. My mother and sister both lived back of the Union depot, and they were burned out. I tried to help them get their things away.

Q: During the fire, were you ever called on by the chief of fire department, or by anybody connected with the fire department, to protect them in their attempts to put out the fire?

A: No, sir.

Q: Do you know of any other officer of the police force being called upon to assist them?

A: No.

Q: Did you take any measures to prevent this destruction?

A: We could not do anything after the first firing was done. With what police force we had, we could do nothing at all. They commenced breaking into houses, and gun stores, &c., and we tried to prevent them from doing that.

Q: Did you see them breaking into any gun stores?

A: Yes; on Penn street I saw a couple of men breaking into a pawn shop. I heard of the mob coming, and I hurried up the officers, and placed men in front of different gun stores, but on Wood street they got into one in spite of the men. Before that, we had notified the different parties to put their guns away, that the excitement was very great, and that the soldiers had fired upon the men, and that they would be apt to break into places to try to get arms. I notified the different parties to put their goods away that the mob should not get them.

Q: Who composed that crowd—did you recognize any of them?

A: They seemed to be working men—men that came from the south side. One squad that came from the south side—I saw them going down the street—a couple of young men—the same that I saw marching down Penn street. Some of them have been arrested since.

Q: You think the men were principally from the south side who broke into the gun stores?

A: About the time that they broke into them, at different places, I had squads of men. On Fifth street a couple of young men came down firing off guns, and I went to the mayor's office for more men, and I was not there two minutes when word came that Brown's gun store was broke into. I then got some men and placed them in front of the door.

Q: Did you succeed in keeping the crowd out then?

A: Yes; but it was not much good then, for the things were gone. They had ransacked the place.

Q: What time was that?

A: It was on Saturday night. It was just about dusk when this party came down, and went in on Liberty street and on Penn street. I was going up that way towards Twenty-eighth street, when I saw this mob coming down. I followed on down to see what they proposed to do.

2 United States Strike Commission, Report on the Chicago Pullman Strike, 1894[2]

George Pullman was an entrepreneur who developed a fleet of railroad sleeping cars, which he leased to railroad operators throughout the nation. He built a company town (Pullman, Illinois) near Chicago and, in his usual profit-making fashion, sold shares in the town to investors and rented the houses to his workers. He sold food, gas, and water to his renters at a 10 percent markup.

The Pullman strike of 1894 was the first national labor strike, and it caused discussions about the need to balance the interests of labor and capital. The immediate cause of the strike was the financial panic of 1893 and the resulting economic depression. When the economic downturn occurred, Pullman laid off one-third of his labor force and cut wages and hours by 25 percent for the remaining workers. Many of the workers joined the American Railway Union, a new union led by Eugene V. Debs that had led a successful strike against the Great Northern Railway in early 1894. In May 1894, the Pullman workers struck, and Debs was able to widen the strike to other railroad companies by getting workers to agree not to move trains that carried Pullman cars.

The railroad owners demanded federal troops to break the strike, but the governor of Illinois, John P. Altgeld, refused to comply. The owners appealed to the US attorney general, Richard Olney, who issued an injunction against the strike, and when strikers refused to comply, President Grover Cleveland ordered federal troops to break the strike. When fighting broke out between the two sides, the soldiers killed a dozen strikers and injured many more.

The strike was effectively broken, but Debs was radicalized by his involvement and arrest, subsequently becoming a member of the Socialist party and running for president five times in the early twentieth century. The message to workers that the federal government would not tolerate strikes remained until the 1930s.

---

[2]   (Washington: Government Printing Office, 1895), pp. xxxii–xxxix.

THE STRIKE

The reductions at Pullman after September, 1893, were the result of conferences among the managers; the employees for the first time knew of them when they took effect. No explanations or conferences took place until May 7 and 9 in regard thereto between the employees and the officers of the company. For the reasons stated the employees at Pullman were during the winter in a state of chronic discontent. Upon May 7 and 9 a committee of 46 from all the departments waited upon the management and urged the restoration of wages to the basis of June, 1893. The company refused this, and offered no concession as to wages whatever, maintaining and explaining that business conditions did not justify any change. . . .

The demand of the employees for the wages of June, 1893, was clearly unjustifiable. The business in May, 1894, could not pay the wages of June, 1893. . . .

On the evening of May 10 the local unions met and voted to strike at once. The strike occurred on May 11, and from that time until the soldiers went to Pullman, about July 4, three hundred strikers were placed about the company's property, professedly to guard it from destruction or interference. This guarding of property in strikes is, as a rule, a mere pretense. Too often the real object of guards is to prevent newcomers from taking strikers' places, by persuasion, often to be followed, if ineffectual, by intimidation and violence. The Pullman company claims this was the real object of these guards. . . .

As soon as the strike was declared the company laid off its 600 employees who did not join the strike, and kept its shops closed until August 2. During this period the Civic Federation of Chicago, composed of eminent citizens in all kinds of business and from all grades of respectable society, called upon the company twice to urge conciliation and arbitration. The company reiterated the statement of its position, and maintained that there was nothing to arbitrate; that the questions at issue were matters of fact and not proper subjects of arbitration. The Civic Federation suggested that competition should be regarded in rents as well as in wages. The company denied this. . . .

RAILROAD STRIKE

Between June 9 and June 26 a regular convention of the American Railway Union was held with open doors at Chicago, representing 465 local unions and about 150,000 members, as claimed. The Pullman matter was publicly discussed at these meetings before and after its committees above mentioned reported their interviews with the Pullman company. On June 21 the delegates, under instructions from their local unions, unanimously voted that the members of the union should stop handling Pullman cars on June 26 unless the Pullman company would consent to arbitration. On June 26 the boycott and strike began. The strike on the part of the railroad employees was a sympathetic one. No grievances against the railroads had been presented by their employees, nor did the American Railway Union declare any such grievances to be any cause whatever of the strike. . . .

On July 7 the principal officers of the American Railway Union were indicted, arrested, and held under $10,000 bail. Upon July 13 they were attached for contempt of the United States court in disobeying an injunction issued on July 2 and served on the 3d and 4th, enjoining them, among other things, from compelling, or inducing by threats, intimidation, persuasion, force, or violence, railroad employees to refuse or fail to perform their duties.

ACTION OF FEDERATED UNIONS

Upon July 12, at the request of the American Railway Union, about 25 of the executive officers of national and international labor unions affiliated with the American Federation of Labor met at Chicago. The situation was laid before them. The conference concluded that the strike was then lost; that a general sympathetic strike throughout the country would be unwise and inexpedient, and, at the time, against the best interests of labor. This conference issued a strong and temperate address to members, expressing sympathy with the purposes of the American Railway Union, advising those on strike to return to work, and urging that labor organize more generally, combine more closely, and seek the correction of industrial evils at the ballot box. To some extent the trade unions of Chicago had struck in sympathy, but this movement was checked by the action of the conference of the 12th and extended no further. This action indicates clearer views by labor as to its responsibilities, the futility of strikes, and the appropriate remedies in this country for labor wrongs.

Upon July 13 the American Railway Union, through the mayor of Chicago, sent a communication to the General Managers' Association offering to declare the strike off, provided the men should be restored to their former positions without prejudice, except in cases where they had been convicted of crime. The General Managers' Association in advance advertised that it would receive no communication whatever from the American Railway Union, and when received returned it unanswered. With reference to this, John M. Egan, strike manager of the General Managers' Association, testified as follows:

. . . . At this date, July 13, and for some days previous, the strikers had been virtually beaten. The action of the courts deprived the American Railway Union of leadership, enabled the General Managers' Association to disintegrate its forces, and to make inroads into its ranks. The mobs had worn out their fury, or had succumbed to the combined forces of the police, the United States troops and marshals, and the State militia. The railroads were gradually repairing damages and resuming traffic with the aid of new men and with some of those strikers who had not been offensively active or whose action was laid to intimidation and fear. At this juncture the refusal of the General Managers' Association to treat with the American Railway Union was certainly not conciliatory; it was not unnatural, however, because the association charged the American Railway Union with having inaugurated an unjustifiable strike, laid at its door the responsibility for all the disorder and destruction that had occurred, and, as the victor in the fight, desired that the lesson taught to labor by its defeat should be well learned.

The policy of both the Pullman company and the Railway Managers' Association in reference to applications to arbitrate closed the door to all attempts at conciliation and settlement of differences. The commission is impressed with the belief, by the evidence and by the attendant circumstances as disclosed, that a different policy would have prevented the loss of life and great loss of property and wages occasioned by the strike.

ACTION OF THE GENERAL MANAGERS' ASSOCIATION

From June 22 until the practical end of the strike the General Managers' Association directed and controlled the contest on the part of the railroads, using the combined resources of all the roads to support the contentions and insure the protection of each. On June 26 we find in the proceedings of the association the following statement:

A general discussion of the situation followed. It was suggested that some common plan of action ought to be adopted in case employees refused to do switching of passenger trains with Pullman cars, but were willing to continue all of their other work, and it was the general expression that in case any man refused to do his duty he would be discharged.

Headquarters were established; agencies for hiring men opened; as the men arrived they were cared for and assigned to duty upon the different lines: a bureau was started to furnish information to the press; the lawyers of the different roads were called into conference and combination in legal and criminal proceedings; the general managers met daily to hear reports and to direct proceedings; constant communication was kept up with the civil and military authorities as to the movements and assignments of police, marshals, and troops. Each road did what it could with its operating forces, but all the leadership, direction, and concentration of power, resources, and influence on the part of the railroads were centered in the General Managers' Association. That association stood for each and all of its 24 combined members, and all that they could command, in fighting and crushing the strike.

VIOLENCE AND DESTRUCTION OF PROPERTY AND MILITARY PROCEEDINGS

The figures given as to losses, fatalities, destruction of property, and arrests for crime tell the story of violence, intimidation, and mob rule better than it can be described. Chicago is a vast metropolis, the center of an activity and growth unprecedented in history, and combining all that this implies. Its lawless elements are at present augmented by shiftless adventurers and criminals attracted to it by the Exposition and impecuniously stranded in its midst. In the mobs were also actively present many of a certain class of objectionable foreigners, who are being precipitated upon us by unrestricted immigration. No more dangerous place for such a strike could be chosen.

The strike, as a strike and as is usual with strikes, presented an opportunity to these elements to burn and plunder, and to violate the laws and ordinances of the city, State, and nation. Superintendent of Police Brennan swears as follows:

On the 26th of June the mayor directed me to use the whole police force in preserving the peace, protecting property, and preventing violence, and from that time on until the arrival of the troops I think I succeeded pretty well. So far as I understand, there had not been very much violence or depredations committed prior to the 3d of July, when the troops arrived. At that time the indications looked bad and the arrival of the troops, I think, was opportune.

3 Constance D. Leupp, "The Shirtwaist Makers' Strike," 1909[3]

Constance D. Leupp was a labor and health reformer and suffragist who wrote a number of articles in the early twentieth century for leading investigative magazines, among them McClure's *and* The Survey. *From a*

---

[3] *The Survey* (December 18, 1909).

*well-to-do family in Manhattan, she summered in the Berkshires at the
Lenox Club, a place where cottage owners and guests of local hotels
gathered for social events. In this article, Leupp wrote about the famous
shirtwaist strike of November 1909–February 1910, which occurred in the
garment industry of New York City. One of the largest manufacturing
businesses in the city in the early twentieth century, the garment industry
mostly employed young Jewish and Italian immigrant women. The women
labored in small factories throughout the city for long hours, receiving low
wages.*

*The Triangle factory was one of the largest in the industry, and, when
some of the Jewish workers there voted in September 1909 to join the
United Hebrew Trades, an association of Jewish labor unions, they were
fired from their jobs. Triangle workers walked off the job in retaliation, and
they began to picket in front of the factory. The company hired
strikebreakers and the police helped to disperse and arrest the picketers.
The International Ladies' Garment Workers' Union (ILGWU) called a
general meeting to discuss the situation at which the labor leader Samuel
Gompers spoke. A garment worker, Clara Lemlich, who had been beaten
earlier that year for her union activities, called for a general strike, and,
within days, 20,000 garment workers from 500 factories had walked off the
job. Most smaller factories had settled with their workers within the first
month, adding better pay, shorter hours, and more safety standards, but the
larger factories held out until February 1910, when the majority of those
also settled and the strike ended. Triangle, however, refused to accept the
conditions, and women returned to work there without improved
conditions or union recognition by the owners. The Triangle Shirtwaist
factory was the scene of a terrible fire about a year later, in March 1911
(see Document 10.4).*

"We'd rather starve quick than starve slow." Such is the battle cry of the
30,000 striking shirtwaist makers (mostly girls) who since November 22 have
made Clinton hall the busiest and most interesting spot in New York city.

Since the union movement began among women, nothing so significant as
this general strike has happened, and for generalship, obedience and good
conduct under circumstances which would break a less determined and courageous host, these Jewish, Italian and American girls from the East Side can
give points to trades practiced in striking.

The members of the trade in New York are estimated at 40,000; between
30,000 and 35,000 have joined the Ladies' Shirtwaist Makers' Union.
Already 18,000 girls are again at their machines on their own terms, 236
firms having taken them back into closed shops. It is the smaller shops that
have settled. The bitterest part of the fight is still ahead.

The history of the trouble has not been fairly given to the public. A few facts about the wholesale trade of machine shirtwaist making will make the whole story more comprehensible. . . .

Sub-contracting is a system whereby the firm never makes any dealing directly with the operators. The sub-contractor undertakes to produce a definite amount of work for a definite price, and makes what bargains he sees fit with his girls. He can slave-drive and underpay as he pleases, and even if his intentions are of the best, he represents an extra profit; the burden of which falls on the operator rather than the consumer.

Curiously enough, it was a sub-contractor who started the strike. Some eighteen months ago at the Triangle shop on Washington place (Harris and Blank's) this man because he "was sick of slave-driving" protested to the manager, saying he wanted to go and take his girls with him. He was not allowed to speak to the girls after he had expressed himself, but was told to report to the cashier for his pay. Fearful of a slugging on the way up in the elevator, he asked to have someone go with him, and was not only refused, but set upon and dragged out of the shop—the original "assault." As he was dragged along he shouted, "Will you stay at your machines and see a fellow worker treated this way?" And impulsively 400 operators dropped their work and walked out.

The union at that time numbered only about 500 members and the trade was in no way organized; so when secretary Schindler suggested conciliatory methods, and the firm seemed willing to treat, it was not difficult to fill the shop again. The managers formed a society of the more intelligent workers, and with its members in council, terms were hit upon. "The society and a job or the union and no job" was the demand of the firm. The society having a membership limited to one hundred, there were five non-members to one member. By degrees it was discovered that the members got most of its benefits, and in frightened twos and threes the girls began to drift down to union headquarters and ask for help in organizing. Discontent grew even among the members, so that when last September a meeting was held at Clinton hall to discuss the situation, all but seven members of the society were asking for help from the union. . . .

This was the situation with the Triangle company on the first of October. Meanwhile there was a local strike at Leiserson's, and the trade at large, seething with discontent, needed no further encouragement to go out *en masse*. Probably the only consideration that had held them in check before was the fear on the part of the Jewish girls—the larger part of the trade— that the Italians would "scab." Employers had made clever use of race and religious antagonism to keep the girls from uniting.

The resolution for a general strike was taken at mass meetings held November 22. At Cooper Union Mr. Gompers spoke, and a procession of speakers, mostly Yiddish, for two hours implored their attentive audience to go about the thing soberly and with due consideration; but, if they decided to strike, to stand by their colors and be loyal to the union. The dramatic climax of the evening was reached when Clara Lemlich, a striker from Leiserson's who had been assaulted when picketing, made her way to the platform, begged a moment from the chairman and after an impromptu Philippic in Yiddish, eloquent even to American ears, put the motion for a general strike and was unanimously endorsed. The chairman then cried, "Do you mean faith? Will you take the old Jewish oath?" And up came 2,000 right hands with the prayer: "If I turn traitor to the cause I now pledge, may this hand wither and drop off at the wrist from the arm I now raise."

Several weeks before this eventful night, the arresting of pickets had begun, and members of the Women's Trade Union League had begun to take a hand. Picketing as practiced by these strikers consists in sentry duty performed by union members before the doors at a shop at opening and closing hours, telling the scabs that a strike is on,—among the newly arrived foreigners there are many who do not know this—and asking them to come to union headquarters and learn about it. . . .

The girls are showing an unusual pluck and unity of spirit. It is a unique spectacle anywhere to see Jews, Italians and Americans working shoulder to shoulder for a common cause. The management at headquarters is excellent. Mr. Baroff with an office and clerical force adapted to a membership of 500 has handled the affairs of 30,000.

Headquarters have been opened for the Italians, and the Americans gather at the Women's Trade Union League. Strike benefits are paid only to those who ask for them. A few of the strikers are married women; a small number are men, but the overwhelming majority are girls under twenty-five. On the evening of December 4 alone, these amounted to $137, representing twenty-six arrests for technical assaults and twenty-three fines.

The most spectacular features of the whole event have been the visit of several thousand workers to the mayor to ask for fair play from the police, and Mrs. Belmont's woman suffrage meeting on December 5. When called upon by the delegation the mayor promised fair play but when invited by Mrs. Belmont two days later to attend her meeting, he stated his inability to be present and his lack of interest.

These are the demands in which the mayor has no interest:

1. A fifty-two hour week and not more than two hours' overtime on any one day. (The law allows sixty hours a week, and not more than three day's a week overtime.)

2. The closed shop (i.e. no non-union labor employed).
3. Notice of slack work in advance, if possible, or at least promptly on arrival in the morning.
4. In a slack season to keep all hands on part time rather than a few operators on full time, so far as possible.
5. All wages to be paid directly by the firm (i.e., the abolition of the sub-contractor system).
6. A wage scale to be adjusted individually for each shop, but the terms to be determined definitely in advance for all forms of work.

The strikers' demands throw much light on conditions that have previously prevailed in the shops. At the Triangle shop, for instance, in rush seasons the girls worked until eight or nine o' clock at night with no time off for supper; while in slack season not infrequently a girl reported for work at the usual time and sat idle all the morning, to be told at noon that she was not needed.

It is impossible to say how much longer the strike will last and on just what terms it will end. Already the New England cotton mills are feeling the dearth of orders from the city in whose shops and factories one half the ready-made clothing in the country is made. So rapidly are the manufacturers giving in, however, that it is difficult to believe the girls will not win the majority odds in the end. It is safe to prophesy that if they arbitrate they may compromise on every other point, but not on the main most vital issue of the whole struggle—the closed shops.

It is easy to say that the closed shop demand is an unjust one, but in a sweated industry where a union exists it is the best defense of the manufacturer as well as of the worker. If our shirtwaists are going to be made on fair terms, either the profit to the manufacturer must be reduced, or the prices must go up. So long as there are manufacturers in the trade who employ sweated labor, they can always underbid union shops. On the other hand, employers with the best intentions, who use both scab and union labor, will in a rush season will make demands to which union members cannot accede and thus by degrees they are driven out of the mixed shop.

But through and about all this discussion of union and scab labor, looms a larger even more important problem—that of the constitutional right of free speech. The conduct of the police officers and magistrates in their seeming conspiracy of curtailing the liberty of American citizens, is one that must attract the attention of even those who are not interested industrial disputes. . . .

RULES FOR PICKETS

Don't walk in groups of more than two or three.

Don't stand in front of the shop; walk up and down the block.

Don't stop the person you wish to talk to; walk alongside of him.

Don't get excited and shout when you are talking. Don't put your hand on the person you are speaking to. Don't touch his sleeve or button. This may be construed as a "technical assault."

Don't call anyone "scab" or use abusive language of any kind.

Plead, persuade; appeal, but do not threaten.

If a policeman arrest you and you are sure that you have committed no offence, take down his number and give it to your union officers.

From a circular issued by the Ladies' Shirtwaist Makers Union.

4 Photographs of the Triangle Shirtwaist Factory Fire, 1911[4]

On March 25, 1911, fire broke out in the Triangle Shirtwaist factory in Lower Manhattan, New York City. In all, 146 women garment workers died, many leaping to their deaths from the factory windows to the pavement below. Many died trying to escape through the stairwell doors, either because the doors were locked to prevent theft by workers or the panicked workers mobbed the exits and prevented the doors from opening inward. The fire resulted in the passage of factory safety regulations and acceptance of the new International Ladies' Garment Workers' Union (ILGWU), which fought against sweatshop working conditions. A fire-prevention division was added to the New York Fire Department. Before the fire, state and federal governments had largely avoided regulating industry, but the tragedy led to the gradual institution of safety regulations. The factory building is now part of New York University and is a National Historic Landmark.

---

[4]   http://www.ilr.cornell.edu/trianglefire/photos/photo_display.html?sec_id=3

Figure 10.1   Family members arrive at the New York City morgue to identify the bodies of victims of the Triangle Shirtwaist Company Fire.
Source: Photo Bettmann/Corbis.

Figure 10.2   On March 25, 1911, 146 immigrant garment workers were killed after they were trapped on the upper floors of the Asch Building after the Triangle Shirtwaist factory caught fire.
Source: Photo Bettmann/Corbis.

Figure 10.3   A sidewalk cellar's skylight was shattered by the fallen bodies of panic-stricken workers. This photograph shows the gutted remains of the tenth floor, with only the floors and walls intact.
Source: Photo Bettmann/Corbis.

Discussion Questions: Chapter 10

1   What were the objectives of labor protest in the Gilded Age? What did it seek to accomplish?
2   How similar and how different were labor protests in 1878, 1894, and 1909?
3   How much power did corporations exert over working people in the Gilded Age?

Part IV   Reform

Chapter 11 Rebuilding American Institutions

1 John Dewey, from *The School and Society*, 1899[1]

John Dewey (1859–1952) was born in Burlington, Vermont, and graduated from the University of Vermont. He then attended the Johns Hopkins University, where in 1884 he received a PhD in philosophy and psychology. On the faculty at the University of Michigan and later the University of Minnesota, in 1894 Dewey was appointed to the University of Chicago, where he became head of the department of philosophy. He was also appointed head of the department of pedagogy.

At Chicago, Dewey became interested and involved in new ideas of reform that focused on schools, and in 1896 he founded a new laboratory school, the basic premise of which was that schools should be integrated into the needs of society by incorporating the needs of an urban–industrial society. Dewey promoted the philosophy of pragmatism, which included a practical, socially responsible life. A thinker whose ideas profoundly influenced education in the United States, Dewey opposed the accepted practice of learning by rote and instead encouraged a system of learning by doing.

We are apt to look at the school from an individualistic standpoint, as something between teacher and pupil, or between teacher and parent. . . . What the best and wisest parent wants for his own child, that must the

[1] (Chicago: University of Chicago Press, 1899), pp. 19–44.

The Gilded Age and Progressive Era: A Documentary Reader, First Edition.
Edited by William A. Link and Susannah J. Link.
© 2012 Blackwell Publishing Ltd. Published 2012 by Blackwell Publishing Ltd.

community want for all of its children. Any other ideal for our schools is narrow and unlovely; acted upon, it destroys our democracy. All that society has accomplished for itself it puts, through the agency of the school, at the disposal of its future members. All its better thoughts of itself it hopes to realize through the new possibilities thus opened to its future self. Here individualism and socialism are at one. Only by being true to the full growth of all the individuals who make it up, can society by any chance be true to itself. . . .

Whenever we have in mind the discussion of a new movement in education, it is especially necessary to take the broader, or social view. Otherwise, changes in the school institution and tradition will be looked at as the arbitrary inventions of particular teachers; at the worst, transitory fads, and at the best merely improvements in certain details—and this is the plane upon which it is too customary to consider school changes. . . .

[The school is] a miniature community, an embryonic society. This is the fundamental fact, and from this arise continuous and orderly sources of instruction. Under the industrial regime described, the child, after all, shared in the work, not for the sake of the sharing, but for the sake of the product. The educational results secured were real, yet incidental and dependent. But in the school the typical occupations followed are freed from all economic stress. The aim is not the economic value of the products, but the development of social power and insight. It is this liberation from narrow utilities, this openness to the possibilities of the human spirit that makes these practical activities in the school allies of art and centers of science and history. . . .

When occupations in the school are conceived in this broad and generous way, I can only stand lost in wonder at the objections so often heard, that such occupations are out of place in the school because they are materialistic, utilitarian, or even menial in their tendency. It sometimes seems to me that those who make these objections must live in quite another world. The world in which most of us live is a world in which everyone has a calling and occupation, something to do. Some are managers and others are subordinates. But the great thing for one as for the other is that each shall have had the education which enables him to see within his daily work all there is in it of large and human significance. How many of the employed are today mere appendages to the machines which they operate! This may be due in part to the machine itself, or to the regime which lays so much stress upon the products of the machine; but it is certainly due in large part to the fact that the worker has had no opportunity to develop his imagination and his sympathetic insight as to the social and scientific values found in his work. At present, the impulses which lie at the basis of the industrial system are either practically neglected or positively distorted during the school period. Until the instincts of construction and production are systematically laid hold of in the years of childhood and youth, until they are trained in social directions, enriched by historical interpretation, controlled and illuminated by scientific methods, we certainly are in no position even to locate the source of our economic evils, much less to deal with them effectively. If we go back a few Centuries, we find a practical monopoly of learning. The term possession of learning was, indeed, a happy one. Learning was a class matter. This was a necessary result of social conditions. There were not in existence any means by which the multitude could possibly have access to intellectual resources. These were stored up and hidden away in manuscripts. Of these there were at best only a few, and it required long and toilsome preparation to be able to do anything with them. A high-priesthood of learning, which guarded the treasury of truth and which doled it out to the masses under severe restrictions, was the inevitable expression of these conditions. But, as a direct result of the industrial revolution of which we have been speaking, this has been changed. Printing was invented; it was made commercial. Books, magazines, papers were multiplied and cheapened. As a result of the locomotive and telegraph, frequent, rapid, and cheap intercommunication by mails and electricity was called into being. Travel has been rendered easy; freedom of movement, with its accompanying exchange of ideas, indefinitely facilitated. The result has been an intellectual revolution. Learning has been put into circulation. While there still is, and probably always will be, a particular class having the special business of inquiry in hand, a distinctively learned class is henceforth out of the question. It is an anachronism. Knowledge is no longer an immobile solid; it has been liquefied. It is actively moving in all the currents of society itself.

It is easy to see that this revolution, as regards the materials of knowledge, carries "with it a marked change in the attitude of the individual. Stimuli of an intellectual sort pour in upon us in all kinds of ways. The merely intellectual life, the life of scholarship and of learning, thus gets a very altered value. Academic and scholastic, instead of being titles of honor, are becoming terms of reproach.

But all this means a necessary change in the attitude of the school, one of which we are as yet far from realizing the full force. Our school methods, and to a very considerable extent our curriculum, are inherited from the period when learning and command of certain symbols, affording as they did the only access to learning, were all-important. The ideals of this period are still largely in control, even where the outward methods and studies have been changed. We sometimes hear the introduction of manual training, art and science into the elementary, and even the secondary schools, deprecated on the ground that they tend toward the production of specialists—that they detract from our present scheme of generous, liberal culture. The point of this would be ludicrous if it were not often so to make it tragic. It is our present which is highly specialized, one-sided and narrow. It is an education dominated almost entirely by the mediaeval conception of learning. It is something which appeals for the most part simply to the intellectual aspect of our natures, our desire to learn, to accumulate information, and to get control of the symbols of learning; not to our impulses and tendencies to make, to do, to create, to produce, whether in the form of utility or of art. The very fact that manual training, art and science are objected to as technical, as tending toward mere specialism, is of itself as good testimony as could be offered to the specialized aim which controls current education. Unless education had been virtually identified with the exclusively intellectual pursuits, with learning as such, all these materials and methods would be welcome, would be greeted with the utmost hospitality. . . .

The obvious fact is that our social life has undergone a thorough and radical change. If our education is to have any meaning for life, it must pass through an equally complete transformation. This transformation is not something to appear suddenly, to be executed in a day by conscious purpose. It is already in progress. Those modifications of our school system which often appear (even to those most actively concerned with them, to say nothing of their spectators) to be mere changes of detail, mere improvements within the school mechanism, are in reality signs and evidences of evolution. The introduction of active occupations, of nature study, of elementary science, of art, of history; the relegation of the merely symbolic and formal to a secondary position; the change in the moral school atmosphere, in the relation of pupils and teachers—of discipline; the introduction of more active, expressive, and self-directing factors—all these are not mere accidents, they are necessities of the larger social evolution. It remains but to organize all these factors, to appreciate them in their fullness of meaning, and to put the ideas and ideals involved in complete, uncompromising possession of our school system. To do this means to make each one of an embryonic community life, active of occupations that reflect the life of society, and permeated throughout with the spirit of art, history, and science. When the school introduces and trains each child of society into membership within such a little community, saturating him with the spirit of service, and providing him with the instruments of effective self-direction, we shall have the deepest and best guarantee of a larger society which is worthy, lovely, and harmonious.

2 Walter Rauschenbusch, from *Christianity and the Social Crisis*, 1907[2]

Walter Rauschenbusch (1861–1918), a major influence in the Social Gospel movement, was born in Rochester, New York, the son of a German Lutheran missionary. Becoming a Baptist minister, he had pastorates in Louisville, Kentucky, and New York City. In New York, from 1886 to 1897 Rauschenbusch ministered to the poor in the Hell's Kitchen area of the city. In these experiences, Rauschenbusch became intensely interested in applying ideas of evangelical Christianity to solving social problems. In 1892, he organized the non-denominational Brotherhood of the Kingdom, which emphasized reform efforts that tried to apply Christian principles to solving social problems – and paving the way for a new Kingdom of God on earth. Serving on the faculty of the Rochester Theological Seminary from 1902 until his death in 1917, he argued for a new theology emphasizing the social responsibilities of Christianity. When his book, Christianity and the Social Crisis, *was published in 1907, it immediately became one of the popular religious works of its day, selling 50,000 copies.*

What social changes would be involved in such a religious reorganization of life? What institutions and practices of our present life would have to cease? What new elements would have to be embodied? What social ideal should be the ultimate aim of Christian men, and what practical means and policies should they use for its attainment? . . . .

One of the most persistent mistakes of Christian men has been to postpone social regeneration to a future era to be inaugurated by the return of Christ. . . . It was at the outset a triumphant assertion of faith against apparent impossibilities. It still enshrines the social hope of Christianity and concedes that some time the social life of men is to pass through a radical change and be ruled by Christ. But the element of postponement in it to-day means a lack of faith in the present power of Christ and paralyzes the religious initiative. It ignores the revelation of God contained in nineteen centuries of continuous history. It is careful not to see the long succession of men and churches and movements that staked all their hopes and all their chances of social improvement on this expectation and were disappointed. It is true that any regeneration of society can come only through the act of God and the presence of Christ; but God is now acting, and Christ is now here. To assert that means not less faith, but more. It is true that any effort

2   (New York: Macmillan, 1907), pp. 343–421.

at social regeneration is dogged by perpetual relapses and doomed forever to fall short of its aim. But the same is true of our personal efforts to live a Christ-like life; it is true, also, of every local church, and of the history of the Church at large. Whatever argument would demand the postponement of social regeneration to a future era will equally demand the postponement of personal holiness to a future life. We must have the faith of the apostolic Church in the triumph of Christ over the kingdoms of the world, plus the knowledge which nineteen centuries of history have given to us. Unless we add that knowledge, the faith of the apostles becomes our unbelief. . . .

In personal religion the first requirement is to repent and re-believe in the gospel. As long as a man is self-righteous and complacently satisfied with his moral attainments, there is no hope that he will enter into the higher development, and unless he has faith that a higher level of spiritual life is attainable, he will be lethargic and stationary.

Social religion, too, demands repentance and faith: repentance for our social sins; faith in the possibility of a new social order. As long as a man sees in our present society only a few inevitable abuses and recognizes no sin and evil deep- seated in the very constitution of the present order, he is still in a state of moral blindness and without conviction of sin. Those who believe in a better social order are often told that they do not know the sinfulness of the human heart. They could justly retort the charge on the men of the evangelical school. When the latter deal with public wrongs, they often exhibit a curious unfamiliarity with the forms which sin assumes there, and sometimes reverently bow before one of the devil's spider-webs, praising it as one of the mighty works of God. Regeneration includes that a man must pass under the domination of the spirit of Christ, so that he will judge of life as Christ would judge of it. That means a revaluation of social values. Things that are now "exalted among men" must become "an abomination" to him because they are built on wrong and misery. Unless a man finds his judgment at least on some fundamental questions in opposition to the current ideas of the age, he is still a child of this world and has not "tasted the powers of the coming age." He will have to repent and believe if he wants to be a Christian in the full sense of the word. . . .

The older conception of religion viewed as religious only what ministered to the souls of men or what served the Church. When a man attended the services of the Church, contributed money to its work, taught in Sunday-school, spoke to the unconverted, or visited the sick, he was doing religious work. The conscientiousness with which he did his daily work also had a religious quality. On the other hand, the daily work itself, the ploughing, building, cobbling, or selling were secular, and the main output of his life was not directly a contribution to the kingdom of God, but merely the necessary method of getting a living for himself and his family. The ministry alone and a few allied callings had the uplifting consciousness of serving God in the total of daily work. A few professions were marked off as holy, just as in past stages of religion certain groves and temples were marked out as holy ground where God could be sought and served. . . .

If a man follows the mind of Jesus Christ in his judgments, he will have to appear partial in a social world which is by no means built on a line with the mind of Christ. It is a different matter entirely for a minister to follow the mind of a political party and make himself liable to the charge of partisanship. It may happen at long intervals in the history of a nation that a political party so thoroughly embodies the righteous instincts of the nation that its cause is almost identified with the triumph of justice. In such a juncture a minister may wisely decide that he must throw his influence publicly with that party and risk a loss of influence in other directions. But it is questionable if that situation has confronted ministers in our country these many years. A man may well doubt if the machinery of our great parties has ground out social progress or ground it up, and whether party loyalty has propagated patriotism or poisoned it. . . .

The doctrine of "Christian stewardship" has been strongly emphasized in church life in recent years, but mainly from the churchly point of view. It is a new formula designed to give our modern men of wealth a stronger sense of responsibility and to induce them to give more largely to the Church and its work. But if a rich man withdraws a million from commerce and gives it to a missionary society or a college, that simply shifts the money from one steward to another, and from one line of usefulness to another. The ecclesiastical idea of stewardship needs to be intensified and broadened by the democratic idea. Every man who holds wealth or power is not only a steward of God, but a steward of the people. He derives it from the people and he holds it in trust for the people. If he converts it to his own use, the people can justly call him to account in the court of public opinion and in the courts of law. If the law has hitherto given an absolute title to certain forms of property and has neglected to insist on the ingredient of public property and rights involved in it, that does not settle the moral title in the least. The people may at any time challenge the title and resume its forgotten rights by more searching laws. The Christian Church could make a splendid contribution to the new social justice if it assisted in pointing out the latent public rights and in quickening the conscience of stewards who have forgotten their stewardship. In turn, the religious sense of stewardship would be reenforced by the increased sense of social obligation. Our laws and social institutions have so long taught men that their property is their own, and that they can do what they will with their own, that the Church has uphill work in teaching that they are not owners, but administrators. Our industrial individualism neutralizes the social consciousness created by Christianity.

. . .

In asking for faith in the possibility of a new social order, we ask for no Utopian delusion. We know well that there is no perfection for man in this life: there is only growth toward perfection. In personal religion we look with seasoned suspicion at any one who claims to be holy and perfect, yet we always tell men to become holy and to seek perfection. We make it a duty to seek what is unattainable. We have the same paradox in the perfectibility of society. We shall never have a perfect social life, yet we must seek it with faith. We shall never abolish suffering. There will always be death and the empty chair and heart. There will always be the agony of love unreturned. Women will long for children and never press baby lips to their breast. Men will long for fame and miss it. Imperfect moral insight will work hurt in the best conceivable social order. The strong will always have the impulse to exert their strength, and no system can be devised which can keep them from crowding and jostling the weaker. Increased social refinement will bring increased sensitiveness to pain. An American may suffer as much distress through a social slight as a Russian peasant under the knout.[3] At best there is always but an approximation to a perfect social order. The kingdom of God is always but coming.

3 Charles Davenport, from *Heredity in Relation to Eugenics*, 1915[4]

Popularized at the end of the nineteenth century, eugenicists sought to remove "undesirable" genetic characteristics in the population by managing reproduction and, in some instances, by forced sterilizations. The eugenics movement focused on the mentally unfit, sexual deviants, and racial and sexual minorities. Its worst form of application came in Nazi Germany, which enthusiastically adopted its principles.

Charles B. Davenport (1866–1944) was a leading biologist and advocate of eugenics, which in twentieth-century America became the science or pseudo-science of managing genetic development of peoples and races. A distinguished zoologist, Davenport received a doctorate from Harvard, and was later appointed to its faculty. He published widely about

---

[3] A whip used in Czarist Russia to punish criminals or political dissenters.
[4] Charles B. Davenport, *Heredity in Relation to Eugenics* (New York: Henry Holt & Co., 1911), pp. 1–5.

eugenics and was especially interested in limiting racial mixing, which he believed degraded human development. Late in life, during the 1930s and 1940s, Davenport maintained contact with German eugenicists, who provided an intellectual rationale for Adolf Hitler's policies of racial extermination.

Eugenics is the science of the improvement of the human race by better breeding or, as the late Sir Francis Gallon expressed it:— "The science which deals with all influences that improve the inborn qualities of a race." The eugenical standpoint is that of the agriculturalist who, while recognizing the value of culture, believes that permanent advance to be made only by securing the best "blood." Man is an organism—an animal; and the laws of improvement of corn and of race horses hold true for him also. Unless people accept this simple truth and let it influence marriage selection human progress will cease.

Eugenics has reference to offspring. The success of a marriage from the standpoint of eugenics is measured by the number of disease-resistant, cultivable offspring that come from it. Happiness or unhappiness of the parents, the principal theme of many novels and the proceedings of divorce courts, has little eugenic significance; for eugenics has to do with traits that are in the blood, the protoplasm. The superstition of prenatal influence and the real effects of venereal disease, dire as they are, lie outside the pale of eugenics in its strictest sense. But no lover of his race can view with complaisance the ravages of these diseases nor fail to raise his voice in warning against them. The parasite that induces syphilis is not only hard to kill but it frequently works extensive damage to heart, arteries and brain, and may be conveyed from the infected parent to the unborn child. Gonorrhea, like syphilis, is a parasitic disease that is commonly contracted during illicit sexual intercourse. Conveyed by an infected man to his wife it frequently causes her to become sterile. Venereal diseases are disgenic agents of the first magnitude and of growing importance. The danger of acquiring them should be known to all young men. Society might well demand that before a marriage license is issued the man should present a certificate, from a reputable physician, of freedom from them. Fortunately, nature protects most of her best blood from these diseases; for the acts that lead to them are repugnant to strictly normal persons; and the sober-minded young women who have had a fair opportunity to make a selection of a consort are not attracted by the kind of men who are most prone to sex-immorality. . . .

The human babies born each year constitute the world's most valuable crop. Taking the population of the globe to be one and one-half billion, probably about 50 million children are born each year. In the continental United States with over 90 million souls probably 2½ million children are annually born. When we think of the influence of a single man in this country, of a Harriman, of an Edison, of a William James, the potentiality of these 2½ annually can be dimly conceived as beyond computation. But for better or worse this potentiality is far from realized. Nearly half a million of these infants die before they attain the age of one year, and half of all are dead before they reach their 23rd year—before they have had much chance to affect the world one way or another. However, were only one and a quarter million of the children born each year in the United States destined to play an important part for the nation and humanity we could look with equanimity on the result. But alas! only a small part of this army will be fully effective in rendering productive our three million square miles of territory, in otherwise utilizing the unparalleled natural resources of the country, and in forming a united, altruistic, God-serving, law-abiding, effective and productive nation, leading the remaining 93 per cent of the globe's population to higher ideals. On the contrary, of the 1200 thousand who reach full maturity each year 40 thousand will be ineffective through temporary sickness, 4 to 5 thousand will be segregated in the care of institutions, unknown thousands will be kept in poverty through mental deficiency, other thousands will be the cause of social disorder and still other thousands will be required to tend and control the weak and unruly. We may estimate at not far from 100 thousand, or 8 per cent, the number of the non-productive or only slightly productive, and probably this proportion would hold for the 600 thousand males considered by themselves. The great mass of the yearly increment, say 550 thousand males, constitute a body of solid, intelligent workers of one sort and another, engaged in occupations that require, in the different cases, various degrees of intelligence but are none the less valuable in the progress of humanity. Of course, in these gainful occupations the men are assisted by a large number of their sisters, but four-fifths of the women are still engaged in the no less useful work of homemaking, the ineffectiveness of 6 to 8 per cent of the males and the probable slow tendency of this proportion to increase is deserving of serious attention.

It is a reproach to our intelligence that we as a people, proud in other respects of our control of nature, should have to support about half a million insane, feeble-minded, epileptic, blind and deaf, 80,000 prisoners and 100,000 paupers at a cost of over 100 million dollars per year. A new plague that rendered four per cent of our population, chiefly at the most productive age, not merely incompetent but a burden costing 100 million dollars yearly to support, would instantly attract universal attention. But we have become so used to crime, disease and degeneracy that we take them as necessary evils. That they were so in the world's ignorance is granted; that they must remain so is denied. . . .

The general program of the eugenist is clear—It is to improve the race by inducing young people to make a more reasonable selection of marriage mates; to fall in love intelligently. It also includes the control by the state of the propagation of the mentally incompetent. It does not imply destruction of the unfit either before or after birth. It certainly has only disgust for the free love propaganda that some ill-balanced persons have sought to attach to the name. Rather it trusts to that good sense with which the majority of people are possessed and believes that in the life of such there comes a time when they realize that they are drifting toward marriage and stop to consider if the contemplated union will result in healthful, mentally well-endowed offspring. At present there are few facts so generally known that they will help such persons in their inquiry. It is the province of the new science of eugenics to study the laws of inheritance of human traits and, as these laws are ascertained, to make them known. There is no doubt that when such laws are clearly formulated many certainly unfit matings will be avoided and other fit matings that have been shunned through false scruples will be happily contracted.

4 Margaret Sanger, *"Morality and Birth Control,"* 1918[5]

Margaret Sanger (1879–1966) was a reformer who became the leading advocate in the United States of women's ability to have universal access to birth control. Born Margaret Louise Higgins to a family of 11 children, she saw the consequences of frequent pregnancy on women. Trained as a nurse in White Plains, New York, she married William Sanger, an architect, in 1902, and they eventually moved to Greenwich Village, in New York City, where they associated with cultural and political radicalism during the years just before World War I, and Sanger participated in the Women's Committee of the New York Socialist party. As part of her feminism, Sanger became a vocal advocate of legal birth control. In most parts of the United States, the sale and distribution of birth control was illegal, and efforts to provide birth-control education met with social and sometimes legal disapproval. In this article, she makes the case for legal birth control as a means of social improvement and social engineering.

[5] Margaret Sanger, "Morality and Birth Control," February, 1918, Margaret Sanger Papers Project (http://www.nyu.edu/projects/sanger/secure/documents/speech_morality_and_bc.html). Courtesy of the Margaret Sanger Papers, New York University.

Throughout the ages, every attempt woman has made to strike off the shackles of slavery has been met with the argument that such an act would result in the downfall of her morality. Suffrage was going to "break up the home." Higher education would unfit her for motherhood, and co-education would surely result in making her immoral. Even today, in some of the more backward countries reading and writing is stoutly discouraged by the clerical powers because "women may read about things they should not know." We now know that there never can be a free humanity until woman is freed from ignorance, and we know, too, that woman can never call herself free until she is mistress of her own body. Just so long as man dictates and controls the standards of sex morality, just so long will man control the world. Birth control is the first important step woman must take toward the goal of her freedom. It is the first step she must take to be man's equal. It is the first step they must both take toward human emancipation. The Twentieth Century can make progress only by fighting the superstitions and prejudices created in the Nineteenth Century—fighting them in the open with the public searchlight upon them. The first questions we must ask ourselves are: Are we satisfied with present day morality? Are we satisfied with the results of present day standards of morality? Are these so satisfying that they need no improvement? For fourteen years I worked as a nurse in the factory and tenement districts of New York City. Eight years ago I was called into a home where the father, a machinist by trade, was earning eighteen dollars a week. He was at the time the father of six living children, to all appearances a sober, serious and hard working man. His wife, a woman in the thirties toiled early and late helping him to keep the home together and the little ones out of the sweatshops, for they were both anxious to give their children a little schooling. Two years ago I came across this same family, and found that five more children had been added in the meantime to their household. The three youngest were considered by medical authorities to be hopelessly feeble-minded, two of the older girls were prostitutes; three of the boys were serving long term sentences in penitentiaries, while another of the children had been injured by a fall and so badly crippled that she will not be able to help herself for years to come.

Out of this family of eleven children only two are now of any use to society, a little girl of seven, who stays at home and cares for her crippled sister during the day while the mother scrubs office floors, and a boy of nine who sells chewing gum after school hours at a subway exit. The father has become a hopeless drunkard, of whom the mother and children live in terror.

This is but one illustration of the results of our present day morality. Here was an opportunity for society to develop and preserve six children for human service; but prudery and ignorance added five more to this group, with the result that two out of eleven are left to fit the struggle against pauperism and charity. Will they succumb? Another case I should like to cite shows how shallow is the concern of society in regard to the over-crowded tenements, where thousands of little children occupy sleeping quarters with parents and boarders whose every act is visible to all. Morality indeed! Society is much like the ostrich with its head in the sand. It will not look at facts and face the responsibility of its own stupidity. I recall the death-bed scene, when the patient, a woman of twenty-six, passed away during the birth of her seventh child. Five out of the seven were girls, the eldest being about ten years old. Upon the death this woman, this girl began to assume the duties of her mother and continued to keep the four men roomers who had lodged in their home for years. A few years later, I found this girl suffering from the ravages of syphilis, although she had only just entered the period of puberty. She told me she could not remember when she had not dressed before the roomers, and on winter nights she often slept in their beds. She was already old—old in ignorance, in vulgarity, in degeneracy. Another womanhood blighted in the bud, battered by ignorance, another soul sunk in despair. These five girl-women did not ask society to fill their minds, as it was willing to do, with a useless knowledge of Greek, Latin or the Sciences. But they did need and unconsciously demand the knowledge of life, of hygiene and sex psychology which is so prudishly and shamefully denied them. No doubt these five sisters will soon represent the ruins of an ancient prejudice, and five more derelicts will be added to that particular relic heap of humanity.

Again, is there anything more sickening to truth than the attitude of society toward that catch phrase "Sacred Motherhood"? Take another illustration and lay bare the living facts and view them for awhile. Two sisters lived in an upstate town, members of a large family, where the older daughters worked in factories, in order that the younger girls might have educational advantages. The youngest fell in love with a good-for-nothing fellow, with the result that she had an illegal child. Disgrace, ostracism and remorse drove her out into the world, and together with her baby she drifted from house to house in the capacity of a servant, until finally the baby died, leaving the mother free to enter upon another vocation.

During this time, however, due to the condescending treatment accorded to her by the women who employed her, she had become so accustomed to look upon herself as an outcast that soon, with other companions of her frame of mind, she began trafficking . . . on the streets of New York. Now the second sister, a few [years] older, also fell in love with one of the "town heroes," and came to grief; but owing to the "disgrace" of the youngest sister and sympathy for the elder members of the family, who were completely anguish stricken over this second mishap, the old family physician took her in charge and sent to her a place where an illegal operation was performed upon her. She returned, a sadder but wiser girl, to her home, finished the high school course, and several years later she became the principal of a school. Today she is one of the most respected women in that county. She devotes her life outside school hours to a sympathetic understanding of the needs of young boys and girls, and her sordid early experience, put to good use, has helped many boys and girls to lead clean lives. These cases represent actual modern conditions. Our laws force women into celibacy on the one hand, or abortion on the other.

Both conditions are declared by eminent medical authorities to be injurious to health. The ever ascending standard and cost of living, combined with the low wage of the young men of today, tend toward the postponement of marriage. Has knowledge of birth control, so carefully guarded and so secretly practiced by the women of the wealthy class—and so tenaciously withheld from the working women—brought them misery? Rather, has it not promoted greater happiness, greater freedom, greater prosperity and more harmony among them? The women who have this knowledge are the women who have been free to develop, free to enjoy in its best sense, and free to advance the interests of the community. And their men are the ones who motor, who sail yachts, who legislate, who lead and control. The men, women and children of this class do not form any part whatever in the social problems of our times. Had this class continued to reproduce in the prolific manner of the working people in the past twenty-five years, can human imagination picture what conditions would be today? All of our problems are the result of overbreeding among the working class, and if morality is to mean anything at all to us, we must regard all the changes which tend toward the uplift and survival of the human race as moral. Knowledge of birth control is essentially moral. Its general, though prudent, practice must lead to a higher individuality and ultimately to a cleaner race.

5   Frances E. Willard, from *Women and Temperance*, 1883[6]

Frances E. Willard (1839–1898) was an educator, temperance activist, and suffragist, who served as head of the Women's Christian Temperance Union (WCTU), which she helped to found in 1873, serving as its president after 1879. The WCTU served as one of the important anti-alcohol organizations in the United States, and it helped to organize temperance efforts across the

---

[6]   (Chicago: Park Publishing Co., 1883), pp. 630–8.

*country which focused on persuading people to give up drink by moral
suasion. Led mostly by white women, it assembled hundreds of thousands of
members by the 1890s. The WCTU became an important vehicle for
activism by women in various social reform campaigns against vice, labor
exploitation, public health, and education. It adopted the white ribbon as a
symbol of moral purity and the protection of the home – two important
objectives of the organization – with the slogan "Agitate, Educate, Legislate."
Some of the WCTU activists, such as Willard, were ardent feminists and
became leaders of the movement for woman suffrage.*

*Willard was born in Churchville, New York, but as a child moved with her
family to Oberlin, Ohio, then Janesville, Wisconsin, and finally to Evanston,
Illinois. She was an advocate of separate spheres for men and women, so she
argued that opportunities for women in education and in public service
could help them accomplish change in their areas of influence. She remained
a strong Christian and did not engage in criticism of religion and the Bible,
unlike some other suffrage activists, such as Elizabeth Cady Stanton.*

HOW OUGHT A LOCAL W. C. T. U. TO CONDUCT A PUBLIC MEETING?

Not on the hap-hazard method, which too often prevails in our temperance meetings. It is found in those of men, notwithstanding fifty years experience, and naturally enough, but most unfortunately, in those of women also. "Who shall preside?" "What shall we sing?" "Who shall take the collection?" Questions like these asked under fire of the eyes in the audience, might do for children, but are pitiable from "grown folks."

Not on the "cut and dried" method, where the President reads every word she says, and if her sight is blurred, or her spectacles are mislaid, finds herself all out at sea.

"Mrs. Secretary of—no—Treasurer of the Woman's Association, no—the Female National—no—National Female—no—the W. C. T. U." That comes of "losing your mind." Put somebody to the fore who don't lose hers (or his).

The common sense method is the right one.

1. Plan matters thoroughly beforehand. Rehearse if necessary—you do this for a wedding, and we shall never wed the W. C. T. U. to the people's heart until we conduct our meetings without hitch or flaw. Keep the machinery out of sight. Let everything be natural, but let it be clear-cut, systematic, "ship shape." For instance: 1. Advertise well, insist on an opportunity for Sunday announcements from the pulpits and schools.

Don't make the blunder of ignoring the children. They can be instructed, grounded, confirmed, and this is the place to do it in. Some speaker may miss the old folks, but if he has any skill at all in taking aim, he will be sure to hit the youngsters. Childhood is the fortress of the future—furnish it with rations and with weapons, and it will hold the fort when we are mustered out.

2. Don't be afraid to hold your meetings in a church, you may warm up a cold one; enlist their apathetic but well-meaning minister, elder, or deacon; touch the conscience of a drowsy layman or woman. The church is a good place in which to do good work.

3. Don't let your music go by default. You discount your speaker one-half at the start by this culpable neglect. Reformers are a sympathetic, natural, poetic sort of folk. Besides, don't forget that a hymn with the gospel ring in the united voices that sing it; a solo from some sweet woman's heart and voice, or from that of some good and true man, a chorus lifting the audience to concert pitch, will utterly transform your audience as to its receptivity, its support, its mental elevation. The poor, tired talker goes into the church hoping for a benediction from psalm, and prayer, and song. If you have no method, no music, no amenity, it will all be taken patiently, turned to account as a means of discipline by the disappointed speaker, but you will lose, and lose immeasurably, in the results you had hoped to witness, and (gently be it uttered) you deserve to. . . .

4. Make the place fair and gracious with flowers. See the saloon windows decked with vines and potted plants. Notice the desecration of the arbor vitae—that noblest of evergreens—to be a mere sign-post for bloated, beery, old King Gambrinus.[7] Shall we not claim the tender and ennobling ministry of God's thought in plant life and flower language for these meetings, held in His name and for the good of His dear, benighted children? I would have also the flag of my country always before my eyes when I speak in her sacred name, but though the request is regularly made, it is complied with on an average once a year.

5. Let the President of the W. C. T. U. preside and go forward, quietly to her duty, as a matter of course. Provide seats in pulpit and chancel for the pastors, and ask them to participate in the opening exercises, on call of the President. We desire to treat them with special courtesy; we need their help; we shall almost invariably have it if we are considerate and

---

[7] Known as "the patron saint of beer," King Gambrinus served as a symbol for brewing and beer production in nineteenth-century America.

wise. Do not have long opening exercises—there is so much "more to follow." The remark is often made (often by the minister, I am sorry to say), "We will omit Bible reading." No, we will not. This, of all others, is not the o'clock o' the century for Christians to leave the keystone out of the arch, or for W. C. T. U. women to adjourn the "Home Book" lesson. On the other hand, let the reading be brief and appropriate to the occasion. . . .

6. Immediately on the conclusion of the address take your collection. Wait for a hymn at this juncture and your audience will file out. Now comes the crucial test of your "level headedness," dear manager. Choose, with all the wisdom of the united society, the man (or woman, and the latter usually succeeds best), who shall attend to this part of your religious exercises. Who in your town has "a gift" for showing to the people the sacred side of this dedication of their substance to the Lord? Who can, while doing this, interest and perhaps, later on, harmlessly amuse and "hold the people?" That is the man for you (or the woman—usually the last). Give to this blessed genius a list of those who are to take the collection, and just where they are to begin (make a draft on your best soldiers of rank and file in the W. C. T. U.), and let them go forth promptly.

   Let the collection baskets be ready beforehand in front of the pulpit. An audience very properly criticises those who bungle with it. An audience is the guest of the W. C. T. U. for the time, and everything should be made just as lovely and pleasant for this guest as possible. Don't keep it waiting for your incoherent whispered consultations; don't let it feel uncomfortable by reason of your own lack of poise and mastership. Rehearse, practice, become perfect. A well-appointed meeting is a work of art. Treat your audience as carefully and charmingly as you would a guest in your own home. I am always sure you will do beautifully by me; treat your audience as well. It will take thought, planning, courage that comes of consecration and prayer. In asking the collection, set forth clearly the objects of your society. It helps to familiarize the public with them. Public intelligence as to your aims and good will, as to your motives, forms a large share of your capital stock for the cause. Be definite; business men like that. But to this end you need not make a scape-goat of your poor lecturer, drag him (or her) to the front and expatiate on the "needs of the hour" in a bold and literal sense. You may state in general terms that a temperance meeting does not "happen"—it is not a sort of spontaneous, fungus growth, but comes as the result of definite aims and engagements. . . .

7. But now, while the collection proceeds, let all work to secure membership in your society. Send out eight or ten or twelve ladies with our " Enrolling Tablets"—half of them going to the rear of the church, half to the front, and meeting in the middle of the house. . . .

Now then, we approach the close. Let the President cordially thank the audience for its presence and attention; for the memberships and collection. If she can put in a kind remembrance of the children and their good behavior, it will not be lost. Also thank the choir. Then have a good, full-chested doxology, and then the benediction.

Postscript.—Don't forget the following items either: To entertain your speaker in a quiet home (with a fire in the room always, in winter). Not to expect much socially, in the way of calls, invitations to tea, etc.; for if you do, your already over-worked talking machine will have so little vitality left that you will be punished by a sleepy speech at night. One of the most distinguished lecturers in this country always says, when invited to meet callers or go out to a meal: "You, my dear friends, love the cause—so do I. You shall take your choice. I will put myself into colloquial talking or into the evening lecture,—just which you think is best. I cannot do you any credit in both of these roles!" Dear friends, remember this, the best rule is: "Enter into one house and there abide." Finally: report your lectures,—not in the way of compliment, but give your best points to the editors. Get your quickest, brightest members to do this for all the papers of your town. Thus you mould public sentiment in the great class that does not move, and therefore must be moved upon; that will not hear with its ears, but will with its eyes, if you put the thoughts before them in the pages of their local paper. Utilize the public meeting by distributing temperance literature at the close, and advertising National and State Temperance papers. Yet again: When you introduce your speaker, give the full name, the official status (if he has one), and where he "hails from." It does a stranger good to be announced as from somewhere in particular.

6 Chicago Vice Commission, The Social Evil in Chicago, 1911[8]

During the Progressive Era, reformers were especially concerned with the moral condition of cities, especially prostitution and, to some extent, homosexuality. There was a widespread scare about "white slavery," a supposed conspiracy to keep white women in prostitution. In 1910, Congress

[8] *A Study of Existing Conditions with Recommendations by the Vice Commission of Chicago* (Chicago: Gunthorp-Warren Printing Co., 1911), pp. 289–306.

*enacted the White Slave Traffic Act, known as the Mann Act, which prohibited
the transportation of women across state lines for "immoral purposes."*

*Across the country, vice commissions were organized to identify the
sources of moral depravity and to recommend policy solutions. In July 1910,
the mayor of Chicago, Fred A. Busse, formed a vice commission made up of
30 members to study recommendations made that January by a gathering of
clergy from over 600 churches in Chicago. The church leaders suggested that
the commission be "made up of men and women who command the respect
and confidence of the public at large . . . to investigate thoroughly the
conditions as they exist." The commission was formed, $5,000 was
appropriated by the city council to help with expenses, and the work of the
commission began. On April 5, 1911, the commission presented its report on
vice to the city council. The following are excerpts from the report.*

No phase of the social evil can be demonstrated with more scientific certainty
than the physical aspect. It has been clearly proved through many and accurate
sources that no danger to the integrity of the race is so great as the diseases
which accompany prostitution. The greatest attention must be paid to every
means which makes for the control of venereal diseases and of dissemination
of reliable information concerning them for the protection of the innocent.

With these facts in mind let us study the various classes of men and
women who are involved in this vice.

The Professional Female Prostitute. The testimony shows that the professional female prostitute is broken down within ten years after she begins to
ply her trade. No better argument as to physical harm could be offered than
this statement. Practically all professional prostitutes have had syphilis or
gonorrhoea or both. It is the exception when either of these diseases is completely cured. During a certain part of the time they are communicable. Not
infrequently these diseases are communicable and at the same time difficult
to recognize. Therefore, a professional prostitute having intercourse with
from ten to sixty men in a single night will infect a large number of men.
Drug habituation also is more widespread amongst prostitutes than amongst
any other class of society.

Occasional Prostitutes. Occasional prostitutes are frequently infected
with venereal disease. They are highly dangerous when so infected. Venereal
diseases are bacterial in origin. From the epidemiologic standpoint they
belong in the category with smallpox, diphtheria and scarlet fever. They
cause most of the sterility, most of the peritonitis in females, most of the
salpingitis. They cause a large part of the joint inflammations—a large part
of the insanity and nervous diseases and a long train of diseases which go by

other names but have syphilis as an underlying factor. Congenital defects and deformities are largely syphilitic in origin.

In spite of all this a study of mortuary statistics does not give us much information, since the immediate or determining cause is usually some factor other than the venereal disease. The group of men who are infected by occasional prostitutes are somewhat more liable to spread venereal disease to innocent women, children and men than those who are infected by professional prostitutes.

Clandestine Prostitutes. Clandestine prostitutes spread infection. They get peritonitis and salpingitis. They are prone to have babies born with infected eyes and therefore they increase blindness. They are frequently sterile. Amongst this and the preceding class are most of the illegitimate children. The death rate amongst illegitimate children is barbarously high. The morbidity rate amongst clandestine and occasional prostitutes is higher than amongst moral women of the same age-periods and in the same strata of society.

Amongst the medical phases of these forms of prostitution is their tendency toward professional prostitution.

Male Prostitutes. (Principally perverts.) They spread infection. They have a high mortality and morbidity rate. They increase the number of drug habitues.

Occasional and Clandestine Male Prostitute. They spread infection. An infected man will not infect as many people as an infected woman, but an infected woman usually infects non-virtuous people; a large part of those infected by men are virtuous—wives and young children. An infected man usually takes infection into a clean home—an infected woman seldom does. . . .

VENEREAL DISEASES

How to Diminish Venereal Diseases. The time is ripe for a united attempt to diminish venereal diseases. To accomplish this both sexes should be taught the social and personal dangers of the black plague, far more to be dreaded than the white plague—venereal disease. They should be taught with emphasis that these diseases, like all other contagious diseases, may be innocently acquired and transmitted. Woman peculiarly needs such instruction, not only that she may protect herself, but that she may protect her child against danger from those to whose care it may be intrusted. Both sexes should be so instructed that they may teach sexual hygiene in all its relations. Innocence is too often dangerous ignorance. . . .

Infection of the Innocent. No marriage should be legal unless both parties furnish certificates of health and freedom from venereal diseases given by legally qualified physicians. In these certificates, the physician giving them should assume all civil and criminal responsibility for them. The person officiating at a marriage ceremony should be obliged by law to require such certificate. . . .

Health Department and Venereal Diseases. Under the police powers now granted by the State, except where specifically limited by statute, the Department of Health could quarantine persons when notified of venereal diseases in them by physicians. To secure proper enforcement of this right, it should be specifically guaranteed by statute. . . . That the Health Department should have the right to inspect prostitutes by a legal extension of the right granted it to inspect other persons exposed to contagious disease. This will require an amendment of the statute which interferes with the logical right of the Health Department in this particular. . . .

Hospitals and Venereal Diseases. . . . The hospitals and dispensaries should be instructed to issue educational leaflets informing patients as to the means of preventing and spreading the disease and of its dangers, such as are now issued in regard to tuberculosis. . . .

Inheritance of Venereal Diseases. . . . All other things being equal, defective parentage will give rise to a defective environment. The majority of defectives are a product not of heredity directly, but of arrested development due to defect. In this the mother plays a larger part than the father since the ovum before fecundation is the chief factor in the future being, while the ovum after fecundation is nourished by her alone, and the child when born is nourished by her alone for some time after birth. While paternal defect plays a large part, much of its alleged influence is due to the bad environment in which it keeps the mother. The mass of the prostitutes, as has been shown in this country, in Italy, in France, in Russia, and in Germany, belong to the defectives.

Sex Perversion. While the subject of sex perversion is included under the heading of this chapter it must be understood that, correctly speaking, it should come under the subject of crime and be treated as such. The law specifically states that these practices are "infamous crimes" and provides certain punishments, among which is the loss of citizenship. Because no chapter was devoted to crime it was decided to incorporate this subject in the report where it now stands.

At the very outset of the Commission's investigation, its attention was called by several persons to a condition of affairs with regard to sexual perversion which was said to be enormously prevalent and growing in Chicago. In reporting their impression of their work on the Municipal bench at the Harrison street court, Judges . . . said that the most striking thing they had observed in the last year was the great increase of sex perversion in Chicago.

Police officers state the same thing. The testimony of others, and the results of investigations by the Commission corroborate these statements. The Commission already had considerable information, including estimates which seemed incredible before an investigator was put in the field to find out the nature and extent of this form of vice. . . .

It appears that in this community there is a large number of men who are thoroughly gregarious in habit; who mostly affect the carriage, mannerisms, and speech of women; who are fond of many articles ordinarily dear to the feminine heart; who are often people of a good deal of talent; who lean to the fantastic in dress and other modes of expression, and who have a definite cult with regard to sexual life. They preach the value of non-association with women from various standpoints and yet with one another have practices which are nauseous and repulsive. Many of them speak of themselves or each other with the adoption of feminine terms, and go by girls' names or fantastic application of women's titles. They have a vocabulary and signs of recognition of their own, which serve as an introduction into their own society. The cult has produced some literature, much of which is uncomprehensible to one who cannot read between the lines, and there is considerable distribution among them of pernicious photographs.

In one of the large music halls recently, a much applauded act was that of a man who by facial expression and bodily contortion represented sex perversion, a most disgusting performance. It was evidently not at all understood by many of the audience, but others wildly applauded. Then, one of the songs recently ruled off the stage by the police department was inoffensive to innocent ears, but was really written by a member of the cult, and replete with suggestiveness to those who understood the language of this group.

Some of these men impersonate women on the cheap vaudeville stage, in connection with disorderly saloons. Their disguise is so perfect, they are enabled to sit at tables with men between the acts, and solicit for drinks the same as prostitutes.

Two of these "female impersonators" were recently seen in one of the most notorious saloons . . . . These "supposed" women solicited for drinks, and afterwards invited the men to rooms over the saloon for pervert practices.

The Commission hesitates about making recommendations for the specific amelioration of the evils which it has learned about. It desires, however, to insist that first and foremost, as a remedy stands the thoroughly practical ideal of a straight and pure sexual life both before and after marriage. . . . It would appear very doubtful, however, whether any spread of the actual knowledge of these practices is in any way desirable. Probably the purity and wholesomeness of the normal sexual relationship is all that is necessary to dwell on.

Discussion Questions: Chapter 11

1 What assumptions about social problems did reformers share in common? How did they differ?

2 In Rauschenbusch's opinion, what is the role of Christians in society? What is the significance of the Kingdom of God?

3 What did Progressive Era reform mean for black people?

4 How did women participate in Progressive Era reform? How did the views of women such as Margaret Sanger and Frances Willard differ about reform? How was woman suffrage connected to social reform?

5 What did reformers see as the root causes of prostitution? How did they see this social problem as ending?

Chapter 12   The Political System

1 Robert M. La Follette, "Peril in the Machine," 1897[1]

*Robert La Follette (1855–1925), a US Senator from Wisconsin, was an
important proponent of Progressive Era political reform. La Follette
believed that political machines and special interests destroyed democracy
by taking advantage of an electorate that was not engaged enough with the
issues to vote for their own interests and the interests of the country as a
whole. As a reform-minded Republican congressman, governor, and senator
who eventually joined the new Progressive party, La Follette believed that the
domination of politics by machine bosses and railroads hurt democracy and
the entrepreneurial spirit. Political machines were especially strong in parts of
the country where immigrants made up a large proportion of the population,
and, by 1890, immigrants made up 80 percent of the citizens of Milwaukee.*

*The idealism of Progressive politicians caused them to overlook the
genuine help that machine politics gave to immigrants, albeit in exchange for
votes. Machine politicians helped immigrants obtain employment, housing,
and other constituent services, and they often were more supportive
advocates of immigrants than were Progressive reformers. However,
Progressives believed that large numbers of immigrants and the presence
of political machines encouraged voter fraud. They argued that changes in
voting procedures, including the ballot box and the blanket ballot, would*

[1] "Peril in the Machine," speech to students at the University of Chicago, reprinted in *Chicago
Times-Herald*, February 23, 1897.

The Gilded Age and Progressive Era: A Documentary Reader, First Edition.
Edited by William A. Link and Susannah J. Link.
© 2012 Blackwell Publishing Ltd. Published 2012 by Blackwell Publishing Ltd.

eliminate much of the corruption. They supported state and local measures, such as the direct primary and civil-service reforms that would limit the influence of antidemocratic powers. La Follette favored the growth of labor unions as a check on the dominance of corporations. The nation's economy, he argued, was dominated by a small group of business leaders, which reduced democratic control.

In every democracy men will affiliate with one or the other of two great political parties. The ballot must determine which party shall administer government, enact new legislation, adjust the laws to all the complex social relations of life, to all the complicated business transactions of millions of human beings with order and justice. The ballot can achieve the kind of administration desired, establish the economic and financial policies essential, only through the election of men of integrity and ability, embodying the ideas expressed in the ballot. That the voter may be thoroughly informed upon the questions involved and upon the men to be chosen as the representatives of his convictions there should be the widest discussion and the most searching investigation.

The fundamental principle of a republic is individual responsibility. The responsibility is personal at the point in our political system where the citizen comes in direct contact with the system itself. This is the initial point of all legislation, all administration. In all the activities preliminary to the primary, and in the primary itself, the citizen is an elementary force in government. Here the voter can lay his hand directly upon the shoulder of the public servant and point the way he should go. But this ends with the adjournment of the primary or caucus. From that moment the citizen in a representative democracy, under a caucus, delegate and convention system, does not again come in direct personal touch with the work either of legislation or administration. How essential, then, if he is to be a factor in government, that he take part, and intelligently, too, in this fundamental work. If there be failure here, there is failure throughout. If through inattention or indifference, through mistake or misrepresentation, through trickery or fraud, or 'fine work,' the minority control the caucus, the laws will be made and executed by the agent of the minority, and the first principle of our government falls.

Individual Interest Required

To enlist the interest of every individual, encourage research, stimulate discussion of measures and of men, prior to the time when the voter should discharge this primary duty of citizenship, offers political organization opportunity for the highest public service. Teaching the principles of the party, reviewing political history, discussing pending and proposed legislation, investigating the fitness of candidates for office, quickening the sense of obligation and personal responsibility in all the duties of citizenship, commanding the continuous, intelligent, personal interest of the individual voter—and, when the campaign is on, conducting the canvass—these are the legitimate functions of political organization.

Such organizations cannot be used as a political machine for individuals or factions. Wherever such organizations are maintained political slates are shattered and political bargains fail of consummation. Cliques, rings, machines thrive upon the citizen's indifference to the plain duties of representative government.

There is no likeness or similitude between political organization that appeals to every voter in the party and a machine that appeals only to the most skillful and unscrupulous workers of the party.

That a political organization can exist without degenerating into a political machine; that it can serve the cause of good government, sometimes in defiance of the machine, is very recent political history.

It is well known that for a long time prior to the last republican national convention the conditions prevailing throughout the country were such as to occasion a widespread and profound interest in the selection of a republican candidate for the presidency. It is well known that this interested centered upon Major McKinley.[2] It is well known that the political machine in every state where it controlled party organization conspired to defeat his nomination. The ensuing contest was one of the most interesting in American politics, and well illustrates the distinction I would make, between machine politics designed to control in defiance of the desires of a majority and legitimate political organization which seeks only a fair and honest expression of the people's will.

The admitted choice of nine-tenths of his party, without wise leadership and perfect organization Major McKinley would have been defeated. The time and opportunity were ripe for a victory over the worst elements in the party. The people were in earnest and ready, but the field covered a continent, and it was a prodigious undertaking to marshal the masses, untrained in the arts of political management, against the disciplined veterans of the machine; to force the contest out into the open field; to leave no opportunity for surprise or betrayal; to make every politician wear his colors and declare his choice.

Hard pressed, the machine reverted to the usual plan of dividing the people by inspiring the candidacy of a favorite son in each of as larger a number of states as possible. Failing in this the last desperate trick was

[2]   President William McKinley.

attempted of securing delegates nominally for McKinley, but, in fact, for any candidate to defeat McKinley. This expedient was promptly met by instructing delegates to vote in convention for the people's choice. And the convention which finally assembled at St. Louis in June, 1896, simply recorded the result determined months before.

Since the appearance of the machine in politics this is the most notable instance of its defeat. It brings with it a lesson for this hour. Probably not twice in a generation would the existence of the people be of such a character, be so general and extend over such a period of time, as to make the members of one party so unitedly of one mind, so fused together in one mass. Never before was the power of machine influence so strongly shown in concerned movement over such a wide field of action. From the control of great cities and great states, of legislatures and of seats in the United States senate—unless speedily arrested—it is manifest that ultimately the machine will acquire supreme control of government. Right-minded, thoughtful, patriotic men observe the rapid and almost irresistible advance of this era of misrule with serious apprehension and misgiving.

Lincoln at Gettysburg

Nov. 10 thirty-three years ago a great concourse of people gathered on a Pennsylvania hillside, and overran the cleared wheat fields adjoining. All about them were the fresh evidence of mighty conflict—leveled fences, demolished buildings, dismounted guns, trees torn and blasted, on every side the newly turned earth in broken billows, marked the places where rested the uncounted dead. A tall form towered above the multitude, and all eyes were turned toward a face, plain and careworn to sadness. A deeper stillness fell upon as those immortal words were borne to their expectant ears on that gray November day.

"We here highly resolve that these dead shall not have died in vain; that this nation, under God, shall have a new birth of freedom, and that the government of the people by the people and for the people shall not perish from the earth."

"The government of the people by the people and for the people." It was reserved for this highest product of the American Republic—this embodied spirit of all the nobility and simplicity, all the wisdom and sentiment, all the courage and patience, all the serious earnestness and quaint humor, all the fear of God and faith in the plain people, in American character—to immortalize at once the profoundest and most philosophical, yet simplest and most popular definition of American democracy. . . .What sacrifices we were freely making for that kind of government! How ready were we to give our fortunes, mortgage our future, march our brave men to battle, blot our individual homes and hopes, clothe the dead in glory and the living in mourning—all to preserve a government of the people by the people and for the people. Who would then have believed that before a generation of time should pass this would gradually become a government of the people by the machine and for the machine?

The modern political machine is impersonal, irresponsible, extralegal . . . . It is without conscience and without remorse. It has come to be enthroned in American politics. It rules caucuses, names delegates, appoints committees, dominates the councils of the party, dictates nominations, makes platforms, dispenses patronage, directs state administrations, controls legislatures, stifles opposition, punishes independence and elects United States senators. In the states where it is supreme the edict of the machine is the only sound heard, and outside is easily mistaken for the voice of the people. If some particular platform pledge is necessary to the triumph of the hour the platform is so written and the pledge violated without offering excuse or justification. If public opinion be roused to indignant protest some scape-goat is put forward to suffer vicariously for the sins of the machine and subsequently rewarded for his service by the emoluments of machine spoils. If popular revolt against the machine sweeps over the state on rare occasions and the machine finds itself hard pressed to maintain its hold on party organization, control conventions and nominate its candidates—when threats and promises fail—the "barrel" is not wanting and the way is cleared.

It Is Machine Despotism

The wrongs inflicted by the machine do not end with the appropriation of offices. It does not secure the offices for salaries primarily. The salary is merely an incident. Government by the machine is machine despotism. It administers the laws, through its subjects, after its own interpretation. It is independent of the people and fears no reckoning. In extreme cases, where it becomes necessary to meet arraignment, it has its own press to parry or soften the blow. Having no constituency to serve, it serves itself. The machine is its own master. It owes no obligation and acknowledges no responsibility.

Its legislatures make the laws by its schedule. It names their committees. Behind the closed doors of its committee-rooms it suppresses bills inimical to its interests. It suppresses debate by a machine rule and the ready gavel of a pliant speaker. It exploits measures with reform titles designated to perpetuate machine control. It cares for special interests and takes tribute from its willing subjects, the private corporations.

Grave danger lies not in waiting for this republic to destroy its life or change its character by force of arms. The shock and heat of collision will ever rouse and solidify patriotic citizenship in defense of American liberty. It is insidious, creeping, progressive encroachment that presents the greatest peril.

The machine—this invisible empire—does its work so quietly. There is no explosion, no clash of arms, no open rebellion, but a sly covert nullification of the highest law of the land. It incurs some of the risks of armed assault; escapes the personal dangers and swift public retribution—provoked by organized violence and intimidation. So long as the methods were the methods of Boss Tweed it was more notorious but infinitely less dangerous. It would in time go down beneath the overpowering weight of decent, loyal, public condemnation. But when adroit, skilled, talented men, schooled in practical politics, devised a system that had in the beginning the semblance of serving its party, but mastered it instead: that openly lauded allegiance to party principle and artfully violated every principle of humor; that had its secret agents in every community and its cunning operatives in every caucus; . . . [that] defeated majorities, debauched politics and drove thousands of good citizens away from the primaries to stay—then, indeed, was the danger to the republic greatly augmented. But more than all this, when they worked into the political thought and life of people by the thousands, young men and old, ignorant men and educated, the pernicious, monstrous doctrine that the violation of the sacred principle of representative government, the spirit and letter of the constitution, is highly commendable, if it is only successful; that the American citizen's ballot, his defense, his power, his hope, his prophecy is the legitimate, rightful spoil and plunder of the political machine—then they corrupted the very springs of national life and pol[l]uted them in their courses as they flow on to meet the coming generations.

Remedy Is Suggested

What, then, shall we do to be saved?

Waste no more time in vain sermons on the duty of attending the caucus. It is too late for that. Except at long intervals, when in a sort of frenzy the citizen strikes at the machine shackles, men can be no longer drafted into caucus attendance. They have seen the game before. They know the dice are loaded. Th[e]y are no longer indifferent to their duties, nor ignorant of the situation. They well understand that their only part in government is to vote the ticket prepared for them and bear the machine rule of their own party, or the machine rule of the other party. They know they do not get the kind of government they vote for, but they do the best they can. They still attend the elections. They are as vitally interested in good government as ever. They are only waiting to find the way to achieve it. Here is our final safety. Here is the ultimate overthrow of the machine. If we provide the same safeguards, the same certainty, the same facility for expressing and executing the will of the people at the primaries as now prevail at the elections, we shall have the same general interest, the same general participation in the one as in the other. . . . If we guarantee the American citizen a full voice in the selection of candidates, and shaping the policy of his party and the administration of government incident thereto, then shall we invest not only the primaries, but the elections as well, with an abiding interest for him, . . . we shall make the primary and the election of vastly deeper significance, appealing in a new way to his deliberate judgment, his patriotism and his personal responsibility.

It is as much the interest and as plainly the duty of the state to as carefully perfect and guard a system of nominating candidates as it perfects and guards the system of electing them.

The caucus, delegate and convention system is inherently bad. It invites to manipulation, scheming, trickery, corruption and fraud. Even if the caucus were fairly conducted, the plan of which it is a part removes the nomination too far from the voter. Every transfer of delegated power weakens responsibility, until finally, by the time it is lodged in the hands of a nominating convention, the sense of responsibility has been lost in transit, unless it has been ticketed through by instructions from its original source. And even then all along the journey, from the primary to the convention, the confidential agents of the machine are introducing delegates to the mysteries of 'gold brick' and 'three card' political schemes.

The convention under most favorable conditions is anything but a deliberative body. Its work is hurried and business necessarily transacted in confusion. There is great excitement. It is the storm center of a political tempest . . . .

There is no time for investigation and no opportunity to distinguish the real issue from the false issue. Charges are withheld and 'sprung' in the convention purposely to avoid disproval and mislead delegates; and the dark horse is ever in reserve, waiting a favorable opportunity to take the convention unawares. Add to this all the corruption which comes with machine domination of a convention and you have political disaster and political crime as a result.

If, after long suffering and misrepresentation, the people by tremendous and united effort could succeed in defeating and even destroying the machine, the opportunity offered by the caucus and convention plan would simply restore the old or build up a new machine in its place.

Drop Caucus and Convention

No, no! Beginning the work in the state, put aside the caucus and the convention. They have been and will continue to be prostituted to the service of corrupt organization. They answer no purpose further than to give respectable form to political robbery. Abolish the caucus and the convention. Go back to the first principles of democracy. Go back to the people. Substitute for the caucus and the convention a primary election—held under all the sanctions of law which prevail at the general elections—where the citizen may cast his vote directly to nominate the candidate of the party with which he affiliates and have it canvassed and returned just as he cast it.

Provide a means of placing the candidates in nomination before the primary and forestall the creation of a new caucus system . . . .

Provide a ballot for the primary election and print on it the names of all candidates for nomination who have previously filed preliminary nomination papers with a designated official.

Provide that no candidate for nomination shall be entitled to have his name printed on the primary election ticket who shall not have been called out as a candidate by the written request of a given percentage of the vote cast at the preceding election in the district, county or state in which he is proposed as a candidate in the same manner that judicial candidates are now called out in many states.

Provide for the selection of a committee to represent the party organization and promulgate the party platform by the election at the primary of a representative man from the party for each county in the state. . . .

Do this and the knell of the political machine has sounded in the state.

Then every citizen will share equally in the nomination of the candidates of his party and attend primary election as a privilege as well as a duty. It will no longer be necessary to create an artificial interest in the general election to induce voters to attend. Intelligent, well-considered judgment will be substituted for unthinking enthusiasm; the lamp of reason for the torchlight. . . .

The nominations of the party will not be the result of 'compromise' or impulse or evil design—the barrel of the machine—but the candidates of the majority honestly and fairly nominated.

To every generation some important work is committed. If this generation will destroy the political machine, will emancipate the majority from its enslavement, will again place the destinies of this nation in the hands of its citizens, then, 'under God this government of the people, by the people and for the people shall not perish from the earth.'"

2 Isaac F. Marcosson, The Dayton Plan, 1914[3]

One of the lasting reforms from the Progressive Era was the city-manager form of government. Under this plan, a professional expert, trained in municipal government, was appointed by the elected officials in order to minimize corruption and partisanship. In 1908, the city of Staunton, Virginia, was the first to employ this form of government, but "the manager movement received national impetus only after a northern city, Dayton, Ohio, adopted the plan in 1913. Thereafter, the 'Dayton Plan' spread rapidly, and in six years more than 130 cities had put through manager charters."[4]

Clearly to understand the peculiar importance which attaches to Dayton's position it is first necessary to refer briefly to the institution of commission government. Most people are familiar with the straight plan, born at Galveston, developed by Des Moines, and now employed by nearly three hundred places. Its main features are the election of a non-partisan commission by the short ballot, the initiative, the referendum, and the recall; in short, an agency for real popular rule without the aid of political machinery.

Under this form each commissioner—and there are usually five—becomes the head of one of the operating branches of city work.

But Dayton has taken a distinct and progressive step forward in the development of the whole commission idea, and because of this really epochal innovation, combined with the dramatic fight made for it, the procedure becomes invested with value for every citizen, no matter where or under what kind of city government he happens to live.

The Commission-Manager Plan

Why should there be any change in a proved antidote for the ills that have so long assailed municipal life? Simply because the generally accepted commission plan, admirable as it is, is neither flawless nor completely businesslike. The chief objection has been the combination—in the commissioners—of the legislative and administrative functions. Running a city is purely an expert job. Yet everywhere, under old and new systems, men without experience or the necessary technical training are being called to it.

Technical experts, and especially those in city matters, do not usually run for office, and when they do run they are not likely to be good vote getters.

---

3   "Business-Managing a City," *Colliers, The National Weekly* 52, No. 16 (January 3, 1914): 5–6.
4   James Weinstein, "Organized Business and the City Commission and Manager Movements," *Journal of Southern History* 28, No. 2 (May 1962): 166–82.

Hence came the inspiration to modify the stereotyped commission plan along the line of a business corporation; that is, to elect commissioners whose sole task is to create policy and then have a hired expert manager to carry it out.

The little town of Lockport, up New York State, was really the pioneer in devising a charter that divorced the representative and legislative wings and called for a hired city operator.

It was an adaptation of the German professional mayor process, but an unsympathetic Legislature prevented action on the scheme.

The idea bore fruit, and strangely enough, in the heart of an ancient conservatism. Down in South Carolina was the bustling town of Sumter with less than ten thousand people, struggling with misrule under the old Federal elective plan. The citizens wanted commission government.

"Why not get an expert to operate the town?" asked the Chamber of Commerce.

So a charter was framed to answer the question and make possible what came to be called the commission-manager or "controlled-executive" system of government. Sumter adopted the charter and hired a Virginia civil engineer with wide railway experience to take hold. He proved the efficacy of the project by saving half of his salary the first year on two items of expenditure. Other Southern communities took up this plan. They were small and obscure, however, and attracted little attention.

The Dayton Upheaval

But events were shaping to give this new freedom from partisan inefficiency its fullest and largest scope. In Dayton, where the smoke curled from a thousand factories, lay the opportunity.

Dayton was no better or no worse than the average city with the old-time elective mayor and council system. The hand of the "machine" lay heavy on the public service; city-hall inadequacy and greed knew no party line. The treasury was always empty; government was by deficit.

In ten years the public debt had grown from $26.37 per capita to $46.13. To obtain funds for street lighting during a single year meant the issue of bonds running for thirty. Similarly, bonds to pay for moderate street construction long outlived the highways. And so on down the familiar line of extravagance and mismanagement.

Then began a movement that, in the completeness of its organization, in the big drama that punctuated its progress, and in the moral of education that it carries for every other city struggling to be free, is almost with precedent. The approach to the Dayton charter was along the path of remarkable preparedness, and it is well worth explaining. It is the business prelude to a business era.

Along in the fall of 1912 the Chamber of Commerce, appalled by the failure of city government, appointed a committee headed by Leopold Rauh and including John H. Patterson, E.A. Deeds, Frederick H. Rike, and E.C. Harley—five representative business men with widely differing interests and experience—to investigate and recommend some new plan. . . .

Choosing a City Manager

The very personnel of the commission—upstanding men who stood shoulder to shoulder amid flood and famine—typifies the spirit of this new working democracy. Four are self-made merchants and the fifth a printer, who still works at the case.

The way they went about their first and most important task—the selection of a city manager—shows their appreciation of high responsibility. Their initial choice was Colonel George W. Goethals, the master builder. They felt that he incarnated the ideal of what a city builder should be. When the news of the invitation to him became known the country suddenly awoke to the significance of this bloodless municipal revolution.

After Colonel Goethals declined the place the commission set systematically about filling it. They had, indeed, set a lofty standard. On the theory that home rule did not necessarily mean home talent, they scoured the country. The list of eligibles included chief engineers and general superintendents of railroads; men with military training and experience; managers of great corporations; university presidents (the White House was the cue here)[5]; experts in budget making and budget saving; even ex-mayors of proved worth and wide technical opportunity. Expert administration in Dayton is to be a condition, not a theory.

I was present when one of these eligibles appeared by invitation at the bar of the commission. It was an event that might easily have happened in the board room of a great corporation. The commissioners sat as directors, and to all intents, they were quizzing a possibility for general manager. When the commissioners entered the assembly room they left their politics, their business interests, their personal prejudices, and their religion outside. The amazing thing about the whole session was that the word politics was never mentioned. Instead, the commissioners probed into their guest's experience,

[5]   Marcosson refers here to President Woodrow Wilson, who had been president of Princeton University.

grasp of civic affairs, method of handling men, and last but not least, his vision of the city-manager domain. So with all the rest of those who seemed to measure up to this epoch-making post. Fitness was the first consideration.

After many such meetings and a month's careful combing of the field, the commission selected Henry M. Waite, of Cincinnati, to take up the duties which will doubtless set a new mark in the conduct of the American city.

Mr. Waite is a trained engineer who has constructed and operated railroads, developed coal fields, and had big part in the actual operation of a metropolitan community. His most recent activity fits him peculiarly for the Dayton work, for he has been one of Mayor Hunt's chief aides in the physical rehabilitation of Cincinnati under the reform era which ended all too soon. He has built streets and sewers, handled large groups of men, and built up an organization that is a model. He knows buildings and he knows business. Big of bone, deep of chest, and keen of eye, he looks as if the terrific task of blazing a whole fresh city path would be bread and meat to him.

This stocky, spectacled man who now sits as city manager in the gray and weather-beaten City Hall down on Main Street in Dayton is in reality the general superintendent of a humming and far-flung corporation of 125,000 stockholders. It is up to him to produce the dividends of service.

How are these dividends to be earned? By the most businesslike system of city government yet devised for an important community in this county. The keynote is centralization of administrative authority. One man—the city manager—is head and front of city operation, and what is more, he is responsible for it. He can appoint, discharge, and fix the salaries of all his immediate subordinates, including the heads of the five principal departments of law, finance, public safety, and public welfare. He can choose them wherever he pleases. Their one qualification must be training.

This unification of power not only enables the city to have a permanent expert, and professional administrator, but permits him to name a cabinet that will be sympathetic as well as efficient. Having no political enemies to punish and no friends to reward, he can proceed with one idea—to get the largest service for the best cost.

Why concentrate so much power in one man, you ask? Simply because business experience proves that centralization of authority in one man and the subsequent decentralization in his chief aids is the best formula for efficiency. The city manager can never usurp his power because, like the commission, he is subject to recall.

The commission, therefore, sits as a legislative body. It decides what the community job is, and the city manager sees that it is done. For example, if a new street is to be built, the commission, certain that the improvement is needed, calls in the city manager and tells him what is to be done. He in turn summons the chief of the Department of Public Service and gives the necessary instructions. If the work lags the commission can jerk up the city manager. Thus responsibility is definitely fixed.

This is a big advance on the cumbersome old Federal councilmanic plan with its waste and delay on public work. Dayton has knocked the bottom out of the municipal "park barrel."

3 Helen Valeska Bary, The Suffrage Movement in Southern California, 1910–1911[6]

Among the most important social reforms of the Progressive Era was the enfranchisement of women. The first serious call for woman suffrage occurred at the Seneca Falls Convention in 1848, but after the Civil War a national movement of women emerged. In 1890, the National American Woman Suffrage Association was created out of two rival groups. Meanwhile, women became involved in women's clubs, temperance organizations, and reform groups, and their involvement heightened their experience in public affairs and politics. It was only natural that Progressive Era women would see the vote as natural, and their exclusion from politics as harmful – and insulting.

From the 1890s into the twentieth century, the woman suffrage movement gathered supporters around the country. For the most part, it emphasized a strategy to obtain votes for women through state legislation or constitutional amendment. Later, that strategy would change: during World War I, suffragists sought the vote through the Nineteenth Amendment, and in August 1920 it was finally ratified and adopted as part of the Constitution. This document is an oral history interview, conducted in 1973 with California suffragist Helen Valeska Bary (1888–1973). California conducted a statewide referendum on woman suffrage, and, in a special election on October 10, 1911, it passed. In this interview, which was conducted by Jacqueline K. Parker, Bary explains her reasons for becoming a suffragist, the characteristics of the movement, and the strategies used to win the vote.

PARKER How was it that you got out of the home eventually, or found your own career?

BARY I did not want to stay at home. I wanted to get out. I worked. After my mother got a bit better, I got a job in a bookstore. I enjoyed meeting people.

[6] Interview with Helen Valeska Bary, December 29, 1972–January 14, 1973, Suffragists Oral History Project, Regional Oral History Office, Bancroft Library, UC-Berkeley (copy at http://content.cdlib.org/xtf/view?docId=kt6z09n8m9&doc.view=frames&chunk.id=doe152&toc.depth=1&toc.id=doe152&brand=calisphere).

I loved books. Then I quit that job after a year or so and I went into the suffrage campaign. . . . I went down to the headquarters to find out what they were doing and what they felt and all that. I got talking with the people down there; and I was talking with Mrs. Seward Simons who was president of the Political Equality League, the outstanding organization. Mrs. Simons said they needed somebody in the office and would I go to work for them. So I did, and I got $10 a week.

PARKER And you were the general secretary for the Political Equality League in 1910 and 1911?

BARY Yes. That was in the spring or so, and the election was coming along in October. The Political Equality League was organized by the leading women of the Friday Morning Club, which was a great institution in Southern California. It was about the biggest of the women's clubs and it was interested in public affairs. They carried on a campaign for pure milk and things like that.

The women's club movement was something. There were hundreds of clubs all over Southern California. Some of them were purely social, a great many of them were. Southern California was being settled up very rapidly, mostly from the middle western states of Iowa, Kansas, Nebraska, some from Illinois, and then a lesser number from other states.

There were all these people who wanted to get acquainted. I think almost every woman seemed to belong to at least one club. Some of the clubs were based on their neighborhoods and some were based on point of origin. They went in for everything. Some of them went in for culture; they studied fifteenth century Spanish architecture, things like that. Some of them were much more practical.

The women's club movement was built up so rapidly because in the farm belt the Department of Agriculture had organized a Home Economics Service to reach the farm women of the wheat and corn states who were living isolated lives and who needed help and companionship. They carried that experience of having been organized into groups with them. When they came to California, they just kept on belonging to clubs. . . . The Friday Morning Club had gone in for suffrage. The women who were members of the league were largely the wives of professional people. They were not so much Middle Westerners. . . . At any rate, they were largely upper middle class, professional class, whose husbands, for the most part, were rather conservative businessmen or professional men—doctors, lawyers. They were very respectable. . . . It represented a certain clash because the *Los Angeles Times*, at that time, dominated business and it was the leading paper in

Southern California. It was conservative. It was opposed to suffrage. It showed its opposition largely by belittling the campaign and sneering at it. As a league we all hated the Times, which is really quite interesting because later on in the campaign when I analyzed it, the area where the women lived went strongly against suffrage. . . .

PARKER What was your work in 1910 as general secretary of the Political Equality League?

BARY I talked to people who came to the office. Mrs. Simons came every day; she would talk to people, but there were too many for her to talk to everybody. I talked to people and I managed a number of volunteers who addressed envelopes and did chores like that. They were my charge. I had general charge of the office. We had a woman on publicity whose name was Bess Munn, a newspaper woman, but we did not get too much publicity.

PARKER Through the *Times*. They ignored you?

BARY Yes. The best the *Times* could do was to ignore us. We did have the support of the *Record*, which was a liberal sort of workingclass paper.

PARKER Socialist labor supported you in Los Angeles, is that right?

BARY Oh, yes. Socialist labor supported us. The league subsidized sub rosa a suffrage organization called the Wage Earners Suffrage League, which was directed by a Mrs. Frances Noel who was a liberal—a socialist, a German-born socialist. A very fine person.

PARKER Can you tell us about her?

BARY She was married to a man in one of the banks who was a minor executive. He was a socialist but kept quiet about it because the bank would not have approved if he hadn't.

Frances Noel made speeches. She helped with everything around the labor temple in the way of organizing women to help in case of strikes or anything of that kind. She was the outstanding woman connected with labor.

The Political Equality League subsidized this Wage Earners League. Sometimes Mrs. Noel came to our office and got her money, and sometimes I went down to the labor temple.

PARKER How much did this amount to, this subsidy?

BARY I don't know. We paid minor expenses. When it came to Labor Day, we put on two floats for suffrage; we paid for those. I might say that some of the members of the board of the league thought I was very brave to be willing to go down to the labor temple.

The labor temple was east of Main Street. Main Street divided Los Angeles so that east of Main was considered a working-class district. Probably most of the women in the Political Equality League had never been east of Main Street. I went down there and I found that there were human beings that lived down there. I also found that when I went to some of their meetings that these labor unions could talk intelligently. They were talking the socialist line of talk. They talked economics from a socialist point of view, and I was quite surprised to find out how well they did talk.... We had meetings all over Southern California and we sent out lots of literature. That was mostly what the volunteers did, they stuffed envelopes and addressed envelopes.

PARKER You sent this out to women's clubs?

BARY Oh, yes. We tried to get all the women's clubs to work for suffrage.

PARKER Did you also send out literature to churches and other groups?

BARY Oh, yes. We sent literature out very generally. We really did not spend much money. In those days, a few thousand dollars was quite a lot of money. Now campaigns run to millions. We collected money from people who came to the office. That was one of my jobs, to encourage people to contribute. Finally, it came to the vote. On election night, the earliest returns we got were from San Francisco. And Orange County came in very early. Those were very much against us.

PARKER Against suffrage?

BARY Against suffrage. By 11 p.m. not enough had come in to counteract it. We thought that not enough would come in so we conceded. Then everybody went home.

The next morning I went down to open up the headquarters. That was one of the most interesting days of my life. Nobody else from the league appeared; they were all flat. People streamed into the office. They were people I had never seen before. They were not our regulars. Many of them said they had never heard of the suffrage campaign; they did not know about it until they saw in the paper that it had lost.

They began to hand me money. I began to recruit people to help me. I had a couple of telephones and these people milling around and giving me money. I took in more money that day than we ever took in before, and I got all these pledges—hundreds of people came in and signed up for the next campaign. We all thought we had lost, you see.

Then on Thursday morning early, around four or five o'clock, one of the newspaperwomen, who was an ardent suffragist, called me and woke me up and said that we had won. The last of the cow counties had come in, and we had won by a margin of, I think it was 240 votes out of a couple of million.

PARKER So the cow counties pulled you through on the suffrage vote?

BARY Every other county voted for suffrage excepting San Francisco and Orange. You see, in San Francisco labor was not socialist. There were some socialists but San Francisco had had union labor for many years. The leaders were P. H. McCarthy and Eugene Schmits. They were labor men but they were not socialists.

They took the general viewpoint that labor was run by men, it was a man's world, and that women should be protected and rather put behind them while they carried on the fight. Also, there was a strong feeling among a great many of them that if women had the vote, they would vote for prohibition. That was not what San Francisco wanted.

PARKER There was a strong Catholic element also in San Francisco's population?

BARY Yes, and the Catholic element was not for suffrage. A woman's place was in the home.

PARKER So you found yourself with a victory. You were victorious.

BARY Yes, we were. Well, then the women decided that we should go ahead. I stayed on. We had a huge map of California, showing every precinct, and I colored that to show where we had won and where we had lost. Where we had won outstandingly was real red; where we had won by a narrow margin got down to a pale pink; and where we had lost went the same way with blue.

PARKER What characterized the strong districts for suffrage?

BARY The labor part. East of Main Street in Los Angeles voted heavily for suffrage. The respectable, stylish West Side voted against it; still the county came in for it. This huge map showed that every place where we had worked and sent literature and all that, we lost. We won in the places that we had neglected. It was quite wholesome and the ladies took it with interest. They did not blame me.

4 Seventeenth Amendment to the US Constitution (direct election of senators), 1913[7]

The framers of the Constitution intended for senators to be elected by the state legislatures for two primary reasons: that the attachment of states to the federal government would be stronger, making more likely the chance for ratification of the Constitution, and that the Senate would be able to conduct its business without direct pressure from voters. By the 1850s, however, conflicts within state legislatures over slavery and related issues led to numerous vacancies in the Senate.

After the Civil War, complaints about inconsistencies among states in the election of senators led to passage of a federal law in 1866 that standardized some aspects of these elections. However, corruption and pressure on state legislators continued to escalate during the late nineteenth century. The direct election of senators was first proposed in the 1820s, and the reform was promoted throughout the rest of the century. In 1907, Oregon and Nebraska became the first states to adopt the direct election of senators. More states began to follow, aided by muckraking articles about corrupt senators, and in 1911, Joseph Bristow, a senator from Kansas, proposed a constitutional amendment to provide for direct election of senators. Following passage in the Senate and then the House, the amendment was ratified by three-quarters of the states and became part of the Constitution in 1913.

Clause 1. The Senate of the United States shall be composed of two Senators from each State, elected by the people thereof, for six years; and each Senator shall have one vote. The electors in each State shall have the qualifications requisite for electors of the most numerous branch of the State legislatures.

Clause 2. When vacancies happen in the representation of any State in the Senate, the executive authority of each State shall issue writs of election to fill such vacancies: Provided That the legislature of any State may empower the executive thereof to make temporary appointments until the people fill the vacancies by election as the legislature may direct.

---

[7]   http://www.archives.gov/exhibits/charters/constitution_amendments_11-27.html

Clause 3. This amendment shall not be so construed as to affect the election or term of any Senator chosen before it becomes valid as part of the Constitution.

5 Marie Jenney Howe on Women's Public Role, 1910[8]

Marie Jenney Howe (1871–1934) was an ordained minister and activist feminist, who, in 1904, married prominent social reformer Frederick Howe. Marie Howe wrote this parody for dramatic presentation in New York City. In the monologue, she makes fun of traditional feminine values – and asserts a new public role for women. Two years after she published this piece, in 1912, Howe helped to found the Heterodoxy Club, a group of avant-garde feminists in New York. The 25 members met every Saturday night to discuss issues that related to rights for women. Rather than social workers, these women were concerned with achieving their fullest individual potential. Among the members were Mabel Dodge Luhan, Emma Goldman, Mary McLeod Bethune, Charlotte Perkins Gilman, Gertrude Vanderbilt Whitney, Crystal Eastman, Mary Heaton Vorse, Elsie Clews Parsons, and Eleanor Roosevelt.

The members represented a diverse group of women in terms of age, race, sexuality, and class, but they all were well-educated and shared the ideal of feminism. These new feminists believed in the necessity of economic independence for women, and, although the majority of them came from bourgeois backgrounds, they identified with socialism and the working class. Sexual freedom was also an important aspect of the new feminism, and the issue of heterosexual marriage remained an obstacle and an issue of continual discussion.

Please do not think of me as old-fashioned. I pride myself on being a modern up-to-date woman. I believe in all kinds of broad-mindedness, only I do not believe in woman suffrage because to do that would be to deny my sex. Woman suffrage is the reform against nature. Look at these ladies sitting on the platform. Observe their physical inability, their mental disability, their spiritual instability and general debility! Could they walk up to the ballot box, mark a ballot, and drop it in? Obviously not. Let us grant for the sake of argument that they could mark a ballot. But could they drop it in? Ah, no. All nature is against it. The laws of man cry out against it. The voice of God cries out against it—and so do I.

[8]   Marie Jenney Howe, *An Anti-Suffrage Monologue* (New York: National American Woman Suffrage Association, 1913).

Enfranchisement is what makes man man. Disfranchisement is what makes woman woman. If women were enfranchised every man would be just like every woman and every woman would be just like every man. There would be no difference between them. And don't you think this would rob life of just a little of its poetry and romance?

Man must remain man. Woman must remain woman. If man goes over and tries to be like woman, if woman goes over and tries to be like man, it will become so very confusing and so difficult to explain to our children. Let us take a practical example. If a woman puts on a man's coat and trousers, takes a man's cane and hat and cigar, and goes out on the street, what will happen to her? She will be arrested and thrown into jail. Then why not stay at home?

I know you begin to see how strongly I *feel* on this subject, but I have some reasons as well. These reasons are based on logic. Of course I am not logical. I am a creature of impulse, instinct, and intuition—and I glory in it. But I know that these reasons are based on logic because I have culled them from the men whom it is my privilege to know.

My first argument against suffrage is that the women would not use it if they had it. You couldn't drive them to the polls. My second argument is, if the women were enfranchised they would neglect their homes, desert their families, and spend all their time at the polls. You may tell me that the polls are only open once a year. But I know women. They are creatures of habit. If you let them go to the polls once a year, they will hang round the polls all the rest of the time.

I have arranged these arguments in couplets. They go together in such a way that if you don't like one you can take the other. This is my second anti-suffrage couplet. If the women were enfranchised they would vote exactly as their husbands do and only double the existing vote. Do you like that argument? If not, take this one. If the women were enfranchised they would vote against their own husbands, thus creating dissension, family quarrels, and divorce.

My third anti-suffrage couplet is—women are angels. Many men call me an angel and I have a strong instinct which tells me it is true; that is why I am anti, because "I want to be an angel and with the angels stand." And if you don't like that argument take this one. Women are depraved. They would introduce into politics a vicious element which would ruin our national life.

Fourth anti-suffrage couplet: women cannot understand politics. Therefore there would be no use in giving women political power, because they would not know what to do with it. On the other hand, if the women were enfranchised, they would mount rapidly into power, take all the offices from all the men, and soon we would have women governors of all our states and dozens of women acting as President of the United States.

Fifth anti-suffrage couplet: women cannot band together. They are incapable of organization. No two women can even be friends. Women are cats. On the other hand, if women were enfranchised, we would have all the women banded together on one side and all the men banded together on the other side, and there would follow a sex war which might end in bloody revolution.

Just one more of my little couplets: the ballot is greatly over-estimated. It has never done anything for anybody. Lots of men tell me this. And the corresponding argument is—the ballot is what makes man man. It is what gives him all his dignity and all of his superiority to women. Therefore if we allow women to share this privilege, how could a woman look up to her own husband? Why, there would be nothing to look up to.

I have talked to many woman suffragists and I find them very unreasonable. I say to them: "Here I am, convince me." I ask for proof. Then they proceed to tell me of Australia and Colorado and other places where women have passed excellent laws to improve the condition of working women and children. But I say, "What of it?" These are facts. I don't care about facts. I ask for proof.

Then they quote the eight million women of the United States who are now supporting themselves, and the twenty-five thousand married women in the City of New York who are self-supporting. But I say again, what of it? These are statistics. I don't believe in statistics. Facts and statistics are things which no truly womanly woman would ever use.

I wish to prove anti-suffrage in a womanly way—that is, by personal example. This is my method of persuasion. Once I saw a woman driving a horse, and the horse ran away with her. Isn't that just like a woman? Once I read in the newspapers about a woman whose house caught on fire, and she threw the children out of the window and carried the pillows downstairs. Does that show political acumen, or does it not? Besides, look at the hats that women wear! And have you ever known a successful woman governor of a state? Or have you ever known a really truly successful woman president of the United States? Well, if they could they would, wouldn't they? Then, if they haven't, doesn't that show they couldn't? As for the militant suffragettes, they are all hyenas in petticoats. Now do you want to be a hyena and wear petticoats?

Now, I think I have proved anti-suffrage; and I have done it in a womanly way—that is, without stooping to the use of a single fact or argument or a single statistic.

I am the prophet of a new idea. No one has ever thought of it or heard of it before. I well remember when this great idea first came to me. It waked me in the middle of the night with a shock that gave me a headache. This is it: woman's place is in the home. Is it not beautiful as it is new, new as it is true? Take this idea away with you. You will find it very helpful in your daily lives. You may not grasp it just at first, but you will gradually grow into understanding of it.

I know the suffragists reply that all our activities have been taken out of the home. The baking, the washing, the weaving, the spinning are all long since taken out of the home. But I say, all the more reason that something should stay in the home. Let it be woman. Besides, think of the great modern invention, the telephone. That has been put into the home. Let woman stay at home and answer the telephone.

We antis have so much imagination! Sometimes it seems to us that we can hear the little babies in the slums crying to us. We can see the children in factories and mines reaching out their little hands to us, and the working women in the sweated industries, the underpaid, underfed women, reaching out their arms to us—all, all crying as with one voice, "Save us, save us, from Woman Suffrage." Well may they make this appeal to us, for who knows what woman suffrage might not do for such as these. It might even alter the conditions under which they live.

We antis do not believe that any conditions should be altered. We want everything to remain just as it is. All is for the best. Whatever is, is right. If misery is in the world, God has put it there; let it remain. If this misery presses harder on some women than others, it is because they need discipline. Now, I have always been comfortable and well cared for. But then I never needed discipline. Of course I am only a weak, ignorant woman. But there is one thing I do understand from the ground up, and that is the divine intention toward woman. I *know* that the divine intention toward woman is, let her remain at home.

The great trouble with the suffragists is this; they interfere too much. They are always interfering. Let me take a practical example.

There is in the City of New York a Nurses' Settlement, where sixty trained nurses go forth to care for sick babies and give them pure milk. Last summer only two or three babies died in this slum district around the Nurses' Settlement, whereas formerly hundreds of babies have died there every summer. Now what are these women doing? Interfering, interfering with the death rate! And what is their motive in so doing? They seek notoriety. They want to be noticed. They are trying to show off. And if sixty women who merely believe in suffrage behave in this way, what may we expect when all women are enfranchised?

What ought these women to do with their lives? Each one ought to be devoting herself to the comfort of some man. You may say, they are not married. But I answer, let them try a little harder and they might find some kind of a man to devote themselves to. What does the Bible say on this subject? It says, "Seek and ye shall find." Besides, when I look around me at the men; I feel that God never meant us women to be too particular.

Let me speak one word to my sister women who are here to-day. Women, we don't need to vote in order to get our own way. Don't misunderstand me. Of course I want you to get your own way. That's what we're here for. But do it indirectly. If you want a thing, tease. If that doesn't work, nag. If that doesn't do, cry—crying always brings them around. Get what you want. Pound pillows. Make a scene. Make home a hell on earth, but do it in a womanly way. That is so much more dignified and refined than walking up to a ballot box and dropping in a piece of paper. Can't you see that?

Let us consider for a moment the effect of woman's enfranchisement on man. I think some one ought to consider the men. What makes husbands faithful and loving? The ballot, and the monopoly of that privilege. If women vote, what will become of men? They will all slink off drunk and disorderly. We antis understand men. If women were enfranchised, men would revert to their natural instincts such as regicide, matricide, patricide and race-suicide. Do you believe in race-suicide or do you not? Then, isn't it our duty to refrain from a thing that would lure men to destruction?

It comes down to this. Some one must wash the dishes. Now, would you expect man, man made in the image of God, to roll up his sleeves and wash the dishes? Why, it would be blasphemy. I know that I am but a rib and so I wash the dishes. Or I hire another rib to do it for me, which amounts to the same thing.

Let us consider the argument from the standpoint of religion. The Bible says, "Let the women keep silent in the churches." Paul says, "Let them keep their hats on for fear of the angels." My minister says, "Wives, obey your husbands." And my husband says that woman suffrage would rob the rose of its fragrance and the peach of its bloom. I think that is so sweet.

Besides, did George Washington ever say, "Votes for women?" No. Did the Emperor Kaiser Wilhelm ever say, "Votes for women?" No. Did Elijah, Elisha, Micah, Hezekiah, Obadiah, and Jeremiah ever say, "Votes for women?" No. Then that settles it.

I don't want to be misunderstood in my reference to woman's inability to vote. Of course she could get herself to the polls and lift a piece of paper. I don't doubt that. What I refer to is the pressure on the brain, the effect of this mental strain on woman's delicate nervous organization and on her highly wrought sensitive nature. Have you ever pictured to yourself Election Day with women voting? Can you imagine how women, having undergone this terrible ordeal, with their delicate systems all upset, will come out of the voting booths and be led away by policemen, and put into ambulances, while they are fainting and weeping, half laughing, half crying, and having fits upon the public highway? Don't you think that if a woman is going to have a fit, it is far better for her to have it in the privacy of her own home?

And how shall I picture to you the terrors of the day after election? Divorce and death will rage unchecked, crime and contagious disease will stalk unbridled through the land. Oh, friends, on this subject I feel—I feel, so strongly that I cannot think!

Discussion Questions: Chapter 12

1   What characteristics did social and political reformers share? How were they different?
2   Why was La Follette opposed to political machines?
3   What were some of the political and social reforms of the Progressive Era that are mentioned in these documents?
4   Compare the views of feminism presented by Bary and Howe.

Part V   Imperialism and War

Chapter 13   Imperialism and Anti-Imperialism

1 Mayo W. Hazeltine, "What Shall Be Done about the Philippines?" 1897[1]

Mayo W. Hazeltine (1841–1909) was an editor and writer for the
New York Sun, who focused much of his attention on US foreign policy
in the Asian Pacific region. As an imperialist, Hazeltine favored the United
States' acquisition of the Philippines, but he also believed that, once the
United States and Spain had signed the peace treaty ending the Spanish-
American War, the United States could not honorably take the Philippines
by force. Instead, he supported a proposal to pay Spain's debts in the region
in exchange for US control of the islands.

Hazeltine edited a book of speeches by famous men, including William
McKinley, who was president during the war with Spain. With the American
victory, the United States became a military and colonial power in East Asia
based on its presence in the Philippines. The declaration of the Open Door
policy in 1899, which announced that the United States had a stake in
western commercial investment in China and would oppose its partition by
European powers, reinforced the identification of American interests, as
Hazeltine suggests in this document.

---

[1]   *North American Review* DIII (October 1898): 385–92.

The Gilded Age and Progressive Era: A Documentary Reader, First Edition.
Edited by William A. Link and Susannah J. Link.
© 2012 Blackwell Publishing Ltd. Published 2012 by Blackwell Publishing Ltd.

Two or three months ago, the President's uncertainty regarding the course to be pursued in the Philippines was shared by many of his countrymen. Neither in its moral nor in its economical aspects had the problem been thoroughly examined. There is no doubt that those who organized a conference at Saratoga for the purpose of considering the questions opened by the war, expected therefrom a declaration that, by the teaching and practice of the fathers, we were precluded from seeking any trans-marine possessions, and, especially, such as were parted from us by the breadth of the Pacific. As a matter of fact, so rapid was the diffusion of information and the resultant evolution of opinion, that the Saratoga Conference pronounced in favor of annexing not only Porto Rico, but also a port in the Ladrones and the whole, or part, of the Philippines. There is now reason to believe that a large majority of our citizens are thoroughly convinced, first, that, by our victory at Cavite, and the subsequent capture of Manila, we assumed a moral obligation toward the natives of Luzon; secondly, that the obligation can be best discharged by the occupation of all the Philippines, and, thirdly, that no grievous financial burden will be imposed upon our people by the discharge of that obligation, seeing that the natural resources of the Philippines are incalculably great, and that our occupation of them will give us a voice potential in the future regulation of China's trade, wherein we are profoundly interested. From the viewpoint of these prevalent convictions, let us glance at the several ways in which it has been suggested by the various advisers of the President that the Philippine problem shall be solved. Shall we restore the whole of the Philippines to Spain, retaining only for ourselves a station for coaling and repair, as, for example, the city and harbor of Manila? This we cannot do without forfeiting our self-respect and the respect of the world, for the natives of Luzon, the most populous and civilized island in the group, have notoriously suffered more at the hands of Spain than have the Cubans, and we are ourselves responsible for the latest uprising on their part. Moreover, what Spain could not do, when she had a considerable navy and funds relatively adequate, she certainly could not accomplish now that her navy is well nigh extinct and that her treasury is bankrupt; that is to say, establish in the island of Luzon a government which should fulfill the fundamental functions of safeguarding life and property. We may dismiss with a word the fantastic proposal that we should govern Luzon in partnership with Spain. Such a mongrel administration would compel us to share the responsibility for evil doing, while depriving us of power to avert it; Spanish influence, so far as a joint regime permitted its exercise, would be sure to follow the old channels of oppression and embezzlement. Shall we, then, declare the island of Luzon independent, and make over the control of it to Aguinaldo[2] and his followers? It is the consensus of all observers, who have studied at first hand the situation in Luzon, that the Tagals could not establish a durable government of their own. They are an industrious people, docile and easily managed by an administration at once firm and just, but they are very far from possessing the qualifications for self-rule. Shall we, by resigning our own claim to the Philippines, a claim which, being based upon our capture of their capital, was, when the news of the signing of the protocol reached Manila, actually stronger than our claim to Cuba or to Porto Rico, enable Spain to sell them to Russia, France or Germany? By such an act, we should endow with an inestimable coign of vantage[3] in the Far East one of the powers, the whole tendency of whose policy is to minimize our share in China's foreign trade. But Spain, it may be argued, could find a purchaser in Great Britain. We answer that, by the acquisition of the Philippines, Great Britain would acquire the prospect of such preponderance in the Far East that the other powers would feel constrained, by a sense of self-preservation, to avert it by a general war. Our duty to mankind enjoins us not to precipitate a general war, and the surest mode of discharging that duty is to take the Philippines ourselves.

Could we not, however, surmount all difficulties by keeping Luzon, which represents in area rather more than a third of the group, and leaving the rest of the islands to Spain, a promise being exacted from her that they shall not be ceded to any other power? This solution of the problem is said to be favored in influential quarters, but it is open to grave objections. In the first place, it is doubtful if Spain would be able to maintain peace and order in the rest of the archipelago, and, thereby, afford no pretext for foreign intervention. Even when her navy was relatively strong, it was only with difficulty that she was able to repress the pirates, who formerly infested the coasts of Mindanao and the islands of the Sulu group. Suppose, however, that, in the remnant of her possessions, she did contrive to maintain a naval force sufficient for police purposes and gradually did manage to develop a flourishing island empire, we should have at our doors a vindictive neighbor ready to join any coalition that might be formed against us, and, meanwhile, eager to foment disaffection in Luzon, which her profession of a common religion and her familiarity with the customs and the character of the Tagals would facilitate. By such a compromise, in short, we should only invite

[2]   Emilio Aguinaldo (1869–1964), who led resistance against the Spanish and, after the Spanish-American War, against the United States' colonial presence.
[3]   An advantageous position.

future trouble, which we can avoid by assuming control of the whole archipelago. The civilizing of the southern islands, which have, collectively, a superficies of about 75,000 square miles, would be a trivial task to the American people, which, in less than a century, has reclaimed the vast region lying between the Mississippi and the Pacific.

From an economic as well as a humanitarian viewpoint, the work would be worth its cost, for, at the end of a century, the whole Philippine group should be able to support fifty millions of inhabitants, if we may judge by the experience of Java, which, in the course of a hundred years, has seen its population expand from about two to over twenty millions. If it be true, as Mr. Benjamin Kidd contends, that the twentieth century is to witness a vehement struggle for the control of tropical lands upon the part of the nations belonging to the temperate zones, we should enter upon the contest with one of the most valuable prizes attainable in the tropics already in our hands. Nor is it only by their natural resources, capable, as they are, of almost limitless development, nor by the capacious market for our manufactures which they would, eventually, offer, that the Philippines would be of immense utility to the United States. Such is their strategic relation to China that our possession of them would give us an influence at Peking second only to that of Russia and Great Britain, an influence that we could use to thwart such of the European powers as contemplate a thorough-going partition of the Middle Kingdom, and to co-operate effectively with those that are resolved to uphold what is left of China's territorial integrity and to keep at all events an open door to that most populous and resourceful section of the Celestial Empire which is watered by the Yang-tse-Kiang. It is, in a word, freedom of access for American manufacturers to the best part of China which would be powerfully furthered by our retention of the Philippines.

II

To the first question, then, What should we wish to do about the Philippines we answer that we ought to keep not only Manila, not only the whole island of Luzon, but the entire Philippine archipelago, if we are to show ourselves alive to the full purport of our opportunities and to the full scope of our mission in the East. That would be the simplest, safest and cheapest solution of the problem. Is it, however, any longer possible to secure all the Philippines in the new situation created by the protocol?

There is no doubt that President McKinley, before that agreement was signed, could have obtained the Philippines well nigh as easily as he obtained Porto Rico and Cuba, for Manila was known to be upon the point of falling into our hands, which is more than could be said for either San Juan or Havana. Had the Madrid Government proved recalcitrant upon this point, it could have been quickly brought to terms by naval demonstrations against the Carolines, the Canaries, the Balearic Isles and the seaports of the Iberian peninsula. But, when the President forbore to exercise the power which he possessed, and consented to let the fate of the Philippines be determined by a commission, in which Spain should have an equal voice, he, practically, put the retention of all the islands by us out of the question, unless some consideration should be tendered, which would be regarded in Mad-rid as a quid pro quo. For suppose that, in compliance with instructions from Washington, the five American commissioners should concur in demanding the cession to us of all the Philippines, it is absolutely certain that the five Spanish commissioners would, on their part, reject the demand, unless it were coupled with an offer of compensation. We could not blame them for an attitude which must, or should have been, foreseen when the protocol was signed. It is even questionable whether the Spanish commissioners will agree to surrender the whole of the island of Luzon in the absence of any indemnifying proposal. In that event, it may be said, the result of the negotiations will be a deadlock, and, if this cannot be broken, both parties will be relegated to the arbitrament of war. We answer that the public opinion of the world would not justify us in recurring to the arbitrament of war after the solution of the Philippine problem had been formally committed by our Executive to a joint commission. We should be told, justly, that if our President was resolved to keep the Philippines, or at least Luzon, he ought, when the protocol was signed, to have proclaimed his resolution as distinctly as he did in the case of Porto Rico, and that, unless we could and would replace Spain in the position occupied by her when hostilities ceased, we should have no right to recur to war, merely because the Spanish commissioners saw fit to exercise the equal voice which the protocol conferred on them. This is indisputably true. Our Government has, voluntarily, made the disposition of the Philippines a subject for negotiation, and it could not, with any show of decency, make a deadlock the pretext for a recourse to arms.

When the President begins to ponder the methods of escaping from the predicament in which the protocol has placed him, he will find a suggestive precedent in the treatment which Mexico received at the hands of President Polk in 1848. At that time General Scott occupied the Mexican capital, and the entire Mexican republic was undeniably at our mercy. We might have annexed the whole of it, but public opinion in the Northern States would not have tolerated such a sweeping exercise of the right of conquest; indeed, it was even indisposed to brook an extensive mutilation of a sister commonwealth. Under these circumstances, it was decided that, although we had demonstrated the possession of a giant's strength, we would not use it like a giant, and our commissioners were instructed not to exact from Mexico a single acre by right of conquest, but to offer $15,000,000 in cash and the assumption of debts amounting to $3,000,000 due from Mexico to American citizens, in exchange for the tract comprising California, Nevada, Utah, Arizona and New Mexico. The purchase money now seems ludicrously small, but it was eagerly accepted by the provisional Mexican Government, the full extent of the mineral wealth of the ceded territory being, as yet, unguessed at. The result of this remarkable transaction, which, so far as we know, has no counterpart in history, and which presents a striking contrast to the treatment of France by Germany in 1871, disarmed, in a considerable degree, the opposition of our Northern States to the dismemberment of Mexico, and the treaty of peace was ratified by the Senate.

The bearing of this precedent upon the situation created by the protocol is obvious. It is most improbable that, without some compensation, the Spanish commissioners will agree to give up the Philippines, or even the island of Luzon. On the other hand, the maintenance of their authority in the rest of the islands would require an outlay of blood and treasure which they are ill able to afford. The Madrid Government could escape from the dilemma, and, to use the Chinese phrase, "save its face" in the eyes of the Spanish people, if, in return for a cession of all the Philippines, it could secure such a sum of money as would, to a moderate extent, relieve the necessities of its exchequer. As it happens, a relatively insignificant part of the Spanish debt is saddled upon the revenues of the Philippines. This our commissioners might consent to assume, and they might even go a little further, and agree to make the United States, or Independent Cuba, responsible for a fifth part of the so-called Cuban debt. Why do we designate this particular fraction? Because, when the Autonomist government was instituted in Cuba, it was stipulated by the Autonomists that the insular revenues should be liable for only a fifth of the Cuban debt, inasmuch as by the most liberal estimate not more than a fifth of the money borrowed in Cuba's name could be regarded as having been applied to the welfare of the island. The Philippine debt and one-fifth of the Cuban debt would not, together, amount to much more than $100,000,000, a sum which we could borrow at three per cent., or, for that matter, easily spare from our national revenue, distended as this has been by the war taxes. We opine that an offer on our part to assume the indebtedness mentioned would secure the assent of the Spanish commissioners to the relinquishment of all the Philippines, and we doubt if their assent to such a proposal can be gained in any other way.

But why, it may be asked, should we buy what we have conquered? We answer that the question comes too late. It should have been put before the signing of the protocol, whereby in the disposition of the Philippines the Spaniards acquired an equal voice.

2 Platt Amendment, 1901[4]

In 1901, Senator Orville Platt of Connecticut attached to an appropriations bill a set of provisions guiding US–Cuban relations. Cuba reluctantly ratified this amendment to the Cuban constitution in June 1904, at the insistence of the American government, and the provisions ultimately were included in a treaty between the two countries. The treaty provided the United States with control over important aspects of the newly independent country in the Caribbean and provided for the establishment of US military bases on the island, one of which – Guantánamo Bay – is still in operation. At the time this policy was instituted, the United States was engaged in a widespread effort to control yellow fever, and the American government insisted on the right to conduct sanitation efforts on the island. It was the first document to legitimize American imperialism, and set the tone for more than a century of US involvement in Latin America, including economic domination and military forays into the region.

The document, according to supporters, helped the United States to ensure Cuba's independence by prohibiting diplomatic agreements between Cuba and other countries without the prior approval of the US government. Opposition to the treaty coincided with the larger anti-imperialist movement in the United States following the Spanish-American War. The Platt Amendment was abrogated in 1934, during the administration of Franklin Roosevelt, in response to increasing nationalist pressure from Latin American countries, including Cuba.

Whereas the Congress of the United States of America, by an Act approved March 2, 1901, provided as follows:

Provided . . . That in fulfillment of the declaration contained in the joint resolution approved April twentieth, eighteen hundred and ninety-eight, entitled "For the recognition of the independence of the people of Cuba, demanding that the Government of Spain relinquish its authority and government in the island of Cuba, and withdraw its land and naval forces

[4] "The Platt Amendment," in *Treaties and Other International Agreements of the United States of America, 1776–1949*, vol. 8, ed. C.I. Bevans (Washington, DC: US Government Printing Office, 1971), pp. 1116–17.

from Cuba and Cuban waters, and directing the President of the United States to use the land and naval forces of the United States to carry these resolutions into effect," the President is hereby authorized to "leave the government and control of the island of Cuba to its people" so soon as a government shall have been established in said island under a constitution which, either as a part thereof or in an ordinance appended thereto, shall define the future relations of the United States with Cuba, substantially as follows:

"I. That the government of Cuba shall never enter into any treaty or other compact with any foreign power or powers which will impair or tend to impair the independence of Cuba, nor in any manner authorize or permit any foreign power or powers to obtain by colonization or for military or naval purposes or otherwise, lodgement in or control over any portion of said island."

"II. That said government shall not assume or contract any public debt, to pay the interest upon which, and to make reasonable sinking fund provision for the ultimate discharge of which, the ordinary revenues of the island, after defraying the current expenses of government shall be inadequate."

"III. That the government of Cuba consents that the United States may exercise the right to intervene for the preservation of Cuban independence, the maintenance of a government adequate for the protection of life, property, and individual liberty, and for discharging the obligations with respect to Cuba imposed by the treaty of Paris on the United States, now to be assumed and undertaken by the government of Cuba."

"IV. That all Acts of the United States in Cuba during its military occupancy thereof are ratified and validated, and all lawful rights acquired thereunder shall be maintained and protected."

"V. That the government of Cuba will execute, and as far as necessary extend, the plans already devised or other plans to be mutually agreed upon, for the sanitation of the cities of the island, to the end that a recurrence of epidemic and infectious diseases may be prevented, thereby assuring protection to the people and commerce of Cuba, as well as to the commerce of the southern ports of the United States and the people residing therein."

"VI. That the Isle of Pines shall be omitted from the proposed constitutional boundaries of Cuba, the title thereto being left to future adjustment by treaty."

"VII. That to enable the United States to maintain the independence of Cuba, and to protect the people thereof, as well as for its own defense, the government of Cuba will sell or lease to the United States lands necessary for coaling or naval stations at certain specified points to be agreed upon with the President of the United States."

"VIII. That by way of further assurance the government of Cuba will embody the foregoing provisions in a permanent treaty with the United States."

3 Jane Addams, "Democracy or Militarism," 1899[5]

*Jane Addams (1860–1935), founder of Hull House, the famous settlement
house in Chicago, became a strong pacifist and antiwar activist. In 1931,
she became the first American woman to win the Nobel Peace Prize. She
served as a chair of the Women's Peace party during World War I and was
president of the Women's International League for Peace and Freedom
from 1919 to 1929.*

*Opposition to US occupation of Cuba, Puerto Rico, and the Philippines
following the Spanish-American War came from a minority of Americans,
but many of these opponents were well-known and influential. Addams was
among them; others who spoke out against American imperialism were
Andrew Carnegie and Mark Twain. In 1899, the American Anti-Imperialist
League was formed to lobby against US annexation of the Philippine Islands.
Included in the platform of this new organization was concurrence with the
opinion of Abraham Lincoln that "no man is good enough to govern another
man without that other's consent. When the white man governs himself, that
is self-government, but when he governs himself and also governs another
man, that is more than self-government – that is despotism."*

*Opponents of American imperialism were motivated by various factors,
among them a moral opposition to subjugation of non-whites, a fear that
American jobs would be lost to workers overseas, and a concern about
domination of the United States by the military and by corporations. Mark
Twain wrote new, satirical lyrics for the "Battle Hymn of the Republic":
"Mine eyes have seen the orgy of the launching of the sword/He is searching
out the hoardings where the strangers' wealth is stored/He has loosed
his fateful lightning, and with woe and death has scored/His lust is
marching on."*

None of us who has been reared and nurtured in America can be wholly
without the democratic instinct. It is not a question with any of us of having
it or not having it; it is merely a question of trusting it or not trusting it. For
good or ill we suddenly find ourselves bound to an international situation.
The question practically reduces itself to this: Do we mean to democratize
the situation? Are we going to trust our democracy, or are we going to
weakly imitate the policy of other governments, which have never claimed a
democratic basis?

The political code, as well as the moral law, has no meaning and
becomes absolutely emptied of its contents if we take out of it all relation

[5] *Liberty Tracts: Central Anti-Imperialist League of Chicago* No 1 (Chicago: Central Anti-
Imperialist League, 1899), pp. 35–9.

to the world and concrete cases, and it is exactly in such a time as this that we discover what we really believe. We may make a mistake in politics as well as in morals by forgetting that new conditions are ever demanding the evolution of a new morality, along old lines but in larger measure. Unless the present situation extends our nationalism into internationalism, unless it has thrust forward our patriotism into humanitarianism we cannot meet it.

We must also remember that peace has come to mean a larger thing. It is no longer merely absence of war, but the unfolding of life processes which are making for a common development. Peace is not merely something to hold congresses about and to discuss as an abstract dogma. It has come to be a rising tide of moral feeling, which is slowly engulfing all pride of conquest and making war impossible.

Under this new conception of peace it is perhaps natural that the first men to formulate it and give it international meaning should have been workingmen, who have always realized, however feebly and vaguely they may have expressed it, that it is they who in all ages have borne the heaviest burden of privation and suffering imposed on the world by the military spirit.

The first international organization founded not to promote a colorless peace, but to advance and develop the common life of all nations was founded in London in 1864 by workingmen and called simply "The International Association of Workingmen." They recognized that a supreme interest raised all workingmen above the prejudice of race, and united them by wider and deeper principles than those by which they were separated into nations. That as religion, science, art, had become international, so now at last labor took its position as an international interest. A few years later, at its third congress, held in Brussels in 1868, the internationals recommended in view of the Franco-German war, then threatening, that "the workers resist all war as systematic murder," and in case of war a universal strike by declared.

This is almost exactly what is now happening in Russia. The peasants are simply refusing to drill and fight and the czar gets credit for a peace manifesto the moral force of which comes from the humblest of his subjects. It is not, therefore, surprising that as long ago as last December, the organized workingmen of America recorded their protest against the adoption of an imperialistic policy.

In the annual convention of the American Federation of Labor, held that month in Kansas City, resolutions were adopted endorsing the declaration made by President Gompers in his opening address: "It has always been the hewers of wood and the carriers of water, the wealth producers, whose missions it has been not only to struggle for freedom, but to be ever vigilant to maintain the liberty of freedom achieved, and it behooves the representatives of the grand army of labor in convention assembled to give vent to the alarm we feel from the dangers threatening us and our entire people, to enter our solemn and emphatic protest against what we already feel; that, with the success of imperialism the decadence of our republic will have already set in."

There is a growing conviction among workingmen of all countries that, whatever may be accomplished by a national war, however high the supposed moral aim of such a war, there is one inevitable result — an increased standing army, the soldiers of which are non-producers and must be fed by the workers. The Russian peasants support an army of 1,000,000, the German peasants sow and reap for 500,000 more. The men in these armies spend their muscular force in drilling, their mental force in thoughts of warfare. The mere hours of idleness conduce mental and moral deterioration.

The appeal to the fighting instinct does not end in mere warfare, but arouses these brutal instincts latent in every human being. The countries with the large standing armies are likewise the countries with national hospitals for the treatment of diseases which should never exist, of large asylums for the care of children which should never have been born. These institutions, as well as the barracks, again increase the taxation, which rests, in the last analysis, upon producers, and, at the same time, withdraws so much of their product from the beneficient [sic] development of their national life. No one urges peaceful association with more fervor than the workingman. Organization is his only hope, but it must be kept distinct from militarism, which can never be made a democratic instrument.

Let us not make the mistake of confusing moral issues sometimes involved in warfare with warfare itself. Let us not glorify the brutality. The same strenuous endeavor, the same heroic self-sacrifice, the same fine courage and readiness to meet death, may be displayed without the accompaniment of killing our fellow men. With all Kipling's insight he has, over and over, failed to distinguish between war and imperialism on the one hand and the advance of civilization on the other.

To "protect the weak" has always been the excuse of the ruler and tax-gatherer, the chief, the king, the baron; and now, at last, of "the white man." The form of government is not necessarily the function itself. Government is not something extraneous, consisting of men who wear gold lace and sit on high stools and write rows of figures in books. We forget that an ideal government is merely an adjustment between men concerning their mutual relations towards those general matters which concern them all; that the office of an outside and alien people must always be to collect taxes and to hold a negative law and order. In its first attempt to restore mere order and quiet, the outside power inevitably breaks down the framework of the nascent government itself, the more virile and initiative forces are destroyed; new relations must in the end be established, not only with the handicap of smart animosity on the part of the conquered, but with the loss of the most able citizens among them.

Some of us were beginning to hope that we were getting away from the ideals set by the civil war, that we had made all the presidents we could from men who had distinguished themselves in that war, and were coming to seek another type of man. That we were ready to accept the peace ideal, to be proud of our title as a peace nation; to recognize that the man who cleans a city is greater than he who bombards it, and the man who irrigates a plain greater than he who lays it waste. Then came the Spanish war, with its gilt and lace and tinsel, and again the moral issues are confused with exhibitions of brutality.

For ten years I have lived in a neighborhood which is by no means criminal, and yet during last October and November we were started by seven murders within a radius of ten blocks. A little investigation of details and motives, the accident of a personal acquaintance with two of the criminals, made it not in the least difficult to trace the murders back to the influence of the war. Simple people who read of carnage and bloodshed easily receive its suggestions. Habits of self-control which have been but slowly and imperfectly acquired quickly break down under the stress.

Psychologists intimate that action is determined by the selection of the subject upon which the attention is habitually fixed. The newspapers, the theatrical posts, the street conversations for weeks had to do with war and bloodshed. The little children on the street played at war, day after day, killing Spaniards. The humane instinct, which keeps in abeyance the tendency to cruelty, the growing belief that the life of each human being—however hopeless or degraded, is still sacred—gives way, and the barbaric instinct asserts itself.

It is doubtless only during a time of war that the men and women of Chicago could tolerate whipping for children in our city prison, and it is only during such a time that the introduction in the legislature of a bill for the re-establishment of the whipping post could be possible. National events determine our ideas, as much as our ideals determine national events.

4 Photograph from the Tour of the Great White Fleet, 1907–09

As a display of the United States' arrival as a seapower, President Theodore Roosevelt ordered that four squadrons of the Atlantic Fleet conduct a worldwide tour that would last 14 months between late 1907 and early

1909. Roosevelt was convinced that the key to the United States' status as a world power would be a strong navy, and as president he sponsored a naval buildup and the extension of naval bases around the world. As competition increased with Japan for influence, Roosevelt was intent on demonstrating the ability of the Atlantic Fleet to reach interests around the world.

The tour was especially noteworthy as the first occasion that a steam-power fleet circled the globe. Especially important were the 16 new battleships that had been commissioned since the end of the Spanish-American War leading the way. Departing the naval base at Hampton Roads, Virginia, on December 16, 1907, the fleet travelled 43,000 miles, included the participation of more than 14,000 sailors, and visited 20 ports on six continents. Only after it completed its voyage on February 22, 1909, did the tour of the Atlantic Fleet become known as the "Great White Fleet."

Figure 13.1   Photograph from the Tour of the Great White Fleet, 1907–09, US Naval History and Heritage Commands.
Source: Photograph, Collection of Roy D. France, photo by C.E. Waterman.

Discussion Questions: Chapter 13

1   How did supporters of American imperialism differ from anti-imperialists?
2   What were the characteristics of American empire?
3   How did the Platt Amendment limit Cuban sovereignty?

Chapter 14   The Debate about World War I

1 W.E.B. Du Bois on the Postwar Peace, 1918[1]

Unlike many black leaders, Du Bois supported the entry of the United States into World War I, because, to him, military service by blacks would lead to acceptance by white Americans and a chance to gain the civil rights denied to them. Although Du Bois was a harsh critic of segregation, he was willing to accept the segregated military in the short term in order to achieve the ultimate goal of equality.

The forum that Du Bois used to promote his views was The Crisis, *the journalistic arm of the National Association for the Advancement of Colored People (NAACP), of which he served as editor for almost twenty-five years. The Crisis, under Du Bois, became an important stage for a discussion of issues affecting African Americans and blacks worldwide, such as colonialism and exploitation. In 1919, when the war had ended, Du Bois went to France to cover heroic black soldiers for the paper.*

July 1918

This is the crisis of the world. For all the long years to come men will point to the year 1918 as the great Day of Decision, the day when the world

[1] "Close Ranks," *The Crisis* 16, No. 3 (July 1918): 93; "Opinion of W.E.B. Du Bois," *The Crisis* 17, No. 1 (November 1918): 97.

The Gilded Age and Progressive Era: A Documentary Reader, First Edition.
Edited by William A. Link and Susannah J. Link.
© 2012 Blackwell Publishing Ltd. Published 2012 by Blackwell Publishing Ltd.

decided whether it would submit to military despotism and an endless armed peace—if peace it could be called—or whether they would put down the menace of German militarism and inaugurate the United States of the World.

We of the colored race have no ordinary interest in the outcome. That which the German power represents today spells death to the aspirations of Negroes and all darker races for equality, freedom and democracy. Let us not hesitate. Let us, while this war lasts, forget our special grievances and close our ranks shoulder to shoulder with our own white fellow citizens and the allied nations that are fighting for democracy. We make no ordinary sacrifice, but we make it gladly and willingly with our eyes lifted to the hills.

November 1918

It was a tremendous speech that Woodrow Wilson made in New York City, September 27, 1918. On one point alone was its meaning vague to us of the darker world, who listened with bated breath. Listen to these words:

"Shall the military power of any nation or group of nations be suffered to determine the fortunes of peoples over whom they have no right to rule, except the right of force?

"Shall strong nations be free to wrong nations and make them subject to their purpose and interest?

"Shall peoples be ruled and dominated, even in their own internal affairs, by arbitrary and irresponsible force, or by their own will and choice?

"Shall there be a common standard of right and privilege for all peoples and nations, or shall the strong do as they will and the weak suffer without redress?

Is it possible that these flaming arrows were not aimed at the Vardamans in Mississippi as well as at Huns in Europe? Is it thinkable that President Wilson did not have clearly in mind Kamerun as well as Serbia? It is neither possible or thinkable if English is English and Justice is Justice, and with this true, Mr. Wilson's speech is one of the half dozen significant utterances of human history.

2 Eugene V. Debs, The Canton, Ohio, Anti-War Speech, 1918[2]

Eugene Debs (1855–1926) was born in Terre Haute, Indiana, and worked in the railroad industry as a boilerman. Subsequently, he became involved in union organizing in the conservative railway brotherhoods, but he eventually

[2] Eugene V. Debs, *Eugene V. Debs Speaks*, ed. Jean Y. Tussey (New York: Pathfinder Press, 1970), pp. 243–79. Copyright © 1970 by Pathfinder Press. Reprinted by permission.

helped to organize a more radical group, the American Railway Union, in 1893. Debs became involved in the famous Pullman strike in the Chicago area in 1894, and he was sent to jail for ignoring a court order requiring the unions to return to work. Debs subsequently helped to organize the Socialist Party of America, and he ran as its presidential candidate five times between 1900 and 1920.

Debs, like most other Socialists, opposed American intervention in World War I, and here he denounced the Wilson administration's prosecutions of Socialists for their antiwar activities. In this famous speech, at the state convention of the Socialist party in Canton, Ohio, Debs connected the war with forces of international capitalism. Because of this speech, he was prosecuted under the Espionage Act of 1917 and was sentenced to ten years in federal prison. He served time in the federal penitentiary in Atlanta from April 1919 to December 1921 – and ran for president from prison, attracting nearly a million votes – when President Warren G. Harding commuted his sentence.

Comrades, friends and fellow-workers, for this very cordial greeting, this very hearty reception, I thank you all with the fullest appreciation of your interest in and your devotion to the cause for which I am to speak to you this afternoon. . . .

I realize that, in speaking to you this afternoon, there are certain limitations placed upon the right of free speech. I must be exceedingly careful, prudent, as to what I say, and even more careful and prudent as to how I say it. I may not be able to say all I think; but I am not going to say anything that I do not think. I would rather a thousand times be a free soul in jail than to be a sycophant and coward in the streets. They may put those boys in jail—and some of the rest of us in jail—but they cannot put the Socialist movement in jail. Those prison bars separate their bodies from ours, but their souls are here this afternoon. They are simply paying the penalty that all men have paid in all the ages of history for standing erect, and for seeking to pave the way to better conditions for mankind. . . .

They who have been reading the capitalist newspapers realize what a capacity they have for lying. We have been reading them lately. They know all about the Socialist Party—the Socialist movement, except what is true. Only the other day they took an article that I had written and most of you have read it—most of you members of the party, at least—and they made it appear that I had undergone a marvelous transformation. I had suddenly become changed—had in fact come to my senses; I had ceased to be a wicked Socialist, and had become a respectable Socialist, a patriotic Socialist—as if I had ever been anything else.

What was the purpose of this deliberate misrepresentation? It is so self-evident that it suggests itself. The purpose was to sow the seeds of dissension in our ranks; to have it appear that we were divided among ourselves; that we were pitted against each other, to our mutual undoing. But Socialists were not born yesterday. They know how to read capitalist newspapers; and to believe exactly the opposite of what they read. . . .

They tell us that we live in a great free republic; that our institutions are democratic; that we are a free and self-governing people. This is too much, even for a joke. But it is not a subject for levity; it is an exceedingly serious matter.

To whom do the Wall Street Junkers[3] in our country marry their daughters? After they have wrung their countless millions from your sweat, your agony and your life's blood, in a time of war as in a time of peace, they invest these untold millions in the purchase of titles of broken-down aristocrats, such as princes, dukes, counts and other parasites and no-accounts. Would they be satisfied to wed their daughters to honest workingmen? To real democrats? Oh, no! They scour the markets of Europe for vampires who are titled and nothing else. And they swap their millions for the titles, so that matrimony with them becomes literally a matter of money.

These are the gentry who are today wrapped up in the American flag, who shout their claim from the housetops that they are the only patriots, and who have their magnifying glasses in hand, scanning the country for evidence of disloyalty, eager to apply the brand of treason to the men who dare to even whisper their opposition to Junker rule in the United Sates. No wonder Sam Johnson declared that "patriotism is the last refuge of the scoundrel." He must have had this Wall Street gentry in mind, or at least their prototypes, for in every age it has been the tyrant, the oppressor and the exploiter who has wrapped himself in the cloak of patriotism, or religion, or both to deceive and overawe the people.

They would have you believe that the Socialist Party consists in the main of disloyalists and traitors. It is true in a sense not at all to their discredit. We frankly admit that we are disloyalists and traitors to the real traitors of this nation . . . .

Wars throughout history have been waged for conquest and plunder. In the Middle Ages when the feudal lords who inhabited the castles whose towers may still be seen along the Rhine concluded to enlarge their domains, to increase their power, their prestige and their wealth they declared war upon one another. But they themselves did not go to war any more than the

---

3 The Junkers were the Prussian landed aristocracy who dominated Germany's social, political, and military leadership.

modern feudal lords, the barons of Wall Street go to war. The feudal barons of the Middle Ages, the economic predecessors of the capitalists of our day, declared all wars. And their miserable serfs fought all the battles. The poor, ignorant serfs had been taught to revere their masters; to believe that when their masters declared war upon one another, it was their patriotic duty to fall upon one another and to cut one another's throats for the profit and glory of the lords and barons who held them in contempt. And that is war in a nutshell. The master class has always declared the wars; the subject class has always fought the battles. The master class has had all to gain and nothing to lose, while the subject class has had nothing to gain and all to lose—especially their lives.

They have always taught and trained you to believe it to be your patriotic duty to go to war and to have yourselves slaughtered at their command. But in all the history of the world you, the people, have never had a voice in declaring war, and strange as it certainly appears, no war by any nation in any age has ever been declared by the people.

And here let me emphasize the fact—and it cannot be repeated too often—that the working class who fight all the battles, the working class who make the supreme sacrifices, the working class who freely shed their blood and furnish the corpses, have never yet had a voice in either declaring war or making peace. It is the ruling class that invariably does both. They alone declare war and they alone make peace.

They are continually talking about your patriotic duty. It is not their but your patriotic duty that they are concerned about. There is a decided difference. Their patriotic duty never takes them to the firing line or chucks them into the trenches.

And now for all of us to do our duty! The clarion call is ringing in our ears and we cannot falter without being convicted of treason to ourselves and to our great cause. . . .

Do not worry over the charge of treason to your masters, but be concerned about the treason that involves yourselves. Be true to yourself and you cannot be a traitor to any good cause on earth.

Yes, in good time we are going to sweep into power in this nation and throughout the world. We are going to destroy all enslaving and degrading capitalist institutions and re-create them as free and humanizing institutions. The world is daily changing before our eyes. The sun of capitalism is setting; the sun of socialism is rising. It is our duty to build the new nation and the free republic. We need industrial and social builders. We Socialists are the builders of the beautiful world that is to be. We are all pledged to do our part. We are inviting—aye challenging you this afternoon in the name of your own manhood and womanhood to join us and do your part.

In due time the hour will strike and this great cause triumphant—the greatest in history—will proclaim the emancipation of the working class and the brotherhood of all mankind.

3 Espionage Act, 1917[4]

The Espionage Act, along with an amendment passed in 1918 and often called the Sedition Act, was passed by Congress and signed by Woodrow Wilson as a response to widespread fears in the United States that alleged traitors and anarchists were trying to sabotage the government during World War I. The portion of the law that places rigid restrictions on freedom of speech led to strenuous objection by people concerned about civil liberty. During the discussion of the bill in Congress, Representative Martin Madden of Illinois noted that, "while we are fighting to establish the democracy of the world, we ought not to do the thing that will establish autocracy in America." A number of important Supreme Court cases resulted from this law and the Sedition Act: Schenck v. United States, Frohwerk v. United States, Debs v. United States, and Abrams v. United States. In each of these cases, the Supreme Court upheld the law. In Schenck, Justice Oliver Wendell Holmes wrote the unanimous opinion, which included the doctrine of "a clear and present danger." This doctrine restricted speech that might cause widespread panic, unless there was an immediate danger, as in yelling "Fire!" in a movie theater. In Abrams, Holmes, in a famous dissent, clarified this doctrine when he wrote, "Only the emergency that makes it immediately dangerous to leave the correction of evil counsels to time warrants making any exception to the sweeping command, 'Congress shall make no law abridging the freedom of speech.'"

The law was used especially often against Socialists, such as Eugene Debs, and in western states where the International Workers of the World were active. Because the law could be enforced at the discretion of US attorneys, it was applied unevenly throughout the country. Convicted under the law for making a speech that allegedly restricted military recruiting, Debs was sentenced to ten years in prison (although his sentence was commuted by Warren G. Harding after five years) and ran for president in 1920 from prison. The poet, e.e. cummings, was convicted and served three months of military detention for saying openly that he did not hate Germans. Albert S. Burleson, the postmaster general, used the law as justification for censoring the mail if a local postmaster believed that it constituted antiwar propaganda.

---

4 "Session I, Chapter 30," *Statutes at Large of the United States of America: from April, 1917, to March, 1919, Concurrent Resolutions of the Two Houses of Congress and Recent Treaties, Conventions, and Executive Proclamations Amendment to the Constitution*, Vol. XL, Part I (Washington, DC: Government Printing Office, 1919), pp. 217–19.

Title I

ESPIONAGE

Section 1

That:

(a) whoever, for the purpose of obtaining information respecting the national defence with intent or reason to believe that the information to be obtained is to be used to the injury of the United States, or to the advantage of any foreign nation, goes upon, enters, flies over, or otherwise obtains information, concerning any vessel, aircraft, work of defence, navy yard, naval station, submarine base, coaling station, fort, battery, torpedo station, dockyard, canal, railroad, arsenal, camp, factory, mine, telegraph, telephone, wireless, or signal station, building, office, or other place connected with the national defence, owned or constructed, or in progress of construction by the United States or under the control of the United States, or of any of its officers or agents, or within the exclusive jurisdiction of the United States, or any place in which any vessel, aircraft, arms, munitions, or other materials or instruments for use in time of war are being made, prepared, repaired, or stored, under any contract or agreement with the United States, or with any person on behalf of the United States, or otherwise on behalf of the United States, or any prohibited place within the meaning of section six of this title; or

(b) whoever for the purpose aforesaid, and with like intent or reason to believe, copies, takes, makes, or obtains, or attempts, or induces or aids another to copy, take, make, or obtain, any sketch, photograph, photographic negative, blue print, plan, map, model, instrument, appliance, document, writing or note of anything connected with the national defence; or

(c) whoever, for the purpose aforesaid, receives or obtains or agrees or attempts or induces or aids another to receive or obtain from any other person, or from any source whatever, any document, writing, code book, signal book, sketch, photograph, photographic negative, blue print, plan, map, model, instrument, appliance, or note, of anything connected with the national defence, knowing or having reason to believe, at the time he receives or obtains, or agrees or attempts or induces or aids another to receive or obtain it, that it has been or will be obtained, taken, made or disposed of by any person contrary to the provisions of this title; or

(d) whoever, lawfully or unlawfully having possession of, access to, control over, or being entrusted with any document, writing, code book, signal book, sketch, photograph, photographic negative, blue print, plan, map, model, instrument, appliance, or note relating to the national defence, wilfully communicates or transmits or attempts to communicate or transmit the same and fails to deliver it on demand to the officer or employee of the United States entitled to receive it; or

(e) whoever, being entrusted with or having lawful possession or control of any document, writing, code book, signal book, sketch, photograph, photographic negative, blue print, plan, map, model, note, or information, relating to the national defence, through gross negligence permits the same to be removed from its proper place of custody or delivered to anyone in violation of his trust, or to be lost, stolen, abstracted, or destroyed, shall be punished by a fine of not more than $10,000, or by imprisonment for not more than two years, or both.

Section 2

Whoever, with intent or reason to believe that it is to be used to the injury of the United States or to the advantage of a foreign nation, communicate, delivers, or transmits, or attempts to, or aids, or induces another to, communicate, deliver or transmit, to any foreign government , or to any faction or party or military or naval force within a foreign country, whether recognized or unrecognized by the United States, or to any representative, officer, agent, employee, subject, or citizen thereof, either directly or indirectly any document, writing, code book, signal book, sketch, photograph, photographic negative, blue print, plan, map, model, note, instrument, appliance, or information relating to the national defence, shall be punished by imprisonment for not more than twenty years: Provided, That whoever shall violate the provisions of subsection:

(a) of this section in time of war shall be punished by death or by imprisonment for not more than thirty years; and

(b) whoever, in time of war, with intent that the same shall be communicated to the enemy, shall collect, record, publish or communicate, or attempt to elicit any information with respect to the movement, numbers, description, condition, or disposition of any of the armed forces, ships, aircraft, or war materials of the United States, or with respect to the plans or conduct, or supposed plans or conduct of any naval or military operations, or with respect to any works or measures undertaken for or connected with, or intended for the fortification of any place, or any other information relating to the public defence, which might be useful to the enemy, shall be punished by death or by imprisonment for not more than thirty years.

Section 3

Whoever, when the United States is at war, shall wilfully make or convey false reports or false statements with intent to interfere with the operation or success of the military or naval forces of the United States or to promote the success of its enemies and whoever when the United States is at war, shall wilfully cause or attempt to cause insubordination, disloyalty, mutiny, refusal of duty, in the military or naval forces of the United States, or shall wilfully obstruct the recruiting or enlistment service of the United States, to the injury of the service or of the United States, shall be punished by a fine of not more than $10,000 or imprisonment for not more than twenty years, or both.

Section 4

If two or more persons conspire to violate the provisions of section two or three of this title, and one or more of such persons does any act to effect the object of the conspiracy, each of the parties to such conspiracy shall be punished as in said sections provided in the case of the doing of the act the accomplishment of which is the object of such conspiracy. Except as above provided conspiracies to commit offences under this title shall be punished as provided by section thirty-seven of the Act to codify, revise, and amend the penal laws of the United States approved March fourth, nineteen hundred and nine.

Section 5

Whoever harbours or conceals any person who he knows, or has reasonable grounds to believe or suspect, has committed, or is about to commit, an offence under this title shall be punished by a fine of not more than $10,000 or by imprisonment for not more than two years, or both.

Section 6

The President in time of war or in case of national emergency may by proclamation designate any place other than those set forth in subsection:

(a) of section one hereof in which anything for the use of the Army or Navy is being prepared or constructed or stored as a prohibited place for the purpose of this title: Provided, That he shall determine that information with respect thereto would be prejudicial to the national defence.

Section 7

Nothing contained in this title shall be deemed to limit the jurisdiction of the general courts-martial, military commissions, or naval courts-martial under sections thirteen hundred and forty-two, thirteen hundred and forty-three, and sixteen hundred and twenty-four of the Revised Statutes as amended.

Section 8

The provisions of this title shall extend to all Territories, possessions, and places subject to the jurisdiction of the United States whether or not contiguous thereto, and offences under this title, when committed upon the high seas or elsewhere within the admiralty and maritime jurisdiction of the United States and outside the territorial limits thereof shall be punishable hereunder.

Section 9

The Act entitled "An Act to prevent the disclosure of national defence secrets," approved March third, nineteen hundred and eleven, is hereby repealed.

4 Woodrow Wilson, The Fourteen Points Address, 1918[5]

The Fourteen Points, which Wilson made public in this speech to Congress, became the basis for the terms of peace at the end of World War I that led to the Axis (Germany and its allies) agreeing to an armistice in November 1918. Wilson's outline was based on a report compiled by 150 political and social scientists, who had been asked to participate in the inquiry by Colonel Edward M. House, an adviser to Wilson. However, during the Paris Peace Conference in 1919, nearly every point was eliminated, because the Allies wanted enormous restitution from and punishment of Germany and its allies. The only point that remained relatively intact was the formation of an international organization to preserve world peace, which became the League of Nations. Frustrated by the refusal of the US Congress to join the league, Wilson predicted that nonparticipation by the United States would result in another world war within 25 years.

Gentlemen of the Congress:

Once more, as repeatedly before, the spokesmen of the Central Empires have indicated their desire to discuss the objects of the war and the possible basis of a general peace. Parleys have been in progress at Brest-Litovsk between Russian representatives and representatives of the Central Powers to which the attention of all the belligerents have been invited for the purpose of ascertaining whether it may be possible to extend these parleys into a general conference with regard to terms of peace and settlement.

[5] Delivered in Joint Session of Congress, in Arthur S. Link *et al.* (eds), *The Papers of Woodrow Wilson*, 69 vols (Princeton, NJ: Princeton University Press, 1966–93), Vol. 45, pp. 534–9. Reprinted by permission of Princeton University Press.

The Russian representatives presented not only a perfectly definite statement of the principles upon which they would be willing to conclude peace but also an equally definite program of the concrete application of those principles. The representatives of the Central Powers, on their part, presented an outline of settlement which, if much less definite, seemed susceptible of liberal interpretation until their specific program of practical terms was added. That program proposed no concessions at all either to the sovereignty of Russia or to the preferences of the populations with whose fortunes it dealt, but meant, in a word, that the Central Empires were to keep every foot of territory their armed forces had occupied — every province, every city, every point of vantage — as a permanent addition to their territories and their power.

It is a reasonable conjecture that the general principles of settlement which they at first suggested originated with the more liberal statesmen of Germany and Austria, the men who have begun to feel the force of their own people's thought and purpose, while the concrete terms of actual settlement came from the military leaders who have no thought but to keep what they have got. The negotiations have been broken off. The Russian representatives were sincere and in earnest. They cannot entertain such proposals of conquest and domination.

The whole incident is full of significances. It is also full of perplexity. With whom are the Russian representatives dealing? For whom are the representatives of the Central Empires speaking? Are they speaking for the majorities of their respective parliaments or for the minority parties, that military and imperialistic minority which has so far dominated their whole policy and controlled the affairs of Turkey and of the Balkan states which have felt obliged to become their associates in this war?

The Russian representatives have insisted, very justly, very wisely, and in the true spirit of modern democracy, that the conferences they have been holding with the Teutonic and Turkish statesmen should be held within open, not closed, doors, and all the world has been audience, as was desired. To whom have we been listening, then? To those who speak the spirit and intention of the resolutions of the German Reichstag of the 9th of July last, the spirit and intention of the Liberal leaders and parties of Germany, or to those who resist and defy that spirit and intention and insist upon conquest and subjugation? Or are we listening, in fact, to both, unreconciled and in open and hopeless contradiction? These are very serious and pregnant questions. Upon the answer to them depends the peace of the world.

But, whatever the results of the parleys at Brest-Litovsk, whatever the confusions of counsel and of purpose in the utterances of the spokesmen of the Central Empires, they have again attempted to acquaint the world with their objects in the war and have again challenged their adversaries to say what their objects are and what sort of settlement they would deem just and satisfactory. There is no good reason why that challenge should not be responded to, and responded to with the utmost candor. We did not wait for it. Not once, but again and again, we have laid our whole thought and purpose before the world, not in general terms only, but each time with sufficient definition to make it clear what sort of definite terms of settlement must necessarily spring out of them. Within the last week Mr. Lloyd George has spoken with admirable candor and in admirable spirit for the people and Government of Great Britain.

There is no confusion of counsel among the adversaries of the Central Powers, no uncertainty of principle, no vagueness of detail. The only secrecy of counsel, the only lack of fearless frankness, the only failure to make definite statement of the objects of the war, lies with Germany and her allies. The issues of life and death hang upon these definitions. No statesman who has the least conception of his responsibility ought for a moment to permit himself to continue this tragical and appalling outpouring of blood and treasure unless he is sure beyond a peradventure that the objects of the vital sacrifice are part and parcel of the very life of Society and that the people for whom he speaks think them right and imperative as he does.

There is, moreover, a voice calling for these definitions of principle and of purpose which is, it seems to me, more thrilling and more compelling than any of the many moving voices with which the troubled air of the world is filled. It is the voice of the Russian people. They are prostrate and all but hopeless, it would seem, before the grim power of Germany, which has hitherto known no relenting and no pity. Their power, apparently, is shattered. And yet their soul is not subservient. They will not yield either in principle or in action. Their conception of what is right, of what is humane and honorable for them to accept, has been stated with a frankness, a largeness of view, a generosity of spirit, and a universal human sympathy which must challenge the admiration of every friend of mankind; and they have refused to compound their ideals or desert others that they themselves may be safe.

They call to us to say what it is that we desire, in what, if in anything, our purpose and our spirit differ from theirs; and I believe that the people of the United States would wish me to respond, with utter simplicity and frankness. Whether their present leaders believe it or not, it is our heartfelt desire and hope that some way may be opened whereby we may be privileged to assist the people of Russia to attain their utmost hope of liberty and ordered peace.

It will be our wish and purpose that the processes of peace, when they are begun, shall be absolutely open and that they shall involve and permit henceforth no secret understandings of any kind. The day of conquest and aggrandizement is gone by; so is also the day of secret covenants entered into in the interest of particular governments and likely at some unlooked-for moment to upset the peace of the world. It is this happy fact, now clear to the view of every public man whose thoughts do not still linger in an age that is dead and gone, which makes it possible for every nation whose purposes are consistent with justice and the peace of the world to avow now or at any other time the objects it has in view.

We entered this war because violations of right had occurred which touched us to the quick and made the life of our own people impossible unless they were corrected and the world secure once for all against their recurrence. What we demand in this war, therefore, is nothing peculiar to ourselves. It is that the world be made fit and safe to live in; and particularly that it be made safe for every peace-loving nation which, like our own, wishes to live its own life, determine its own institutions, be assured of justice and fair dealing by the other peoples of the world as against force and selfish aggression. All the peoples of the world are in effect partners in this interest, and for our own part we see very clearly that unless justice be done to others it will not be done to us. The program of the world's peace, therefore, is our program; and that program, the only possible program, as we see it, is this:

I. Open covenants of peace, openly arrived at, after which there shall be no private international understandings of any kind but diplomacy shall proceed always frankly and in the public view.

II. Absolute freedom of navigation upon the seas, outside territorial waters, alike in peace and in war, except as the seas may be closed in whole or in part by international action for the enforcement of international covenants.

III. The removal, so far as possible, of all economic barriers and the establishment of an equality of trade conditions among all the nations consenting to the peace and associating themselves for its maintenance.

IV. Adequate guarantees given and taken that national armaments will be reduced to the lowest point consistent with domestic safety.

V. A free, open-minded, and absolutely impartial adjustment of all colonial claims, based upon a strict observance of the principle that in determining all such questions of sovereignty the interests of the populations concerned must have equal weight with the equitable claims of the government whose title is to be determined.

VI. The evacuation of all Russian territory and such a settlement of all questions affecting Russia as will secure the best and freest cooperation of the other nations of the world in obtaining for her an unhampered and unembarrassed opportunity for the independent determination of her own political development and national policy and assure her of a sincere welcome into the society of free nations under institutions of her own choosing; and, more than a welcome, assistance also of every kind that she may need and may herself desire. The treatment accorded Russia by her sister nations in the months to come will be the acid test of their good will, of their comprehension of her needs as distinguished from their own interests, and of their intelligent and unselfish sympathy.

VII. Belgium, the whole world will agree, must be evacuated and restored, without any attempt to limit the sovereignty which she enjoys in common with all other free nations. No other single act will serve as this will serve to restore confidence among the nations in the laws which they have themselves set and determined for the government of their relations with one another. Without this healing act the whole structure and validity of international law is forever impaired.

VIII. All French territory should be freed and the invaded portions restored, and the wrong done to France by Prussia in 1871 in the matter of Alsace-Lorraine, which has unsettled the peace of the world for nearly fifty years, should be righted, in order that peace may once more be made secure in the interest of all.

IX. A readjustment of the frontiers of Italy should be effected along clearly recognizable lines of nationality.

X. The peoples of Austria-Hungary, whose place among the nations we wish to see safeguarded and assured, should be accorded the freest opportunity to autonomous development.

XI. Rumania, Serbia, and Montenegro should be evacuated; occupied territories restored; Serbia accorded free and secure access to the sea; and the relations of the several Balkan states to one another determined by friendly counsel along historically established lines of allegiance and nationality; and international guarantees of the political and economic independence and territorial integrity of the several Balkan states should be entered into.

XII. The Turkish portion of the present Ottoman Empire should be assured a secure sovereignty, but the other nationalities which are now under Turkish rule should be assured an undoubted security of life and an absolutely unmolested opportunity of autonomous development, and the Dardanelles should be permanently opened as a free passage to the ships and commerce of all nations under international guarantees.

XIII. An independent Polish state should be erected which should include the territories inhabited by indisputably Polish populations, which should be assured a free and secure access to the sea, and whose political and economic independence and territorial integrity should be guaranteed by international covenant.

XIV. A general association of nations must be formed under specific covenants for the purpose of affording mutual guarantees of political independence and territorial integrity to great and small states alike.

In regard to these essential rectifications of wrong and assertions of right we feel ourselves to be intimate partners of all the governments and peoples associated together against the Imperialists. We cannot be separated in interest or divided in purpose. We stand together until the end. For such arrangements and covenants we are willing to fight and to continue to fight until they are achieved; but only because we wish the right to prevail and desire a just and stable peace such as can be secured only by removing the chief provocations to war, which this program does remove. We have no jealousy of German greatness, and there is nothing in this program that impairs it. We grudge her no achievement or distinction of learning or of pacific enterprise such as have made her record very bright and very enviable. We do not wish to injure her or to block in any way her legitimate influence or power. We do not wish to fight her either with arms or with hostile arrangements of trade if she is willing to associate herself with us and the other peace-loving nations of the world in covenants of justice and law and fair dealing. We wish her only to accept a place of equality among the peoples of the world, — the new world in which we now live, — instead of a place of mastery.

Neither do we presume to suggest to her any alteration or modification of her institutions. But it is necessary, we must frankly say, and necessary as a preliminary to any intelligent dealings with her on our part, that we should know whom her spokesmen speak for when they speak to us, whether for the Reichstag majority or for the military party and the men whose creed is imperial domination.

We have spoken now, surely, in terms too concrete to admit of any further doubt or question. An evident principle runs through the whole program I have outlined. It is the principle of justice to all peoples and nationalities, and their right to live on equal terms of liberty and safety with one another, whether they be strong or weak.

Unless this principle be made its foundation no part of the structure of international justice can stand. The people of the United States could act upon no other principle; and to the vindication of this principle they are ready to devote their lives, their honor, and everything they possess. The moral climax of this the culminating and final war for human liberty has come, and they are ready to put their own strength, their own highest purpose, their own integrity and devotion to the test.

Discussion Questions: Chapter 14

1   What did World War I and American involvement mean for black people? How did the war affect Jim Crow?
2   What critique of American intervention did Eugene Debs offer?
3   How did the Wilson administration treat domestic antiwar sentiment? How did the Espionage Act limit free speech?
4   What was Woodrow Wilson's vision of a postwar international order? What were its most important elements?

Further Reading

Part I

Ayers, Edward. *The Promise of the New South*. New York: Oxford University Press, 1992.

Carlton, David L. *Mill and Town in South Carolina, 1880–1920*. Baton Rouge: Louisiana State University Press, 1982.

Cobb, James C. *Industrialization and Southern Society, 1877–1984*. Lexington: University Press of Kentucky, 1984.

Edwards, Rebecca. *New Spirits: Americans in the "Gilded Age," 1865–1905*. New York: Oxford University Press, 2006.

Elliott, Mark. *Color-blind Justice: Albion Tourgee and the Quest for Racial Equality from the Civil War to* Plessy v. Ferguson. New York: Oxford University Press, 2006.

Foner, Eric. *Reconstruction: America's Unfinished Revolution, 1863–1877*. New York: HarperCollins, 1988.

Gilmore, Glenda Elizabeth. *Gender and Jim Crow: Women and the Politics of White Supremacy in North Carolina, 1896–1920*. Chapel Hill: University of North Carolina Press, 1996.

Hahn, Steven. *A Nation under Our Feet: Black Political Struggles in the Rural South from Slavery to the Great Migration*. Cambridge, MA: Belknap Press, 2003.

Hall, Jacquelyn Dowd et al. *Like a Family: The Making of a Southern Cotton Mill World*. Chapel Hill: University of North Carolina Press, 1987.

Hunter, Tera W. *To 'Joy My Freedom: Southern Black Women's Lives and Labors after the Civil War*. Cambridge, MA: Harvard University Press, 1997.

The Gilded Age and Progressive Era: A Documentary Reader, First Edition.
Edited by William A. Link and Susannah J. Link.
© 2012 Blackwell Publishing Ltd. Published 2012 by Blackwell Publishing Ltd.

Jones, William P. *The Tribe of Black Ulysses: African American Lumber Workers in the Jim Crow South*. Chicago: University of Illinois Press, 2005.

Kantrowitz, Stephen. *Ben Tillman and the Reconstruction of White Supremacy*. Chapel Hill: University of North Carolina Press, 2000.

Lears, Jackson. *Rebirth of a Nation: The Making of Modern America, 1877–1920*. New York: HarperCollins, 2009.

Lichtenstein, Alex. *Twice the Work of Free Labor: The Political Economy of Convict Labor in the New South*. New York: Verso, 1996.

Link, William A. *The Paradox of Southern Progressivism, 1880–1930*. Chapel Hill: University of North Carolina Press, 1992.

Painter, Nell Irwin. *Standing at Armageddon: The United States, 1877–1919*. New York: W.W. Norton & Co., 1987.

Richardson, Heather Cox. *West from Appomattox: The Reconstruction of America after the Civil War*. New Haven, CT: Yale University Press, 2007.

Rosen, Hannah. *Terror in the Heart of Freedom: Citizenship, Sexual Violence, and the Meaning of Race in the Postemancipation South*. Chapel Hill: University of North Carolina Press, 2009.

Turner, Elizabeth Hayes. *Women, Culture, and Community: Religion and Reform in Galveston, 1880–1920*. New York: Oxford University Press, 1997.

Woodward, C. Vann. *Origins of the New South, 1877–1913*. Baton Rouge: Louisiana State University Press, 1951.

Part II

Allen, Judith A. *The Feminism of Charlotte Perkins Gilman: Sexualities, Histories, Progressivism*. Chicago: University of Chicago Press, 2009.

Buder, Stanley. *Capitalizing on Change: A Social History of American Business*. Chapel Hill: University of North Carolina Press, 2009.

Cashman, Sean Dennis. *America in the Gilded Age: From the Death of Lincoln to the Rise of Theodore Roosevelt*. New York: New York University Press, 1984.

Levine, Susan. *Labor's True Woman: Carpet Weavers, Industrialization, and Labor Reform in the Gilded Age*. Philadelphia, PA: Temple University Press, 1984.

Trachtenberg, Alan. *The Incorporation of America: Culture and Society in the Gilded Age*. New York: Hill & Wang, 1982.

Wall, James T. *Wall Street and the Fruited Plain: Money, Expansion, and Politics in the Gilded Age*. Lanham, MD: University Press of America, 2008.

Part III

Blackmon, Douglas A. *Slavery by Another Name: The Re-Enslavement of Black Americans from the Civil War to World War II*. New York: Doubleday, 2008.

Brody, David. *Steelworkers in America: The Non-Union Era*. Cambridge, MA: Harvard University Press, 1960.

Giddings, Paula. *Ida: A Sword among Lions: Ida B. Wells and the Campaign against Lynching*. New York: Amistad, 2008.

Goodwyn, Lawrence. *The Populist Moment: A Short History of the Agrarian Revolt in America*. New York: Oxford University Press, 1978.

Green, James R. *Death in the Haymarket: A Story of Chicago, the First Labor Movement, and the Bombing that Divided Gilded Age America*. New York: Pantheon Books, 2006.

Kazin, Michael. *A Godly Hero: The Life of William Jennings Bryan*. New York: Knopf, 2006.

McMath, Robert C. *American Populism: A Social History 1877–1898*. New York: Hill & Wang, 1993.

Montgomery, David. *Workers Control in America: Studies in the History of Work, Technology, and Labor Struggles*. New York: Cambridge University Press, 1979.

Postel, Charles. *The Populist Vision*. New York: Oxford University Press, 2007.

Stowell, David O., ed. *The Great Strikes of 1877*. Urbana: University of Illinois Press, 2008.

Woodward, C. Vann. *Tom Watson: Agrarian Rebel*. New York: Macmillan, 1938.

Part IV

Arnold, Peri E. *Remaking the Presidency: Roosevelt, Taft, and Wilson, 1901–1916*. Lawrence: University Press of Kansas, 2009.

Chambers, John Whiteclay. *The Tyranny of Change: America in the Progressive Years*. New York: St Martin's Press, 1980.

Dennis, Michael. *Lessons in Progress: State Universities and Progressivism in the New South, 1880–1920*. Urbana: University of Illinois Press, 2001.

Flanagan, Maureen A. *America Reformed: Progressives and Progressivism, 1890s–1920s*. New York: Oxford University Press, 2007.

Gould, Lewis L. *America in the Progressive Era, 1890–1914*. New York: Longman, 2001.

Gullett, Gayle Ann. *Becoming Citizens: The Emergence and Development of the California Women's Movement, 1880–1911*. Urbana: University of Illinois Press, 2000.

Link, Arthur S., and Richard L. McCormick. *Progressivism*. Arlington Heights, IL: Harlan Davidson, 1983.

McGerr, Michael E. *A Fierce Discontent: The Rise and Fall of the Progressive Movement in America, 1870–1920*. New York: Free Press, 2003.

Sallee, Shelley. *The Whiteness of Child Labor Reform in the New South*. Athens: University of Georgia Press, 2004.

Sanders, Elizabeth M. *Roots of Reform: Farmers, Workers, and the American State, 1877–1917*. Chicago: University of Chicago Press, 1999.

Southern, David W. *The Progressive Era and Race: Reaction and Reform, 1900–1917*. Wheeling, IL: Harlan Davidson, 2005.

Tichi, Cecelia. *Civic Passions: Seven Who Launched Progressive America (and What They Teach Us)*. Chapel Hill: University of North Carolina Press, 2009.

Unger, Nancy C. *Fighting Bob La Follette: The Righteous Reformer*. Chapel Hill: University of North Carolina Press, 2000.
Wiebe, Robert H. *The Search for Order, 1877–1920*. New York: Hill & Wang, 1967.

Part V

Jacobson, Matthew Frye. *Barbarian Virtues: The United States Encounters Foreign Peoples at Home and Abroad, 1876–1917*. New York: Hill & Wang, 2000.
Kennedy, David M. *Over Here: The First World War and American Society*. New York: Oxford University Press, 1980.
Knock, Thomas J. *To End All Wars: Woodrow Wilson and the Quest for a New World Order*. Princeton, NJ: Princeton University Press, 1995.
Kramer, Paul A. *The Blood of Government: Race, Empire, the United States, and the Philippines*. Chapel Hill: University of North Carolina Press, 2006.
Levin, N. Gordon, Jr. *Woodrow Wilson and World Politics: America's Response to War and Revolution*. New York: Oxford University Press, 1968.
Lewis, David Levering. *W.E.B. Du Bois, 1868–1919: Biography of a Race*. New York: Holt, 1993.
Link, Arthur S. *Woodrow Wilson and the Progressive Era*. New York: Harper, 1954.
Pérez, Louis A. *The War of 1898: The United States and Cuba in History and Historiography*. Chapel Hill: University of North Carolina Press, 1998.
Renda, Mary A. *Taking Haiti: Military Occupation and the Culture of U.S. Imperialism, 1915–1940*. Chapel Hill: University of North Carolina Press, 2001.
Rosenberg, Emily S. *Spreading the American Dream: American Economic & Cultural Expansion, 1890–1945*. New York: Hill & Wang, 1982.
Rosenberg, Emily S. *Financial Missionaries to the World: The Politics and Culture of Dollar Diplomacy, 1900–1930*. Durham, NC: Duke University Press, 2003.
Tuttle, William M., Jr. *Race Riot: Chicago in the Red Summer of 1919*. New York: Atheneum, 1970.
Veeser, Cyrus. *A World Safe for Capitalism: Dollar Diplomacy and America's Rise to Global Power*. New York: Columbia University Press, 2002.

Index

The Gilded Age and Progressive Era: A Documentary Reader, First Edition.
Edited by William A. Link and Susannah J. Link.
© 2012 Blackwell Publishing Ltd. Published 2012 by Blackwell Publishing Ltd.